Gibran Khalil Gibran as Arab World Literature

Edinburgh Studies in Modern Arabic Literature
Series Editor: Rasheed El-Enany

Writing Beirut: Mappings of the City in the Modern Arabic Novel
Samira Aghacy
Women, Writing and the Iraqi State: Resistance and Collaboration under the Ba'th, 1968–2003
Hawraa Al-Hassan
Autobiographical Identities in Contemporary Arab Literature
Valerie Anishchenkova
Gibran Khalil Gibran as Arab World Literature
Ghazouane Arslane
The Iraqi Novel: Key Writers, Key Texts
Fabio Caiani and Catherine Cobham
Contemporary Arab Women's Life Writing and the Politics of Resistance
Hiyem Cheurfa
Sufism in the Contemporary Arabic Novel
Ziad Elmarsafy
Gender, Nation, and the Arabic Novel: Egypt 1892–2008
Hoda Elsadda
The Arabic Prose Poem: Poetic Theory and Practice
Huda Fakhreddine
The Unmaking of the Arab Intellectual: Prophecy, Exile and the Nation
Zeina G. Halabi
Egypt 1919: The Revolution in Literature and Film
Dina Heshmat
Post-War Anglophone Lebanese Fiction: Home Matters in the Diaspora
Syrine Hout
The Modern Arabic Bible: Translation, Dissemination and Literary Impact5
Rana Issa
Prophetic Translation: the Making of Modern Egyptian Literature
Maya I. Kesrouany
Nasser in the Egyptian Imaginary
Omar Khalifah
Conspiracy in Modern Egyptian Literature
Benjamin Koerber
War and Occupation in Iraqi Fiction
Ikram Masmoudi
Literary Autobiography and Arab National Struggles
Tahia Abdel Nasser
Latin American and Arab Literature: Transcontinental Exchanges
Tahia Abdel Nasser
The Libyan Novel: Humans, Animals and the Poetics of Vulnerability
Charis Olszok
The Arab Nahdah*: The Making of the Intellectual and Humanist Movement*
Abdulrazzak Patel
Blogging from Egypt: Digital Literature, 2005–2016
Teresa Pepe
Religion in the Egyptian Novel
Christina Phillips
Space in Modern Egyptian Fiction
Yasmine Ramadan
Gendering Civil War: Francophone Women's Writing in Lebanon
Mireille Rebeiz
Occidentalism: Literary Representations of the Maghrebi Experience of the East–West Encounter
Zahia Smail Salhi
Arabic Exile Literature in Europe: Forced Migration and Speculative Fiction
Johanna Sellman
Sonallah Ibrahim: Rebel with a Pen
Paul Starkey
Minorities in the Contemporary Egyptian Novel
Mary Youssef

edinburghuniversitypress.com/series/smal

Gibran Khalil Gibran as Arab World Literature

Ghazouane Arslane

EDINBURGH
University Press

Edinburgh University Press is one of the leading university presses in the UK. We publish academic books and journals in our selected subject areas across the humanities and social sciences, combining cutting-edge scholarship with high editorial and production values to produce academic works of lasting importance. For more information visit our website: edinburghuniversitypress.com

Edinburgh University Press Ltd
13 Infirmary Street
Edinburgh EH1 1LT

Typeset in 11/15 EB Garamond by
Cheshire Typesetting Ltd, Cuddington, Cheshire, and
printed and bound in Great Britain

A CIP record for this book is available from the British Library

ISBN 978 1 3995 0468 3 (hardback)
ISBN 978 1 3995 0470 6 (webready PDF)
ISBN 978 1 3995 0471 3 (epub)

Contents

Series Editor's Foreword vi
Acknowledgements ix
Notes on Translation, Transliteration and Abbreviations xi

Introduction: Why and How Should We Read Gibran Today? 1
1 The Poetics of Prophetic Writing: Reinventing the Religious in and against Modernity 33
2 The Bilingual Chasm 95
3 Gibran as Nationalist and *Nahḍawī* 141
4 Multiple Horizons of Expectations, Multiple Gibrans: Or, Gibran as World Literature 185
Epilogue: Rereading Gibran and the Question of Reading 241

Bibliography 249
Index 263

Series Editor's Foreword

Edinburgh Studies in Modern Arabic Literature is a unique series that aims to fill a glaring gap in scholarship in the field of modern Arabic literature. Its dedication to Arabic literature in the modern period (that is, from the nineteenth century onwards) is what makes it unique among series undertaken by academic publishers in the English-speaking world. Individual books on modern Arabic literature in general or aspects of it have been and continue to be published sporadically. Series on Islamic studies and Arab/Islamic thought and civilisation are not in short supply either in the academic world, but these are far removed from the study of Arabic literature qua literature, that is, imaginative, creative literature as we understand the term when, for instance, we speak of English literature or French literature. Even series labelled 'Arabic/Middle Eastern Literature' make no period distinction, extending their purview from the sixth century to the present, and often including non-Arabic literatures of the region. This series aims to redress the situation by focusing on the Arabic literature and criticism of today, stretching its interest to the earliest beginnings of Arab modernity in the nineteenth century.

The need for such a dedicated series, and generally for the redoubling of scholarly endeavour in researching and introducing modern Arabic literature to the Western reader, has never been stronger. Among activities and events heightening public, let alone academic, interest in all things Arab, and not least Arabic literature, are the significant growth in the last decades of the translation of contemporary Arab authors from all genres, especially fiction, into English; the higher profile of Arabic literature internationally since the award of the Nobel Prize in Literature to Naguib Mahfouz in 1988; the growing number of Arab authors living in the Western diaspora and writing both in English and in Arabic; the adoption of such authors and others by mainstream, high-circulation publishers, as opposed to the academic publishers of the past; and the establishment of prestigious prizes, such as the International Prize for Arabic Fiction, popularly referred to in the Arab world as the Arabic Booker, run by the Man Booker Foundation, which brings huge publicity to the shortlist and winner every year, as well as translation contracts into English and other languages. It is therefore part of the ambition of this series that it will increasingly address a wider reading public beyond its natural territory of students and researchers in Arabic and world literature. Nor indeed is the academic readership of the series expected to be confined to specialists in literature in the light of the growing trend for interdisciplinarity, which increasingly sees scholars crossing field boundaries in their research tools and coming up with findings that equally cross discipline borders in their appeal.

Gibran Khalil Gibran (1883–1931) may be the best-known Arab writer in the west, apart from being a cult figure especially in the USA, if only for his famous *The Prophet*. He was at the forefront of a group of poets and writers who emigrated at a young age from Lebanon (then part of Syria) in the latter decades of the nineteenth and early decades of the twentieth centuries and settled in the Americas, particularly the United States. They wrote mostly in Arabic and, despite their far-flung location, have come to be regarded as leading figures in the literary *nahda* (or renaissance) of Arabic, especially (but not solely) in poetry. Unlike the majority of these authors, Gibran did not limit his creativity to the Arabic language but also wrote in English and gained a considerable following outside the boundaries of Arab readership, where his Arabic writings exercised a huge influence as well. His writings, especially *The Prophet*, have been compared to Nietzsche's *Thus Spoke Zarathustra* and to William Blake's poetry, as too has his painting style to the latter's. A rebellious spirit, his originality extended from revolutionising the language and content of prose and poetry to questioning institutionalised religion and unmasking its and society's hypocrisies. With his work straddling two languages and his appeal so widespread and pivotal at a critical moment in the evolution of Arabic letters into modernity, it was natural for Gibran to attract scholarly attention in both English and Arabic, some of it further enhanced by interest in his personal life and relationships. As with all colossal figures, no amount of research and study ever will exhaust the possibilities of approach, interpretation and reinterpretation. The current book advances scholarship on Gibran and problematises issues that have long been glossed over, linking together his two writing personas of Arabic and English. It explores in one volume his output in both languages and its reception in both cultures, while examining his place as an Arab writer in the context of approaches to World Literature.

Rasheed El-Enany,
Series Editor,
Emeritus Professor of Modern Arabic Literature,
University of Exeter

Acknowledgements

First of all, I am immensely grateful for the generous scholarship I received from the Algerian Ministry of Higher Education and Scientific Research to pursue a PhD in Comparative Literature at Queen Mary University of London; most of the research I did then forms the basis of this book. I am infinitely thankful and indebted to Galin Tihanov, who has supported me in many formidable ways that I cannot count or describe here; his intelligent supervision and genuine belief in me and my book project sustained my confidence and strengthened my spirit, especially when I had unvoiced doubts about it. I am also thankful to Nadia Atia for her warm support and critical feedback. My enormous thanks and gratitude to Ziad Elmarsafy, Marilyn Booth, Hiyem Cheurfa and Katie da Cunha, who read early drafts and/or chapters of my book and offered me critical comments and suggestions, and to Rehana Ahmad, whose feedback at the early stages of this project broadened the ways I thought about my approach and theoretical framework. Special thanks to Professor Rasheed El-Enany, and to all the editors at Edinburgh University Press, for their impressive professionalism, patience, support and feedback. I also thank the anonymous reviewers who read my book proposal and a chapter and offered me valuable feedback.

I would also like to thank all the colleagues and friends with whom I had wonderful and engaging discussions about the research that led to this book, and especially Katie da Cunha, Andrew Hines, Ellen Jones, Shital Pravinchandra, Ruby Tuke and John Dunn, among many others. My deepest appreciation and gratitude for the warm encouragement and support of my precious family and friends in Algeria, and for the enchanting presence of my beloved Yousra, whose vivacious smile and kind thoughtfulness uplifted my spirit in moments of intense and prolonged concentration.

Parts of this book appeared in *Journal of Arabic Literature* (many thanks to the anonymous reviewers for their brilliant feedback and suggestions), *Concentric: Literary and Cultural Studies* and *Universal Localities: The Languages of World Literature* (edited by Galin Tihanov, J. B. Metzler). I wish to thank the editors and presses for the permission to reprint. I also wish to thank Telfair Museums for granting me the permission to reproduce Gibran's self-portrait (1911) as a book cover.

Notes on Translation, Transliteration and Abbreviations

All translations from the Arabic in this book are mine, unless otherwise noted. Transliterations of titles, words or passages in Arabic follow the Transliteration Guide of the *International Journal of Middle Eastern Studies* (IJMES). For the purpose of convenience and accessibility, names of authors in Arabic are not transliterated following IJMES.

For primary sources, the abbreviations below are used consistently throughout:

CWs: Gibran, *The Collected Works*. New York: Everyman's Library, 2007.
CWs in Arabic: Gibran, *al-Majmūʿa al-kāmila li muʾallafāt Jubrān Khalīl Jubrān bi-l-ʿarabiyya*. Lebanon: Kitābuna li-l-Nashr, 2014.

To the memory of my Mother,
who instilled in me the desire for excellence

Introduction

Why and How Should We Read Gibran Today?

This book offers a new reading and critical appreciation of the bilingual work of Gibran Kahlil Gibran (Jubrān Khalīl Jubrān), the eminent Arab *Mahjari* writer. It aims to 'salvage' Gibran from the snare of biographical studies and approaches, whereby the author's work is not only indissociable from his life but is seen fundamentally through and reduced to that life. It also aims to 'de-mythologise' Gibran, who has become this mysterious mystic poet, especially in the United States, whose work hovers between literature and 'spirituality'. This book does so, however, without falling prey to those culturalist analyses that foreground the question of power and cultural politics at the expense of the essential literary or poetic quality of the text. Rather, it engages with Gibran's *oeuvre* as bilingual Arabic literature by situating it within, without reducing it to, its contexts of emergence and reception, rethinking in the process the relationship between poetics and politics, literature and history, 'form' and 'content'. This approach will reveal those dimensions of Gibran's work that have been obscured in its Euro-American and Arabic histories of reception, although the latter is itself forgotten in Euro-American scholarship. The primary aim of the book, therefore, is to read Gibran in a creative manner that does justice to the multifariousness and complexity of his literary *oeuvre*. In so doing, it goes beyond (while exposing and interrogating) the modes of reading and valuation that confined Gibran to often reductive categorisations, the prophet of the New Age and/or the Romantic and sentimentalist poet.

In modern Arabic literature, Gibran's contributions are canonical and well-known.[1] The *Mahjari* writer experimented with many genres: the short story, poetry, the play and the essay. But what marks this experimentation is the way in which he used language. His signature style is lyrical, energetic, immersive. It uses imagery, repetition and parallelism in a novel fashion that creates a gripping rhythm, immersing the reader in the current of feelings carried through this innovative use of language. This creative spirit, which also turned many social and cultural norms upside-down, is deemed by many notable Arab critics and writers – Adonis (Ali Ahmad Said Esber), Kamal Abu-Deeb and Boutros Hallaq, to mention but a few[2] – a discursive turn in, if not the inaugural eruption of, Arab literary modernity. Adonis, for instance, sees Gibran as the founder of modernity as vision (*al-ḥadātha al-ru'yā*) in Arabic literature and the pioneer of its articulation, in that his innovative mode of writing made possible a new horizon of literary expression. He writes:

> [T]he primary significance of Gibran resides in the fact that he took a trajectory hitherto unknown in Arab writing, in that he *destroyed memory and constructed the sign*. In this sense, he represents *a beginning* [. . .] Arab writing, starting from him, has ceased to contemplate itself in the mirrors of expression, but has begun, instead, to submerge itself in anguish, search and yearning – and hence its energisation; the readers who previously fed on words now feed on the power of renewal and transformation.[3]

What is more, Gibran captivated many Arab readers by virtue of his spirited and inspiring rebelliousness, which is at times tinged with 'idealism'.[4] His writings betray an aversion to all forms of authority that sustain what he calls '*quwwat al-istimrār*' or 'the power of continuity'.[5] In *Ghurbat al-kātib al-ʿarabī* (The Exile of the Arab Writer, 2013), for instance, the Syro-Lebanese novelist and scholar Halim Barakat foregrounds that 'Gibran's writing was primarily an expression of the concerns of the mind, the heart and the apprehensions of the self in a world born of its death. For that reason, it took the form of total rebellion against mainstream culture and institutions'.[6] Barakat is speaking about Gibran in reference to a memorial built for him in an empty, non-descript place between the centre of Washington, DC, and its suburbs in 1989, where Gibran lived in 'an isolation which is not the one he loved and, inspired by it, he wrote, but a poor and stifling isolation that he has not chosen for himself but was, indeed, forced upon him'.[7] That Barakat speaks about Gibran's 'exile' in this manner is not surprising. For Gibran, he maintains, has turned from a poet of 'counterculture' into one of 'peace, understanding, reconciliation and consensus',[8] not just in the US but also in Lebanon, where he has been subject to 'ritualistic celebrations' that robbed him of his counter-cultural significance.[9] Domestication, however, is conventional. And it is the task of criticism, in Edward Said's sense of the word, to de-domesticate, as it were, to scrutinise through the eyes of an exile, to not belong. Gibran lived in two different worlds and wrote in two different languages, feeling at home in neither. This book sets out on a journey, therefore, through these worlds, hoping that what emerges from this journey is a rounded picture of Gibran and a complex understanding of his *oeuvre*, its legacy and its reception.

Gibran Khalil Gibran as Arab World Literature attempts to uncover and probe the domesticated, obscured or overlooked incarnations of Gibran: namely, a post-religious poet who is peculiarly modern and critical of modernity, an anxious bilingual writer who is at once a universal poet and a critical *Nahḍawī* intellectual. This interplay of the national and the universal will inform my reading of Gibran, meaning that I examine Gibran through and across Arabic and English, the Arab cultural geography and the Euro-American one. This is why I also investigate the ways in which his works have thus far been received, both in the US and the Arab world, underscoring the conditions of these modes of reception and their presuppositions, and revealing what is rendered (in)visible by them. The aim is not so much to 'reclaim' Gibran as to de-mystify him, to bring him back to this world, to history, reading his bilingual literary enterprise in a way that does not reduce it to such designations as 'Eastern,' 'spiritual', 'humanist', or even 'Romantic'. For Gibran was neither an inexplicable 'genius'[10] nor an 'Eastern guru', but an important and influential writer whose work has been decontextualised and therefore often misunderstood.

As a bilingual writer or, perhaps more accurately, as an Arab writer in Arabic and in English, Gibran has been subject to divergent modes of reception that have obscured his literary specificity and the value of his work, in ways that are extremely perplexing and at times disturbing. For how can one reconcile the enormous scholarly and literary interest in Gibran in the Arab discursive universe with the dearth of criticism devoted to his work in Anglo-American scholarship, exceptions notwithstanding? In English, the only solid book-length study is Khalil Hawi's *Kahlil Gibran: His Background, Character and Works* (1972), a standard reference in Gibran Studies. For all the breadth, rigour and insightfulness of Hawi's study, its approach reads Gibran's texts as inseparable from the life of their author, such that it is only to their author's 'personal experience' that they owe their ultimate value. Other important books on Gibran in English include two critical biographies, Robin Waterfield's *Prophet: The Life and Times of Kahlil Gibran* (1998) and Suheil Bushrui and Joe Jenkins's *Kahlil Gibran, Man and Poet: A New Biography* (1998), both of which are valuable and illuminating in their study of Gibran as a man conditioned by specific circumstances which he nevertheless attempted to overcome in his work.[11] In Arabic, however, studies of Gibran from a multiplicity of critical perspectives are legion, but the question, meaning and significance of his bilingualism as an Arab writer are generally overlooked. This profound chasm in literary and cultural reception, which is visible in his name itself[12] – on the one hand, the American and global *Kahlil Gibran*, the name he seemed to have reluctantly adopted in the US,[13] and on the other hand, the Arab *Jubrān Khalīl Jubrān* – is what triggered the critical concern that made this book possible. Gibran, I argue, must be read bilingually: any appraisal of his work should rest on a cognizance of the two linguistic, cultural and epistemic spheres in which his work was produced and received, and on a historical awareness of what made that production and reception possible.

To read Gibran in a critical and hospitable spirit, this monograph breaks with the biographical and East–West culturalist perspectives from which Gibran has so far been perceived or studied. Instead, it adopts a nuanced approach of reading that attends to the particularity of literary texts, not as objects that either transcend their historical situatedness or reflect their socio-cultural context, but as texts whose meanings and value are configured and reconfigured depending on the historical, epistemic and cultural contexts of reception and conditions of reading. This means that what the text says and how it does so – which is referred to as its 'singularity', a concept I draw from Derek Attridge's *The Singularity of Literature* (2004) – should be distinguished from the history of its reception in one or more cultural locations. This book offers a reading of Gibran's writings that is both attentive to their singularity as they intervene in their multiple contexts (including our present one) *and* critical of their histories of reception, namely, of what underpins their literary and aesthetic (e)valuation, thereby drawing attention to what has hitherto been absent or absented in this reception. What has often been absented, whether consciously or not, is the tacit connections between his Arabic and Anglophone writings, which this study accentuates and discusses beyond the approaches of biographical criticism, culturalism and, to a lesser extent, post-colonialism.[14] These approaches, I submit, fall short of accounting for, and doing justice to, the singularity of Gibran's work as *Mahjari* Arabic and Arab Anglophone literature – that is, as bilingual Arabic literature.[15]

From the point of view of reception, Gibran's literary singularity may be regarded as a discontinuous one. In other words, if we follow Attridge in positing that a literary work is *creative* when it brings into being something other – that is, hitherto un-thought, un-imagined, or un-formulated – and becomes *inventive* when it alters the literary sphere in which it is accommodated,[16] then Gibran's work is both creative and inventive in Arabic, while creative and not sufficiently inventive in English, given its tepid reception in American literary criticism despite, or because of, its popular celebration. But if approached as bilingual Arabic literature or, as I construe it, as Arab world literature, this discontinuity would cease to appear this way, for his Anglophone work has been translated also into Arabic – and into many other languages – and accommodated as part of its modern literature.[17] While keeping in mind the importance of Gibran's work as 'Arab American', therefore, I read his bilingual text, to invoke Gayatri Spivak, as 'the emergent' that 'persistently and repeatedly undermines the definitive tendency of the dominant [in the Arab world and particularly in the US] to appropriate [it]',[18] as a text that remains, to draw on Attridge, 'a stranger, even and perhaps especially when the reader knows it intimately'.[19]

The argument of the book is enacted by way of reading Gibran's multifarious work – including poems in English and Arabic, as well as letters (read as texts, not as biographical data), short stories, plays and essays in Arabic, some of which were published posthumously – from a perspective that highlights the creative tension between the local or the particular and the universal. The local designates Arabic language and culture as well as Gibran's background and homeland (Lebanon spiritually, Greater Syria politically, the Arab East culturally), while the universal is understood as the poetic that speaks to the human as such, irrespective of the language of writing and of poetry as genre (as Gibran himself conceives of it). This reconfiguration of the local and the universal deconstructs the bond of language-nation-culture: I demonstrate that the universal, in Gibran, begins in the particular and goes beyond it; that is, it is not just adopted by virtue of his switch into English as a language of writing. This reconfiguration, furthermore, has a double aim. On the one hand, it provides an illuminating perspective from which to reengage with his texts and interpret them critically and rewardingly. On the other hand, it allows for a reading that does not decouple his Arabophone and Anglophone writings, uncovering and establishing multiple associations that many critics and scholars have failed to discern thus far.

'Worlding' Gibran

Gibran is approached in this study as a world writer whose texts cannot be dissociated from the modern emergence of 'literature' as a relatively autonomous domain;[20] from the transformation of 'religion' in modernity and the Arab *Nahḍa* or renaissance; from the travelling, circulation and transformation of ideas, concepts and ideologies on a global scale in the nineteenth and early twentieth centuries; and from the interconnected locations – geographical, cultural and imaginative – of enunciation and reception that shaped the status of Gibran's work and its value in multiple and discordant ways. In other words, Gibran's work cannot be dissociated from what Edward Said calls 'the historical experience of empire as a *common* one', the separation between Europeans and non-Europeans notwithstanding.[21] Engaging with Gibran's texts by situating them within this nexus without reducing them to it is, generally speaking, my method in this book. Arriving at this method came after realising that reading and doing justice to Gibran's works as creative products – whatever their limitations – entails attending to them, first, in their literary singularity (that is, by reading them in a creative manner that reveals their unexhausted possibilities of generating meaning and significance); and second, as entangled in the constellation of the worldly forces and conditions that made their emergence, inscription and longevity in the world possible. This is demonstrated in my situated close readings of Gibran's texts throughout the book.

The worldliness that I am emphasising, following Said, is inherent to the being of the text itself: 'It is not only that any text, if it is not immediately destroyed, is a network of often colliding forces, but also that a text in its actually *being* a text is a being in the world'.[22] The text is brought into being and becomes a text in the world, in that it is the reading of it as a published work by multiple subjectivities in one or more cultural locations that makes it possible as a text beyond the control of the author. But what is equally important here are the worldly conditions that make a particular text, a set of texts or an *oeuvre* possible, the historical, discursive and cultural conditions of writing against which writers as agents produce their work. It is the bilingualism of Gibran, his situatedness in two linguistic and cultural spheres at a particular juncture in history that is at once modern, imperial and colonial – in the sense in which these three inter-relate in ways that are not always accounted for in terms of dominant-subordinate structure – and it is the intriguing after-life of his texts in the twentieth and at the beginning of the twenty-first centuries that render his case particularly complex and difficult to approach. The task is therefore to avoid, as much as possible, any sort of interpretative reductionism, which could be countered by being at once hermeneutically careful/hospitable and historically critical when engaging with his texts. This is not an easy task, indeed, but one that I am sure this monograph will not divert from in any conspicuous way, unavoidable limitations notwithstanding.

Reading Approach: Two Planes of Analysis

Attending to the singularity of the Gibranian text in its bilingual (in)visibility and in its multifariousness will be carried out by demarcating *two planes of analysis* which, however inter-related, should not be confused with one another. This is, of course, in addition to the inevitable thematic or perspectival division. What I mean by planes of analysis has to do with my approach in the book. This approach consists of rendering visible the Gibranian text in its necessarily polysemic nature – which is not the same as semantic indeterminacy – by considering its worldly situatedness, but without determining its ultimate value by subduing it to such discursive or contextual over-determinations as the East–West culturalist dichotomy or the biography of the author. What is at stake here is *how* one understands these cultural, discursive and biographical elements – or, in short, the 'context' – in relation or in their manner of relating to the text and *vice versa*. We know after Roland Barthes and Jacques Derrida that the text has more to say than what its author meant or intended to, that the text always exceeds the author-as-cause. This should not mean, however, that the text becomes the new god, as it were. For the text, as emphasised earlier, is a *being in the world*. We read it, that is, in the world and in relation to the world, and the more we know about the world(s) in which it is written and received the more enriched our reading becomes. Furthermore, it is in these worlds that we can locate and understand the conditions which enabled the emergence of Gibran's texts and, most importantly, occasioned their persistence, conditions that resist any monocultural or monolinguistic understanding – hence the necessary plural use of 'world'. The history and modality of this persistence is confounding, as indicated in the reception of *The Prophet*, which is the most popularly visible of Gibran's books but the least inviting of critical attention, at the expense (at least in the US) of his other works in both languages, which suffer both popular and critical attention.

This is why I delineate two planes of analysis: the first has to do with *what* the literary text says and *how* it does so in connection to its general context of emergence – and, of course, to the actual context of reading – and how it intervenes in it as a text; and the second pertains to the location(s) of and the degree to which this changing context of enunciation and reception bears on the manner in which the text is or has been read, evaluated and valued. Both planes inevitably overlap, but it is the topical concern that entails the prioritising of one over the other. Even though my argument would logically require the first plane of analysis, the second will be also crucial when the question of reception is addressed or, at least, is relevant to the discussion. Confusing these two planes, which are inter-connected but distinct, has led, for instance, to the tendency of accounting for the intriguingly popular appeal of *The Prophet* by returning, whether explicitly or not, to the author-as-cause, whereas Gibran had nothing to do with the enormous celebration of the book in the 1930s, the New Age movement and beyond. It is the text that has survived, not its author or any implied authorial intention, despite the writer's inventiveness having brought the book into existence. That this study is not solely concerned with reading but with specific modes of reading/reception and with what they reveal and conceal would, I hope, lend more importance and validity to the notion of Arab world literature, which is obviously meant as a critical intervention into the Anglo-Saxon academic discourse of 'world literature'.

Gibran's *Oeuvre*: Between the Local and the Universal

Gibran began his literary career by publishing a long poetic essay in Arabic, *al-Mūsīqā* (On Music, 1905), which demonstrates an experimentally audacious use of language marked by lyricism, simplicity and emotionalism. This stylistic uniqueness was combined with a celebration of the individual and the values of solitude, exile and madness, a rebellious and anti-authoritarian spirit and a spiritual fascination with nature in his collections of short stories, *ʿArā'is al-murūj* (Nymphs of the Valley, 1906) and *al-Arwāḥ al-mutamarrida* (Spirits Rebellious, 1908), as well as in his novella *al-Ajniḥa al-mutakassira* (The Broken Wings, 1912). All these stories are set in Lebanon, against a backdrop of ecclesiastical tyranny and social injustice in the face of which his protagonists – like Khalil the heretic or Yuhanna the mad, mouthpieces of his poet-prophetic activism – hyperbolically revolt and romantically subvert the social order, without reforming or positing an alternative social vision. Despite the occasional didacticism and sentimentality that characterise these writings, as well as their simplicity of plot and characterisation, they introduced, by virtue of their unique subjective tone, lyrical flow, vivid imagery and rebellious tenor, a new energy in modern Arabic literature – which made Gibran the foremost *Mahjari* Romantic. This first stage of Gibran's writings ends with a publication of a collection of essays and poetic prose, which he wrote for the Arab press over the years preceding the publication, under the title of *Dam'a wa ibtisāma* (A Tear and a Smile, 1914). The second and more mature stage begins with the publication of *The Madman: His Parables and Poems* (1918) and *al-ʿAwāṣif* (The Tempests, 1920), a collection of writings across many genres: the essay, the short story, poetic prose and the play. What characterises these works is an acute sense of social and religious revolt, marked by an unmistakable Nietzschean spirit that exposes and satirises the contradictions inherent in existing norms and moral values, both in the Arab world and in the US. The voice of the Romantic Gibran continues to be heard in this stage, in his long poem *al-Mawākib* (The Processions, 1919), *The Forerunner* (1920), *The Prophet* (1923), *al-Badā'iʿ wa al-ṭarā'if* (Marvels and Masterpieces, 1923), *Jesus the Son of Man* (1928), *The Earth Gods* (1931) and his posthumous work *The Garden of the Prophet* (1932). But what distinguishes most of these writings is a post-Nietzschean impulse in which Gibran and his poets are thinking within the horizon of thought that Nietzsche made possible: exposing the nihilism behind certain values which survived by dint of 'the power of continuity',[23] and reimagining God, the self and the world by way of reclaiming prophetic speech. Furthermore, Gibran wrote many essays and plays for the Arab *Mahjar* press, particularly in the 1910s and in the first half of the 1920s, most of which are collected by John Daye.[24] These texts are important because they reveal another crucial facet of Gibran, that of the intellectual who is committed to the *Nahḍa* or renaissance of the Syrian nation and the Arab East. The material studied, furthermore, includes numerous letters that Gibran exchanged with his American close friend Mary Haskell and, to a lesser extent, with May Ziadeh; American reviews of his books in English; translations of *The Prophet* (1923) into Arabic; and Arabic creative engagements with his Anglophone work, such as Mansur Rahbani's play *Jubrān wa-l-nabiyy* (Gibran and the Prophet, 2010), performed as an operetta in 2005.

Gibran's *oeuvre* is studied in this book in a way that does not focus on the development of his writing career as much as it demonstrates what makes these writings peculiar, namely their poetic reinvention of the religious (Chapter One) and their national-*Nahḍawī* impulse (Chapter Three) – in other words, their universal and national dimensions. These dimensions, I argue, are not antithetical but dialectical; and it is one of the main aims of this book to show exactly how they are dialectical. The question of bilingualism (Chapter Two) is examined in relation to this dialectical relationship between the universal and the local: the universal, which in Gibran is made possible by virtue of the poetic, begins from the local but extends beyond it, in language, culture and audience. The notion of Arab world literature is meant to capture this specific configuration of the local and the universal, which has been lost on many readers and critics.

The scope of this book cannot be stretched to focus on Gibran's art, which consists of numerous drawings and paintings, simply because I do not have the requisite expertise to engage with it critically. One awaits a book that studies his drawing and paintings, that traces and explains the development of his artistic career. I must note, furthermore, that Gibran's reception outside the Arab world and the US is not covered in this book. This is because the American reception occupies much of my analysis in Chapter Four, an unstudied reception that warrants such an attention, not to mention the Arabic afterlife of his Anglophone works, which is an essential and overlooked element that must be brought to the fore, as my overall argument in this book entails.

The Poetic, the Prophetic and the Abrahamic

It is essential to remember that Gibran writes as a poet, even and particularly in his prose. That is to say, it is the poetic, the inventive force by which a language lives and survives,[25] that constitutes the driving force of his writings, beyond the conventional division of genres or of prose and poetry. What is more, poetry is often identified, explicitly or tacitly, with the universal in Gibran, in that the true poet in his text is not only indicative of '*quwwat al-ibtikār*'[26] or 'the power of invention' in a certain language, but also emerges as existentially exiled,[27] necessarily singing and manifesting life as such – what he refers to as 'world-consciousness'.[28] So the prophetic in his writings is essentially poetic; which is to say that his post-religious prophet, as I discuss in Chapter One, speaks primarily as a poet. This is a fundamental point that must be underlined time and again, even when Gibran's national, critical writings are examined. In addition, when I speak of the prophetic, I not only refer to the modern Romantic notion of the poet-prophet, but, most importantly, to the Abrahamic as that mythic-discursive condition that allows for the Romantic appropriation of the poet as a prophet, and for Gibran and the *Mahjar* school to embrace the same notion.[29] And since the Abrahamic points to that which simultaneously unites and divides the three monotheistic religions, of which Christianity and Islam are particularly pertinent to Gibran, it precedes and exceeds not only the Romantic embrace of the trope of the poet-prophet, which is marked by the imprint of Islam and Sufism as far as Gibran and the *Mahjar* Romantic poets are concerned.[30] It also precedes, exceeds and destabilises the reductive culturalist logic of symbolic geography (East and West). Furthermore, Gibran's case is particularly interesting here because, despite his early profound awareness of Greek mythology, he 'wrote no Greek mythological poetry', which means that '[h]e had a clear idea of what he was doing, that is, of the reason he was not writing such poetry'.[31] For the Greeks, as Maurice Blanchot reminds us, had not known the *nabi*s (prophets).[32] The prophetic, in other words, is essentially Abrahamic.

Gibran, the *Mahjari* School and the Arab *Nahḍa*

The worlding of Gibran requires that we study his work within the cultural and discursive universe that made it possible. That world is largely seen as a world affected and interconnected by empire; that is, a world made by European modes of thought, of governance, of knowledge production and identity formation.[33] But this is only one side of the picture. The world of Gibran is the world of the *Nahḍa*, of the Arab renaissance that cannot be understood in isolation from European modernity, but which cannot, in the same breath, be reduced to it.

Along with other influential writers and poets such as Ameen Rihani, Mikhail Naimy and Ilia Abu Madi, Gibran was part of an Arab literary movement in the US that consolidated *al-adab al-mahjarī* (*émigré* literature) as a crucial episode in the modern experience of Arabic literature. These figures in 1920 formed *al-Rābiṭa al-Qalamiyya* (the Pen Bond), known as *Arrabitah*, a literary society whose aim was to infuse a new creative spirit in Arabic literature. Gibran was elected the president of *Arrabitah* and remained so until his demise in 1931. His work, as a *Mahjari* writer, reflects the stance of *Arrabitah* in its self-conscious literary activity of 'breaking with the past', yet this orientation, as Naimy stresses, embodies not so much a complete rupture with 'the ancients' or tradition as an interdiction of 'imitation':

> For there be some among them [the ancients] who will remain to us and to those who follow a source of inspiration for many ages to come. To revere them is a great honour. To imitate them is a deadly shame. For our life, our needs, our circumstances are far different from theirs. We must be true to ourselves if we would be true to our ancestors.[34]

Problems of the present and the past, thus, of how to conceive of 'tradition' and its place and function in the present, were central concerns for the *Mahjari* movement's call for the rejuvenation and rekindling of creativity in Arabic literature. Crucially, the movement, which was remarkable in its influence on literary expression in the Arabic literary field, cannot be dissociated from the Arab *Nahḍa* that had begun in the nineteenth century.

The *Nahḍa* was essentially a reform movement, institutionally, culturally and economically. While its initiation is usually associated with Napoleon's invasion of Egypt in 1798, the 'modernisation' process had already begun in the reign of Sultan Salim III (1789–1809).[35] The need to reform was fundamental to its articulation as a modernising process by various thinkers, intellectuals and literati and to its bureaucratic, institutional and educational enactment in the Ottoman Empire, under the immense pressure of imperial Britain and France. Intellectually and philosophically speaking, the *Nahḍa* witnessed an active movement of travelling ideas and concepts – mostly of European provenance – that were appropriated and hybridised in the Arab cultural discourse.[36] Chief among these concepts are nationalism, Darwinism (especially in its social and metaphysical variations) and socialism.[37] The peculiar domestication of Darwinism and nationalism in the *Nahḍa* is particularly relevant to Gibran's enterprise, as I will show in Chapters One and Three.

The renaissance project, as is well-known, was premised on the notion that Arabo-Islamic identity and civilisation must be rejuvenated *à l'Europeénne* after what became known as centuries of *inḥiṭāṭ* (decadence)[38] under the Ottoman Empire, a notion that had taken root in the work of early erudite reformers such as Rifa'a Rafi' al-Tahtawi, Ahmad Faris al-Shidyaq, 'Ali Mubarak and Butrus al-Bustani in the nineteenth century.[39] Gibran and the *Mahjari* Romantics were part of the 'modern' phase of the renaissance at the turn of the twentieth century. This phase, which broke with the revival (*iḥyā'*) of the premodern genres of the *maqāma* (with Ibrahim al-Yajizi and Muhammad al-Muwaylihi) and the pastiche (*mu'āraḍa*) of the Abbasid poetry of al-Buhturi and al-Mutanabbi (with such important poets as Ahmad Shawqi and Mahmud Sami al-Barudi), had begun with the gradual introduction of new genres and modes of writing in *fin-de-siècle* Egypt and Greater Syria. Prominent examples of this literary transformation include the social novels of Salim al-Bustani, the historical novels of Jurji Zaydan, the plays of Ya'qub Sannu' and the satires of 'Abdallah al-Nadim.[40] Breaking with 'traditional' forms of writing, these modern changes nevertheless did not break with (even though they occasionally and variously questioned) the reformist formula tied to the paradigm of civilisation and progress as laid down by the first generation of reformers.[41] However, witnessing the colonisation of the MENA region and the authoritarian reign of the Ottoman Sultan 'Abd al-Hamid intensified the need for alternative reform agendas, now that a whole new cultural and institutional infrastructure was in place, partly thanks to the early reformers.

The Romantics were averse to what became known as the nineteenth-century neo-classical trend, mainly because they considered its mode of writing to be out of touch with the contemporaneous Arab individual. For them, this mode embodied less the concerns, ordeals and aspirations of the poet as a socially and culturally conditioned being than a nostalgia for the past evinced in the 'revival' of the classical style. In its emphasis on poetry and literature as the expression of the poet's soul or interiority, therefore, Romanticism was partly occasioned by the revivalist poetics of exteriority; the latter's concern with resuscitating the rhetorical potency and linguistic richness of the Abbasid high poetry was regarded by the Romantics as a mere echo of the past, rather than a true and authentic poetic engagement with the present.[42] Beyond this literary concern, which is of course not solely or strictly literary, Stephen Sheehi argues that the Arab Romantics strove to break with the rationalist, reformist project of the renaissance, whose telos was the civilisational model of the West – civilisation *qua* urbanity. They did so by emphasising the transcendental unity with nature and reintegrating tradition as a metaphysical plane of moral purity and cultural authenticity, in response to the split in Arab subjectivity ushered in by the *Nahḍa*.[43] This thesis is only partly tenable, because the positing of Romanticism against reformist rationalism in the context of the *Nahḍa*, and particularly in relation to Gibran, creates a rigid binary of rationalism and Romanticism that my reading in Chapter Three will show to be reductive. For while the Romantic paradigm accounts for the break with reformist rationalism in the fictional works of the Romantics,[44] it does not exhaust the range of representational and intellectual engagement within their *oeuvres*, in this case Gibran's. Neither does it explain Gibran's crucial difference in conceptualising the *Nahḍa* itself: a change from conceiving of 'knowledge' as the basis of the renaissance[45] to positing 'moral independence' as the premise of acquiring/producing knowledge and establishing an original *Nahḍa* or modernity.

Essentially literary but broadly national and civilisational in its commitment, thus, the literary school of the *Mahjar* was part and parcel of this history of the *Nahḍa*, and the work of influential bilingual writers such as Gibran cannot be adequately examined and appreciated in Arabic or in English without a cognizance of the *Nahḍa*'s discursive field and the worldly forces that enabled its emergence and what it itself enabled, beyond the polarity of either local agency or foreign presence as instigators. The *Nahḍa*, hence, is understood as an at once local and imperial manifestation of modernity beyond Europe. Situating Gibran in this historical-discursive context is a necessary step towards a better understanding of his literary enterprise and its legacy.

East–West Identitarianism, the Problem of 'Agency' and the Study of Modern Arab(ic) Literature

Gibran's peculiarity lies in the fact that he wrote in both Arabic and English, that he wrote, that is, as an Arab writer in English. This bilingual and bicultural feature is often articulated through the frame of the Orient–Occident dichotomy, one which therefore necessitates some critical comments here. This is not the space to discuss this problem in detail, yet this identitarian division – which is inseparable from both modernity and Orientalism (themselves indissociable) – is pertinent to Gibran and his historical, discursive and imaginative universe. My concern is with *why* and *how*, precisely, this is pertinent here. In the introduction to his still-debated book *Orientalism* (1978), Said begins by giving three definitions to Orientalism, the first academic, the second imaginative and the third historical and material. It is the second definition that interests me here:

> *Orientalism is a style of thought based upon an ontological and epistemological distinction made between 'the Orient' and (most of the time) 'the Occident'.* Thus a very large mass of writers, among whom are poets, novelists, philosophers, political theorists, economists, and imperial administrators, have accepted the basic distinction between East and West as the starting point for elaborate theories, epics, novels, social descriptions, and political accounts concerning the Orient, its people, customs, 'minds', destiny, and so on.[46]

This style of thought, thus, divides the world into two distinct categories of identification, both ontologically and epistemologically. In other words, this style projects trans-historical and unchanging essences onto the identitarian categories in question, and based on this essentialist distinction, knowledge about the Other is produced by – and bears on the definition of – the same. But Said's concern is with writers from the Western hemisphere; that is, with representations of the Orient by Occidental writers. Considering what Said in *Culture and Imperialism* (1993) calls the common experience of empire, what was the impact of this 'style of thought' on Arab 'Oriental' writers in and after the *Nahḍa*, for instance? In what ways did they react to or interact with it? How did they think about or represent themselves? These questions are beyond the scope of Said's book, the contours and limitations of which he clearly demarcates in *Orientalism*'s introduction. They are also beyond the scope of this book. Yet, since this issue pertains to Gibran as an Arab Oriental writer in the American Occident, some clarifications need to be made.

While the division of the world into two identitarian spheres – articulated in civilisational and cultural terms – was commonplace and went largely unquestioned in the nineteenth and most of the twentieth century, the distinction between Orient and Occident has not always been an ontological and epistemological one. This is evidenced in the *Nahḍa* itself and what became known in the late nineteenth century as 'the Eastern question' (*al-masʾala al-sharqiyya*); this unsurprisingly coincided, as Marwa Elshakry has shown, with the pervasiveness of evolutionist thought in the same period, where discourses about 'civilisation' and progress gained unprecedented currency.[47] In this context, civilisations and cultures were understood as subject to the law of evolution, which entails that 'identity' is a variable (not a stable) entity, the division of 'us' and 'them' notwithstanding. Yet identity, insofar as it is produced by narratives that define the same in opposition to the Other, often functions as that which anchors subjectivity/community in an imagined stability/continuity in changing time and space. For that reason, it invites less a complex and open than a static understanding of it. And because of the modern, imperial ubiquity of the concepts of 'civilisation' and 'culture',[48] the identification of the self and the Other, in modernity and late modernity, took on an *essentially* civilisational and cultural designation. This identification, thus, would predetermine and constitute subjecthood itself; identity, that is, would precede and define the self *a priori*. The problem, however, was that because the Occident was *materially* more advanced than the Orient – one potent factor that led the former to rule territorially and epistemologically over the latter – this identification was fundamentally hierarchical and oppositional. Said shows how 'European culture gained in strength and identity by setting itself off against the Orient as sort of surrogate and even underground self'.[49] What is intriguing, however, is that most of the Arab Oriental writers in the *Nahḍa* and post-*Nahḍa* would refute Orientalist claims about Oriental cultural and civilisational inferiority – Europe being the normative yardstick here – without questioning the civilisational nature of the distinction and its underpinning epistemology; that is, even if they interrogated or repudiated certain ontological features attributed to the Arab Orient.[50] In other words, the Occident–Orient division of the world was – and is – a modern, imperial phenomenon shared by both 'Occidentals' and Arab 'Orientals'. What is meant by Oriental or Occidental outside Europe, however, complicates the distinction and the way in which it is employed, entailing closer attention to who uses these entities as identitarian markers, how, why and in what context. The importance of this observation lies in the fact that an Arab Oriental writer in the nineteenth or early twentieth century was an *active* agent in a specific cultural and social milieu, however limited the effectiveness of her text on the ground, and not simply the European's 'Other'.

A telling anecdote from Gibran's life will illustrate my point. In a letter to Mary Haskell that dates back to 1912, Gibran informs his beloved companion that he met Pierre Loti, the French novelist and naval officer who travelled extensively in Africa and Asia and was known for his exoticist novels. This is what Gibran had to say about the meeting:

> Pierre Loti is here and I had a charming hour with him on Thursday. We talked about 'his beloved East'. He said he saw my *Broken Wings* and ended by saying, 'You are becoming more brutal and less Oriental – and it is too bad, too bad!' I love my country too well to be like her other children. But he does not see that; he is too delicate, too sensitive. He has all the beautiful Oriental diseases in his soul.[51]

Gibran goes on to describe him as an 'Orientalised occidental', a designation that encapsulates the dramatic irony of this encounter. For Loti's 'beloved East' is obviously not Gibran's. Loti speaks as a Westerner for whom the East, at that time, represents docility, submissiveness, cooperation and – this is implicit but crucial – availability. The East, for Loti, is a place of mythic and exotic escapism, and the possibility of its autonomy or unavailability is inconceivable. For Gibran, however, the East is in dire need of reform and must rise again as a civilisational power. That an Easterner could be 'brutal' in his criticism, that an Easterner could be self-critical, is unfathomable for Loti. The irony of the exchange peaks when Gibran diagnoses Loti's 'artistic soul' as suffering from 'all the beautiful Oriental diseases', for we do not know whether those diseases are Loti's invention or actual diseases that crept into his soul, rendering him an 'Orientalised occidental'. As will be discussed in Chapter Three, however, Gibran regards the East as suffering from eradicable (historical) maladies such as 'despotism', not inherent (ontological) ones. The East, for him, is neither a 'career'[52] nor an exotic escapist place, but his own civilisational sphere to which he belongs and for which he spends his intellectual energy as an engaged writer and intellectual. As he writes in his essay 'al-ʿAhd al-jadīd' (The New Age, 1923), the East is torn between regressive and progressive forces, and for him the latter should prevail.[53] That Gibran cannot *completely* escape Orientalism as a style of thought – the division of the world into East and West – is unsurprising, given that it is part of the larger paradigm of imperial modernity; that he resists it is in equal measure unsurprising, given that resistance to cultural imperialism is an integral feature of that imperial modernity.

While Said's critique of Orientalism has laid bare the consequences and dangers of adopting that essentialist style of thought, the persistence of entities such as the West and the East, however, indicates the persistence of modern identitarian reason, which often confuses inherited and narrated identity with subjecthood. National and/or civilisational identity is something that has emerged in and with modernity, with the scientific, economic and imperial ascendency of Europe in the seventeenth and eighteenth centuries – Europe taking on the name of 'the West' in the nineteenth[54] – and the concurrent colonial conquering of the world and of what became known, more specifically, as 'the Orient'. Hence, identitarian reason cannot be dissociated from the rise of modern forms of knowledge and sovereignty. Because it still lends power and persistence to entities such as the West and the East, the former obviously more potently consolidated and used in public and academic discourse than the latter (which is now referred to, more or less euphemistically, as 'the non-West' or 'the global South'), it is something that we should heed with great caution. Despite the globality of the Earth that renders such entities geographically relative or even invalid, their continuance ought to be critiqued but not easily dismissed, precisely because they are a human invention rather than an inert fact of nature. The West and the East are signifiers whose usage is problematic but, alas, at times unavoidable; this is to say that one should be aware that these loose identitarian poles, which saturate geography with symbolic and imaginative significations, are necessarily marked by semantic instability, despite the fictional homogeneity and opposition that essentialist discourse, whether Orientalist or not, imputes to them. This depends, I should reiterate, on who uses, claims and questions them, and how, why, when and where – that is, on the set of conditions and power relations underpinning their usage[55] – beyond or because of the fact of their being 'an invention',[56] and this is particularly relevant to my analysis in Chapters Two, Three and Four. It bears reminding, however, that my analysis begins *with the Gibranian text*, not with the Orient–Occident polarity as a starting point of analysis or object of critique. For this Gibranian text, as I shall attempt to demonstrate, is irreducible to such general entities, and the poetic impulse that animates it disrupts such vacuous generalities. Yet, Gibran could not escape this entrenched identitarian reason, and I also try to show how and why.

A historically critical reading of Arab (Anglophone) literature, therefore, should pay attention to the fact that the role and influence of Orientalism as a form of identitarian reason in the modern, imperial juncture on, in particular, 'Oriental' subjects, is *necessarily different* from the way in which it operates in a 'post-colonial' one, especially after the publication of Said's *Orientalism* and the institutionalisation of Post-Colonial Studies in the Anglo-Saxon academy. This vital historical shift means that one should not be quick in making retrospective historical-critical judgements on Arab, Oriental writers at that particular point in history – which should *not* mean absolving them of criticism – while forgetting the privileged historical and institutional vantage point (post-colonial and post-*Orientalism*, respectively) from which the judgement is made. More specifically, the task is not so much to reduce what they write to culturalist readings that interpret texts through the sole lens of colonial discourse analysis in a retrospectively evaluative or judgmental manner, as *to better understand* what is textually produced through, within or beyond Orientalist imagination as we understand it today. For there are so many aesthetic, cultural, political and religious concerns in modern Arabic literature that do not lend themselves to post-colonialist readings.[57] Hence the kind of reading I try to perform in this study: that of attending to the Gibranian text in its literary particularity as it intervenes in (and is affected by) its context of emergence and reception, while keeping in mind the modern experience of empire in which 'all cultures are involved in one another; none is single and pure, all are hybrid, heterogenous, extraordinarily differentiated, and unmonolithic'.[58] My point, to put it differently, is *not* to look at Arabic and Arab, Anglophone literature, and at Gibran's text in particular, from a strictly post-colonial, culturalist lens, which at times runs the risk of falling (unwittingly) into the sort of reductionism against which Said himself warned.[59]

This leads me to foreground the problem 'difference' in a modern world in which cultures and traditions are imperially and translationally inter-related, but unevenly and unequally visible and influential. Hosam Aboul-Ela reminds us that 'contemporary Arabic poetry presents a challenge for postcolonial studies, which is far more comfortable with novels, especially ones written in English', and that, most importantly, 'non-European poetics raises issues of difference that are not easily understood through the frame of colonialism'.[60] This is why I earlier demarcated two planes of analysis which, however inter-related, should not be confused with one another. For to start with the awareness of the text's own difference that calls for the reader's ethical responsibility of reading, which consists of attending at once to its own textual particularity and its worldly situatedness, is not the same as starting with an *a priori* notion of cultural difference that interprets/appropriates the text by flattening – whether unwittingly or not – its own literary or poetic singularity in the name of 'context'.

It is essential, therefore, to point out that the concept of 'the Other' in my critical orientation is primarily understood as the ontologically universal Other whose essence – if there is any – is inaccessible and whose singularity cannot be fully exhausted or appropriated. This means that the Other has an infinite ethical claim on the same, as Emmanuel Levinas would say.[61] This notion of Otherness precedes, exceeds and therefore resists – as opposed to negating the existence of – the culturally, racially and socially constructed notion of Otherness in which the Other is another term for the exotic, the inferior, the backward, the barbarian, the colonised, the infidel and so on, which is unfortunately not waning. Textual difference is of course not the same as (although it overlaps with) human and cultural difference, yet both are equally important and relevant to my reading of Gibran in this book. In this respect, I follow Attridge's conception of literature as 'the reader's Other', which he sharply distinguishes from reader-response criticism. The Other, in this conception, is 'a relating':

> [I]t is not the text 'itself' but my singular and active relation to the particular configuration of possibilities represented by the text that is the site of alterity. However old the text, however familiar to me, it can always strike me with the force of novelty if, by means of a creative reading that strives to respond fully to the singularity of the work in a new time and place, I open myself to its potential challenge. Rather than the familiar model of the literary work as friend and companion, sharing with the reader its secrets, I propose the work as stranger, even and perhaps especially when the reader knows it intimately.[62]

One last thing must be mentioned regarding my theoretical orientation in this book. When I refer to identitarian reason, I rely mostly on Fethi Meskini's critique of this modern kind of reason (*naqd al-ʿaql al-huwawī*). According to the Tunisian philosopher, the modern notion of national and cultural 'identity' displaces the classical ontological notion of *al-huwiyya* or ipseity, as understood in Greek and Arabic philosophy. His critique of identitarian reason is a critique of, on the one hand, the modern paradigm of sovereign subjectivity, in which the world turns from a divine 'sign' into an 'object' for domination by the transcendental subject (that is, modernity as a new form of *monotheism*),[63] and, on the other hand, of the anthropological/cultural concept of 'identity', which generated the post-modern and post-colonial obsession with cultural 'authenticity' and identitarian narratives. This obsession with identity, thus, has obscured the fundamental question that must concern the post-Kantian subject everywhere: freedom, or the horizon of a self that transcends inherited identity.[64] This critique orients the debate towards a phenomenological probing of ipseity – that is, of the question 'who?' – which precedes and informs any sense of subjecthood and 'identity', from both a classical Arab and post-modern philosophical perspectives.[65] Meskini's complex argument has been necessarily simplified for usage here. His philosophical and theoretical work, however, is particularly important here, for two reasons. The first is that Meskini is steeped in Arabic literature and philosophy, and Gibran is no exception (I critically highlight Meskini's reading of Gibran's parable 'How I became a Madman' in Chapter Four as a creative instance of reception). The second is because he thinks within the horizon of global, contemporary philosophy but from an Arab vantage point; that is, he is thinking universally in Arabic. Thus, philosophising and theorising in Arabic for him should interrupt the kind of reason that bears the stamp of symbolic geography, whether 'Western' or 'Eastern', all the while acknowledging the particular 'hermeneutical situation' of contemporary Arab thought, where the 'sources of the self'[66] – the Qur'ān, classical poetry and the extremely large repertoire of theological, jurisprudent, philosophical and Sufi heritage – inevitably belong to, and ought to be creatively and universally reclaimed by, the modern Arabs. His critique of identitarian reason, thus, is both a local and universal critique,[67] hence its pertinence here.

The universal is crucially understood as that 'pluriversal',[68] global or world horizon of knowing, sensing and believing in which are *shared* various local ways of thinking around the globe, which are inevitably steeped in a certain form of life or tradition. A shared normative multiplicity, therefore, not relativism, is the horizon of the universal, which nevertheless always carries a certain contextual, symbolic, perspectival, linguistic *et cetera* signature.[69] This is the sense in which I use 'the universal' in this book, especially in relation to the poetic, the religious or the spiritual in Gibran's text. I rely and draw, of course, on various theoretical sources and reflections throughout my work, both Arab and Euro-American, with particular attention to Derrida – his insights on ethical issues such as giving, hospitality, invention and language have been instructive and inspiring. I am especially indebted to Meskini, however, and the kind of nuanced thinking that his work displays, in ways that I had not been able to imagine before embarking on this research project.

Chapter One of this book demonstrates how many of Gibran's writings in Arabic and English constitute a poetic attempt to reinvent the religious within the epistemic conditions of modernity and in resistance to its predominant calculative reason. This reinvention is post-religious, I argue, in that it adopts the Abrahamic mode of prophetic speech as a poetic form of enunciation, while breaking with monotheism's vertical metaphysics of creation, fatherhood and morality. The chapter discusses how this poetic reinvention is enabled by the interpretative horizons made possible by Darwinian evolutionism – as domesticated in the *Nahḍa* discourse – and Nietzsche's *Thus Spoke Zarathustra*, which allow Gibran to reclaim and reinvent

Christian and Islamic-Sufi concepts in evolutionist terms. Teasing out the creative particularity of this enterprise and some of its limitations, the chapter shows how many of Gibran's poetic texts echo the fragmented evolutionary worldview that he expresses in some of his letters. It also investigates the ways in which his modern protagonists and character-poets reclaim and reactivate, in Arabic or in English, the Abrahamic pre-institutional force of religion as disruption, migration and event.

Chapter Two discusses what is continuous and discontinuous in Gibran's shift from one language to another, or the concurrent use of the two. It demonstrates how the switch into English retains the universal spirit of his early Arabic writings and effaces their aesthetic inventiveness. This switch is characterised by uneasy self-translation, which is textually manifested in Gibran's conscious adoption of the English biblical style that, for him, bears the trace of the Syriac Bible. This bilingual movement, as the chapter also shows, entails that the originary hospitality of English as a foreign language occasion Gibran's inscription into the host(ile) culture, which appropriates both the language and the foreign writer in essentialist terms. This is where the chasm occurs, where the Orient as Outside becomes the identitarian entity that veils the textuality of his English writings. This bilingual chasm, thus, creates different and *seemingly* irreconcilable incarnations or functions of Gibran, yet only a close attention to his texts would render, so the chapter insists, what this (in)visible chasm makes invisible, namely the text itself: the interpretative horizon of the text that is irreducible to – albeit inseparable from – the writer's identity and the culture of the foreign language in which he writes.

Chapter Three foregrounds the national and civilisational concern in Gibran's Arabic writings as warranted by, but also beyond, the question of bilingualism. Reading essays and one-act plays spanning the period before, during and after World War I, as well as posthumously published letters, the chapter thoroughly examines the politics and ethics of the nation in Gibran. It demonstrates that Gibran's nationalism is imagined and defined *territorially*, in that it is the territory of Greater Syria as a pre-national, pre-state *waṭan* (homeland or dwelling) that grounds his nationalism, not sect, religion, or ethnicity. Gibran's specificity, the chapter argues, lies in his constant emphasis on *al-istiqlāl al-maʿnawī* or *moral independence* as the universal condition for the hoped historical ascendancy of Syria and the Arab East as national and civilisational entities, respectively. This emphasis for Gibran critiques the notion of Euro-America as the civilisational telos of history, calling for an Eastern originality of innovation, framed at times in essentialist and social Darwinist terms, seen as *the* prerequisite of an authentic *Nahḍa* or renaissance. The discussion of the latter reveals how Gibran's vision is enabled by, and diverges from, other prominent *Nahḍawī* intellectuals.

Chapter Four investigates the reception of Gibran's Anglophone work in both the US and the Arab world. Excavating the early reviews of Gibran's books in the US, the chapter discusses how and why they were received as monolithically 'Oriental' and 'spiritual', a modality of reception that flattens his text and predetermines its value in that cultural location. Also, the chapter examines the problem of *The Prophet* in American literature and culture, underscoring the ways in which cultural translation and exoticism produce the symbolic value of Gibran's text in America, and how this value-coding has decontextualised it by obscuring both its literary polysemy and the visibility of works other than *The Prophet*, leaving Gibran uncanonised. The chapter, furthermore, highlights the recontextualisation of Gibran in the Arab cultural geography. It discusses how Gibran is reclaimed as a poet of modern vision and rupture by Arab modernist poets such as Adonis and Yusuf al-Khal, going on to highlight the significance of the 'Arabisations' of *The Prophet* and the creative and philosophical afterlife of the Anglophone Gibran in Arabic. This movement reveals another regime of value that reconfigures how Gibran's text is read and valued. It therefore compels us to disrupt the putative correlation between 'English' and the concept of 'world literature', and to de-privilege the Euro-American epistemic location in literary and aesthetic evaluation.

To read Gibran in this manner is to accentuate the worldliness of an important Arab writer who is often shrouded in ambiguity or misunderstanding in Euro-American cultural and academic discourses. Admired, avoided, championed, dismissed, domesticated, or simply decontextualised, Gibran awaits a critical examination that is alive to the literary, cultural and historical specificities of his literary *oeuvre*, to its relevance and significance as bilingual Arabic literature. *Gibran Khalil Gibran as Arab World Literature* attempts to furnish that critical examination, aiming not just to do justice to Gibran but to intervene, by 'worlding' Gibran, in critical debates that concern the discourse of 'world literature' today.

Notes

1 See, for instance, Salma Khadra Jayyusi, *Trends and Movements in Modern Arabic Poetry, Volume Two* (Leiden: Brill, 1977), 91–107.

2 See, for instance, Adonis, 'Jubrān Khalīl Jubrān, aw al-ḥadātha al-ru'yā', in *al-Thābit wa-l-mutaḥawwil: baḥth fi-l-ittibāʿ wa-l-ibdāʿ ʿinda al-ʿarab: Ṣadmat al-ḥadātha* (The Fixed and the Changing in Arabic Poetics: The Shock of Modernity) (Beirut: Dār al-ʿawda, 1978), 160–211; Kamal Abdel-Malek and Wael Hallaq (eds), *Tradition, Modernity, and Postmodernity in Arabic Literature* (Leiden: Brill, 2000), 315–20, 342. Boutros Hallaq, *Gibran et la refondation littéraire arabe: Bildungsroman, écriture prophétique, transgénérisme* (Arles: Sindbad-Actes Sud, 2008).

3 Adonis, 'Jubrān Khalīl Jubrān', 210 [emphasis in the original].

4 For a reading of Gibran's *oeuvre* as an expression of a geographical, social and metaphysical alienation, manifesting itself in social criticism and mystical idealism, see Nadim Naimy, 'The Mind and Thought of Kahlil Gibran', *Journal of Arabic Literature* 5 (1974): 55–71.

5 Gibran, 'al-ʿUbūdiyya' (Slavery), in *al-Majmūʿa al-kāmila li mu'allafāt Jubrān Khalīl Jubrān bi-l-ʿarabiyya* (The Collected Works in Arabic) (Beirut: Kitābuna li-l-Nashr, 2014), 215. Henceforth abbreviated as *CWs in Arabic.*

6 Halim Barakat, *Ghurbat al-kātib al-ʿarabī* (London: Saqi Books, 2011), 124.

7 Ibid., 123.

8 Ibid., 126.

9 Ibid., 127.

10 Bahraini poet Qassim Haddad has recently lamented the fact that Gibran, in the Arab world, was ignored in his lifetime and mythologised as 'genius' after his death, a condition from which many Arab writers and poets, such as the Iraqi poet Badr Shakir al-Sayyab, suffered. See Qassim Haddad, 'Jubrān Khalīl Jubrān: Namūdhaj al-uṣṭūra al-wāqiʿiyya' (Gibran as a Model of Realistic Myth), al-Quds al-ʿArabī (10 April 2021), https://www.alquds.co.uk/جبران-خليل-جبران-نموذج-الأسطورة-الواق/

11 Waterfield homes in on the psychology of Gibran as an immigrant writer with 'multiple personalities' striving for recognition in order to show that his creativity owes its success to his being a 'troubled man' who was 'crucified' on the dichotomies of 'East' and 'West' and 'Man' and 'Myth'. Waterfield takes pains, while exposing Gibran's troubled personality, to demonstrate the value of his English work, which is wrongly underestimated in his assessment. See Robin Waterfield,

Prophet: The Life and Times of Kahlil Gibran (London: Allen Lane, 1998). Bushrui and Jenkins's biography, however, is much more celebratory of the Arab *Mahjari* writer. Bushrui has immensely contributed to Gibran's studies in Arabic and specifically in English, and his biography is the acme of his life-long preoccupation with Gibran. The biography finds in Gibran that figure who, despite his ambivalence, reconciled 'East' and 'West'. Over-emphasised in the biography is the 'spiritual' source and value of Gibran's work, which, in a century that witnessed the intensification of the East–West collision and of local, imperial and world wars, remains relevant and important. See Suheil Bushrui and Joe Jenkins, *Kahlil Gibran, Man and Poet: A New Biography* (Oxford: OneWorld, 1998).

12 I use the name 'Gibran Khalil Gibran' in this book as a middle ground, so to speak, between his Arabic and American names.

13 For a historical account of the Americanisation of his name as Kahlil Gibran, see Francesco Medici, 'Tracing Gibran's Footsteps: Unpublished and Rare Material', in *Gibran in the 21st Century: Lebanon's Message to the World*, ed. H. Zoghaib and M. Rihani (Beirut: Centre for Lebanese Heritage, LAU, 2018), 93–145.

14 Examples of culturalist and postcolonial readings of Gibran include Waïl S. Hassan, 'The Gibran Phenomenon', in *Immigrant Narratives: Orientalism and Cultural Translation in Arab American and Arab British Literature* (New York; Oxford: Oxford University Press, 2011), 59–77; and Jacob Berman, '*Mahjar* Legacies: A Reinterpretation', in *Between the Middle East and the Americas: The Cultural Politics of Diaspora*, ed. by Ella Shohat and Evelyn Alsultany (Ann Arbor: University of Michigan Press, 2013), 65–79. Hassan's article is particularly important because it examines Gibran's status and legacy in the US as a 'minor' bilingual writer with a pivotal emphasis on his role as a 'cultural translator', demonstrating the complexity of his enterprise as an Arab writer in the US. Yet, his reading, as well as Berman's, highlight the East–West politics of culture in a manner that tacitly privileges the American context and marginalises Gibran's Arabic works, whose prophetic dimension is forgotten or belittled and attributed essentially to his Anglophone writings. This attribution implies that the trope of the prophet is less an aesthetic choice than a political acquiescence to Orientalist discourse, obfuscating the aesthetic and ethical centrality of the prophetic in Gibran's poetic imagination in both languages, and flattening out the relationship between aesthetics and politics.

15 In considering Gibran's *oeuvre* as bilingual Arabic literature, I share John Walbridge's significant and neglected argument: 'Books like *The Prophet* are

Arabic literature written in English. The literary standards of twentieth century English literature are extreme in their demand for cool authorial detachment. Extended metaphor, elaborate rhetorical devices, earnest intensity – if they are used at all in modern English literature – tend to be ironic or political. It is not an aesthetic ideal that Gibran shared. He was not writing bad English books; he was writing good, extremely original Arabic books. It is a distinction that readers understood far better than critics'. John Walbridge, 'Gibran: His Aesthetic, and His Moral Universe', *Al-Hikamat* 21 (2001), 52 [emphasis added].

16 Derek Attridge, *The Singularity of Literature* (London: Routledge, 2004), 42.

17 By 'world literature', following David Damrosch, is meant any literary work that travelled in the original or translation beyond its linguistic and cultural 'origin'. David Damrosch, *What is World Literature?* (Woodstock: Princeton University Press, 2003), 5. Gibran's case, however, complicates this definition. This is due, first, to his bilingualism (that is, the initial enunciation and situatedness of his work in two literary and cultural spheres); second, to the travelling of his work in translation between these two distinct spheres, which are unevenly related in terms of power differentials; and, third, to the translation of his work into more than a hundred languages and the reception that ensued, which is beyond the scope of this book.

18 Gayatri Spivak, *Death of a Discipline* (New York: Columbia University Press, 2003), 100.

19 See Derek Attridge, 'Innovation, Literature, Ethics: Relating to the Other', *PMLA* 114, no. 1 (January 1999), 26.

20 See Michel Foucault, *The Order of Things: An Archaeology of the Human Sciences* (New York: Vintage, 1973), 299–300; see also Raymond Williams, *Keywords: A Vocabulary of Culture and Society*, revised ed. (New York: Oxford University Press, 1983), 183–88.

21 Edward Said, *Culture and Imperialism* (London: Vintage, 1994), xxiv [emphasis added].

22 Edward Said, *The World, the Text, and the Critic* (New York: Vintage, 1982), 33 [emphasis in the original].

23 Gibran, 'al-ʿUbūdiyya', in *CWs in Arabic*, 215.

24 Gibran, 'Wathā'iq' (Manuscripts), in John Daye, *'Aqīdat Jubrān* (The Doctrine of Gibran) (London: Dār Surāqia, 1988), 225–429. See also Gibran, *al-Majmūʿa al-kāmila li muʾallafāt Jubrān Khalīl Jubrān: Nuṣūs khārij al-majmūʿa* (The Collected Works of Gibran: Texts outside the Main Collection), ed. Antoine al-Qawwal (Beirut: Dār al-Jīl, 1994).

25 See Gibran, 'Mustaqbal al-lugha al-'arabiyya' (The Future of the Arabic Language), in *CWs in Arabic*, 317–22.

26 Ibid.

27 In *al-'Awāṣif*, he writes: 'A Poet am I. I bring together in verse what life scattered in prose, and I strew in lines of prose what life has rendered in verse. Wherefore I shall ever be the stranger, and an exile I shall remain until death snatches me away and whisks me back to my homeland'. *Kahlil Gibran: An Illustrated Anthology*, trans. and ed. by Ayman A. El-Desouky (London: Spruce, 2010), 210.

28 After meeting Rabindranath Tagore in New York, Gibran wrote to Mary Haskell: 'Tagore speaks against nationalism while his work does not show or express a world-consciousness'. KG to MH, 03 January 1917, in *Beloved Prophet: The Love Letters of Kahlil Gibran and Mary Haskell*, ed. Virginia Hilu (London: A. Knopf Inc., 1972), 283. I shall henceforth refer to the date of the letter or of Haskell's journal entry whenever I cite a quote from this book.

29 The influential *Mahjar* literary society, *al-Rābiṭa al-Qalamiyya* (The Pen Bond), which was formed by expatriate Arab writers and poets in the US, led by Gibran himself, to rejuvenate Arabic literature, had in the centre of its logotype a hadith (saying) attributed to Prophet Muhammad: 'How wonderful the treasures beneath God's throne which poets' tongue can unlock'. See Jean Gibran and Kahlil G. Gibran, *Kahlil Gibran: His Life and World* (New York: Interlink Books, 1998), 339.

30 In his remarkable study on Arabic Romantic poetry, Muhammad 'Abd al-Hayy writes: 'The Christian *émigrés* used it [Sufi diction] extensively; and, indeed, it was due to them that it reached the degree of aesthetic transformation and poetic transparency that made it part of the language of Arabic romantic poetry'. He gives Gibran's poem 'Sukūtī inshād' (My Silence is a Hymn), written in classical rhyme and meter, as an illustrative example, which resonates with one of the poems of the Sufi legendary poet Ibn al-Farid. He goes on to stress that '[i]t is this close and vital proximity to the traditional language of Sufism that gives the language of Arabic romantic poetry curves and tones characteristic to it when compared to English romantic poetry. In Arabic, Sufism is not an occult; it is a living tradition'. See Muhammad 'Abd al-Hayy, *Tradition and English and Romantic Influence in Arabic Romantic Poetry: A Study in Comparative Literature* (London: Ithaca, 1982), 110–11.

31 'Abd al-Hayy adds: 'In a letter to Mary Haskell in 1913, he [Gibran] expresses his idea of the difference between the Greeks and the ancient people of the Middle East as far as their artistic creations are concerned. For him, *Greek art is visual,*

the other is visionary. The Greek artist lacked the 'third eye', which the Chaldean or the Phoenician or the Egyptian artist possessed. Michelangelo's David overpowers Dionysius and Apollo; and Astarte or Isis are certainly more powerful than Venus or Minerva'. Ibid., 146 [emphasis added]. See also Tawfiq Sayigh, *Aḍwā' jadīda 'alā Jubrān* (Gibran under New Spotlights) (London: Riad el-Rayyes, 1990), 250–51.

32 Maurice Blanchot, 'Prophetic Speech', in *The Book to Come*, trans. Charlotte Mandell (Palo Alto: Stanford University Press, 2003), 79.

33 Said, *Culture and Imperialism*, especially the Introduction and Chapter One: 'Overlapping Territories, Intertwined Histories'.

34 Mikhail Naimy, *Kahlil Gibran: A Biography* (New York: Philosophical Library, 1988), 156.

35 Stephen Sheehi, *Foundations of Modern Arab Identity* (Gainesville: University of Florida Press, 2003), 4.

36 See Albert Hourani's classic, *Arabic Thought in the Liberal Age* (Oxford: Oxford University Press, 1983).

37 See Marwa Elshakry, *Reading Darwin in Arabic, 1860–1950* (Chicago: University of Chicago Press, 2013); Dyala Hamzah (ed.), *The Making of the Arab Intellectual (1880–1960): Empire, Public Sphere and the Colonial Coordinates of Selfhood* (London: Routledge, 2013).

38 That the *Nahḍa* as operative concept and project presupposes *inḥiṭāṭ* as an Orientalist historiographical generalisation should be questioned, yet one should also ask: what kind of *inḥiṭāṭ* are we talking about? More precisely, is it literary, social or material? Does the material bear on the way in which the cultural and the historical are understood and examined? And what is the normative yardstick here – is it simply 'Europe'? These difficult questions are of course beyond the scope of this book. Nevertheless, I venture to bring them up here in an attempt to do justice to the complexity of the *Nahḍa* as a project without making retrospective historical judgements. Perhaps the following crucial observation by Sadiq Jalal al-Azm is necessary to mention, but this is only an indication of what is at stake here: 'That 19th century Europe was superior to Asia and much of the rest of the world in terms of productive capacities, social organization, historical ascendency, military might and scientific and technological development is indisputable as a contingent historical fact. Orientalism, with its ahistorical bourgeois bent of mind, did its best to eternalize this mutable fact, to turn it into a permanent reality past, present and future – Hence Orientalism's essentialistic ontology of East and West'. See Sadiq Jalal al-Azm, 'Orientalism and Orientalism

in Reverse', in *Orientalism: A Reader*, ed. A. L. Macfie (New York: New York University Press, 2000), 227–28.

39 For more on this, see Hourani, *Arabic Thought*. For a different perspective on the *Nahḍa* that highlights the role of indigenous humanists by building on recent studies challenging the 'decline paradigm' that informs Hourani and his students, see Abdulrazzak Patel, *The Arab Nahḍah: The Making of the Intellectual and Humanist Movement* (Edinburgh: Edinburgh University Press, 2013).

40 The richness of the *Nahḍa*'s cultural production cannot be captured here. For a recent anthology, see *The Arab Renaissance: A Bilingual Anthology of the Nahda*, ed. Tarek El-Aris (New York: The Modern Language Association of America, 2018).

41 For more on this, see Sheehi, *Foundations of Modern Arab Identity*.

42 Boutros Hallaq has cogently demonstrated how Gibran's conception and practice of literature as an autonomous entity ruptured with the dynamics of the *Nahḍa*. See Hallaq, *Gibran et la refondation littéraire arabe*, 28–45.

43 Sheehi, *Foundations*, 98–102. See also his article 'Modernism, Anxiety and the Ideology of Arab Vision', *Discourse* 28, no. 1 (Winter 2006), 73–74.

44 Sheehi, *Foundations*, 133–34.

45 Foundational reformers such as Butrus al-Bustani saw the acquisition and application of secular and scientific knowledge as essential to cultural and civilisational progress. Ibid., 20–21.

46 Said, *Orientalism*, 2–3 [emphasis mine].

47 'Indeed, for many popularizers [of Darwin in Arabic], evolution was understood as *the* preeminent doctrine of empire (which also helps to explain the later eclipse of Darwin – particularly by Marx – in the age of decolonization). After all, the most intense phase of the debate over Darwin in Arabic coincided precisely with the intensification of the Eastern Question after 1876 and the British occupation of Egypt in 1882. It was at this time that the laws of evolution – from natural selection to the struggle for survival – made their way into discussions of contemporary affairs'. Elshakry, *Reading Darwin*, 10.

48 These concepts emerged and gained currency in Europe in the eighteenth and nineteenth centuries. See Williams, *Keywords*, 87–93. For a critical engagement that draws on Williams's historicisation of 'culture' as both a category and an object of analysis and relates it to Orientalism, the colonial juncture and the Arab *Nahḍa*, see Joseph Massad, *Desiring Arabs* (Chicago: University of Chicago Press, 2007), 1–5 (especially).

49 Said, *Orientalism*, 3.

50 Massad, *Desiring Arabs*, 3–6. See, in particular, his discussion of the Arab intellectual debates about sex that the *Nahḍa* spawned, which were mostly framed in civilisational terms, in the chapter 'Anxiety in Civilization', 51–98.

51 KH to MH, 29 September 1912.

52 This is Benjamin Disraeli's phrase – 'The East is a career' – that Said cites as an epigraph to *Orientalism*.

53 Gibran, 'al-'Ahd al-jadīd', *CWs in Arabic*, 323–26.

54 For a brief but remarkable account of the complex history of the idea of the 'west' as 'heritage and object of study', which 'doesn't really emerge until the 1890s, during a heated era of imperialism', see Kwame Anthony Appiah, 'There is No Such Thing as Western Civilisation', *The Guardian* (9 Nov 2016), https://www.theguardian.com/world/2016/nov/09/western-civilisation-appiah-reith-lecture

55 Since, imperially and materially speaking, the Occident dominated and ruled over the Orient, the meaning and performativity of the latter as an identitarian marker for an Oriental writer or reformer in the *Nahḍa*, for instance, are not the same for an Occidental or an Orientalist using the same marker to designate or study the Other – whether in negative or positive terms. The disparate material and discursive conditions that undergird the way in which one claims and uses those markers very often determine their semantic and performative content.

56 I follow Said's insistence, who draws on Vico, that men make and invent their own history, and that the Occident or the Orient, therefore, are 'not merely *there*' but are indeed man-made. Said, *Orientalism*, 4–5 [emphasis in the original].

57 See Mohamed-Salah Omri, 'Notes on the Traffic between Theory and Arabic Literature', *International Journal of Middle East Studies* 43, no. 4 (November 2011): 731–33; and Hosam Aboul-Ela, 'Is There an Arab (Yet) in This Field? Postcolonialism, Comparative Literature, and Middle Eastern Horizon of Said's Discourse Analysis', *MFS Modern Fiction Studies* 56, no. 4 (Winter 2010): 729–50.

58 Said, *Culture and Imperialism*, xxix.

59 Said, *Orientalism*, 46.

60 Hosam Aboul-Ela, 'Is There an Arab (Yet) in This Field?' 744–45.

61 See Emmanuel Levinas, 'Ethics as First Philosophy', in *The Levinas Reader*, ed. Sean Hand (Oxford: Basil Blackwell, 1989), 75–87.

62 Attridge, 'Innovation', 26.

63 See Fethi Meskini, *al-Huwiyya wa-l-ḥurriya: Naḥwa anwār jadīda* (Identity and Freedom: Towards a New *Aufklärung*) (Beirut: Dār Jadāwil, 2011), 208–10.

64 'Modern philosophy from Hegel to Ricoeur', so Meskini argues, 'has failed to realise this promise, in that it only displaced the foundation of the self to found a host of [implicit] narratives of identity'. Ibid., 12.

65 See Meskini, *al-Huwiyya wa al-zamān: Ta'wīlāt finuminulujia li mas'alat al-naḥn* (Identity and Time: Phenomenological Interpretations of the 'We' Question) (Beirut: Dār al-Talīʿa, 2001), 7–12; see also his *al-Huwiyya wa-l-ḥurriya*, 9–19.

66 Meskini adopts this term from Charles Taylor as a 'quiet substitute' for various and fragile categories like *turāth*, religion, origin, foundation and so on. See his *al-Huwiyya wa-l-ḥurriya*, 21.

67 I briefly sketch out his critical orientation in the last section of Chapter Four.

68 See Walter Mignolo, *Local Histories/Global Designs: Coloniality, Subaltern Knowledges, and Border Thinking* (Princeton and Oxford: Princeton University Press, 2000), xiv, xxii.

69 Meskini differentiates between *al-kawnī* and *al-kullī*, both of which translate as 'universal' in European languages. While *al-kullī* is the Arab translation of the Greek notion of 'to katholou', or the one of science, *al-kawnī* refers to the normative multiplicity of the universal which is precariously but necessarily shared by humanity. See Meskini, 'al-Kawnī wa al-kullī, aw fī hashāshat al-mushtarak', in *al-Huwiyya wa-l-ḥurriya*, 159–76.

1

The Poetics of Prophetic Writing: Reinventing the Religious in and against Modernity

Everything still remains open after Nietzsche.

Paul Ricoeur[1]

The prophet is a normative device of an exceptional kind. It is the last of the Abrahamic inventions, after those of Adam, God the Creator, the Created World, the Sacred Books and the Thereafter . . . etc. This is not merely a question of religion. Rather, it concerns a wide-ranging spiritual apparatus of legislation invented by peoples of the ancient Middle East who were, by virtue of it, transformed into nomadic and open spiritual groups. The descendants of Abraham insist that the normative validity of this apparatus is universalisable, because it is a form of life that remains habitable.

Fethi Meskini[2]

This chapter examines the prophetic dimension in Gibran's work as a form of poetic writing. Starting from the premise that – as Gibran himself avers – 'style and ideas are one',[3] I offer a reading that highlights a paramount and often overlooked aspect of his multifarious work: that of the modern poet who reinvents the religious in and against modernity. The religious here designates the Abrahamic force of religion as disruption, migration and event. The notion of 'event' signifies a singular, irregular and inexhaustible rupture, not just in time but also in perception, which at once enables, and is enabled by, an inventive use of language.[4] As this chapter will illustrate, this dimension of 'the event' in Gibran's writings is made possible by none other than the poetic, which reinvents the religious insofar as it refers to the prophetic in its Abrahamic sense – and I say 'Abrahamic'[5] in full awareness of the marked differences between the three monotheistic religions, which nevertheless share this specific prophetic dimension. What interests me here is the 'form' of this poetic reinvention: the adoption of an Abrahamic prophetic trope in a modern world where myth-making is no longer possible. I argue that, for Gibran, the poetic is understood as a 'prophetic form'[6] (his expression) that reframes and reimagines the boundaries of God, the self and the world, exploring their new or unexhausted possibilities of meaning and embodiment. The meaning of the world is thought anew, precisely because new historical, cultural and epistemological conditions call for such a rethinking, one which is poetic in this case. Going beyond Romanticism as an explanatory 'movement' and category of analysis, but without dismissing it as a viable philosophical framework and way of reading, this perspective attends to the wider implications of Gibran's prophetic form of writing: its simultaneous embeddedness *in* modernity – and the *Nahḍa* – and thrust *against* the positivist, rationalist and identitarian forms of reason that dominate and shape the modern world. Such a perspective scrutinises Gibran's work in a manner that does not dissociate 'form' and 'content'; in so doing, it demonstrates, rather than obscures, its historical or worldly relevance.

What makes possible this poetic reinvention of the religious and, more specifically, the prophetic style of this reinvention? What results from it? And why is it still relevant and important? These are the core questions with which this chapter is concerned. But before I address these questions, I wish to explain why I use *reinvention* as interpretative and analytical prism. It is obvious that reinvention implies a reworking of older and more authoritative ideas, therefore invoking the notion of influence. To reinvent is to adopt, rethink, rework and repurpose – in a word, to transform – the old in a new context. To reinvent, in other words, is to interrogate or, at least, to complicate the notion of 'influence' and its authorial and theological implications – that of origin and the obsession with finding the sources of influence. My approach, thus, emphasises reinvention as a way of reading that probes the *travelling* of ideas, forms, styles, tropes, motifs and the like, not just from one 'author' to another, but from one worldly context to another, from one set of historical, linguistic and cultural conditions to another, highlighting destination rather than origin, all the while acknowledging the commonness of the modern, imperial world. Hence my focus on modernity and the *Nahḍa* as historical and discursive frames for my discussion here, as well as on the ways in which Gibran is reinventive, as it were, within the specific conditions of his own location in the world.

The chapter, furthermore, demonstrates that underlying Gibran's work is a worldview, however disjointed or incomplete, that Gibran writes as a poetic thinker. My focus on reinvention is further substantiated when this worldview is pieced together and, most importantly, discussed in the form or style of its poetic embodiment. This reading of Gibran is analogous to, albeit far more modest than, Northrop Frye's well-known study of William Blake's system of thought in *Fearful Symmetry*,[7] in that, like Frye reading Blake, I show that Gibran's work is the product of a poet who sought to *remake* the world, to think it anew as a poet or a poetic thinker,[8] not a philosophical one. In this respect, I read his letters as texts that illuminate rather than explain or justify aesthetic and thematic choices in his poetic and creative work; that is, I do not make a fundamental distinction between his creative and non-creative writings, which for me form one long text that is neither unified nor completely fragmented. I consider the letters themselves literary or poetic in the broad sense of the term – that is, as works of the creative mind rather than mere biographical or autobiographical information.[9]

The Prophetic as a Mode of Writing

What does it mean to adopt the prophetic as a form of poetic writing in the modern juncture? To address this question, one must think through and beyond the Romantic notion of the poet-prophet. For Romanticism itself, whether European or Arab, is a product of modernity; and in the Arab context, one cannot study Romanticism in isolation from the discursive field of the *Nahḍa*. What interests me here is not the prophetic as a Romantic trope, but the prophetic itself as a form of poetic writing and thinking that proved compelling and necessary in the modern world. Maurice Blanchot's reflections on prophetic speech are instructive here: 'When speech becomes prophetic, it is not the future that is given, it is the present that is given away, and with it the possibility of a firm, stable, and lasting presence'.[10] This is, of course, the prophetic as an Abrahamic mode of speech. 'The word "prophet" – borrowed from the Greek to designate a condition foreign to Greek culture – would deceive us if it invited us to make the *nabi* the one who speaks the future',[11] Blanchot writes. In other words, what is peculiar to Abrahamic prophecy is its revelatory announcement of an *impossible* future, impossible in the sense that it is beyond the binary opposition of possible and non-possible – that is to say, absolute transcendence, God as the Infinite and the wholly Other. The impossible thus understood disrupts the present and destabilises all forms of idolatry – namely, fixed and humanly graspable or rationalisable forms of thinking. It shakes up linear temporality and rigid forms of rationality by opening up a space of transcendence beyond the logos, a space in which the infinite becomes a question, or rather *the* question, that demands but exceeds rational thinking. Hence the poetic as a prophetic form, as a mode of thinking that always seeks to transcend the limits imposed on the notion of the world in a given place and time, that seeks to offer or imagine a liberating way of dwelling in the world.

Note that I do not provide any specifiable 'content' here, at least not yet, in that I underscore what the prophetic does rather than what it is, what it suggests rather than what it contains. We should therefore ask: Why does the figure of the Abrahamic *nabi* insist on reappearing in a new guise? Why, in other words, does the prophetic appear as a form that inspires modern poets, those who think with(in) 'literature' as a modern invention? And why was the prophetic form so compelling – so indispensable, one might argue – for an Arab Christian writer living in the United States in the early decades of the twentieth century? Gibran, as Ayman El-Desouky reminds us, is amongst an array of 'self-begetting' modern writers for whom poetry or literature is a way of inhabiting and reshaping the world, 'a new way of living that emerged when the writer used his creativity to explore and recover from unendurable personal and historical circumstances'.[12] This new way of living takes shape in the mind of the poet as a prophetic thinker.

Thinking after Nietzsche and Darwin, Gibran reinvents the religious by espousing an Abrahamic prophetic trope beyond the eschatological and moral dimensions of monotheistic theology. This poetic reinvention reclaims and repurposes many Christian and Islamic-Sufi concepts by inscribing them in an evolutionary worldview, which is made possible, at least in part, by the domestication of Darwinian evolutionism in the discourse of the *Nahḍa*. Gibran, as I will demonstrate in the next section, developed such a worldview in the early 1910s; and this worldview is echoed everywhere in his work, particularly in *The Madman*, *al-ʿAwāṣif* (The Tempests) and the works published thereafter. This does not mean, however, that his early work is irrelevant. It is in Gibran's early short stories and poetic prose that one encounters the prophetic as a mode of social, aesthetic and metaphysical intervention, which is later transformed into a mode of existential intervention, one that seeks the universal reframing of the boundaries of God, the self and the world. And all of this cannot be appreciated without studying the ways in which Gibran's texts, understood primarily as poetic, intervene in the world or worlds in which they are historically produced.

To reinvent the religious presupposes that 'religion' itself has undergone a profound transformation. Under the epistemic force of modernity, religion loses its *epistemological* authority over explanations of the world, but its existential, experiential and interpretative power and affect remain inexhaustible.[13] In this context, Nietzsche's Zarathustra, as a post-religious poet-prophet, provided a horizon for Gibran to think the religious anew. And this creative encounter with Nietzsche is one that allowed Gibran, as I will show later in this chapter, to nurture and extend his prophetic imagination *beyond* Nietzsche.

Reimagining God, the Self and the World

By the beginning of World War I, Gibran's own conception of God begins to manifest itself clearly in his letters to Mary Haskell, and this is specifically relevant to his work after *Damʿa wa ibtisāma* (A Tear and a Smile). But we will see how this worldview actually integrates elements from his early work, which is explicitly and uniquely Romantic in orientation, while attempting to offer a more sophisticated vision of God, the self and the world. He writes: 'If God the Power, God the force, God the mind, God the subconsciousness of Life, is in all the struggles that take place on this planet, He must be in this war of nations. *He is this war*'.[14] To think of God in these terms is to radicalise and repudiate the notion of God as a Perfect Being, even as *agape* in Christian and Islamic Sufi traditions, the profound bearing of both upon his intellectual formation and work notwithstanding. What interests me here, primarily, is how he conceives of the notion of God as such, not its rational or theological validity; that is, how he reconceptualises the notion of God as a poetic thinker. Gibran speculates that 'the *Mind* [God] of this world is not free from its body [the Earth] – and as long as the body is struggling for more life, the mind will go on struggling for more life, more mind. *There is no such thing as struggle for death*'.[15] God, the 'subconsciousness' of Life,[16] is not, in this case, separate from Life, as He is the struggle itself. Gibran goes on to assert that 'there is nothing on this planet but a struggle for Life', which characterises 'every physical or mental movement, every wave of the sea and every thought or dream'.[17] This radical understanding of Life as an eternal struggle renders man 'elemental', a part of nature where 'the elements declare war on each other'.[18] This is how Gibran justifies the act of war, conceiving of violence, albeit implicitly, as natural as the struggle for Life itself, and reducing man to a mere element in nature, albeit one whose soul is endowed, unlike the elements, with 'the desire for more of itself, hunger for that which is beyond itself'.[19] This emphasis on the struggle for Life is an evidently evolutionist notion and has its echoes in Gibran's Arabic work.

Situating Gibran within the *Nahḍa* discourse will help us illuminate this social and metaphysical interpretation of evolutionism. The latter was so prevalent a notion during the *Nahḍa* that 'evolution [for Arab readers of Darwin] was about much more than biology and more even than history: the new universal history for which it provided the blueprint was one with the power to recast the future'.[20] In the *Nahḍa* discourse, thus, . . .

> . . .discussions of religion were also increasingly attached to notions of the evolution of the 'idea of God' and assigned a 'social function' that could be considered and compared across a universal timeline. The coming of Darwin was thus accompanied by reconceptualizations of the meaning of 'religion' itself.[21]

Evolutionism, as Marwa Elshakry has shown, gained currency in the *Nahḍa* thanks largely to *al-Muqtaṭaf*, a popular scientific journal whose role in disseminating European scientific theories and discoveries from 1870s onwards was widely influential. This induced a host of debates and discussions around the interpretation and validity of evolutionism in the Arab East.[22] Shibli Shumayyil, an influential *Nahḍa* intellectual and one of the pioneering proponents of Darwinism,[23] translates and reflects on evolutionism as *Falsafat al-nushūʾ wa-l-irtiqāʾ* (Philosophy of Evolution and Progress), the title of one of his books that was published in 1910. Shumayyil's interpretation of evolutionism is strictly materialist, albeit with mystical and pantheistic overtones to it.[24]

In a one-act play published by Gibran in *al-Funūn* in 1913 and signed, intriguingly, 'One of the Grave-Digger's Disciples',[25] Shumayyil is included as a character. In the play, Gibran, Shumayyil, Ameen Rihani and Sheikh Iskandar al-ʿAzzar (a Lebanese poet), sitting in a café in Lebanon, are discussing a medley of topics that revolve around Darwinism (natural selection), Turner, Keats and Nietzsche – in relation to the nature of religion, poetry and imagination – each of whom represents a particular way that seeks or reveals 'truth'. This discussion is joined by an ordinary man speaking in the Lebanese dialect (*al-ʿāmmī*),[26] who ultimately deems himself in a better existential status than they are. What is pertinent to my discussion here is that Gibran, in response to Shumayyil's espousal of natural selection as a principle of social reality, asserts:

> Your reason, Doctor [in reference to Shumayyil], moves between the teachings of Darwin and the principles of Nietzsche, and I share this conviction with you. However, were Darwin or Nietzsche able to truly demonstrate what is the best or the fittest? For what Nietzsche deems full of will and nobility may actually bring about weakness and abjectness. Who can say with absolute confidence that the distant visions that visit the soul of a Sufi is not one of the elements that nature selects as a mechanism to preserve the fittest and maintain the best? I am a worshipper of Power [*al-quwwa*], but I love all the manifestations of Power, not one of them only.[27]

In 'al-Jabābira' (The Giants), furthermore, an Arabic poetic essay published in *al-ʿAwāṣif*, Gibran explicitly expresses his belief in evolutionism. He writes:

> I am an advocate of the law of evolution and progress [*sunnat al-nushūʾ wa-l-irtiqāʾ*], which, to me, applies to both immaterial and material (sensory) living entities, for it transforms religions and nations to the better as much as it transforms all creatures from the fitting to the fittest. Hence, there is only retrogression in appearance and decadence in the superficial.
>
> The law of evolution has diverse channels that are at bottom unified. Its manifestations, which are adverse, dark and unfair, are repudiated by limited thoughts and renounced by weak hearts. Its invisible force, however, is just

> and enlightening, for it embraces a right that is higher to the rights of individuals, aims for an end that is loftier than the goal of the group, and listens to a voice that overwhelms, in its immensity and pleasantness, the sighs of the ill-fated and the agonies of the tormented.[28]

For Gibran, thus, evolutionism is not only a philosophy but also a historical, social and metaphysical law (*sunna*). The expression itself (*al-nushūʾ wa-l-irtiqāʾ*), however, is Shumayyil's. In another context, that of the future of the Arabic language, Gibran asserts that 'languages, like everything else, are subject to the law of the survival of the fittest',[29] with the fittest understood as the inventive, what he calls *quwwat al-ibtikār* or the power of invention. My contention is that Gibran's espousal of evolutionism as a metaphysical law was an offshoot of the *Nahḍa*, the Arab manifestation of modernity. In this context, Herbert Spencer was another celebrated figure, and the Spenserian interpretation of evolutionism was embraced to account for what became known as 'the Eastern question' (*al-masʾala al-sharqiyya*).[30] Thus, '[c]ivilizational progress – like evolution – was [. . .] seen as a law of nature in the age of Darwin and Spencer, and commentators who seemed to offer scientific insights into this process were seized upon by those seeking to promote their particular policies of social reform'.[31] Gibran is part and parcel of this particular historical and intellectual context. His writings in the Arab press – to be discussed at length in Chapter Three – demonstrate that he was acutely aware of the *Nahḍa*'s intellectual and cultural enterprise and actively interacting with it. His rethinking of God, the self and the world, in Arabic or in English, was therefore *primarily* occasioned by this intellectual context, where evolutionism was at times subject to transcendental interpretations that made it religiously acceptable. What is peculiar about Gibran is that he went as far as rethinking the idea of God itself, pushing it beyond the confines of orthodox religion. It was, in other words, his own idea of God, with all the weight, and perhaps the weakness, that accompanies this reinvention.

Gibran's conception of God as an ever-evolving absolute reflective of all struggles in and for Life is nevertheless tinged with ambiguity. The relationship between God and Life is left unexplained (apart from God being the 'subconsciousness' of Life in the instance of war). Moreover, the organic and implicit justification and purification of the violence ensued by wars and struggles seems to reduce man to a passive element in nature, one who is impotent in the face of the will to Life imputed to God – which does not mean, however, that man is unimportant. Gibran's encounter with Nietzsche may elucidate this reimagining of God.[32] Gibran, like Nietzsche, glorifies Life as such, Life as all there is; Life, that is, as Being. In other words, Life for Gibran represents everything that exists, while death is simply a passage from one stage in life to another, as shall be explained in relation to his peculiar embrace of the notion of reincarnation. This is reminiscent of what Nietzsche once declared: 'Being – we have no idea of it other than "living". – How can anything dead be?'[33] While Nietzsche's Zarathustra despises 'the preachers of death',[34] Gibran hails true poets as preachers of Life:

> The saints and the sages of the past ages were seldom in the presence of the God of this world, because they never gave themselves to life but simply gazed at it. The great poets of the past were always one with Life. They did not seek a point in it nor did they wish to find its secrets. They simply allowed their souls to be governed, moved, played upon by it. The wise man and the good man are always seeking safety – but safety is an end and Life is endless.[35]

In another context, Gibran scorns the desire for peace and the 'tiresome, illogical, flat, and insipid' insistence on universal and international Peace. 'Why should man speak of Peace when there is much *ill-at-easeness* in his system that *must* go *out* one way or another? Was it not Peace disease that crept into the Oriental nations and caused their downfall?'[36] Gibran was in favour of a Syrian revolution against the Ottoman Empire, a disposition that few nationalists advocated at the time. This political context aside, what is interesting here is that Gibran speaks of war in evolutionist terms: 'Peace is the desire of old age, and the world is still too young to have such a desire. I say, let there be *wars*; let the Children of the Earth fight one another until the last drop of impure, animal blood is shed'.[37] He then goes on to stress that 'those who *live*, those who know what it is to *be*, those who have knowledge in the Life-in-Death do not preach Peace: *They Preach Life* [. . .] There is no Peace in the art of Being'.[38] The evolutionist struggle for Life becomes a Nietzschean, aesthetic affirmation and celebration of Life. God does not die in this picture; rather, 'He, the mighty one, is fighting for a mightier self, a clearer self, a self of higher life'.[39]

God for Gibran ceases to be the Prime Mover, the Necessary Being, the God of morality and monotheistic eschatology, the God who simultaneously loves and judges,[40] or the God of what Martin Heidegger calls 'onto-theology'.[41] This conception of God dies silently in Gibran. And this silent death – for 'when gods die, they die several kinds of death'[42] – gives way to *another* notion of God, an ever-evolving God, an absolute seeking more absolution and crystallisation, as he would say. As Nietzsche once announced, '[h]ow many new gods are still possible!'[43] This new conception of God enables a space of transcendence which is *horizontally* reimagined – that is, one which is conceived *within* Life, not beyond it. But is such a transcendence possible? Or is Gibran's God an immanent pantheistic God whose immanence is Life itself? How does Gibran conceive of the human self after the silent death of the transcendent god of morality? And what kind of temporality is possible after the silent death of this transcendent god of monotheistic eschatology and messianism? To begin with, Gibran tackles the absence of eschatology by embracing reincarnation,[44] a notion around which his early short story 'Ramād al-ajyāl wa al-nār al-khālida' (The Ashes of Generations and Eternal Fire) is structured, as I will demonstrate below. His conception of the human is not that of the finite being, but of the being whose existence is infinite by virtue of reincarnation. The latter can be thought of in terms of ontological *and* narrative return (as in the figure of the prophet). In the Abrahamic monotheisms, death does not designate finitude; it is a passage, a step, a bridge to the afterlife. This conception of death as passage is the crux of the notion of reincarnation, too, espoused by Gibran after breaking, quietly, with the Abrahamic notion of the afterlife. In an important letter to Mary Haskell, Gibran posits his new perception of God:

> God is not the creator of man. God is not the creator of the earth. God is not the ruler of man nor of earth. God desires man and earth to be like Him, and a part of Him. God is growing through His desire, and man and earth, and all there is upon the earth, rise towards God by the power of desire. And desire is the inherent power that changes all things. It is the law of all matter and all life.[45]

The universe of Gibran, where Life is all there is, is hierarchical. Every element in this hierarchy strives for what is higher than it, which means that pantheism is not the proper qualifier for this cosmology. By conceiving of God as a desiring force, a force that grows by virtue of desire and to which the lower elements, including the soul, *long* to rise by virtue of the same power of desire, Gibran reinvents the Sufi notion of longing or *al-shawq*[46] in that he inscribes it in an evolutionary cosmology. Desire/longing, thus, comes to assume a fundamental ontological importance in a cosmology in which all the elements are willy-nilly evolving. It becomes 'the law of all matter and all life'. This desire is not born out of lack or need; it is an originary ontological force. In this worldview, there is no transcendent realm beyond Life, but this does not mean that there is no transcendental experience. For God, being the higher and most refined element in this universe, 'the furthest form of life',[47] is reinvented as a beyond *within* Being, as it were. How does this understanding of God bear upon the notion of the human self?

The soul, for Gibran, compared to God is 'a newly developed element in Nature',[48] a refined form of matter whose inherent properties – for it has its own inherent properties, like other elements in nature – are 'the desire for more of itself' and 'the hunger for that which is beyond itself'.[49] Gibran sums up these properties in one word: consciousness. And consciousness, in Gibran's Arabic fiction and non-fiction, is usually equated with '*al-dhāt al-waḍ'iyya*' or '*al-dhāt al-ma'nawiyya*' (authentic or ethical self) as opposed to '*al-dhāt al-muqtabasa*' (inauthentic or, literally, borrowed self). Other equally significant properties of the soul include 'the power [. . .] and the desire to seek' God, even as heat seeks height or water seeks the sea'.[50] Thus, a primordial and impersonal metaphysical desire is attributed to the soul. This impersonality is an essential element in Gibran's worldview, for 'it [the soul] never loses its path, any more than water runs upwards'.[51] Gibran articulates this constitutive impersonality as follows: 'That which is more than we think and know is always seeking and adding to itself while we are doing nothing – or think we are doing nothing'.[52] Echoing the Sufi highest stations of annihilation, *fanā'*, and persistence (or subsistence), *baqā'*, in God (the ultimate Desirer), 'the soul', speculates Gibran, 'never loses its inherent properties when it reaches God. Salt does not lose its saltness in the sea; its properties are inherent and eternal'.[53] Although the potentiality of the soul to 'be in God' is attainable, it does not mean that the soul becomes God; it becomes *in* God, annihilates in His Infinity, while retaining its above-mentioned properties, persisting in God, as in Sufism.[54] This insight resonates with the distinction that al-Hallaj, the famous Sufi poet, also known as the Martyr of Divine Love, makes between *nāsūt*, human nature, and *lāhūt*, the Divine. As Reynold Alleyne Nicholson remarks, 'though mystically united, they [*nāsūt* and *lāhūt*] are not essentially identical and interchangeable. Personality survives even in union: water does not become wine, though wine be mixed with it'.[55]

For Gibran, however, 'the absolute seeks more absoluteness, more crystallization', and 'God too is growing and seeking and crystallizing',[56] whereas God in Islam and Sufism is the Perfect Being, that which in His incomparability is beyond conceptualisation, or Being as such. Apart from that, Gibran asserts that 'we cannot fully understand the nature of God because we are *not* God, but we can make ready our consciousness to understand, and grow through, the visible expressions of God'.[57] This is, in other words, an understanding of God as *both* immanence *and* transcendence, which echoes the Sufi philosophy of, among others, Ibn al-ʿArabi, in which God is understood as He/not He. William C. Chittick explains:

> 'Where can I find God?' Wherever He is present, which is everywhere, since all things are His acts. But no act is identical with God, who encompasses all things and all acts, all worlds and all presences. Though he can be found everywhere, He is also nowhere to be found. He/not He.[58]

The acts and attributes of God in Islamic Sufism – that is, God in His similarity and knowability – turn into the visible expressions of God in Gibran. But God as such remains inaccessible and beyond conceptualisation. If Gibran abstains from speaking of God as such[59] – 'because we are *not* God'[60] – then his statement that 'God is everything and everywhere'[61] is best interpreted, in his own words, as 'the visual expressions of God'; that is to say, God as not He. Gibran, however, is not interested in *creatio ex nihilo*, nor is he concerned with God as He – that is, with the transcendent essence of God who is Being itself. As a poet, he is interested in God as expression; he once told Mary Haskell that crucifixion matters to him insofar as it is an expression.[62] This expression is one that simultaneously transforms and transcends language, and as such is irreducible to what he calls, in *al-Ajniḥa al-mutakassira (The Broken Wings)* and elsewhere, 'the world of measures and quantity' – which is posited against the realm of the poetic as such, the inexpressible, the spiritual or supra-sensuous, whose importance I shall later discuss. Breaking with the narrative of God as Father and Creator, Gibran rethinks God's transcendence horizontally and temporally; that is, as the impossible horizon of being as becoming: meaning not the non-possible, but that which is possible, paradoxically, in its unattainability. Put differently, God as such is temporally reinvented as the impossible future of the human self, which is expressed in the notion of the 'Greater Self' that comes to us from the future, not from above. No longer spatially imagined or locatable, except for his immanence, God as such, for Gibran, is no longer the transcendent vertical Being who loves and commands obedience from above, a point upon which I will touch in my discussion of his prose poem 'God' in the next section.

In Gibran's worldview, thus, there is no authority of a Supreme Being over the cosmos or beings; 'God and the universe are two universes occupying the same space. They are but one universe'.[63] Desire, in this speculative cosmology, constitutes the primordial impetus or determinant of the way in which every element (from low to high) grows and evolves. The soul is the highest form of matter, endowed with this intrinsic craving to reach God, and God is the furthest form of Life, who wants man and the earth to become like Him and a part of Him. These speculations, however, are not elaborated: how the soul is the highest form of matter or God the highest form of Life, we do not know. But one can discern a genuine and assiduous endeavour to reinvent God and the human self without a radical transcendence at once separating and bonding them. There can be no radical transcendence if Life is all there is; transcendence, rather, becomes horizontal and temporal – an unending process that stems from necessity, not obedience. While Gibran reconfigures Sufi-Islamic and Christian concepts by reappropriating them in an evolutionist fashion, his vision of God, the self and the world breaks with the fundamental pillars of Abrahamic monotheism: God as Prime Mover, as Creator and/or as a Father, eschatology and the transcendental discourses of values, of good and evil, and of reward and punishment. Yet he does so in a specific modern context that calls for a new configuration of values. His conception that perfection is limitation led him to purge God of any conceptual and ontological perfection, instead espousing an evolutionist notion of God who becomes at once the utmost horizon of the human self to dwell anew in this world and the immanent God who manifests himself everywhere spatially. Even more radical is the notion of the soul as the highest form of matter, which is part of Gibran's own version of the Unity of Being/Life, where all the old dualities – such as body-soul, mind-matter, immanence-transcendence – are radically (and at times loosely) rethought and reconciled, albeit not completely abolished.

My attempt to piece together a certain *Weltanschauung* out of Gibran's fragments of thought is interpretative, not strictly philosophical or religious. I use interpretative not in the sense of revealing something hidden, but in the sense of making connections and associations between disparate elements by way of zooming in and out of multifarious texts, hoping to lend a new understanding and significance to Gibran's works as texts that express a specific vision and literary configuration. Gibran never endeavoured to put together a coherent picture of this worldview. Yet, as discussed above (and as will be discussed in the following sections), some elements in this worldview are evidently recurrent and bespeak an attempt – however limited or conceptually undeveloped – to forge an original vision, to reimagine the world. What is crucial to my discussion here is that this evolutionist vision reconfigures some Christian and Sufi existential concepts – atonement, crucifixion, metaphysical longing/desire, the interplay of *fanā'* (annihilation) and *baqā'* (subsistence) and being as giving – in a modern context where religion and the fundamental notions of God, the self and the world were undergoing a radical transformation. Gibran's literary enterprise should be situated in this context of modernity as a whole and of the Arab *Nahḍa* in particular. His poetic work is not merely symbolic or loosely mystical, nor is his fiction strictly allegorical. There is a vision that underpins and informs his literary output and a worldly context of travelling ideas, concepts and forms within which it ought to be located. It is to his literary output that I now turn.

The Poet as a Post-religious Prophet in Modern Times

How does Gibran reimagine God, the self and the world poetically? What does it mean to speak prophetically as a poet in the context of modernity? And why poetry as that which articulates the prophetic? Let us begin with 'God', a prose poem published in *The Madman*, in which Gibran speaks of God as neither Creator nor Father, echoing his above-mentioned speculations. In the poem, the speaker tells us that, when he 'ascended the holy mountain and spoke unto God, saying, "Master, I am thy slave. Thy hidden will is my law and I shall obey thee for ever more"', God made no answer. And God made no answer when, a thousand years later, the speaker ascended the mountain calling unto God: '"Creator, I am thy creation. Out of clay thou fashioned me and to thee I owe mine all"'. Still God made no answer when, after another thousand years, the speaker called unto him, saying: '"Father, I am thy son. In pity and love thou hast given me birth, and through love and worship I shall inherit thy kingdom"'.[64] In other words, God as Master, Creator and Father has died, and this death, to reiterate what I said in the previous section, is a quiet death. A noiseless death: God simply made no answer. What dies in Gibran is the conception of God as Creator and Father, not God as such. More precisely, what dies is the consciousness of God as Creator and Father *inside* the speaker, in the mind of the speaker, in the history of the speaker as a human self – and it is no wonder that this speaker is the madman, one of Gibran's recurrent prophetic figures who speak as post-religious poets, those who take it upon themselves to reinvent their own notions of God. Yet this death is implicit, not even announced or spoken about but only hinted at, for God simply made no answer. What dies is the past of God, the history of God as Creator, Father, Master and Commander, the Christian god of love, pity and worship. This means that the speaker is no longer the 'slave', the 'creation' and the 'son' of God; what is more, the intimation here is that he has never been, for all this transpired 'in the ancient days, when the quiver of speech came to [his] lips'.[65] The poem, however, is written against the backdrop of a specific worldly and historical context, that of the modern world in which it intervenes. If religion, in this context, loses its epistemological grip over the fundamental notions of God, the self and the world, which were radically questioned and transformed in the epistemic paradigm of modernity, then poetry becomes *the* realm in which the religious is rethought and reimagined. By reinventing his own conception of God, the poet is thereby reinventing his own values, quietly destroying the Master-slave, Creator-created, Father-son relational structure. What kind of structure does this relationship take then?

That a certain notion – and history – of God dies in Gibran means that he was not merely 'influenced' by Nietzsche but was thinking with and after Nietzsche, in that he was writing poetically within the horizon of thought that Nietzsche's *Thus Spoke Zarathustra* opened up: the radical rethinking of the religious by way of reclaiming its prophetic mode of speech. In other words, he was, as a poet, engaging with Nietzsche, not appropriating or instrumentalising him. Towards the end of the poem, the speaker tells us that he climbed the mountain again, this time uttering the following words: 'My God, my aim and my fulfilment; I am thy yesterday and thou art my tomorrow. I am thy root in the earth and thou art my flower in the sky, and together we grow before the face of the sun'. It is only then that 'God leaned over [him], and in [his] ears whispered words of sweetness, and even as the sea that enfoldeth a brook that runneth down to her, he enfolded [him]'.[66] Purged of absolute authority and of radical and vertical transcendence, God no longer signifies a divine Fatherhood nor is He, for Gibran, a divine Creator. Rather, God is one's tomorrow insofar as one is God's yesterday: this is the form that one's relationship with God now takes. As one's 'aim and fulfilment' – that is, as one's beyond, as it were – God names the future as a form of horizontal transcendence[67] that is temporally (un)fulfillable. Coming from the future, becoming the impossible future – 'a future never future enough', to borrow a phrase from Emanuel Levinas[68] – God as such is reinvented as a transcendental condition of being *qua* becoming for the human self. After Nietzsche and Darwin – or a certain interpretative horizon that Nietzsche and Darwin made possible – Gibran reimagines God as an ever-evolving desiring force the mystical yearning for which has not died. Rather, this mystical yearning, finding its roots in the Sufi embodied concept of *al-shawq*, is reinvented in a post-religious fashion. This God, furthermore, is not only horizontally transcendent, but spatially immanent as well: 'And when I descended to the valleys and the plains', the speaker tells us, 'God was there *also*'.[69] This 'also' means that God is both the deferred tomorrow of the human self – God as a horizontal form of transcendence – and that which is 'there', that is, everywhere – God as a 'visual expression', Gibran would say. God as immanence.

The madman, who announces this new relationship with God, is one of many other figures in whose name Gibran's prophetic imagination is articulated. The madman, the forerunner, Almustafa (the prophet), the wanderer and Āmina (the principal Sufi character of his one-act play *Iram dhāt al-ʿimād*) – and some of the main characters of Gibran's early fiction in Arabic, including Yūḥanna al-majnūn (Yuhanna the mad), Warda al-Hāni, Khalīl al-Kāfir (Khalil the heretic) and Salma Karāma – are prophetic figures who name and reclaim the radicality of religion in its fundamental and pre-institutional sense of rupture, migration and event. In reclaiming this Abrahamic heritage of prophecy in a modern context, these figures name the (im)possibility of repeating 'religion without religion',[70] so to speak, of religion without any theological foundation. As my discussion below will demonstrate, religion here is restated, by virtue of the poetic, as a disruptive force that seeks to demolish the new idols or masks of modernity. It is also reclaimed, in Gibran's Arabic fiction, as the realm of universal nomos or law (*al-nāmūs al-kullī*), which seeks to subvert or disrupt the oppressive manifestation of bourgeois morality and/or religious instrumentalism in Beirut and Mount Lebanon, through the embodiment of love understood and acted out as a metaphysical sacrifice. Speaking in the name of these prophetic figures, who name an Abrahamic ethical horizon whose universal validity has not been exhausted,[71] Gibran rejuvenates the prophetic as a powerful poetic and aesthetic motif through which the religious and the ethical are radically rethought within and against modernity.

The madman – residing 'outside' the predominant modes of reason, morality, identity and value, for the prophetic always speaks from an Outside[72] – begins his discourse by relating to us how he became a madman: one day he wakes up to find out that all his masks, the self-fashioned masks he wore in the past seven lives, were stolen. Walking around the crowded streets and looking for the thieves who stole his masks, he is identified as a madman by 'a youth standing on a house-top'. As soon as he looks up, however, 'the sun kiss[es] [his] own naked face for the first time'.[73] Thus he discovers the nakedness of his face for the first time. Thus he becomes a madman, in that he discovers the capacity to belong to himself without any veiling masks, the capacity to reside and be 'outside' the reigning social institutions of reason and identity: madness as event.[74] This event is tantamount to what the Sufis call *kashf* (disclosure) or 'unconcealment', in the Heideggerian sense of truth as *aletheia*.[75] And, in Gibran's short stories, this event usually manifests itself as an epiphanic episode in consciousness that links love, sacrifice and death. This event of madness, the discovery of the face that exists beneath and beyond all identitarian and normative veils, epitomises Gibran's predominant concern in *The Madman*: belonging to oneself with no prior identifications or designations. In this respect, the 'Seventh Self' of the madman, reacting against his other six selves that wish to rebel against him with a preconceived intention and purpose, declares:

> How strange that you all would rebel against this man, because each and every one of you has *a pre-ordained fate to fulfil*. Ah! could I be but one of you, *a self with a determined lot*! But I have none, I am the do-nothing self, the one who sits in the dumb, empty nowhere and nowhen, while you are busy re-creating life. Is it you or I, neighbours, who should rebel?[76]

No wonder that the second piece in *The Madman* is the one in which God is reimagined beyond the vertical metaphysics of creation, fatherhood and morality. For only a madman, speaking 'in the ancient days' and 'before many gods were born', could intervene from the 'outside' of history, as it were, from below or behind the history of the gods of morality, authority and value, to announce the arrival of his own God. Retrieving and resuscitating the prophetic as a mode of poetic and ethical intervention, this madman is what Fethi Meskini would call an 'impossible believer': 'the *other* believer who reinvents the notion of God from within and does not consume it from without, nor does s/he borrow it from anyone'.[77] The madman, furthermore, is one who laughingly buries his 'dead selves',[78] and this grave-digging, which is a recurring metaphor in Gibran, is the prerequisite condition to overcome the history and concept of 'man' – as Nietzsche would say – and create new values.

This metaphor of grave-digging is usually coupled with the metaphors of the night and the tempest, all of which are used by Gibran to designate or announce a new mode of thinking, being and dwelling in the world. It is as a poet that Gibran thinks, as a post-religious poet for whom the poetic is synonymous with the creative. The creative here is understood in the fundamental sense of autonomous (self-)creation, which produces a conception of poetry as an aesthetic expression of moral and spiritual autonomy.[79] This radical poetic thinking usually takes place in the night, the night which becomes thought's condition of possibility and the enabling nothingness where the 'ghost of the mad god' becomes the thinking horizon of the poet.[80] This is the gist of Gibran's short story 'Ḥaffār al-qubūr' (The Grave Digger). In it, the poet is walking alone at night, 'in the valley of life's shadow that is lined up with bones and skulls'. While standing 'on the banks of the river of blood and tears which flows like a speckled serpent [. . .] gazing at the nothingness', the poet is suddenly visited by 'a giant, august ghost'.[81] Frightened, the poet shouts, 'what do you want from me?' Thereupon the ghost declares that he wants nothing and everything from the poet, that he is 'aloneness itself' and that which the poet fears and fears to fear – a 'double fear',[82] that is, that the poet must confront and overcome in order to think. What emerges here is a dialogue between the poet and the ghost that essentially revolves around the poet's name, vocation, marital status and religion. It is the discourse of the giant ghost that makes 'Ḥaffār al-qubūr' such a powerful piece and a pioneering reflection 'through and against nihilism' in modern Arab thought.[83] The ghost begins by unravelling what lies beneath the name of the poet, 'Abdallah (God's servant). The poet says that this name was given to him by his father, to which the ghost responds: 'The misfortune of children lies in the gifts of their parents, and those who do not deprive themselves from the gifts of their parents and ancestors remain slaves to the dead until they die'.[84] The ghost, in other words, is laying bare that which is concealed by the act of naming itself: the metaphysics of the name that absents the named, the poet himself, by perpetuating the presence of the absent and absenting name, which implicitly bears the father's heritage.[85] The possibility of life itself, thus, is predicated on the will and courage to say 'no' to the father's gift, a gift that creates and necessitates, whether the child is aware of it or not, a feeling of indebtedness to the father, a gift that perpetuates the values of the father and thereby obscures the creative 'yes' of the child.

The ghost, then, goes on to devalue the poet's vocation – writing poetry – by considering it 'old, deserted, neither useful nor harmful'.[86] When the poet wonders what he could do to be useful to people, the ghost urges him to become a 'grave digger' so 'he could relieve the living from the piled corpses of the dead around their houses, courts and temples'.[87] He is asking him, that is, to bury the dead values of the self, the law and the holy, which he cannot see because he looks with a 'deluded eye' that 'sees people shivering in the tempest of life, thinking that they are alive while dead they have been since birth'.[88] Which is to say that life for them is still lived according to the dead and the values of the dead, not according to themselves, still shivering as they are in front of life's tempest. It bears pointing out that it is not the destruction of the self, the law and the holy that is called for here, but the burying of what is dead 'around' them, the burying of that which lost the ethical, normative and spiritual capacity to orient the living. A new life, therefore, must be reinvented and created. The tempest, moreover, is not merely a metaphor of destruction, rupture, radical change and transformation; the tempest is life itself in that it represents the antithesis of death: 'The dead shiver in the tempest, while the living march with it running and only halt when it does',[89] declares the ghost. This is the major task of the poet in modern times then: to preach life as a relentless tempest, to create the possibility of life by digging graves for that which is dead around people's houses, courts and temples, to *be* and *think* only as a tempest, which is the condition of being in the world insofar as it means thinking it anew and creating it again every time.

'What is your religion?' is the last question that the ghost asks. The poet answers: 'I believe in God, I honour his prophets, I love virtue and I have hope in a thereafter'.[90] The ghost's response is worth quoting here:

> You are only saying these words, which were laid out by ancient generations, by a mere act of borrowing that placed them upon your lips. The naked truth, however, is that you believe only in yourself, you honour none other than it, you love nothing save what it desires, and you hope only for its immortality. Man has worshipped himself since time immemorial, yet this worshipped self has taken on as many names as his wishes and desires: at times he called it Lord or Jupiter, at others he called it God.[91]

With irony, however, he adds, 'but how strange are those who worship themselves, and their selves are nothing but rancid corpses',[92] suggesting that what one believes in matters less than the lack of creative self-expression, which can only be born out of an arduous experience of self-creation. This ghost turns out to be the 'mad god' who, averse to wisdom which he deems a sign of human weakness, is the god of his own self, born in every place and in every time. How can such a god – a god who curses the sun and the humans, mocks nature and kneels in front of himself and worships it, a god who, along with time and the sea, does not sleep but eats the corpses of people, drinks their blood and snacks on their gasps[93] – be the thinking horizon of the poet? How can this thinking horizon, the nocturnal horizon of the tempest, be a positive breakthrough for the poet?

This god, being a mad god, points to the utmost possibility of self-creation in an age in which the regnant modes of reason, authority and value are no longer alive. The mad god bespeaks a different direction of thought; that is, a different direction of reason and not the opposite of reason, that the poet must have the courage and will to take: the direction of self-creation that must begin by gravedigging – that is to say, by burying his dead selves, laws and values, not the self, the law and values as such. The poet can no longer be a crafter of poetry in this age. The poet must face the nihilism that lies behind it and overcome it. The poet must sing life as a tempest that destroys what is no longer alive, what is no longer capable of inspiring and orienting a creative life. Otherwise he will remain a slave to the dead, a mere repetition of the past that is embodied in his name, his poetry and his religion, unable to bear – in the double sense of carrying and enduring – the possibility of life as a new creation of values. Thus, unlike the Christian god of morality that dies in Nietzsche, Gibran's god becomes a mad god, the terrible thinking horizon in the night of the poet, the madness that can make possible a new kind of reason, attained only if the poet overcomes his 'double fear' of radically rethinking and remaking the world.

The night itself becomes the madman's unattainable self-image in 'Night and the Madman'.[94] 'I am like thee, O, Night', declares the madman time and again. Yet the speaking Night denies him this resemblance and identification, pointing to that which he must yet become and/or overcome. For he, so the Night reminds him, still looks backwards at his own large footsteps, shudders before pain and the terrifying song of the abyss, unable as he is to befriend his 'monster-self' and become a law unto himself. Gibran's celebration and fascination with the night as a metaphor of overcoming, self-becoming and – as evinced in his Arabic prose poem 'Ayyuha al-layl' (O Night)[95] – mystical self-disclosure should be located, hermeneutically, in the context of modernity. To be more precise, it is against a particular modern regime of reason and identity, where one's personhood is predetermined and plainly demarcated in the light of the modern day, so to speak, that the madman conjures up the night as the abyss whose terrifying song the moderns are unable to bear and to listen to. In the 'destitute time' of modernity, as Heidegger writes in relation to Hölderlin,[96] the abyss of the night, the night as a revealing abyss, consists in the unbearable ordeal of giving oneself one's law and of building a throne 'upon the heaps of the fallen Gods'.[97] The madman, this post-religious poet, is the one who, building this throne, strives to think the 'untamed thoughts' of the night and speak its 'vast language'.[98] This is the poet of destitute times who, as Heidegger would say, 'attend[s], singing, to the trace of the fugitive gods'.[99] Only in the night of the modern day can one retrieve the vastness of language and the abyssal, transformative power of thought, which have been tamed, as Gibran's powerful prose poem '"The Perfect World"' suggests, by modernity's calculative and instrumental reason. The madman is the poet who, against the flattening order of the modern day, invokes the night's immeasurable capacity to reveal space; that is to say, to reveal his irreducible and immeasurable soul[100] – the soul that cannot be reduced to, or measured by, 'recording' and 'cataloguing'.[101]

In '"The Perfect World"', the madman laments and castigates the rigidly mathematical and rationalistic order by which human life is preordained, regulated and experienced in modernity. What is initially intriguing here is that the madman's discourse is addressed to 'the God of lost souls [. . .] who [is] lost amongst the gods'.[102] What are these gods? And why is God lost amongst these gods? 'Hear me', the madman says to this 'Gentle Destiny that watchest over us, mad, wandering spirits'.[103] 'Hear me': thus is addressed God in the modern times, thus addresses the madman, who 'dwell[s] in the midst of a perfect race, [he] the most imperfect', his lost God. The madman, as a post-religious poet, is the one who addresses God amidst the proliferation of the gods, the new idols of modernity: order, perfection and calculative reason. In other words, God becomes the *addressee* of the post-religious poet, the madman who speaks from the Outside, who is an outsider to this 'perfect world' of the moderns. Because this poet is overwhelmed by the new, secular gods of modernity, following which this 'perfect race' dwells in the world, he has no addressee but God. For God, albeit lost amongst those gods, can still be addressed. Yet God can still be addressed insofar as He, in these destitute times, *can only be addressed*. Prophetic speech, as reclaimed by the madman, is addressed to God, not the other way around. Put differently, prophetic speech no longer comes from the Outside but speaks *to the Outside*, such that it is – and can only be – a summoning of the trace of this Outside. 'Hear me', says the madman to 'the God of lost souls':

> I, a human chaos, a nebula of confused elements, I move amongst finished worlds – peoples of complete laws and pure order, whose thoughts are

> assorted, whose dreams are arranged, and whose visions are enrolled and registered.
> Their virtues, O God, are measured, their sins are weighed, and even the countless things that pass in the dim twilight of neither sin nor virtue are recorded and catalogued.
> Here days and nights are divided into seasons of conduct and governed by rules of blameless accuracy.
> [. . .]
> It is a perfect world, a world of consummate excellence, a world of supreme wonders, the ripest fruit in God's garden, the master-thought of the universe.[104]

The madman's speech betrays an acute disillusionment with what Heidegger calls *Gestell*, the (en)framing that structures modern technological Being.[105] This rigid mathematical and technological regulation of modern life erases any empowering possibility of imperfection, being the essential condition for Life as a 'never-finished building'.[106] For to be human, Gibran firmly believes, is to long insatiably for a Greater Self – at once desiring more of the self and striving to go beyond it. To long presupposes imperfection, an enabling imperfection, because perfection, according to him, is nothing but a limitation. This is not solely reflective of the primordial longing that defines the human as a potentiality that lies ahead, a longing for 'the Greater Sea' that always lies beyond the other seas, the absolute desiring Other.[107] It concerns the fundamental manner of dwelling in the world: one cannot dwell perfectly; one can truly dwell, to draw on Heidegger again, insofar as one dwells poetically, poetry here being that dwelling which lets dwelling itself be,[108] an opening up of Being that cannot frame or measure in calculative terms.[109]

The madman – this outsider who, being an outsider, speaks to the Outside – ends his speech with a rhetorical question that announces the impossible character of being in the modern, 'perfect world': 'But why should I be here, O God, I a green seed of unfulfilled passion, a mad tempest that seeketh neither east nor west, a bewildered fragment from a burnt planet? Why am I here, O God of lost souls, thou who art lost amongst the gods?'[110] God in this 'perfect world' becomes the addressee – and the sole addressee

– of the post-religious poet. For God here bespeaks an alternative mode of being, one of potentiality and openness, not of rigidity and closure. As such, God becomes the sole addressee of the poet, who endeavours to colour the 'perfect world' with a much-needed trace of lost divinity. Thus, to address God is to invoke the (im)possibility of rupture, of event, of the unknown and the unexpected, to make the world more habitable or less rationalisable. Albeit lost amongst the many new gods that emerged in the modern world, God is invoked as the trace of an Outside that could be reached by way of questioning. This questioning is much more than rhetorical. It points to the fundamental question of being itself: the mode of being that befits the human in this modern world where everything, as the madman bitterly points out, is predetermined, arranged, demarcated, pigeon-holed, catalogued, recorded and numbered. God, in this context, becomes the trace of the Outside whose invocation aims to question and disrupt this modern mode of being. And this interrogatory invocation beckons to that which lies outside these 'finished worlds', to a world where one can never be reduced to a mathematical, rationalist order. Thus, human essence, albeit obscured by the emergence of the new idols of modernity, is still recoverable and, therefore, must be recovered. It is the post-religious poet who attends to the retrieval of this essence, of that which remains ungraspable and unknowable as such, and in this sense transcendental, in man. This poetic retrieval – for only poetry can retrieve the ungraspable and sing it – is possible by way of invoking the lost trace of God insofar as it allows for a mode of being and dwelling in the world that is beyond calculation and 'pure order'.

The madman, this 'impossible prophet'[111] who must become a law unto himself, also sets out to reclaim and reinvent 'crucifixion' as a necessary condition for an 'exaltedness' without atonement. By dissociating the name from the named, or the signifier from the signified, Gibran attempts to reactivate the radical, disruptive force of religion itself – a religion that announces itself only by, as it were, effacing itself – such that its name or the names that point towards it are taken beyond the history of meaning, value and authority that saturate them. Thus crucifixion, stripped of its essential meaning in Christianity – that is, of the elements of sin and retribution that lend it its Christian particularity – is transformed into a metaphor of overcoming, divorced from any discourse of good and evil or reward and punishment:

> I cried to men, 'I would be crucified!'
> And they said, 'Why should your blood be upon our heads?'
> And I answered, 'How else shall you be exalted except by crucifying madmen?'
> And they heeded and I was crucified. And the crucifixion appeased me.[112]

Crucifixion becomes a metaphor of rebirth and self-creation, an expression of the self beyond original sin and salvation. This is another element that places Gibran in proximity with – because thinking after – Nietzsche, who 'had at times signed himself "Dionysus" and at others "*Der Gekreuzigte*" ['The Crucified One'], likewise extending these aliases beyond good and evil'.[113] Arousing the perplexity of the crowd who is unable to fathom this act of crucifixion, the smiling madman asserts:

> 'Remember only that I smile. I do not atone – nor sacrifice – nor wish for glory; and I have nothing to forgive. I thirsted – and I besought you to give my blood to drink. For what is there to quench a madman's thirst but his own blood? I was dumb – and I asked wounds of you for mouths. I was imprisoned in your days and nights – and I sought a door into larger days and nights. And now I go – as others already crucified have gone. And think not we are weary of crucifixion. For we must be crucified by larger and larger men, between greater earths and greater heavens.'[114]

This motif, that of seeking 'larger' and 'greater' selves, will feature again and again in Gibran's writings after *The Madman*. It is not difficult to discern in this longing for a Greater Self the Nietzschean echoes of overcoming as redemption: 'To redeem those who lived in the past and to recreate all "it was" into a "thus I willed it" – that alone should I call redemption',[115] says Zarathustra. Gibran's specificity here lies in reclaiming crucifixion as an *expressive* act of self-redemption delinked from the discourse of good and evil and the after-life eschatology of reward and punishment, from any messianism except that of the larger self of this world, of this Life. Like grave-digging (burying that which is dead but still directing the being of the self), crucifixion is reconfigured as a post-religious metaphor of tireless self-fashioning, whose horizon is the future of the self as a Greater Self. This crucifixion does not need any transcendent vertical morality that bestows meaning on it and accords it a certain teleology. It is rather turned into a Nietzschean 'thus I willed it', so to speak, but without any Nietzschean resentment towards Christianity.[116]

The Prophetic in Gibran's Early Fiction: Love, Epiphany and Sacrifice

Before discussing the prophetic as it expresses itself in the poetics of 'the Greater Self' in Gibran's late work, from *The Forerunner* onwards, it is necessary first to explore its manifestation in his early Arabic fiction. This is where the prophetic in Gibran finds its initial, powerful expression both narratively and aesthetically, notwithstanding the occasional sentimentalism and flatness of characterisation. The narrative and aesthetic elements are indissociable from the Lebanese and Arab contexts, albeit one also discerns the universal dimension of this vision – concerning the nature of poetry, the human self, religion and law, love and marriage, nature and culture, among other things. What is peculiar about this phase is Gibran's fusion of Phoenician mythology with an Abrahamic prophetic imagination – predominantly Biblical – in a manner that transforms our understanding of tradition in relation to the present and the future. Prophetic imagination here often manifests itself in epiphanic moments that simultaneously embody Love[117] as a transformative event in consciousness seeking to disrupt the social order and, thereby, entail self-sacrifice as Love's ultimate metaphysical expression.

In Gibran's early short stories, the narrative is usually structured around a character or a couple who is alienated because of the unjustness of society in the form of social, economic and religious oppression. Love, the highest manifestation of what Gibran calls the ethical or authentic/innate self (*al-dhāt al-maʿnawiyya* or *al-dhāt al-waḍʿiyya*,[118] respectively), functions as an antidote to oppression. In this context, Love is understood neither as erotic subversion nor as Christian agape, but as that which represents the soul or essence of natural or universal law (*al-nāmūs al-kullī*) as opposed to religious, traditional or customary laws (*sharāʾiʿ*). These laws, in the stories, are inseparable from a materialistic modernity in the Levant. Understood this way, Love can be equated with consciousness oriented towards the subversion, or at least the disruption, of a traditional law or custom used to justify social and economic oppression. This is especially the case in 'Mārtha', 'Yūḥanna al-majnūn', 'Warda al-Hāni' and 'Maḍjaʿ al-ʿarūs' (The Bridal Couch), all of which are short stories in which the protagonists are victims of oppressive social mores that stifle the realisation of their authentic selves, and this reveals to themselves, to others or to the narrator a consciousness enlightened by Love and thereby sacrificed in its name. The sacrifice takes either the form of death, which strikes the bride and her beloved in 'Maḍjaʿ al-ʿarūs' and the eponymous protagonist of 'Mārtha', or the form of ostracisation, as reflected in the fate of the eponymous protagonists of 'Yūḥanna al-majnūn' and 'Warda al-Hāni'. In either case, Love manifests itself as an *event* in consciousness – hence its metaphysical nature – that disturbs or seeks to disturb an oppressive state of affairs.

The short story as a form supplies this 'content' with a concentration of emotional and affective force. The form condenses a long narrative only to leave us with a story whose tragic end is related as an inevitable disruption. This sense of inevitability, which usually links the enactment of enlightened or authentic consciousness with death or ostracisation, may justify the choice of form. And this choice, it seems to me, is a conscious one, experimental though it may be. Of interest to Gibran, first and foremost, is the epiphanic moment, the disruptive force, the subversive event, which are given this sense of inevitability in, or by virtue of, his short stories. This interest, furthermore, is simultaneously metaphysical, social and aesthetic, as the epiphanic moment is articulated in a lyrical language whose unique poetic flow and Romantic imagery are marked by novelty and vitality in style, arguably the signature contribution of Gibran to modern Arabic literature. Yet this occurs at the expense of complexity on the level of characterisation. One discerns, as many commentators have remarked, an almost clear demarcation between the world of the oppressors and that of the oppressed in Gibran's early work (and also in his long poem *al-Mawākib*), between 'Tradition' and 'Love', an allegorical opposition mediated, as Boutros Hallaq has cogently shown, by death.[119] But it is not so much tradition that Love opposes as the instrumental use of sanctified traditional and religious codes to buttress the socio-economic power of the bourgeoisie and upper-middle-classes as well as the clergy, which seeks to control both bodies and souls. In Gibran's fiction, thus, Love serves as a counterforce to a modern, bourgeois morality (in Beirut) and religious instrumentalism (in the Christian countryside of Lebanon), or a combination of both. What is more, it acquires a metaphysical dimension: the manifestation of an authentic self that is destined to die in the material and social world and survive elsewhere. The short story's sense of inevitability, as a form, hastens the arrival of this death, the culmination of Love as an epiphanic, disruptive event.[120]

Love, in Gibran's Arabic fiction, also expresses itself as a revelatory event in an individual consciousness that retrieves and reinvents a mythical trace of divinity which is no longer possible in the modern world. In 'The Ashes of Generations and Eternal Fire', for instance, narrative time is episodic and mythical rather than historical or sociological. The story relates – in the double sense of narrating and connecting – two events in consciousness that occur in two different points in time, linking two different bodies by way of reincarnation. As mentioned earlier, reincarnation serves both an ontological and narrative purpose in Gibran. The first part of the story takes place in the autumn of 16 BC in Baalbek, the city of Baal or the sun god. It narrates the tragic fate of Nathan, son of the priest Hiram, who prays for his dying beloved in the temple of Astarte, the Phoenician goddess of love and beauty. His beloved dies, but on her deathbed she tells him that Astarte 'resurrects the souls of lovers who left for eternity before relishing the pleasures of love and the joys of youth'.[121] Fast forward to the spring of 1890 AD, the second part of the story also takes place in Baalbek but revolves around a shepherd called Ali al-Husaini, who is taking a rest with his herd in the ruins of Astarte's temple. There, half-awake, he experiences a transformative, epiphanic moment in which his true, authentic self, the one that 'transcends the laws and teachings of man', substitutes for his 'borrowed' or inauthentic one, so that 'the circles of vision broadened before his eyes'.[122] This epiphany is described as an individuation in which 'the self isolates itself from the procession of time that seeks nothingness'. Thus, 'standing alone [. . .] he [Ali] knew or almost knew for the first time in his life the reasons behind the spiritual hunger overtaking his youth'.[123] This 'strange sensation', we are told, was awakened by the ruins of the temple. Such an awakening expresses itself in Love experienced as a metaphysical, unsettling force that 'reveals to the self the secrets of the self and separates the mind from the world of measures and quantity'.[124] Understood this way, Love represents the embodiment of mythological time in history. The individual here experiences in himself an estranging revelation whereby he is reunited with his reincarnated beloved and is thereby liberated. If this experience is articulated in a mystical language reminiscent of Sufism, it is nevertheless post-religious in its celebration of human Love, with divinity *felt* as a trace or a dimension of Love irreducible to positivist reason – or to the 'perfect world' in which the madman cannot belong – rather than an aim in itself. What is more, reincarnation serves the narrative function of return as a liberating reinvention of myth in a modern world where myth-making is no longer possible; for, as the narrator tells us, the old gods are dead. The temple, as my reading of *al-Ajniḥa al-mutakassira* will also demonstrate, is the space in which this trace of divinity is resurrected in the individual who experiences it as an epiphanic moment that reveals her true, authentic self to her, the one that does not abide by human-made law, be it religious or customary, or by positivist reason. That the temple links two moments in history by way of myth bespeaks Gibran's awareness of what Charles Taylor calls the 'sources of the self',[125] Phoenician mythology being one of those sources whose summoning indicates the extent to which Gibran understands their complementarity or enriching multiplicity as *moral* sources. What enables the reinvention of the divine trace (and the sources of the self, more generally) is precisely the poetic: poetic words whose prophetic power it is to turn the *ruins* of the ancient temple into a modern, individual experience of Love as a transformative self-revelation, one which is irreducible to 'the world of measures and quantity'.

In *al-Ajniḥa al-mutakassira*, the story of a tragic beauty of love sacrificed in the face of oppressive social codes, the distinction between the ethical, authentic self and the sensuous, borrowed self, between the irreducible and transcendental world of the former and the quantifiable or measurable world of the latter, is central to it both structurally and thematically. The authentic self is the self that transcends the senses and reaches towards a higher realm of reality, which is nevertheless within Life, which for Gibran is all there is. Hence the inexpressible that haunts Gibran's texts, since to go beyond the senses is to enter a space beyond language. And because language is the only resource available to embody the beyond, that which cannot be expressed in words casts its shadow over the text. When the narrator attempts to describe Salma, his beloved, he does so but with a note that Salma's beauty is one that does not lend itself to 'human-made measures of beauty', in that it is 'a kind of poetic genius whose spectres we discern in great verses of poetry and timeless painting and music'.[126] One may interpret this in Platonic terms – Salma's indescribable beauty as reminder of True Beauty – but this is less about essence *versus* appearance than it is about the finite and the infinite, the measurable and immeasurable, both of which for Gibran are of the here and now; the difference is one of degree, not of kind. The soul, the vision, the creative idea, beauty and so on, in Gibran, are by their very nature unamenable to what he calls 'mechanical' reason, whose limited validity he nevertheless acknowledges.[127] But the Absolute, for which art and the soul strive, is within Life, even if it is not within reach. Therefore, to invoke 'poetic genius' in the attempt to describe the beauty of Salma is not merely a rhetorical gesture; it bespeaks a worldview in which the sensible matters to the extent that it suggests what transcends it, the inexpressible and the immeasurable.

The other implication here is that poetic genius assumes an autonomy irreducible to positivism. The poetic, in this worldview, is a manifestation of natural or universal law (*nāmūs kullī*), not human-made ones (*sharī'a bashariyya*), be they religious or secular. Unconstrained by sanctified codes, the poetic reflects the purity of the inexpressible, which does not abide by *a priori* standards. But 'tradition' is nevertheless indispensable insofar as it designates a reservoir of *individual* works of art[128] (both religious and secular) that simultaneously instantiate and suggest the Absolute, that represent exemplary attempts at expressing the inexpressible – a modern, Romantic notion in which Gibran wholeheartedly believed. This is alluded to, for instance, in the forgotten temple in which Salma and the narrator, following her unwanted marriage, decide to meet once a month. On the walls of this ancient, unknown temple are painted or sculpted images of both Astarte and Jesus Christ. The temple, thus, stands for the (overlooked) mythological and Abrahamic sources of the self, which are reinvented in a modern context by virtue of the poetic words that invoke them. What matters as far as the temple is concerned, therefore, is not what it reminds one of, 'the fate of bygone generations and the procession of people from one condition to another and one religion to another',[129] as much as what it bespeaks – namely the world beyond the senses, which enables one 'to feel what one does not see and imagine what one does not sense'.[130] And, as the narrator tells us, this is expressed in art, which simultaneously manifests itself in and transcends history.

The novella itself, as I construe it, is about innocence and experience. This innocence is not necessarily associated with young age, but with the purity or essence of a world beyond the senses, which is posited against the experience of social oppression. Love triumphs and survives in death – the death of Salma, her baby and her father – because social norms in modern Lebanon are dominated by a materialistic ethos that is at odds with authenticity understood as moral autonomy or independence. As I show in Chapter Three, this moral autonomy for Gibran is the *sine qua non* of an original or creative *Nahḍa*, be it in poetics or politics. The tragic beauty of *The Broken Wings* stems from the sacrificial nature of a Love that transcends the senses, that derives from the immeasurable realm of the soul (*al-dhāt al-maʿnawiyya*) as manifested in Salma's sacrifice of a possible, future happiness with the narrator for his own sake: 'Finite love', she tells him, 'seeks the possession of the beloved, but infinite love seeks nothing but itself'.[131] This notion of Love as sacrifice is later echoed in *The Prophet*: 'Love gives naught but itself and takes naught but from itself./ Love possesses not nor would it be possessed;/ For love is sufficient unto love'.[132] Salma, thus, speaks prophetically, and her prophetic speech is vindicated by the sacrifice that she makes in the name of Love, choosing 'the cross of Jesus Christ over the joys of Astarte' and thereby embodying *the* impossible: 'the ability to sacrifice something great for the sake of something greater'.[133] That Love here is a metaphysical sacrifice and not just a tragic occurrence is a notion that the narrator himself suggests, whose self 'submits in silence before the higher Law [*al-nāmūs al-ʿulwī*] that took as a temple the chest of Selma and as an altar her own self'.[134]

The Spiritual as a Worldly Ethics of Belonging

The impossible character of Gibran's prophetic vision lies also in the unhomeliness it preaches. This unhomeliness does not imply alienation, nor does it suggest what Freud calls the *Unheimlich* (the uncanny).[135] Rather, it designates a necessary detachment from place, familiarity, repetition, habit, sameness and limitation, emphasising the spiritual as the imaginative horizon that allows for a mode of dwelling which shakes any stable relationship with place. This unhomeliness, the condition of a dwelling that attends to space rather than place, is essentially prophetic. As Blanchot points out, '[p]rophetic speech is a wandering speech that returns to the original demand of movement by opposing all stillness, all settling, any taking root that would be rest'.[136] The spiritual is that which names this movement. As such, it should not be understood as the antithesis of the earthly or the bodily. The spiritual, for Gibran, names the unity of Being/Life, the unity of body and soul, the unity of sight (*al-baṣar*) and insight (*al-baṣīra*). It names the *disclosure* of Being in this life and in this world. This is particularly show-cased in his one-act play *Iram dhāt al-ʿimād* (Iram, City of Lofty Pillars), published in 1921. The title of the play is taken from the Qurʾān, in which it is described as a city the likes of which were never created,[137] to signify a place or rather a space of spiritual disclosure. My reflections on the spiritual here, which is reclaimed beyond any facile connotation of it, are primarily based on this play.

The main character of *Iram dhāt al-ʿimād*, Āmina al-ʿAlawiyya, a name whose Islamic resonance is unmistakable,[138] is a female spiritual figure whom Najeeb, the Lebanese writer, is searching for, as he is seeking her knowledge. That this Sufi figure is a female should not go unnoticed. Āmina is a prophetic figure who has attained the knowledge – in the sense of gnosis – that her father, who 'was the imam of his time in spiritual and esoteric matters',[139] did not. That is, her 'gender' does not matter here, and the masculinist monopoly of knowledge production and attainment is tacitly destroyed and overcome – let us remember that the play, published in 1921, is set in 1883. Zain al-ʿAbidin of Nahavand, the Persian character who is known as the Sufi, tells Najeeb that, when Āmina turned twenty-five, she set out with her father to Mecca to fulfil the duty of pilgrimage. On their way, however, her father caught a fever and passed away. Āmina buried him at the foot of a mountain and stayed by his grave for seven nights, 'calling unto his soul and seeking to discover the secrets of the unseen world and what lies beyond the veil'.[140] On the seventh night, the soul of her father inspired her to head to the heart of the Arab peninsula, the Rubʿ al-Khali desert. The desert, indeed, is 'not time, or space, but a space without place and a time without production', so Blanchot ruminates, 'this outside, where one cannot remain, since to be there is to be always already outside, and prophetic speech is that speech in which the bare relation with the Outside could be expressed'.[141] This relation is essentially one of disclosure or unveiling (*kashf*). Āmina confronts this bare Outside on her own and *reveals* it. Āmina represents the prophetic figure of a post-religious *Iram dhāt al-ʿimād*, where Being as such is disclosed to her – insofar as her vision reveals it – in the bare desert of Arabia. After five years of disappearance, Āmina was seen in Mosul, where her emergence was 'something akin to the falling of a meteor from space'.[142] In the circles of the ulama (religious scholars), she spoke about divine matters and described what she saw in *Iram dhāt al-ʿimād* with a unique eloquence hitherto unknown to the people of Mosul. Because her followers increased and her name became a threat to the city's ulama, the governor of Mosul summoned her, offered her a packet of gold and asked her to leave the city. Disappointed, she left without taking the gold. The same thing happened to her in Istanbul, Aleppo, Damascus, Homs and Tripoli, where her knowledge did not please the imams and religious jurists. As a result, she decided to lead a reclusive life in northeast Lebanon, where she is sought out by Najeeb, the Lebanese writer.

Āmina appears at some point, and both Najeeb and Zain are enraptured by her, 'as though they were in the presence of one of God's prophets'.[143] The dialogue that unfolds between Āmina and Najeeb reveals in an unambiguous fashion most of Gibran's central ideas as far as the religious is concerned, which are basically drawn from Sufism: truth as *kashf* or disclosure, Longing (*al-shawq*) as the arduous bridge towards the witnessing (*mushāhdat*) of the self, understood as the microcosm of Being,[144] the Unity of Being, imagination as a disclosing insight (*baṣīra*)[145] and the transcendent unity of religions.[146] Āmina tells Najeeb that she 'entered the veiled city with her body, which is [her] visible soul, and with [her] soul, which is her invisible body. And whoever tries to separate the particles of the body has been plainly led astray [*kāna fī ḍalālin mubīn*]. For the flower and its fragrance are one'.[147] This notion of the Unity of Being and its 'imaginal' disclosure is one that finds its roots in Sufism.[148] This Unity of Being, insofar as it is a Unity of Life, is nevertheless devoid from any reference to good and evil and reward and punishment or to any eschatological afterlife. Āmina is not a moral preacher of the afterlife; she preaches the infinitude of the human self insofar as it is a microcosm in this Life, which is essentially endless, since 'every existent shall remain, and the being of the existent is proof of its eternal subsistence'.[149]

What deserves attention here is the Sufi idea of primordial displacement or estrangement (*ghurba*) as a necessary condition of being in the world. Both Āmina and Zain were nomadic and migrant before settling in a small forest in northeast Lebanon. Zain tells Najeeb that he was born in Nahavand (modern-day Iran). After growing up in Shiraz and being educated in Nishapur, he went on to travel the world east and west, only to find out that everywhere he is a stranger (*gharīb*). When Najeeb responds by saying that 'all of us are strangers to all places', Zain demurs: 'No! I have met and conversed with thousands of people, and I have only seen those who are content with their environs, finding warmth and familiarity in their limited corner of the world by turning their backs to the world'.[150] This estrangement is not a negative one. It is not an estrangement *vis-à-vis* the nation. Nor is it an estrangement in the sense of being uprooted and unable to belong to the 'mother country' after immigrating or being forced into exile. Rather, it is a primordial estrangement or exile imposed by the originary inability to be content with a place, which is necessarily limited and demarcated as a territory in the world – that is, by the inability to feel a sense of belonging anywhere insofar as this 'where' is a place (a city, a country, a nation and so on). When Najeeb asserts that 'people are naturally inclined to be attached to their place of birth', Zain retorts: 'Only those who are limited in vision are naturally inclined to be attached to that which is limited in life. The short-sighted can see no more than a cubit on the track upon which they tread and a cubit on the wall upon which they support their backs'.[151] In other words, the limits of one's vision (*ru'yā*) are the limits of one's world. The spiritual here is that which denotes the possibility of the body to go beyond itself and the regime of life into which it was 'thrown'. It does not signify a transcendent realm beyond Being, but a disclosure of Being that allows for an expanded experience of the world in the here and now. *Iram dhāt al-ʿimād*, the 'veiled city' which is 'a spiritual state (*ḥāla rūḥiyya*)', comes to designate a universal promise for the stranger (*al-gharīb*) to transcend place – the modern city or the nation – not to a transcendent realm, but to an internal space of vision that stretches the limits of the stranger's world. In other words, the spiritual is not that which rises above the body, but the language *of* the body that widens the limits of its world. It is in this sense that we ought to understand Gibran's reclamation of Sufism as a post-religious and supra-national mode of being in the world, whether in Arabic or in English. For Almustafa, like Āmina, affirms a mode of living where space precedes and expands place:

> But you, children of space, you restless in rest, you shall not be trapped or tamed.
>
> Your house shall be not an anchor but a mast.

It shall not be a glistening film that covers a wound, but an eyelid that guards the eye.
[. . .]
You shall not dwell in tombs made by the dead for the living.
And though of magnificence and splendour, your house shall not hold your secret nor shelter your longing.
For that which is boundless in you abides in the mansion of the sky, whose door is the morning mist, and whose windows are the songs and the silences of the night.[152]

The Greater Self, or the Prophetic as *the* Impossible

To speak prophetically for Gibran, as we have seen thus far, is to suggest or incarnate the impossible; that is, to sacrifice the attainable possibility for the sake of the greater, metaphysical potentiality. This is what the notion the Greater Self conveys, which recurs in Gibran's works written in English and in *al-Badāʾiʿ wa al-ṭarāʾif* (Marvels and Masterpieces). If the madman, Salma Karāma and Āmina al-ʿAlawiyya sacrifice themselves for the sake of a Greater Self, the forerunner celebrates a 'giant-self' which one builds towers for its foundation, until it becomes itself a foundation: 'Always have we been our own forerunners, and always shall we be. And all that we have gathered and shall gather shall be but seeds for fields yet unploughed. We are the fields and the ploughmen, the gatherers and the gathered'.[153] The forerunner's self is recast as a beginning whose destination – that for which it yearns – will become a beginning in itself. This ontological conception of the self implies a fundamental infinitude, an essential unendingness to its quest of becoming: Being is becoming, and *vice versa*. This embrace of beginning is posited against the notion of 'origin'. The forerunner is a beginning without origin. Yet even when Gibran breaks with the Abrahamic story of creation (*creatio ex nihilo*), in its three *different* versions in Judaism, Christianity and Islam, a trace of this narrative, as interpreted by Ibn al-ʿArabi, can still be discerned here, a secularised trace that is inevitably ambiguous:

When you were a wandering desire in the mist, I too was there, a wandering desire [. . .] And when you were a silent word upon Life's quivering lips, I too was there, another silent word. Then Life uttered us, and we came down the years throbbing with memories of yesterday and with longing for tomorrow, for yesterday was death conquered and tomorrow a birth pursued.[154]

Gibran uses Life in the sense of Being, through whose 'quivering lips' one is 'uttered' into existence. Life, in other words, is the force that lets beings be and enables their presence. But being a silent word that awaits Life's utterance presupposes what Ibn al-ʿArabi calls the 'eternal individuality'[155] of the self. In one of his early Arabic pieces of poetic prose, 'Nashīd al-insān' (The Hymn of Man), Gibran writes, 'I WAS [*sic*], from before time!/ And, behold me now, I AM! And I SHALL BE [*sic*] till the end of time! And my being shall be without end!'[156] This piece, interestingly, begins with a quote from the Qurʾān: 'and you were dead and He [Allah] gave you life, then He shall make you dead, then He shall give you life, then unto Him you shall be returned'.[157] The Qurʾānic verse notwithstanding, Gibran dissociates this eternal individuality of the self from the metaphysics of creation. What we observe in the 'The Forerunner', however, is something similar to, yet by no means as sophisticated as, the notion of 'genesis' in Ibn al-ʿArabi, which is not exactly a *creatio ex nihilo* but a complex 'process of increasing illumination, gradually raising the possibilities eternally latent in the original Divine Being to a state of luminescence'.[158] All beings, that is, exist as possible or latent beings (*mumkināt*) in God's eternal knowledge; their coming into actual existence lies in their being revealed or manifested, and not in being *stricto senso* created from nothingness.

This notion of manifestness is one that frequently recurs in Gibran's late work, but without reference to God as Creator or to any metaphysics of creation. It is rather articulated through the image of the Mist, the primordial Mist which is the ground of all beings: 'Life, and all that lives, is conceived in the Mist and not in the crystal'.[159] The Mist is therefore Life in its hiddenness, not manifestness. It articulates the fundamental ambiguous space at the heart of Being, that from which all beings as 'wandering desires' emerge or manifest themselves, since desire for him is 'the inherent power that changes all things [and] the law of all matter and all life',[160] and to which they shall also return, as Almustafa says in *The Garden of the Prophet*: 'O Mist, my sister, white breath not yet held in a mould,/ I return to You, a breath white and voiceless, a word not yet uttered'.[161] This figural image is central to Gibran's reinvention of the self and the world. Its particularity, being at once phenomenal and symbolic, is strangely reminiscent of the ontological status accorded to 'the creative Active Imagination' in the metaphysics of Ibn al-ʿArabi, 'the Primordial Cloud' exhaled by the Divine Breathing (*Nafas al-Raḥmān*), which '*receives* all forms and at the same time *gives* beings their forms'.[162] Yet, while for Ibn al-ʿArabi this Primordial Cloud – which is at once hidden in the Creator (*bāṭin*) and revealed as creature (*ẓāhir*), or the 'Creator-Creature'[163] – is inseparable from the Divine Being, for Gibran the Mist is devoid of any metaphysical conceptual density or narrative of creation. The Mist becomes a post-religious name of God that alludes to Him without naming Him, because it (the Mist) still carries the Abrahamic structural signification that the name of God evokes: that from which one emerges or is revealed into Life and to which one returns until Life's second day.[164] The Mist for Gibran becomes the destiny of the self that renders it once more a beginning, the 'greater freedom' of the self.[165] As such, it is the necessary transition from one life to another, the passage to another reincarnation:

> O Mist, my sister, my sister Mist,
> I am one with you now.
> No longer am I a self.
> The walls have fallen,
> And the chains have broken;
> I rise to you, a mist,
> And together we shall float upon the sea until life's second day,
> When dawn shall lay you, dewdrops in a garden,
> And me a babe upon the breast of a woman.[166]

In a worldview where the Abrahamic afterlife (the eschatological narrative of the judgment day, heaven and hell and so on) is abandoned, death remains a passage but to another life; and one does not die but returns to the primordial Mist. Drawing on the Sufi tradition and breaking with its dense metaphysics of creation, Gibran's vision is aesthetically creative but metaphysically and ontologically weak, because the Mist remains an ambiguous image with no specific content save its fogginess – in the literal and figural sense, as the form *is* the content here. The quiet death of the moral and vertical notion of God gives way to an empty space filled only by the Mist, the promise of 'our greater freedom'[167] and of the mystical union with a post-religious God who does not bear His name. The image of the Mist, in other words, repeats the possibility of God without God, so to speak. This ambiguity is, perhaps, what a prophetic poet *can* offer us in the destitute times of modernity; whether it is convincing or not is another question that does not interest me here.

The faith of this post-religious poet, however, even after reinventing his Abrahamic God, remains essentially Abrahamic. In his parable 'The Two Learned Men', the madman casts his irony over the futility of rationally debating the existence of the gods. We are told that two men, 'who hated and belittled each other's learning', met one day in the marketplace and argued for hours 'about the existence and non-existence of the gods'. In the evening, 'the unbeliever [among the two learned men] went to the temple and prostrated himself before the altar and prayed the gods to forgive his wayward past', whereas the other learned man, 'the believer', 'burned his sacred books' and became an unbeliever.[168] The madman suggests that a rationally validated or nullified faith is a false and untenable kind of faith, for what matters here is not the actual existence or non-existence of the gods and whether their existence can be proven or refuted with rational arguments. Rather, faith as such is an *experience* of the visionary imagination, what Gibran calls 'the Eye'[169] or *al-baṣīra*; it goes beyond this mode of reason in that it is located on a supra-rational level of human experience. This experience is not reducible to statements or arguments that correspond (or not) to certain 'objective' facts in the outside world. It is, as he writes in *The Forerunner*, a 'skyward' movement of a bird rising out of the forerunner's 'deeper heart' and growing higher and larger – 'at first it was but like a swallow, then a lark, then an eagle, then as vast as a spring cloud'[170] – eventually filling 'the starry heavens', without, however, leaving his heart. This paradoxical movement, which structures the prose poem, is one that the forerunner describes without referring explicitly to 'God':

> Out of my heart a bird flew skywards. And it waxed larger as it flew. Yet it left not my heart.
>
> O my faith, my untamed knowledge, how shall I fly to your height and see with you man's larger self pencilled upon the sky?
>
> How shall I turn this sea within me into mist, and move with you in space immeasurable?

> How can a prisoner within the temple behold its golden domes?
> How shall the heart of a fruit be stretched to envelop the fruit also?[171]

This paradoxical movement is *the* movement of faith, and it is one that simultaneously bewilders and frustrates, perplexes and stupefies, going beyond the heart without leaving it. This faith cannot be a lazy answer but is lived as a paradoxical movement that generates questions; the poem's form here is essential to its meaning, for only in the form of questions, however rhetorical they may be, can one live out one's own faith. This is the kind of faith that can be solely experienced, to invoke Ibn al-ʿArabi again, as 'neither/nor' or 'both/and',[172] one that is irreducible to the Greek rationalist principle of the excluded middle – which does not mean that it is 'irrational'. In other words, this faith, even in its post-religious configuration, remains at bottom Abrahamic, since it can only happen, to draw on Kierkegaard, 'by virtue of the absurd'.[173] Kierkegaard's fascinating reading of the Abrahamic story of sacrifice offers us a remarkable way of understanding Abrahamic faith as such, which he describes as the impossible movement of faith.[174] Gibran, pursuing this Abrahamic legacy, was aware of this fundamental and necessary paradox of faith.

This faith, nevertheless, is no longer directed towards the Christian, moral God whose authority revolves around accusation, consolation, condemnation and protection.[175] It is a post-religious faith that entails breaking with the form of religion which is based on prohibition and punishment,[176] yet not with religion as such. As Paul Ricoeur argues, this faith is still possible after the death of ontotheology's god:

> Only a preacher, or, I should say, a prophetic preacher, with the power and freedom of Nietzsche's Zarathustra would be able to make a radical return to the origins of Jewish and Christian [Abrahamic, I would say] faith and, at the same time, make of this return an event which speaks to our own time. Such preaching would be both originary and post-religious.[177]

Almustafa, whose name is the most prophetic among Gibran's post-religious figures,[178] would go as far as announcing an impossible dwelling in the world. This impossibility has been readily interpreted as 'idealism'. Yet an Abrahamic, post-religious prophet cannot be a realist. He must herald, he must preach the impossible as the ultimate possibility of freedom. Let us attend to his words:

> At the city gate and by your fireside I have seen you prostrate yourself and worship your own freedom, [. . .]
> And my heart bled within me; for you can only be free when even the desire of seeking freedom becomes a harness to you, and when you cease to speak of freedom as a goal and a fulfilment.
> [. . .]
> And how shall you rise beyond your days and nights unless you break the chains which you at the dawn of your understanding have fastened around your noon hour?
> In truth that which you call freedom is the strongest of these chains, though its links glitter in the sun and dazzle your eyes.[179]

Only a radical freedom that tirelessly questions itself as it enacts itself can combat its modern fetishisation and trivialisation. Almustafa is drawing attention to the conditions of freedom rather than to freedom itself. For freedom not to turn into 'a yoke' and 'a handcuff' worn by the 'freest among you', these conditions must be radically and constantly interrogated and unchained, to use his metaphor. That is to say, alertness to the conditions of freedom *is* the primary condition of freedom as such, what he calls 'greater freedom'. The latter remains a deferred possibility and can never be an attained actuality; it is realised insofar as it is hopelessly yearned for, a yearning whose hopelessness lies in relentless self-interrogation. Like faith, freedom is experienced as a paradox, at once a chain and a breaking-free from the chain, an impossible movement whose condition of possibility is the persistent awareness of this very paradox. For it must never turn, Almustafa suggests, into a doctrine or an idol that people worship, into something other than itself, in allusion to its idolisation and instrumentalisation in modern politics.

The qualifier 'greater' is much more than a qualifier here; it represents the kernel of Gibran's thought: conquering oneself constantly, slaying one's 'burdened selves'[180] in longing to attain larger and freer selves, themselves the premise of yet larger and freer selves: 'And what is it but fragments of your own self you would discard that you may become free'.[181] The passage ends by pointing out, in a charming poetic style, that the dialectical relationship between freedom and greater freedom is characteristic of 'all things [which] move within your being in constant half embrace, the desired and the dreaded, the repugnant and the cherished, the pursued and that which you would escape'.[182] This post-religious poet articulates his idea by resorting to the image of light/shadow:

> These things move within you as lights and shadows in pairs that cling.
> And when the shadow fades and is no more, the light that lingers becomes a shadow to another light.
> And thus your freedom when it loses its fetters becomes itself the fetter of a greater freedom.[183]

Thus spoke Almustafa, preaching the always already 'not yet'[184] of one's freedom, its utmost potentiality that should not be confused with an 'ideal freedom'. Prophetic speech does not just preach ideals: it points to the impossible as the condition of being and dwelling in the world. Prophetic speech radically questions the present and its conditions by shaking it up and heralding an impossible future. This is what *The Prophet* is fundamentally announcing.

It bears emphasising in this respect that freedom, in Gibran's Arabic fiction, designates more than a quest for social emancipation, because Gibran's protagonists are not merely social outcasts but mouthpieces of his prophetic imagination. In 'Khalil the Heretic', Khalil is not just a Romantic hero who rebels against the oppressive clergy. He calls for autonomy and self-dependence in matters of faith. Against a specific governing of 'bodies' by the political governor ('the Sultan has appointed me as a ruler over your bodies [*waṣiyyan ʿalā ajsādikum*]'[185]) and of 'souls' by the priest ('God has appointed me as a custodian over your souls [*waliyyan ʿalā arwāḥikum*]'[186]), Khalil vents his social criticism and enacts his rebellion. He calls for free faith, one inspired from the spirit of Jesus as a prophetic figure. He is therefore at once a figure of Enlightenment and a Romantic outcast. What is more, he speaks in a prophetic register, for which this oppressive biopolitical state of affairs calls. His final 'speech', which is a supplication, is addressed to freedom, interestingly, not to God. In this sense, Khalil's prophetic speech is post-religious – that is, his concern is secular, not strictly religious. But the form derives from the disruptive power of Abrahamic prophecy. Hence the reinvention of the prophetic in a modern context where freedom is the central cause. *The Prophet* pursues and deepens this vision but in a more abstract manner.

What characterises *The Prophet*, furthermore, is its 'positive ontology',[187] to use Paul Ricoeur's phrase, which resides in a vision that de-transcendentalises ethics – that is to say, it divorces ethics from the sphere of morality and the horizon of reward and punishment. Almustafa, in this respect, could be described as what Nietzsche's Zarathustra calls 'an esteemer', one who gives himself his own good and evil and *creates* his own values.[188] Seen from this perspective, *The Prophet* is a logical sequel to *al-'Awāṣif*, *The Madman* and *The Forerunner*, whose short stories, parables and prose poems radically place into question so many old values by way of laying bare the inherent contradictions that inhabit them. In those works, one discerns a glimpse of the post-religious poet's capacity to reclaim and reinvent the religious and create his own values. Yet it is in *The Prophet* that this poet fully assumes this prophetic role of value-creation, now that the destructive forces of grave-digging and the slaying of one's burdened selves have been exhausted in the discourses of the poet's mad god, the madman and the forerunner. In other words, there is no discontinuity here. To be thinking fruitfully as a poet along the horizon of thought that Nietzsche's Zarathustra made possible requires that one not only annihilate but create values – however thin or unconvincing those values may be. And Gibran does so, as we have seen, with no vengeance or resentment against the god of morality or theology, who either goes mad or dies quietly without anyone reporting the news, as it were. For the notion of God itself does not die but is reinvented as a horizontal form of transcendence whose name is the greater, larger and freer self. What further distinguishes *The Prophet* is that there is no antipathy towards the 'last men' or 'the herd' that Zarathustra loathes. For Almustafa is *not* Zarathustra, albeit thinking with and after him. Rather, Almustafa celebrates Life insofar as it is a 'longing for your giant self [wherein] lies your goodness: and that longing is in all of you'.[189]

Almustafa, moreover, reclaims 'religion' as 'all deeds and all reflection', conceiving of it in 'your daily life' where 'you take with you your all'.[190] In other words, he is re-naming religion by un-naming it: un-naming religion insofar as it represents, on the one hand, a differentiated social sphere (in a presumably secular society) and insofar as it refers, on the other hand, to a theologico-political community (*al-milla*, not *dīn* or religion[191]) where morality is vertically imposed.[192] This un-naming of religion beyond the modern secular-religious binary does not mean that it loses its transcendental particularity, for it is also 'that which is neither deed nor reflection, *but a wonder and a surprise springing in the soul*, even while the hands hew the stone or tend the loom'.[193] This wonder and surprise of the soul is that transcendental element of the religious which is horizontally experienced in one's daily life, that which remains, that is, transcendental about the religious: the perplexity of faith. As a horizontal kind of transcendence, it is one that springs from the soul and does not necessarily refer to a transcendent realm that commands, from above, the being of the religious self. This is what Meskini has recently called 'free faith', which 'expresses an ancient actuality that pertains to the Abrahamic experiences of the holy: that faith, unlike pagan belief, is the art of acquiring the space of transcendence that exists in the crux of the self's relationship to itself'.[194] Almustafa, un-naming and renaming religion, is positing this (im)possibility of free faith by reorienting the transcendental experience.

The de-transcendentalising of ethics is most apparent in Almustafa's discourse on giving. Preaching Life as giving, Almustafa dissociates giving from the authority of the giver, much in the same way as he dissociates God from the absolute authority of vertical transcendence. The ethical here is severed from any transcendental moral discourse. The ethical as such becomes, paradoxically, a non-ethical mode of being that consists in giving as being or being as giving. In response to a rich a man who asked him to 'speak to us of Giving', Almustafa begins by foregrounding self-giving as authentic giving: 'It is when you give of yourself that you truly give'.[195] He then proceeds to declare that 'those who have little and give it all' are 'believers in life and the bounty of life'.[196] Yet, most importantly, he asserts:

> There are those who give and know not pain in giving, nor do they seek joy,
> nor give
> with mindfulness of virtue;
> They give as in yonder valley the myrtle breathes its fragrance into space.
> Through the hands of such as these God speaks, and from behind their eyes
> He smiles upon the earth.[197]

This is giving in its impossible embodiment, or, to draw on Derrida, the gift as *the* impossible,[198] in that it is possible as a gift, paradoxically, only when the giver ceases to be a source of giving, when the giver is not recognised as giver and the given or the gift are not identified as gift: 'See first that you yourself deserve to be a giver, and *an instrument of giving*. For in truth it is life that gives unto life – while you, who deem yourself a giver, are but a witness',[199] writes Gibran. No giver means no authority, the authority of the subject who gives, and the centrality of this giving subject is de-centred here, as the giver becomes merely an instrument of giving. In other words, the ethical as such is conceived beyond any circuit of exchange, beyond any transcendental discourse of good and evil and reward and punishment. The ethical becomes ontological: to give is to be insofar as being is living. This prophetic speech is thereby announcing an impossible ethics, one that can only enact itself by effacing itself: 'They give as in yonder valley the myrtle breathes its fragrance into space'. In this configuration, God speaks through the hands of those who give unmindful of virtue. Which is to say that one does not ask God to be: God *is* the giving itself. God does not command but manifests Himself *in* and *as* impossible giving: God is giving as such. This view of giving is strikingly reminiscent of Ibn al-ʿArabi's equation of giving with Being: '*ʿan al-jūd ṣadara al-wujūd* [from bountiful giving (*al-jūd*) emanated existence (*al-wujūd*)]', he famously wrote.[200] Almustafa, echoing Ibn al-ʿArabi, affirms that the essence of Life/Being is giving: 'You often say, "I would give, but only to the deserving."/ The trees in your orchard say not so, nor the flocks in your pasture./ *They give that they may live, for to withhold is to perish*'.[201]

Yet Almustafa goes as far as reversing the logic of giving and receiving, because 'you are all receivers', emphasising the 'courage and confidence, nay the charity, of receiving'.[202] Gibran shifts attention from the giver, from the *possible* hostility and oppression of the giver – his/her self-consciousness as a giver – to the *impossible* hospitality and openness of the receiver as a host towards the incomprehensibly bountiful Other that is Life. 'Assume no weight of gratitude, lest you lay a yoke upon yourself and upon him who gives',[203] says Almustafa, preaching the impersonality of Life as the source of all personal giving, preaching, that is, the self-effacement of the ethical subject if it is to be truly ethical.

But *The Prophet*'s didactic form and optimistic 'message' – 'you are far, far greater than you know, and All is well'[204] – in an age which had lost faith in all certainties made it at once appealing and questionable. The need for a poet speaking as a post-religious prophet concerned with the fundamental issues of life, not one who is 'cool,' 'detached' and wittily 'intellectual' in the manner of modernists, may explain the book's popular appeal in the Unites States – and elsewhere – as well as some of the critical disdain towards it. Yet the problem of reception, as will be discussed at length in Chapter Four, is inseparable from the socio-cultural and epistemic conditions specific to its location. Of relevance here is that *The Prophet*'s didactic form, albeit didactic in an unassumingly authoritative manner, may have watered down the richness and complexity of its 'content'; *what* is said in literature is always indissociable from *how* it is said. Gibran himself had doubts about the style of this didacticism, as he checked with Mary Haskell 'if anywhere it [*The Prophet*] sounded preachy'.[205] The prophetic for Gibran is partly modelled after Nietzsche's Zarathustra, but without the 'analytical' mind of Nietzsche.[206] Gibran always seeks simplicity in style, which for him is a prerogative of poetry.

This poetic combination of didacticism, optimism and simplicity, which made the book at once modern and anti-modern, therefore at once appealing and questionable, has the unmistakable and poignant undertow of exile. One cannot help but discern the exilic fate and underlying tragic tone of Almustafa, especially in the introductory and final sections of the book. Almustafa does not belong. But he wishes, precisely because he does not belong, to make the world more habitable. Hence the prophetic form that seeks to offer a poetic – that is, a liberating and irreducible – dwelling in the world. That Almustafa speaks as a late Romantic and in a biblical register is not a stylistic regression but an enactment, an expression, of his exile. That is, the style itself, belated but relevant, speaks of his exile. In this sense he is post-religious *and* post-Romantic, but not, of course, modernist, for Gibran writes in English but does not 'belong' to the 'Western tradition'; only to poetry does he belong, if he belongs at all (the name for poetic verse in Arabic, *bayt*, also means house or home). *The Prophet* is thus a book that speaks and bespeaks, in its belatedness and ironic fate, exile – that is to say, the Outside.

Gibran's late book *The Earth Gods* (1931) turns this exile into an existential problem in which Gibran's worldview, by virtue of the poem's dialogic form, itself is problematised. The book is a long poem in which three 'earth-gods' speak of man and existence from three divergent perspectives that reflect (on) the variations of Gibran's prophetic imagination and metaphysical universe. While the first god expresses his weariness 'of all there is', of his 'earth-bound mortality' which he strives to 'rise beyond', the second god, who is reminiscent of the mad god in 'The Grave Digger', is invigorated by 'the scent of death', by the 'sacrifice' of man (echoing the notion of sacrifice as a metaphysical act of self-realisation), by the hunger for that which is more than human:

> All that is human counts for naught if human it remain;
> The innocence of childhood, and the sweet ecstasy of youth,
> The passion of stern manhood, and the wisdom of old age;
> The splendour of kings and the triumph of warriors,
> The fame of poets and the honour of dreamers and saints;
> All these and all that lieth therein is bred for gods.
> And naught but bread ungraced shall it be
> If the gods raise it not to their mouths.
> And as the mute grain turns to love songs when swallowed by the
> nightingale,
> Even so as bread for gods shall man taste godhead.[207]

The third god, however, is one who listens to the sky-piercing song of love, sung by a youth in 'yonder valley' and heard by a girl who, enchanted, later finds him. This earth-god records what he hears and sees – the song and sight of love – in a style that combines simplicity with assurance. These three gods can only be understood within the metaphysical universe of Gibran. The gods are 'sons of the beginning', 'when out of chaos came the earth'.[208] As such, they represent divinities insofar as that means the primal potentialities of humanhood, man's horizon of becoming: power (second god), infinity (first god) and love (third god). And, interestingly, this becoming is described as the 'self-fulfilment' of the gods. To illustrate this, it is worth quoting a long passage uttered by the second god:

> Man, the faint hearted, overbold by our purpose,
> Ventures with lyre and sword,
> Ours is the will he heralds,
> And ours the sovereignty he proclaims,
> And his love trodden courses are rivers, to the sea of our desires.
> We, upon the heights, in man's sleep dream our dreams.
> We urge his days to part from the valley of twilights
> And seek their fullness upon the hills.

Our hands direct the tempests that sweep the worlds
And summon man from sterile peace to fertile strife,
And on to triumph.[209]

If this sounds a bit familiar, it is because it echoes *al-'Awāṣif* and personifies as gods the forces of being as becoming, which, as exemplified in the notion of the Greater Self, is central to Gibran's worldview. But this personification also humanises the gods, who are either unsatisfied of being themselves, hungry for self-fulfilment, or attentive to the human song of love. After all, these are *earth*-gods. As human possibilities of divinity, they stand between man and the 'Supreme Godhead': 'But you are neither human, / Nor the Supreme above us',[210] the first god lamentingly points out. The gods represent or personify, in different ways, the Greater Self of Gibran's prophetic imagination:

In our eyes is the vision that turns man's soul to flame,
And leads him to exalted loneliness and rebellious prophecy,
And on to crucifixion.
Man is born to bondage,
And in bondage is his honour and his reward.
In man we seek a mouthpiece,
And in his life our self-fulfilment.
Whose heart shall echo our voice if the human heart is deafened with dust?
And what would you do with man, child of our earliest heart, our own
self-image?[211]

This is a dramatisation of the relationship between man and the earth-gods, man and his potential greater selves. If the aim of the earth-gods is to lift man out of his 'sterile peace' into 'fertile strife', into the 'exalted loneliness' of 'rebellious prophecy' and 'crucifixion', all of which are expressions of sacrifice as self-realisation, then the earth-gods are also in need of man, without whom they cannot simply be.

What is interesting about *The Earth Gods* is therefore not just the way in which Gibran's worldview finds poetic expression in it, but – most importantly – the manner in which that poetic expression *problematises* this worldview. We have three earth-gods, three forces as it were, each one of whom articulates a peculiar vision, a different idea of the divine that lies within man. This dialogic style thus lends more force to the uncertainty or anxiety of becoming, which emerges as problem here rather than an answer or, as in *The Prophet*, as a potentiality latent within everyone. That love, 'human and frail', should 'command the coming day' as the final line of the poem tells us, does not so much undermine or resolve the dialogic nature of the poem as it foregrounds it. The song of love – recorded by the third god, who simply watches and asks the other gods to 'behold' what plays out on earth, in the here and now – triumphs in the end, precisely because the giant forces of power, sacrifice and infinity are caught between weariness and hunger. The return to the 'human and frail' love is a *late* assertion by Gibran of the uncertainty of the idea of becoming through prophecy and self-sacrifice. The frailty and humanness of love, which the singing of it signifies, has gone unnoticed and unheard: 'heedless' and 'unhearing' are the first and second gods until the third god addresses their 'affliction of knowing' and 'armies of reasoning' by reminding them that the gods' 'measures' are unable to 'subdue' man's 'passion to stillness, / Or to our own passion'.[212] But the discourses of the first and second gods are possible precisely because they do not heed the first god. *The Earth Gods* therefore offers less a synthesis than a dissonance, for their 'questioning' is not so much resolved as 'outsoared' by love. Only the song of love offers hope eventually, but a rather fragile hope – unconvincing yet inevitable. Is that not an allusion to the simplicity of the lyrical, to poetry as the necessary but fragile home of hope? This is *lateness*, to draw on Edward Said, as lack of transcendence or unity, lateness as a 'lost totality'.[213] Even though Gibran started working on the book's manuscript in the 1910s, its late publication (the latest book published in Gibran's lifetime) attests to the power of late style 'to render disenchantment and pleasure without resolving the contradiction between them'.[214] The artist's 'mature subjectivity', by virtue of late style, is 'stripped of hubris and pomposity, unashamed either of its fallibility or of the modest assurance it has gained as a result of age and exile'.[215]

Gibran's prophetic imagination, as the foregoing discussion has tried to demonstrate, resumes the Abrahamic mode of prophetic speech in a modern context that compels a poetic reinvention of the religious. This reinvention, occasioned by both evolutionism (as domesticated in the *Nahḍa*) and Nietzsche, breaks with monotheism's vertical metaphysics and morality. It simultaneously reclaims, by virtue of the poetic, central Christian and Sufi motifs beyond the eschatological realm of good and evil and reward and punishment. The Gibranian post-religious poet or fictional protagonist therefore represents a modern prophetic figure who insists on the capacity of the religious, which is reinvented by virtue of modernity, to question the positivist, calculative and identitarian forms of reason prevalent in modernity. This is by 'burying' the dead values that preclude the possibility of a new life, sacrificing oneself in the name of Love understood as a metaphysical force that disturbs materialistic social norms, and/or reinventing God as the horizon of a radical and deferred form of becoming. The prophetic is thus embraced and transformed by Gibran to redirect the moderns' attention towards an alternative possibility, which is made possible by poetry, of being in the world. This alternative mode of being is one that reinvents the moral sources of the self in order to broaden the limits of one's world that are willy-nilly imposed on us as veiling 'masks' or sanctified social codes since birth. Gibran's, thus, is a genuine poetic attempt – whatever its limitations or weaknesses – to unveil and herald this alternative (im)possibility. Yet, his bilingualism (that is, his dwelling in two linguistic and cultural geographies) has obscured the prophetic peculiarity of, and the worldview that informs, his poetic and literary enterprise, particularly in Euro-America. His switch from Arabic into English is both creative and problematic, and it is to this switch that I will turn my attention in the next chapter.

Notes

1 Paul Ricoeur, 'Religion, Atheism, and Faith', trans. Charles Freilich, in *The Conflicts of Interpretations: Essays in Hermeneutics*, ed. Don Ihde (Evanston: Northwestern University Press, 1974), 447.

2 Meskini, 'al-Nabiyy al-mustaḥīl' (The Impossible Prophet), in *al-Īmān al-ḥurr aw mā baʿda al-milla: Mabāḥith fī falsafat al-dīn* (Free Faith, or Post-*Milla*: Studies in the Philosophy of Religion) (Rabat: Mominoun Without Borders, 2018), 395–96. *al-Milla* for Meskini is not religion, but a theologico-political community which is based on a certain religion.

3 'It's hard, he [Gibran] said, to separate style and subject – What a man wants to say determines how he says it. If he has a vision of life he is always putting that vision before us – in different form. We unconsciously contradict ourselves when we say we like a man's style and not his ideas. Style and ideas are one'. MH Journal, 2 June 1912.

4 This notion of the event is not concerned with its 'content', but with the way in which 'form' and 'content', in the configuration of the event, 'the un-happening

[that] is the dazzling reality of the happening itself', are interdependent. For more on 'the event' in relation to literature, especially in the wake of Martin Heidegger, Jacques Derrida, Maurice Blanchot (drawn upon in this chapter) and Jilles Deleuze, see Ilai Rowner, *The Event: Literature and Theory* (Lincoln: University of Nebraska, 2015).

5 I use this category, following Carol Bakhos, as a critical alternative to 'Western', 'elective' and 'Semitic' monotheism. The Abrahamic is a modern concept, and it gained academic currency thanks mainly to French scholar and Orientalist Louis Massignon in the mid-twentieth century. See Carol Bakhos, *The Family of Abraham: Jewish, Christian, and Muslim Interpretations* (Cambridge, MA: Harvard University Press, 2014), 1–5.

6 The prophetic form for Gibran was 'the really great form'. See Jean Gibran and Kahlil G. Gibran, *Kahlil Gibran: Beyond Borders* (Northampton, MA: Interlink Books, 2017), 288.

7 Northrop Frye, *Fearful Symmetry: A Study of William Blake* (Princeton: Princeton University Press, 1974 [1947]).

8 I mean a thinker whose thought is expressed poetically, not philosophically or systematically. One cannot gloss over the poetic nature of his reflections in the letters he exchanged with Mary Haskell, which are reminiscent of his poetic prose in Arabic.

9 One cannot, of course, overlook the fact that those letters were not meant to be published; that is, that there was no intention on the part of Gibran to make them public, but that does not disqualify them from being treated as creative or literary.

10 Blanchot, 'Prophetic Speech', 79.

11 Ibid.

12 *Kahlil Gibran: An Illustrated Anthology*, ed. Ayman A. El-Desouky (London: Spruce, 2010), 9.

13 *After* Copernicus, Newton, Kant, Hegel, the Romantics, Nietzsche, Darwin and Freud – to name but a few 'founders of discursivity', as Foucault would say – the premodern cosmological worldview in which the three fundamental notions of God, the self and the world were articulated and experienced no longer held sway. This does not mean, of course, that the religious was brushed aside in modernity. The religious, rather, is reinvented, transformed and articulated anew and multifariously within a modern secular space that compels this reinvention, but with no *complete* rupture with the premodern past, now conceived as 'mythic'. It is important to underscore in this context that under the discursive relative

autonomy of what the moderns call 'literature', the religious is experienced as at once religious and secular. See Talal Asad, *Formations of the Secular: Christianity, Islam, Modernity* (Palo Alto: Stanford University Press, 2003), 8–9.

14 KG to MH, 14 October 1914 [emphasis in the original].

15 Ibid. [emphasis in the original].

16 I capitalise 'Life', following Gibran, to designate the ontological connotation it takes on for him, that of Being itself.

17 KG to MH, 14 October 1914.

18 Ibid.

19 Gibran conceives of the universe as a hierarchy, and man, although below God in this hierarchy, is above Earth and the elements. Yet, they are all interconnected in a way, constituting what he calls Life, which signifies all there is.

20 Elshakry, *Reading Darwin*, 12.

21 Ibid, 15–16.

22 'The journal was novel and expensive and attracted contributions from renowned literary and public figures such as Ali Mubarak, Mahmud al-Falaki, Riaz Pasha, Shibli Shumayyil, Salama Musa, and Jurji Zaydan – Egyptian and Syrian intellectuals, technocrats, and politicians. It quickly became a prominent forum for what the historical novelist and popular intellectual Zaydan and others termed *al-nahda al-ʿilmiya* (the renaissance of knowledge or science)'. Ibid., 31.

23 In a letter to May Ziadah, Gibran writes: 'Like yourself I am an admirer of Dr Shumayyil, one of the few men the Lebanon has produced who can bring about the new renaissance in the Near East, and I believe the East is in dire need of men like Dr Shumayyil to counteract the influences left in both Egypt and Syria by the "righteous and the Sufis"'. *The Love Letters of Kahlil Gibran to May Ziadah*, trans. and ed. Suheil Bushrui and Selma H. al-Kuzbari (Oxford: OneWorld, 1995), 2–3. It is interesting that Gibran fully supports the intellectual efforts of Shumayyil against 'the righteous and the Sufi', an indication of the extent to which he felt the need to reinvent the religious as a modern writer and poet.

24 Shumayyil begins his book by citing the twelfth-century Sufi philosopher Ibn al-ʿArabi: 'See Him in a tree, see Him in a stone, and see Him in everything, that is God'. His materialism, thus, was monistic and pantheistic. Elshakry, *Reading Darwin*, 99.

25 See Gibran, 'Mudāʿaba' (A Merry Conversation), in Daye, *'Aqīdat Jubrān*, 238–42.

26 This is perhaps one of the earliest texts in modern Arabic literature that includes whole passages in the Syrian dialect. Gibran also does that in an anecdote entitled

'al-Majnūn' (The Madman), who is represented as an old man speaking in the Syrian dialect, published in the periodical *al-Sā'iḥ* (23 September 1918). The anecdote is included in John Daye, *Lakum Jubrānukum wa lia Jubrānī* (You Have Your Gibran and I Have Mine) (Beirut: Qub Elias Press, 2009), 338–41. Interestingly, in the same year this anecdote was published, Gibran's first book in English, *The Madman*, was also published.

27 Daye, *'Aqīdat Jubrān*, 240.

28 *CWs in Arabic*, 248.

29 Ibid., 320.

30 See Elshakry, 'Evolution and the Eastern Question', in *Reading Darwin*, 73–88.

31 Ibid., 90.

32 This encounter is well-known in Gibran Studies. Gibran once declared to Mikhail Naimy: 'What a man [Nietzsche]! What a man! Alone he fought the whole world in the name of his Superman; and though the world forced him out of his reason in the end, yet he did whip it well. He died a Superman among pygmies, a sane madman in the midst of a world too decorously insane to be mad [. . .] And what a pen! With one stroke it would create a new world, and with one stroke it would efface old ones, the while dripping beauty, charm and power'. Naimy, *Kahlil Gibran*, 119.

33 See Martin Heidegger, *Poetry, Language, Thought*, trans. Albert Hofstadter (New York: Harper and Row, 1971), 101.

34 Fredrich Nietzsche, *Thus Spoke Zarathustra*, trans. Walter Kaufmann (New York: Penguin, 1966), 44–46.

35 In the same letter, he writes: 'Beloved Mary, You and I and all those who are born with a hunger for Life, are not trying to touch the outer edges of other worlds by deep thinking and deep feeling – our sole desire is to discover *this* world and to become one with *its* spirit. And the Spirit of this world, though ever changing and ever growing, is the Absolute'. KG to MH, 17 July 1915 [emphasis in the original].

36 KG to MH, 16 May 1912.

37 Ibid. [emphasis in the original].

38 Ibid. [emphasis in the original].

39 KG to MH, 14 October 1914.

40 'Whoever praises him as a god of love does not have a high enough opinion of love itself. Did this god not want to be a judge too? But the lover beyond reward and retribution'. Nietzsche, *Thus Spoke Zarathustra*, 261.

41 See Mark A. Wrathall, 'Introduction: Metaphysics and Onto-Theology', in

Religion after Metaphysics, ed. Mark A. Wrathall (Cambridge: Cambridge University Press, 2003), 1–3.

42 Nietzsche, *Thus Spoke Zarathustra*, 261.

43 Friedrich Nietzsche, *The Will to Power*, trans. Walter Kaufmann and R. J. Hollingdale (New York: Vintage books, 1967), 534.

44 For more on Gibran's belief in reincarnation and the possible Druze, Sufi and Christian sources that might have influenced him, see Bushrui and Jenkins, *Kahlil Gibran*, 76–78.

45 KG to MH, 30 January 1916.

46 This term is used in Gibran's one-act play *Iram dhāt al-'imād* (Iram, City of Lofty Pillars, 1921), which illustrates the impact of Sufism on his thought. See *CWs in Arabic*, 327–38.

47 'Some believe God made the world. To me it seems more likely that God has grown from the world because He is the furthest form of Life. Of course, the possibility of God was present before God himself'. MH journal, 18 April 1920.

48 KG to MH, 10 February 1916.

49 Ibid.

50 Ibid.

51 Ibid.

52 KG to MH, 1 March 1916.

53 KG to MH, 10 February 1916.

54 'Inasmuch as human beings are not He, they are annihilated, and inasmuch as human beings are He, they subsist'. William Chittick, *Imaginal Worlds* (Albany: State University of New York Press, 1994), 89.

55 See Reynold Alleyne Nicholson, *Studies in Islamic Mysticism* (Cambridge: Cambridge University Press, 1921), 81.

56 KG to MH, 10 February 1916.

57 KG to MH, 6 January 1916 [emphasis in the original].

58 William Chittick, *The Sufi Path of Knowledge: Ibn Arabi's Metaphysics of Imagination* (Albany: State University of New York Press, 1989), 6.

59 'God can't be demonstrated. I never tried to prove His existence. The idea of God is different in every man, and one can never give another his own religion'. MH Journal, 14 September 1920.

60 In *The Garden of the Prophet*, he writes that 'it were wiser to speak less of God, whom we cannot understand, and more of each other, whom we may understand. Yet I would have you know that we are the breath and the fragrance of

God. We are God, in leaf, in flower, and oftentimes in fruit'. Kahlil Gibran, *The Collected Works* (New York: Everyman's Library, 2007), 540.

61 MH Journal, 26 and 28 December 1922.

62 MH Journal, 10 August 1914.

63 MH Journal, 22 May 1920.

64 *CWs*, 6.

65 Ibid.

66 Ibid.

67 Transcendence is horizontal in that it hinges, on the one hand, on the interplay of necessity and freedom – what Gibran calls 'proud submission' (MH Journal, 5 May 1922) – and, on the other, on the future as the impossible horizon of self-realisation – impossible in that it is always yearned for but deferred.

68 Emmanuel Levinas, *Totality and Infinity: An Essay on Exteriority*, trans. Alphonso Lingiss (The Hague; London: Nijhoff, 1979), 254.

69 *CWs*, 6 [emphasis added].

70 That is to say, 'a thought-provoking genealogy of the possibility and essence of the religious that doesn't amount to an article of faith [. . .] a non-dogmatic doublet of dogma . . .' Jacques Derrida, *The Gift of Death and Literature in Secret*, trans. David Wills (Chicago; London: University of Chicago Press, 2008), 50.

71 Meskini, *al-Imān al-ḥurr*, 204.

72 Blanchot, 'Prophetic Speech', 79–80.

73 *CWs*, 5.

74 See my discussion of Meskini's insightful reading of the parable in the last section of Chapter Four.

75 This is the ancient Greek word on whose etymology Heidegger draws in his rethinking of the concept of 'truth' as 'unconcealement'. See Martin Heidegger, 'On the Essence of Truth', in *Pathmarks*, ed. William MacNeill (Cambridge: Cambridge University Press, 1998), 146. On unveiling as an epiphanic imagination in Sufism, see Henry Corbin, *Alone with the Alone: Creative Imagination in the Sufism of Ibn Arabi* (Princeton: Princeton University Press, 1997).

76 Gibran, 'The Seven Selves', in *CWs*, 14–15 [emphasis mine].

77 Meskini, *al-Īmān al-ḥurr*, 204 [emphasis mine].

78 Gibran, 'The Grave Digger', in *CWs*, 27.

79 See Khalil Gibran, 'Mustaqbal al-lugha al-ʿarabiyya' (The Future of the Arabic Language), in *CWs in Arabic*, 317–22.

80 *CWs in Arabic*, 210–13. See also his poem 'al-Jabbār al-ri'bāl' (The Lonely Giant), written in a classical metric form, but with a distinct rhyme for each

couplet of verses. This giant is another version of the mad god of 'The Grave Digger': he is 'the shadow of destiny', 'the terrifying death', 'the secret that sways between body and soul', Love itself and, most importantly, the elusive reflection of the poet himself: 'Concealed, he said: You are I, so do not ask the earth about me or the sky/ And should you wish to know who am I, keep your eyes upon the mirror day and night', declares the giant to the poet before disappearing, leaving the poet's thought wandering in the night. Ibid., 345–46.

81 Ibid., 210.

82 Ibid.

83 Fethi Meskini, *Falsafat al-nawābit* (The Philosophy of *Nawabit*) (Beirut: Dār al-Ṭalīʿa, 1997), 36. Meskini talks about the Arab thinker, not the poet, as far as 'The Grave Digger' is concerned. His reading, *à la* Heidegger, is a philosophical reflection that takes poetry as that which can open and expand thought's horizon. For him, the ghost or the mad god is the utmost condition of thought itself. My reading, however, places premium on the poet as a thinking poet, for the poet is one who is relating this short story to us. I am nevertheless indebted to Meskini's insightful reading of it.

84 *CWs in Arabic*, 210.

85 Meskini, *Falsafat al-nawābit*, 38–39.

86 *CWs in Arabic*, 211.

87 Ibid.

88 Ibid.

89 Ibid.

90 Ibid., 212.

91 Ibid.

92 Ibid.

93 Ibid., 213.

94 *CWs*, 33–34.

95 'There I saw you, O Night, and you saw me. You have been, with your enormity, a father to me, and I, with my dreams, a son to you. Removed are all the blinds of forms between us and torn are all the veils of doubt and conjecture over our faces. Thus, you divulged your secrets to me, and your intentions, and I disclosed my wishes to you, and my hopes [. . .] You lifted me up to you, placed me upon your shoulders, and you taught my eyes to see and my ears to hear and my lips to speak, and you taught my heart to love what people hate and to hate what they love. Then you touched my thoughts with your fingers whereupon they flowed like a running, chanting river rubbing off the withering grass, and you kissed my

soul with your lips whereupon it glittered like a burning flame that devoured all the ruins of the earth'. *CWs in Arabic*, 221–22.

96 'In the age of the world's night, the abyss of the world must be experienced and endured'. Heidegger, *Poetry*, 92.

97 *CWs*, 34.

98 Ibid., 35.

99 Heidegger, *Poetry*, 94.

100 *CWs*, 35.

101 Ibid., 47.

102 Ibid.

103 Ibid.

104 Ibid.

105 See Heidegger, 'The Question Concerning Technology', in *The Question Concerning Technology and Other Essays*, trans. William Lovitt (London; New York: Harper and Row, 1977), 3–35.

106 This is Mary Haskell's phrase, in a reply to a letter of Gibran. MH journal, 2 February 1915.

107 Gibran, 'The Greater Sea', *CWs*, 37–38.

108 Heidegger, *Poetry*, 215.

109 Let us remember that the word 'verse' in Arabic – in the sense of poetic verse – is *bayt*, a word that also means a house or a dwelling. One reads poetry, one experiences the poetic, by inhabiting it, so to speak.

110 *CWs*, 48.

111 Meskini, 'al-Nabiyy al-mustaḥīl', in *al-Īmān al-ḥurr*, 381–410.

112 *CWs*, 39.

113 Raymond Schwab, 'The Iran of Nietzsche', in *The Oriental Renaissance*, trans. Gene Patterson-Black and Victor Reinking (New York: Columbia University Press, 1984), 346.

114 *CWs*, 39.

115 Nietzsche, *Thus Spoke Zarathustra*, 139.

116 Paul Ricoeur notes that '[Nietzsche's] aggression towards Christianity remains caught up in the attitude of resentment [. . .] Nietzsche's work remains an accusation of accusation and hence falls short of a pure affirmation of Life'. Ricoeur, 'Religion, Atheism, and Faith', 447.

117 I capitalise Love in this section to designate the metaphysical meaning of *maḥabba* which it takes on in Gibran.

118 In contemporary Arabic philosophical discourse, *al-waḍʿiyya* is the estab-

lished translation for the term 'positivist'. But this is not, crucially, what Gibran meant by it. In his worldview, it is used to qualify the self that is innate or authentic, which is in harmony with *al-nāmūs al-kullī* or *universal law.*

119 Boutros Hallaq, 'Love and the Birth of Modern Arabic Literature', in *Love and Sexuality in Modern Arabic Literature*, ed. Roger Allen et al. (London: Saqi Books, 1995), 20–21.

120 Boutrus Hallaq ascribes the incorporation of death to the allegorical nature of Gibran's fiction, which necessitates the inclusion of an element external to the story. But one should not forget the function of the form here.

121 *CWs in Arabic*, 19.

122 Ibid., 20.

123 Ibid.

124 Ibid., 21.

125 Charles Taylor, *Sources of the Self: The Making of the Modern Identity* (Cambridge, MA: Harvard University Press: 2001).

126 *CWs in Arabic*, 98.

127 In an important essay titled 'al-Dawālīb' (Wheels), Gibran, defining the age as a 'mechanical' (*ālī*) one, acknowledges the validity of the empirical sciences but laments the reduction of 'the manifestation of life' – especially 'God', 'Life', 'the soul', 'revelation' and 'eternity' – to mechanical reason. Gibran, 'al-Dawālīb', in *Lakum Jubrānukum*, 353–55.

128 I emphasise the individuality of works of art because 'the works of bygone generations' are never understood as a whole for Gibran, but as a miscellany of artistic works each of which represents a manifestation of individual genius. The same applies to great historical events, which for Gibran are given initial catalyst in the singleness or oneness of a great idea: 'everything of greatness and beauty in this world is born in one single thought or sensation inside man'. See *CWs in Arabic*, 100.

129 *CWs in Arabic*, 120.

130 Ibid.

131 Ibid., 124.

132 *CWs*, 104.

133 *CWs in Arabic*, 125.

134 Ibid.

135 'The uncanny is that class of the frightening which leads back to what is known of old and long familiar'. Sigmund Freud, 'The Uncanny', in *The Standard*

Edition of the Complete Psychological Works Volume XVII, trans. Alix Strachey et al. (New York: Norton, 1961), 220.

136 Blanchot, 'Prophetic Speech', 79.

137 'Hast thou not seen how thy Lord did with Ad, Iram of the pillars, the like of which was never created in the land'. *The Koran Interpreted*, trans. A. J. Arberry (Oxford: Oxford University Press, 1983), 89: 7–9. In a short prologue to the play, Gibran cites the above-mentioned verse from the Qur'ān, a Hadith (saying) believed to be Prophet Muhammad's –'*yadkhuluhā ba'ḍu ummatī* [some of my people shall enter it]' and a long quote that describes the fabulous process of constructing the city of Iram, taken from *Siyasatnama* (The Book of Government), known in Arabic as *Siyar al-mulūk* (The Lives of Kings), by the eleventh-century Persian scholar Nizam al-Mulk. In the Qur'ān, Iram, believed to have been located in the southern part of the Arab peninsula, is the magnificent city of the people of 'Ād and their prophet Hud. Gibran, however, makes of Iram a city or a space of Sufi disclosure or gnosis. In other words, he is reinventing the meaning of Iram in the light of Sufism, practicing a kind of free *ta'wīl* (esoteric interpretation) upon which the play is aesthetically and ethically based.

138 Āmina is the name of Prophet Muhammad's mother.

139 *CWs in Arabic*, 330.

140 Ibid.

141 Blanchot, 'Prophetic Speech', 80.

142 *CWs in Arabic*, 331.

143 Ibid., 332.

144 Āmina asserts that 'Man is able to long [*yatashawwaq*] and long until longing uncovers the veil of phenomena over his sight so that he can contemplate or witness [*yushāhid*] his self [*dhātahu*]. Whoever is able to see his self sees the bare essence of Life'. Ibid., 333 [emphasis mine]. Gibran deliberately employs the verb *yushāhid* here, which is reminiscent of the Sufi *maqām* or station of *mushāhada,* contemplation or witnessing of the Real. The idea that 'everything that exists resides inside you and all that resides inside you exists in Being' (Ibid., 334) resonates with the notion of the 'Perfect Man' in Islamic Sufism, 'who is the miniature of Reality; he is the microcosm, in whom are reflected all the perfect attributes of the macrocosm'. A. J. Arberry, *Sufism: An Account of the Mystics of Islam* (London: Unwin Brothers, 1972), 101.

145 *CWs in Arabic*, 337.

146 'Say there is no God but Allah and there is nothing but Allah and you may remain a Christian'. Ibid., 334.

147 Ibid., 333.

148 The imaginal is Henry Corbin's translation of what Ibn al-'Arabi calls *al-barzakh* or *al-barzakhi*, the realm in which the 'corporealisation of the spirits' (*tajassud al-arwāḥ*) and the 'spiritualisation of the corporeal bodies' (*tarawḥun al-ajsām*) occur. The imaginal world is the world of both; hence, it is the realm of the unveiling of Being. See Chittick, *The Sufi Path of Knowledge*, 15. Gibran's emphasis on the unity of body and soul and the Unity of Being cannot be understood without reference to Sufism, and this play reveals like none of his other texts the powerful Sufi motifs that permeate his work.

149 *CWs in Arabic*, 335.

150 Ibid., 329.

151 Ibid.

152 *CWs*, 118.

153 *CWs*, 53.

154 Ibid.

155 Corbin, *Alone*, 173.

156 *Kahlil Gibran: An Illustrated Anthology*, 157.

157 *The Koran Interpreted*, 2: 26.

158 Corbin, *Alone*, 217.

159 *CWs*, 159.

160 KG to MH, 30 January 1916.

161 *CWs*, 556.

162 Corbin, *Alone*, 185 [emphasis added].

163 Ibid, 186.

164 This is even reiterated in Gibran's posthumously published one-act play *Lazarus and his Beloved*, in which the madman says: 'They are afraid of the mist. And the mist is their beginning and the mist is their end'. Kahlil Gibran, *Lazarus and his Beloved* (New York: Graphic Society, 1973), 43.

165 *CWs*, 517–18.

166 Ibid., 557.

167 'Did I not speak of freedom, and of the mist which is our greater freedom?' Ibid., 518.

168 Ibid., 44.

169 Ibid., 43.

170 Ibid., 73.

171 Ibid.

172 Chittick, *Imaginal Worlds*, 71–72.

173 Soren Kierkegaard, *Fear and Trembling*, trans. Sylvia Walsh (Cambridge: Cambridge University Press, 2006), 39–42.

174 Ibid.

175 Ricoeur, 'Religion, Atheism, and Faith', 445. In this essay, Ricoeur dwells on the dialectic of religion and faith that is mediated by a 'liberating and destructive' atheism. He discusses the themes of religious accusation and consolation and the death of the moral God of Christianity (with reference to Nietzsche's and Freud's hermeneutics of suspicion), going on to posit the possibility of a post-religious faith that goes beyond accusation and protection. His insights, albeit informed by a European 'Judeo-Christian' conception of religion, are illuminating and pertinent to my discussion of Gibran.

176 Ibid., 442.

177 Ibid., 447–48.

178 Almustafa, meaning 'the chosen one', is one of the attributes of the Prophet Muhammad. This reclamation of the name attests to a vision that does not break with the past so much as it reinvents it in the context of the present.

179 *CWs*, 127.

180 Gibran, 'Beyond My Solitude', in *CWs*, 86.

181 *CWs*, 127.

182 Ibid., 128.

183 Ibid.

184 I borrow this phrase from Levinas, who uses it to describe the insatiability of the primordial striving towards un unnameable Beyond. See Levinas, *Totality and Infinity*, 254, 256.

185 *CWs in Arabic*, 74.

186 Ibid.

187 'Our critique of metaphysics and its search of rational reconciliation must give way to a positive ontology, beyond resentment and accusation. Such a positive ontology consists in an entirely nonethical vision, or what Nietzsche described as "the innocence of becoming" (*die Unschuld des Werdens*). The latter is another name for "beyond good and evil". Of course, this kind of ontology can never become dogmatic, or it will risk falling under its own criticisms'. Ricoeur, 'Religion, Atheism, and Faith', 457.

188 Nietzsche, *Thus Spoke Zarathustra*, 59.

189 *CWs*, 140.

190 Ibid., 148.

191 Meskini, *al-Īmān al-ḥurr*, 189–91.

192 'He who wears his morality but as his best garment were better naked./ The wind and the sun will tear no holes in his skin./ And he who defines his conduct by ethics imprisons his songbird in a cage./ The freest song comes not through bars and wires./ And to whom worshipping is a window, to open but also to shut, has not yet visited the house of his soul whose windows are from dawn to dawn'. *CWs*, 148.

193 *CWs*, 148 [emphasis added].

194 Meskini, *al-Īmān al-ḥurr*, 21.

195 *CWs*, 109.

196 Ibid.

197 Ibid.

198 'If there is gift, the *given* of the gift (*that which* one gives, *that which* is given, the gift as given thing or act of donation) must not come back to the giving (let us not already say to the subject, to the donor). It must not circulate, it must not be exchanged, it must not in any case be exhausted, as a gift, by the process of exchange, by the movement of the circulation of the circle in the form of return to the point of departure [. . .]. It is perhaps in this sense that the gift is the impossible'. Derrida, *Giving Time: I. Counterfeit Money*, trans. Peggy Kamuf (Chicago; London: University of Chicago Press, 1992), 7 [emphasis in the original].

199 *CWs*, 110 [emphasis added].

200 Muhy al-Din Ibn al-ʿArabi, *al-Futūḥāt al-makkiyya* (The Meccan Openings) vol 3, ed. Ahmad Shams al-Din (Beirut: Dar al-Kutub al-ʿIlmiyya, 1999), 268–69.

201 *CWs*, 110 [emphasis added].

202 This resonates with Gibran's Arabic piece of poetic prose 'Mā akrama al-ḥayāt' (How Bountiful is Life), in which he poignantly exalts the incomprehensible bounty of Life and laments his incapacity to be receptive of and attentive to its magnitude. Gibran, *al-Majmūʿa al-kāmila: Nuṣūs khārij al-majmūʿa*, 35–39.

203 *CWs*, 110.

204 Gibran and Gibran, *Kahlil Gibran: Beyond Borders*, 345.

205 Ibid., 348.

206 When writing *The Prophet*, Gibran reflects on its introductory section with Mary Haskell by invoking Nietzsche's *Thus Spoke Zarathustra*, which, for all the admiration Gibran has for it, starts with an inadequately 'too short a beginning' according to him. And this, he asserts, comes down to 'a lack of balance in

him [Nietzsche] as an artist. He had an analytical mind [. . .] And the analytical mind always says too much'. Ibid., 338.

207 *CWs*, 420.

208 Ibid., 422.

209 Ibid., 423.

210 Ibid., 434.

211 Ibid., 424–25.

212 Ibid., 439.

213 Edward Said, *On Late Style: Music and Literature against the Grain* (New York: Pantheon Books, 2006), 148.

214 Ibid.

215 Ibid.

2

The Bilingual Chasm

*I spend my days and nights, my friend, in two worlds that are separated by a massive, bottomless abyss. What happens to me in one world, the other does not know. I live in two divergent civilisations [*madaniyyatayn*]: The Eastern that is my mother; and the Western that has adopted me. And what I don't fathom, my friend, is that people in these two divergent civilisations do not agree on any aspect of this small self [*dhāt*] I call 'me' [*anā*]. I find myself lost, therefore, occupied less with life-thinking [*al-tafkīr bil-ḥayāt*] – and this is the vocation that suits me – than with self-thinking [*al-tafkīr bil-nafs*], a vocation from which I seek to absolve myself.*

From Gibran's posthumously published manuscripts[1]

We only ever speak one language – and, since it returns to the other, it exists asymmetrically, always for the other, from the other, kept by the other. Coming from the other, remaining with the other, and returning to the other.

Jacques Derrida[2]

'The gulf between the Syrian work and my own work has to be crossed every day, and that is the thing that tires me',[3] wrote Khalil Gibran to Mary Haskell in 1918, the year he published his first book in English, *The Madman*. Is the gulf attendant on writing in and between two languages, the native and the adopted, so massive that it becomes almost impossible to bridge, or is the bilingual literary enterprise of the Arab *Mahjari* poet and essayist one in which the two languages, to invoke Abdelkebir Khatibi's *Amour bilingue* (1983), occupy a space of eroticism, of mutual enrichment and exchange? Gibran's bilingualism was definitive to his social, literary and intellectual life. A panoramic and close look at his bilingual work and letters testifies to the fact that his bilingual experience as a writer was a strenuous and, at times, an angst-ridden one. In this chapter, I probe this bilingualism by looking at and bringing together several, seemingly distinct but arguably interlaced, aspects and specific moments in his literary and intellectual career. By bilingualism, not only do I mean the fact of dwelling and writing in two languages, but also the attendant straddling of two or more cultures at a specific juncture in history.

This oscillation between two linguistic and cultural geographies is both creative and problematic. Gibran alternates between the urge to rejuvenate Arabic literature and the desire to gain literary cosmopolitan appeal in the United States as an Arab writer in English. His situatedness in the US at that specific historical point entailed representing, perforce, the Orient. This imposed Oriental identity – that is, a *fixed* and *a priori* notion of subjectivity – created a chasm that produced different incarnations of Gibran. His shift from Arabic to English generated, therefore, a discursive multiplication of functions: an Arab 'revolutionary' writer, on the one hand, whose creative output signalled a discursive turn in Arab literary modernity, and an Arab writer in English, on the other, whose texts were filtered through the vessel of the hostile cultural discourse on the *xenos*. In this double linguistic and cultural texture, I trace what is (dis)continuous in Gibran's movement from one language to another. I demonstrate that, while this bilingualism is culturally disjunctive, attending to Gibran's manifold writings in both languages reveals that the chasm at once separates and connects; that is, that the hostility of rigid cultural division could be addressed by the hospitality of critical interpretation, and that the universal in Gibran's case begins from the local and, while going beyond it, still depends on it.

This chapter will journey through a medley of Gibran's writings in both languages and for different purposes all of which are, I argue, interconnected. An itinerary of the chapter is therefore in order. In section one, I attempt to tease out, by closely reading two of Gibran's early pieces of poetic prose in Arabic, how his modern *ru'yā* (vision) is aesthetically staged in writing. This is to show that this vision is embodied in his 'romantic break with the past'[4] as much as in the aesthetics of the literary text – that is, in his endeavour to write 'poetic prose' that 'disperses' (*yanthur*) signifiers by way of an excess of metaphor and imagery – blurring the line between content and form. In section two, I probe this *ru'yā* (vision) in his poetic essay 'Ṣawt al-shā'ir' (The Voice of the Poet) by shedding light on his poetics of universal hospitality and Love (*maḥabba*) *qua* justice. I focus on the textual creativity and universal orientation of Gibran's early Arabic work, not only to point out its significance *vis-à-vis* Arab literary modernity, but also, most importantly, to foreground its importance in connection to his bilingualism as a writer: the later switch into English would carry this universal element and efface the aesthetic particularity of his Arabic writings. Then I move on, in the third section, to underscore the anxieties attendant on his decision to begin writing in English. I address this bilingual anxiety by analysing this movement as one in which English, bearing the 'Syriac' trace of the Bible, represses and displaces, rather than replaces, the 'language of the mother'. In the fourth section, I extend my discussion of Gibran's bilingual experience by looking at it phenomenologically. Drawing on Derrida and Levinas, I posit that language as such is inherently hospitable to the Other. The originary openness of English as a foreign language occasions Gibran's inscription into the host(ile) cultural discourse that appropriates both the language and the foreign writer in its own terms. In the last section, by way of discussing his Arabic essay 'Mustaqbal al-lugha al-'arabiyya' (The Future of the Arabic Language), I demonstrate that the mother tongue for the late bilingual Gibran becomes the locus of his civilisational commitment to the Arab East, arguing that writing in English as an adopted language entails the active preservation of the mother tongue and its universal potentiality. By adopting English as a language of writing, however, Gibran is adopted into the Euro-American culture in a way that masks his English-language texts by the identitarian veil of the Orient. I finish this chapter, therefore, with a reflective reading of his prose poem 'My Friend', in which I show that between 'seeming' and 'being' there lies a gulf that gives rise to an interpretative horizon which is irreducible to the 'identity' of the writer or to the 'culture' of the language in which the text is written. By highlighting and problematising Gibran's literary bilingualism, this chapter aims to show that, while 'all expatriations remain singular',[5] the literary and intellectual experience of Gibran's expatriation offers a fertile ground for universal reflections.

Gibran's Modern Poetics of *Ru'yā*

I examine *vision* (*ru'yā*) in Gibran's Arabic work insofar as it is emblematic of literary modernity (*ḥadātha*); vision as an indicator of poetic and literary innovation (*iḥdāth*) staged in *writing* itself: writing as *the* stage in which vision as event (*ḥadath*) takes place. This *ḥadath* is marked by disclosure or unveiling (*kashf*), itself wedded with innovation (*iḥdāth*). Writing occasions vision (*ru'yā*); it is that which enables his vision to materialise. As such, it is the terrain of linguistic and aesthetic experimentation/innovation. My reading will focus on two pieces of poetic prose, which show-case what came to be known as the Gibranian style in Arabic literature.[6] This field of vision engages and plays with the senses in the text; vision becomes an open field of playful interactions between the senses, especially vision (sight) and voice (or sound), signifiers that are unstable and always merging into one another in the body of the Gibranian text. The visible here is always at the mercy of the invisible, but the invisible, what is seen beyond the senses, that towards which Gibran was vehemently driven and with which he was creatively obsessed, is itself enabled and conditioned – in the domain of writing – by the visible: *ru'yā* (vision *qua* insight) as *ru'ya* (vision *qua* sight) in its metaphoric play with other sensorial signifiers. It is in and through writing – writing as material signs – that the infinite becomes finite, that is, materially circumscribed, only to become infinite again in the play of signs, their difference and deferral[7] (of meaning) by way of metaphor. Gibran's *ru'yā* as *ru'ya*, vision as materialised in writing, can be apprehended and approached through the prism of the imaginal, a Sufi concept to which I referred in the previous chapter, summoned here *vis-à-vis* the Gibranian text insofar as it embodies the space of writing, or the 'isthmus' (*al-barzakh*), where the invisible (the immaterial, the infinite) and the visible (the material, the sensorial, the finite) coincide. The seeming opposites (finite/infinite, corporal/spiritual) coincide in the space of writing by simultaneously negating and affirming each other; in Derridean terms, they coincide in writing by differing from and deferring to each other.[8]

In 'Ru'yā', a piece of poetic prose published in *Dam'a wa ibtisāma* (A Tear and a Smile, 1914),[9] the narrator tells us that 'in the midst of a field by the bank of a crystalline stream [he] *saw* a cage whose *ribs* were crocheted by a cunning hand', in one corner of which is a dead bird and in the other a 'vessel whose water dried up and a plate empty of seeds'.[10] We are later told that the cage has turned into 'a translucent human skeleton' and that 'the dead bird has metamorphosed into a human heart, and in the heart lies a deep bleeding wound, dribbling crimson blood, whose edges bear resemblance [*ḥākat*] to a grieving woman's lips'.[11] The Gibranian narrator often tells us what he sees by emphasising that he sees (*yarā*) and hears what transpires in his vision (*ru'yā*), describing what he sees/hears – the line between vision and hearing becomes blurry – in a metaphorical language: 'I heard a voice coming with the drops of blood out of the wound saying: I am the human heart, prisoner of matter and victim of the laws of earthly man'.[12] There are some words in the passage that I want to stop at; words that, when translated, are necessarily purged of their untranslatable semantic particularity and etymological history.[13] The verb *ḥākat*, from *ḥākā, yuḥākī*, which translates as 'to resemble', is very close in its etymology to *ḥakā, yaḥkī*, to tell or recount (a story), to narrate. Both words share the same root. Thus, embedded in the resemblance that the wound bears to the grieving woman's lips is the act of narration, insofar as it consists of speaking and uttering words that disclose a vision.

Vision (*ru'yā*) is the horizon in which vision (*ru'ya,* sight) and voice (and what is seen and heard) are coupled within the realm of language. It is within language that vision as *ru'yā* materially takes place. Vision is unthinkable without a language into which it is inscribed and disclosed; without language, it remains immaterial, unembodied, non-poetic. The signs of language, of writing, disclose the content of vision and determine its (unstable) semantic sphere. 'I *heard* these words [uttered out of the bleeding wounds of the human heart] and I *saw* them coming out with the drops of blood from the wounded heart, whereupon I no longer saw anything, nor did I hear a sound, so I returned to my reality'.[14] As the heart bleeds, the words are simultaneously heard and seen in this vision. The words are heard and seen *because* and *as* the heart is bleeding (not metaphorically). In other words, the words are produced with the bleeding of the heart. Is it by coincidence that the Arabic word *kalima*, which means 'word', shares its etymological root with *kalm*, wound? Words (*kalimāt*) are, in a sense, the traces of wounds (*kilām*).[15] This Gibranian vision/insight brings vision/sight and voice together in the scene of the bleeding heart which, as it bleeds, utters visible words, a scene that betrays, coincidently or not, the etymological history of the Arabic words *kalima* (word), *kalām* (speech), *kalm* (wound) and *kilām* (wounds). The wounding body of the word is seen and heard, a body whose history is linked with *kalm*, wound. The materiality of language, the sensorial effects of words – words seen and heard – disclose, paradoxically, the immateriality of vision (vision, in Ibn al-ʿArabi's definition, is unveiling). This is also reminiscent, as mentioned earlier, of Ibn Arabi's imaginal world, which corporealises the spiritual and spiritualises the corporeal: vision as the site where the corporeal and the spiritual, that which is supra-sensory, coincide.

This dynamic can be also seen in Gibran's long poetic essay *al-Musīqa* (On Music), published as a pamphlet in 1905, which was his first published work. In it, Gibran embarks on a poetic description and Romantic veneration of music. What interests me here is the textuality and rich imagery of the text. Gibran's vision of music is imbued with metaphors and images that engage the senses. Music here is always described analogically, in a fashion that is melodramatic or overtly imaginative.[16] As such, it attests to what it essentially is, a phenomenon that is only apprehensible – in language – indirectly or through analogy. The latter in this case is exaggerated, amplified and dramatised by virtue of the estranging and defamiliarising of the literary text. Let us not forget that this vision of music is materialised in writing: what matters here is not music itself or *what* the text presumably refers to outside it, but *how* the text discloses what it refers to – that is, its very textuality. What is at play in this vision is the way in which it fuses sound and sight, so much so that music becomes seen by what Gibran calls '*ʿayn samʿī*' or 'my hearing eye': 'I saw the effects of my beloved's heart with my hearing eye, whereupon I became distracted to the content of her speech by the substance of her emotions, which was embodied in music, the voice of the self'.[17] Not only does he hear music when his beloved sighs, but he also sees it with his 'hearing eye', as his beloved's emotions are now embodied in and through music, such that music itself becomes 'the language of the soul'.[18] Again, the immaterial is made material, the emotional is embodied and becomes simultaneously seen and heard. No signifier is stable in the body of the Gibranian text, as Fatima Qandil has also shown.[19] The signifiers of the senses, especially voice and sight (and what is heard and seen), embody one another in the space of writing. The essence of music, if there is any, becomes dispersed in the body of the text, in the play of the senses, signifiers that are made volatile and 'spectral', to use

Qandil's description of the Gibranian texts, as they freely wander and embody one another by way of analogy, metaphor and metonymy. Here is a passage that illustrates this spectrality:

> Music is akin to a lamp [. . .] and the melodies in my space are the spectres of the true self or the shadows [*akhīla*] of animated feelings. And reflected in the self, which resembles a mirror standing before the events of Being and its affects, are the drawings of those spectres and the images of those shadows.[20]

Music is light; that is, is it understood – or rather imagined – as illumination. The melodies it produces are spectres and shadows which spring from the 'true self' and 'animated feelings' whose 'drawings' and 'images' are reflected in the 'soul', that which is (like) a mirror. The melodies, in short, turn into images, (in)visible, spectral images, only because they are now subject to language, language as writing. The field of hearing and listening merges into the field of vision and seeing, and this fusion is encapsulated in what Gibran describes as the 'hearing eye'. The literary/poetic text metamorphoses the melodies, so to speak, into spectres and images. One is therefore lost in signifiers that ceaselessly refer – or, rather, that are made to refer – to other signifiers by means of metaphors and similes such that imagery at once supplements and supplants, following the Derridean logic of the supplement,[21] that which it describes: music becomes everything which it is not in the body of the text. It is even 'the *tongue* of all the nations of the Earth',[22] suggesting that music is a universal language by virtue of everyone's ability to taste it – tongue as language and tongue as organ.[23] The essay abounds in such metaphors and imagery that revolve around a centre (music) whose essence is dispersed or fragmented throughout the text. For it is a centre insofar as it is de-centred, and it is an essence insofar as it is dispersed, a dispersion (*nathr*, which also means 'prose') that is essentially metaphoric and poetic: poetic prose.

By writing a prose that is poetic, Gibran seeks to blur the lines between form and content, prose and poetry, because (Arabic) language for him should not be hampered by the 'laws of poetry' and should even incorporate colloquial expressions in its liberating and liberated flow, as he avers in his late essay 'Lakum lughatukum w lia lughatī' (You Have Your Language and I Have Mine). It is interesting to note that poetry in Arabic is associated with *naẓm* – that is, with versing. In classical Arabic poetry, which is still very much alive today, one verses poetry, as it were, but does not write it. The etymology of *naẓm*, as Abdelfattah Kilito observes, suggests 'order, arrangement, harmony' and so on. The opposite of *naẓm* is *nathr* (that is, prose), but the etymology of *nathr* also suggests 'dispersion, separation, division, fragmentation'.[24] Many of Gibran's early lyric essays are marked by this poetic dispersion: not prose poetry, but a prose that is poetic. The poetic dispersion of his text does not mean that poetry precedes prose or *vice versa*, that in the beginning there was either poetry or prose; these questions of 'origin' do not matter for Gibran. Rather, poetry acquires a new meaning and function in the *Nahḍa* context in which Gibran is writing: poetry is now enabled by and incarnates *ru'yā*, poetry not just as the expression of a 'state of feeling' – which is the case to the extent that one foregrounds his Romanticism – but poetry as 'a problem of vision, which engages in altering the Arab sensibility towards things and life'.[25]

Indeed, Salma Khadra Jayyusi asserts that this kind of 'poetry-in-prose' experiments, which were led by Gibran and Ameen Rihani (another influential Arab *Mahjari* writer in America), prompted 'the gradual disintegration of traditional formal concepts in Arabic poetry'.[26] Bearing immensely on the Arab literary generations of the 1920s and 1930s, '[Gibran's] experiment was initially offered to an audience devoted to the inherited, balanced metrics of Arabic poetry, and this would have created the greatest resistance were it not for the positive outlook Jibran (and al-Rayhani) [*sic*] had towards their homeland'.[27] In the case of Gibran, the 'positive outlook' towards his homeland manifested itself in an idealised version of Lebanon which, as apparent in his poetic essay 'Lakum Lubnānukum wa lia Lubnānī' (You Have Your Lebanon and I Have Mine), serves to denounce the politics of identity and westernisation in Greater Syria. Suffice it to emphasise for now, as Jayyusi reminds us, that thanks to these experiments, 'Jibran laid one cornerstone for the modernist poetry of a much later period [1940s and 1950s]'.[28]

No wonder, therefore, that Adonis refers to Gibran as a visionary writer (*kātib ru'yawī*) whose work was seminal in the experience of modern Arabic poetry and vital in 'erecting the concept of modernity in Arabic literature'.[29] This vision is innovatively modern, I must add, in that it also reconfigures the meaning of belonging: to belong entails a laborious effort of cultivating and carving out a new self from its old sources, such that the rupture with a particular mode of writing or poetry does not mean a rupture with 'tradition', but a rupture with an obsolete mode of being. The new mode of writing, to the extent that it reflects and refracts a new of mode of being, does not break with those 'ancients' who, in their own time, were modern in this peculiar creative sense.[30] It is, in a sense, a continuation of their creative 'modernity' in Arabic.[31] I now wish to demonstrate how this *ru'yā*, apart from its linguistic and aesthetic embodiment and its wider poetic function, is additionally reflected in an Arab cosmopolitan disposition that disrupts the nexus of language, nation and culture, despite or perhaps because of the fact that Gibran was not a citizen of an autonomous nation-state at the time.

Ṣawt al-Shā'ir (The Voice of the Poet): An Arabic Voice of a Universal Vision

In 'Ṣawt al-shā'ir', a short piece of poetic prose published in *Dam'a wa ibtisāma*, we may discern how the vision of the poet is embodied in his voice, a voice whose silence is supplanted, in the body of the text, by the vision that the poet holds. This vision is one in which patriotism and cosmopolitanism become complementary rather than contradictory.[32] The title is, nevertheless, somewhat intriguing: does the poet belong to the world as such, a belonging to which his voice testifies? Why the voice and not, for instance, the words? As discussed earlier, Gibran's *ru'yā* is marked by this tendency to engage the senses, sight and voice in particular. And it does so by destabilising and dispersing, by way of metaphor, imagery and analogy, the signifiers of voice and sight, such that one signifier is almost always made to refer to something other than itself, deconstructing itself, as it were, in its literary, linguistic embodiment. I am now concerned with the universal dimension of this *ru'yā*, since it is relevant to my critical focus in this chapter and in the book as a whole: is the voice of the poet – and should it be – at once local and universal, patriotic and cosmopolitan? If so, how? And what is implied in the metaphor of the poet, or in the poet as metaphor?

Gibran begins the essay by invoking the notion of giving as being which he underscores, as discussed in Chapter One, in *The Prophet* and elsewhere. The poet is the one who 'reaps' what the invisible force 'sows' inside him, the one who lights up the lamp that Heaven has filled up with oil. In other words, the poet, *qua* poet, gives expression to the force of giving itself: 'I do these things because I live by them, and if the days were to thwart me and the nights were to shackle my hands, then death would be better for a prophet cast out in his homeland and a poet exiled amongst his own people'.[33] What is significant to my discussion here is that the poet-prophet, in contrast to 'people [*al-bashar*[34]] who are divided into sects and tribes and belong to countries and regions', is everywhere a stranger and an outsider. 'All the earth is my homeland, and the human family is my tribe', he declares, 'because I have realised that man is weak and is further weakened by dividing upon himself. It is therefore a folly that the earth, which is too narrow, is partitioned into kingdoms and states'.[35] Thus, Gibran proclaims his belonging to the world as such, espousing the Romantic view that the poet, unique and exceptional, is by necessity a hopeless exile. As he goes on to lament humankind's 'destruction of the shrines of the spirit' and 'construction of the temples of the body', a motif prevalent in his early writings, he, 'standing alone in mourning', 'hear[s] a voice of hope from within saying: as Love [*maḥabba*] revives the human heart by means of pains, so does folly show it the ways of knowledge'.[36] The voice of the poet, the voice heard from within, heard by the poet from within himself, is a voice of hope. This is the voice of a poet whose prophetic vision it invokes, a voice that carries words of hope in what he deems a cynical world. A voice of an optimistic vision. This Romantic vision – by virtue of which, its idealism and magnifying of the exceptional role of the poet notwithstanding, the poet is a prophet; the poet whose voice, the voice heard from within the poet, is prophetic – leads to a declaration of what we may call, after a certain reading of Kant, a 'cosmopolitan patriotism':[37]

> I long for my country because of its beauty and I love the people of my country for their misery, but if my people, motivated by what they call patriotism, fell upon the country of my neighbour, plundered its goods, murdered its men, orphaned its children, widowed its women, watered its soil with the blood of its people and fed the flesh of its youth to its prowling beasts, then I would hate my country and the people of my country.[38]

In this passage, one can evidently observe how patriotism – or national belonging in general – are important for Gibran insofar as the land of one's nation is one's place of birth, the home that witnessed one's up-bringing. One's love of one's country, should it become a pretext to invade other countries and conquer other territories under the banner of nationalism, patriotism or jingoism, turns into hate, hatred of one's country. Gibran espouses patriotism to the extent that it is not, or does not become, transgressive and imperialist; to the extent that it holds other nations and territories in respect in that all nations belong to the world; to the extent that one's allegiance and loyalty is to one's nation as much as it is to the world – that is to say, to the world of my nation but also to *the* world, the world *as* other nations, the world *of* other nations. Thus, patriotism and cosmopolitanism, which seem incompatible at face-value, become necessarily complementary. Gibran, it must be reminded, is not concerned with the relationship between the state and its own citizens or with the relationship between one state and another. He is rather proposing an ethics of belonging to the world from the standpoint of the nation: an ethics enabled by poetics, by the universal 'voice of the poet'.

Gibran goes on to bring up another crucial matter in this regard, that of hospitality:

> I sing eulogies for the place of my birth and I yearn for a house wherein I was raised, but if a wayfarer passes by, seeking shelter in that house and ailment from its inhabitants, and is turned away, then I would substitute mourning for eulogy and consolation for longing, and I would say in myself, '*the house* that refuses bread to the needy and a bed to the seeker is most meriting of destruction and ruin'.[39]

This passage is reminiscent of Kant's 'cosmopolitan right' of hospitality, that one should be hospitable, not hostile, to the stranger and the foreigner, the *xenos*, that the latter have the right to hospitality 'by virtue of their common possession of the surface of the earth, where, as a globe, they cannot infinitely disperse and hence must finally tolerate the presence of each other'.[40] The way in which Gibran associates hospitality with one's love for one's country, interestingly, is such that the failure to be hospitable (that is, hostility towards the stranger) entails hatred towards one's country: 'the *house* that refuses bread to the needy and a bed to the seeker is most meriting of destruction and ruin'. This is 'the voice of the poet' that has now become, as the formulation of this statement suggests, the source of an unconditional law. To put it otherwise, and let me invoke Kant again, hospitality is not a matter of philanthropy, but a (matter of) right, and if this right is not received (by the stranger) and not given (by the inhabitant), then the house of the inhabitant, according to

Gibran, had better be destroyed. What is particularly interesting here is that Gibran speaks of the house, not its inhabitants: such a house whose inhabitants are hostile to the stranger should be destroyed, Gibran says, but why the house in particular? As Levinas and Derrida remind us, it is in the nature of a house to be hospitable.[41] Should its inhabitants deny the foreigner who seeks shelter in that house the right to hospitality, then the house is denied its essence, too. For the inhabitants would be acting in such a way that the house is stripped of its essence, 'its essence without essence', that of hospitality: 'The *hôte* [the *host*, the inhabitant, who is also a *guest* in his own house] offers the hospitality that he receives in his home; he receives it from his own home – which, in the end, does not belong to him'.[42] Hence Gibran's assertion that such a house 'is most meriting of destruction and ruin'.[43]

Again, this is the voice of the poet that oscillates between love and hatred, praise and elegy, longing and consolation for his country, depending on the treatment of his country and its own people towards other countries and their people, on the one hand, and towards the stranger and the foreigner who come to his land and seek shelter in it, on the other. It is the voice of an exilic poet – an originary exile – whose longing for his place of birth is far from being blinding in that the longing itself is not (only) subject to the poet's emotional and existential state, but (also) to the manner in which his country, the country of his place of birth, acts towards other countries and people of other countries stopping by his own. Or, perhaps, the voice of an exilic poet whose *blindness* – the Romantic obsession with the poet as essentially solitary, exceptional and exile – is that which, to invoke Paul De Man, enables his *insight*.[44] Gibran, in 'The Voice of the Poet', proceeds: 'I love my birthplace with some of my love for my country, and I love my country [*bilādī*] with a portion of my love for the land of my nation [*waṭanī*]. And I love the Earth with my all [*bi kulliyyatī*], because it is the pastureland of humanity, the spirit of divinity on Earth.'[45] This passage is testimony to the cosmopolitan patriotism I mentioned above. Love of Earth, of the world, for Gibran, outweighs but does not erase – in fact it corroborates – love of one's place of birth and love of one's homeland. Being cosmopolitan, thus, requires one to be patriotic, but patriotic in the strict sense that Gibran attributes to it: to love one's country insofar as the land of one's country and one's place of birth belong to the Earth; to love the Earth is to necessarily love your country, in such a way that the former takes precedence over, but does not eliminate or eclipse, the latter.

In the third part of the short essay, Gibran abruptly shifts attention to address the Other, his 'brother' in humanity: 'You are my brother, and we are both the children of one universal holy spirit [*rūḥ wāḥid quddūs kullī*] [. . .] You are a human being, and I have loved you, my brother'.[46] Gibran goes on to assert that whatever 'you may say of me', 'take from me' or 'do with me', 'you are my brother and I love you', but not before pointing to the limits of transgression that the Other, his brother, can inflict upon him, reminding him that 'you are unable to touch my essence [. . . and] incapable of jailing my thought, because it is as free as a breeze in a space boundless and measureless'.[47] Then he continues: 'I love you when you prostrate yourself in your mosque, when you kneel in your synagogue and when you pray in your church', a statement which, in its belief in a Universal Soul that unites humankind irrespective of religious and ethnic divergences, sounds like a Romantic, humanist manifesto.[48] We should not forget that this is the voice of the poet, an Arabic voice that speaks in a historical period of transformation and turmoil in the Middle East, the poet who takes it upon himself to voice his cosmopolitan and universal ideals of Love and justice – and we shall see why justice is aligned with Love – in a world of constant unrest and enormous promises and threats.

'You are my brother and I love you, but why do you fight me?' wonders Gibran, 'why do you come to my country striving to subjugate me in order to satisfy leaders who seek glory in your words and joy in your labouring?'[49] – in reference to colonialism (Ottoman in the Middle East before World War I, and Western all over the world). Protecting the rights of the Other, Gibran emphasises, is 'the noblest and finest of man's acts', and 'should my survival entail the annihilation of another, then death would be better and sweeter to me [than life]'.[50] The voice of the poet, crucially, is not reactionary or defensive here. Rather, it is one that radically interrogates the universal obsession with the same by foregrounding the responsibility for the Other. It is a voice that, in addressing the Other in the name of Love, *maḥabba*, seeks to transcend the obsession with the individual or collective self, the self that is nevertheless subjected, in his case, to the oppression and subordination of this Other. This *maḥabba*, interestingly, is solely realisable if conceived of as justice, such that it becomes the opposite of selfishness in its primary responsibility for the Other: 'I love you and you are my brother, and Love is justice in its highest manifestations', Gibran writes towards the end of the essay, 'and if I were not just in my love for you everywhere [*fī kulli al-mawāṭin*], then I would be a deceiver who conceals the monstrosity of selfishness beneath love's fine raiment'.[51] Gibran's cosmopolitan and universal vision, thus, is fundamentally ethical is its equation of *maḥabba* and justice, in its very emphasis on Love *qua* justice, whose universality entails that it be enacted *anywhere* on Earth, 'in all lands', not within the boundaries or in the sole interest of one's own nation or country – in allusion to colonialism and the crimes committed and justified in the name of patriotism or national interest. To put it differently, justice is not conditional on place, nationality, time, circumstance, interest and so on; justice as *maḥabba*, justice as such, is unconditional, or else it is not justice: 'Where is the justice of authority', Gibran wonders, 'if it slays the slayer and imprisons the robber then falls upon a neighbouring country to kill thousands of its people and rob many of its goods? What say the zealots of killers who punish murderers and robbers who reward plunderers?'[52]

It should be remembered that this essay was written in Arabic, in one of Gibran's early works, at a time when he was still a monolingual writer. Gibran voices his universal vision in an unambiguous fashion, in a prophetic style that is not tersely symbolic or parabolic, as is the case with his later work in English. The latter does not break from his early work in Arabic, especially in terms of its prophetic register, as the voice of the poet anticipates the multilingual expansion of his universal, prophetic imagination: 'I came to be for all [*lil-kul*] and with all [*wa bil-kul* . . .] and what I say with one tongue now will be uttered by many tongues to come'.[53] His vision in this particular essay – which also testifies to the singularity of a text that demands attentive reading – interrupts the bond of nation, language and culture, in that language becomes disruptive of the bond itself. Having said that, I should point out that the language of writing bears, prospectively speaking, not solely on the mode of writing, on language as a terrain of aesthetic experimentation, but also on language as that which carries a horizon of promise and threat in its connection to culture. As Gibran turns to English as a language of writing, as he becomes a bilingual writer, the second language is the one that will most visibly carry his universal vision, which would be understood, ironically and paradoxically, as *essentially* Oriental in the Euro-American culture that hosted him. If language disrupts the bond of language-nation-culture, it is culture – in its appropriation of language, in its discursive capacity to absorb and contain the different and the subversive – that reaffirms it, and it does so, in this case at least, by veiling the literary particularity of texts deemed 'foreign'. The bilingual fissure that marks Gibran's literary and intellectual enterprise therefore warrants focused and meticulous attention. The rift is created, as I now hope to demonstrate, as soon as Gibran embarks on the endeavour to write poetry in English in the mid-1910s. The switch for him was by no means an easy one, accompanied as it was by some self-interrogatory moments that are particularly relevant and revealing here.

The Decision to Write in English: Bilingual Anxiety

Gibran's bilingualism cannot be probed without considering his status as an Arab *émigré* writer in America. His decision to begin writing in English, after producing works in Arabic – works short in length but wide and influential in terms of their immediate impact on and lasting appeal in modern Arabic literature[54] – was one on which he dwelled a great deal. This is due to his self-consciousness of being a poet who wishes to write in a language that is not his native or 'mother tongue', with the enormous linguistic and cultural challenge that this enterprise entails. It is worth noting that Gibran continued to write in Arabic after publishing his first book in English, *The Madman* (1918). *al-Mawākib* (The Processions), his first serious attempt of writing metric and rhythmic poetry in Arabic was published in 1919, followed by *al-ʿAwāṣif* in 1920 and *al-Badāʾiʿ wa al-ṭarāʾif* in 1923. In the same period, Gibran published *The Forerunner* (1920) and *The Prophet* (1923), going on to write *Sand and Form* (1926), a short book of aphorisms, *Jesus the Son of Man* (1928) and *The Earth Gods* (1931). He continued to write non-fiction essays for the Arab press, however – an aspect of Gibran's writings that is often overlooked in Arabic and English scholarship, despite its significant contribution to debates that concern the Arab *Nahḍa* and Arab literary modernity.

Gibran's decision to write in English was haunted by intermittent anxieties and (self)-doubt. Jean Gibran and Kahlil G. Gibran (a cousin of Gibran) in their biography of the author reveal how unsettling it was for him to write in English, wondering 'what led him to compose in English?'

> When Mary showed him a copy of *Light of Dawn*, the recently published poetry of Aristides Phoutrides, *he was still questioning whether any poet could successfully use a second language.* He was 'much interested in Phoutrides' book', she wrote, . . . but . . . he said, 'He's word ridden – But after all, *foreigners can't write English poetry . . . Yet I keep on trying*'.[55]

What Gibran was questioning is not uncommon. W. B. Yeats, for instance, lambasted Tagore for translating his own poetry into English after initially supporting him, wondering rather condescendingly: 'Tagore does not know English, no Indian knows English'.[56] In a similar vein, T. S. Eliot contended that one cannot be a bilingual poet, asserting his unawareness 'of any case in which a man wrote great poetry or even fine poems equally well in two languages',[57] a reminder of his own failure at writing poetry in French. These dispositions, coming from canonical figures of Western modernism, are not merely personal but may function as taste-makers and gate-keepers. One is reminded, however, of the extraordinarily successful attempts of Vladimir Nabokov and Samuel Becket at writing 'equally well' in two languages, to mention but two towering literary figures that led George Steiner to dwell on what he named the 'exterritoriality' of (exilic) twentieth-century literature.[58]

But if 'foreigners can't write English poetry', why did Gibran insist on doing so? Is it the urge to be recognised as an Arab cosmopolitan writer in America? Will this bear on his writings in Arabic, and if so, how? The above-mentioned biographers attach Gibran's decision to write exclusively in English to the scathing criticism heaped on the form and language of *al-Mawākib*, his long Arabic poem written in classical form but somewhat experimentally. The criticism, they claim, 'did inhibit his Arabic production, and finally ended it'.[59] We read:

> His last truly creative poem had been *The Procession*, and this work, so important to him, was attacked not only for its 'corrupt images' but for its linguistic and metrical weaknesses. Faced with the choice of continuing to struggle for acceptance by the Arabic world of letters or of confining himself to expression in English, he took the latter course. With this decision he resolved the last major dichotomy in his life.[60]

The point is well-taken, but to ascribe Gibran's late exclusive espousal of English as a language of writing poetry to the supposed failure of his Arabic poem is slightly reductive and unconvincing. After all, the poem, for all its weaknesses, was not a failure, but an experimental attempt that helped loosen the then rigid and unquestionable form of classical Arabic poetry.[61]

The poem attracted a great deal of critical attention. 'Abbas Mahmud al-'Aqqad, in his review of the poem, criticised the occasional faultiness of its Arabic grammar and the idealist notion of nature that it espouses, considering Gibran less a poet than one who 'thinks as a poet'.[62] He therefore failed to discern – like many other commentators – the dialogic nature of the poem, meaning the irreducible tension between the two different worldviews its two speakers articulate, and the centrality of this tension to the meaning of the poem. The poem speaks in two different voices – different in tone, style and worldview: that of the youth who celebrates the idyllic and harmonious world of the woods, of Nature, and that of the old man who speaks ironically and bitterly about the world of the city and civilisation, of its hypocrisy and dualism. This duo-phony, so to speak, may be that of the same person, and has an affinity with William Blake's *Songs of Innocence* and *Songs of Experience*.[63] In its dialogic form, however, the poem juxtaposes the youth's singing and blind rebellion with the sage's sober wisdom; the former finding in the woods a world devoid of all dualities (good and evil, body and soul, life and death, freedom and slavery, and so on), the latter reminding us of the deep-seated, ironic and irredeemable manifestation of those very dualities. The juxtaposition is one of temporal and intellectual concomitance, not of innocence restored through and despite experience. The two voices feed off each other, but the tension between both is not resolved, not even by the singing of the *nāy* or the pipe, which the youth describes as 'the mystery of immortality' and that 'which subsists after the annihilation of Being'.[64] This tension, rather, is the central force that informs the structure and meaning of the poem, which, no wonder, ends with the sober voice of the old man, not with the exuberant one of the youth. In its duo-phony, thus, the poem is torn between the bitter reality of dualism, which permeates the world of culture and civilisation, and the mystic aspiration towards oneness and unity, which are only found in nature; between the impurities and constraints of the world of 'quantity and measures' and the freedom of the Universal Spirit, as it expresses itself in the purity of pipe-singing[65] in the woods.

Therefore, to go as far as claiming that Gibran's decision to write – and the fact that he wrote – almost exclusively in English after *al-Mawākib* 'resolved the last dichotomy of his life' is to undermine, on one side, the specificity of the poem and, on the other, Gibran's own status as a foreigner who adopted English, his adopted language, as a language of writing. It is, furthermore, to turn a blind eye to the anxieties that often accompany the bilingual writer who lives in a country and writes in a language both of which are not his native. For Gibran did struggle to be recognised in the US as a writer of poetry in English, and his insistence on improving his use of English attests to his stubborn and strenuous endeavour to challenge his own assumption that 'foreigners can't write English poetry'.

This self-awareness of being a foreigner and a bilingual who inhabits two linguistic and cultural worlds – without fully inhabiting them – deepened his sense of exile, as both realms represented terrains of continuous challenge and incessant struggle for him. Forging a new literary mode of writing in Arabic poetics that would gain recognition and break with the outdated modes of expression was no less laborious than the endeavour to write poetry in a language which was not his native and in a culture that deemed him an outsider. The first enterprise, however, has undeniably left its indelible mark in the history of modern Arabic literature, while he is hitherto uncanonised in American literature despite, or because of, the popular appeal of his work, mainly *The Prophet*.[66] I am aware of the fact that breaking with a certain tradition of writing or thought often triggers sharp counter-reactions, especially at a historical juncture where 'traditional' modes of writing and thought were highly venerated and perpetuated by the political and religious institutional authorities, and that the struggle to revive the Arab literary scene, therefore, was one that he must have anticipated.

That Arabic was his native tongue, however, is a vital element whose role and impact on his English writing should be taken seriously insofar as he is a bilingual writer. His anxieties about his own English haunted him for years. In 1918, he wrote to Mary Haskell:

> *English still fetters me.* I don't think without looking for words. In Arabic I can always say what I want to say. I have coined words and phrases in the Arabic – *to say what I wanted in the way I wanted – in my way.* When I was a boy, it was my desire to write Arabic as well as anybody ever wrote in Arabic. And in all these years, even from the time I first began at sixteen to publish or to be known – with all that has been said and written against my ideas – no one has ever criticized the way I said it or called it poorly said.[67]

Until 1918, Gibran claimed that no one had criticised the way in which he wrote in Arabic; it was the 'what' that had been subject to criticism, not the 'how'. He wanted to achieve the same in English, but, alas, English 'fetters' him. But why this strong insistence and determination to write in English? Is it to do with his creative urge to be acknowledged as a universal poet in the US? Or is it the realisation that any recognition of the work that he produced in the language of the host country would guarantee him the trans-national appeal that would make his work reachable to the Arab world through translation, a reminder of Abdelfatah Kilito's rather poignant remark that 'to be [for an Arab writer] is to be translated [from Arabic to a Western language or the other way around, as the recognition would always involve the West]?'[68] This disquieting question should remain an open one, its rhetorical nature notwithstanding. Now the second language for Gibran, the adopted language which he wanted to adopt as a language of writing, 'fetters' him. Yet he insisted on unfettering himself by way of 'naturalising' it, of making it akin to his native language and the way in which he dwelled in it, by way of de-foreignising it, in short.

Dwelling – speaking and writing – in two languages is not as liberating as one might think, especially if the adopted language is the language of the adopted country whose literary history goes beyond the US (Euro-America) and of whose (then) current poetic usage he was not (perhaps) profoundly aware, as his confession to Mary Haskell in 1922 reveals:

> I have a fear about my English. For years I have wondered about this, but I have not said it to you. Is my English, modern English, Mary, or is it the English of the past? For *English is still to me a foreign language. I still think in Arabic only.* And I know English only from Shakespeare and the Bible and you.[69]

Arabic implacably lurks in the background, devouring, as it were, his second language, to use the metaphor of bestiality that Kilito employs to describe the experience of bilingualism: 'When two languages live side by side, one or the other will always appear bestial. If you do not speak as I do, you are an animal. The "I" in this case must occupy the dominant position; if I am the weaker party, it is I who am the animal'.[70] Yet Gibran's initial experience of bilingualism is not essentially explainable in terms of power. Rather, it is one in which the adopted language would never outweigh the native or 'mother tongue' – even if it appears to do so – but would hopelessly occupy a secondary importance in relation to the first, such that the latter will invariably, often unbeknownst to its user, tinge or haunt the adopted. Kilito's metaphor of bestiality, as far as bilingualism is concerned, is challenged by Abdelkebir Khatibi's metaphor of eroticism in his *Amour bilingue*: the two languages that live side by side in the same tongue inhabit a space of eroticism, of mutual exchange and enrichment.[71] This creative mutual enrichment, however, necessarily takes place somewhere – that is, in a specific cultural, historical and social context, where the text is culturally translated in accordance with the mode of reason and ways of reading dominant in that cultural milieu. More specifically, by adopting the host language as a language of writing, the culture in which Gibran's text is produced would *adopt* the text itself according to its own discursive codes, a point to which I shall return later. Gibran, furthermore, is in a muddle as to whether his English is 'modern' or that 'of the past'. One is inevitably driven to wonder why it was the case that '[he knew] English only through Shakespeare and the Bible and [Mary]' in the cosmopolitan climate of early-twentieth-century New York. Was he not also acquainted with Blake, Keats, Shelley, Carlyle and Whitman, as his letters and writings demonstrate? Or did he confine himself to the heated literary and intellectual debates that captured the Arab scene at the time? The latter case seems to be more plausible, as his various articles and essays on Arabic literature, language and writing reveal. I shall come back to one of these essays later, which is significant in its contribution to those debates and relevant to my concern in this chapter.

Gibran's bilingualism warrants further attention and invites me to raise more disturbing questions, partly because it has been deemed secondary or left unnoticed in critical appraisals of his work. I am raising these questions to disturb, more precisely, the tendency to either 'resolve' or 'politicise' Gibran's bilingual experience, this shift from one language to another that is either taken granted by *forgetting* the question of power, on the one hand, or is accounted for in terms of discursive acquiescence to the dominant culture by *over-emphasising* the question of power, on the other. If, following Derrida, language bears the structure of promise and/or threat,[72] even before it reveals itself, before the disclosure of its content, to push Derrida's formulation a bit further, was the literary adoption of the adopted language in Gibran one that held the promise of what the mother tongue could not offer – namely, universal literary recognition and appeal? Did it not offer, also, the promise of coming to terms with the worldly experience of immigration and exile, of the (painful) pleasure that exile affords the bilingual writer whose concern with his native language and culture is confined to his country or place of birth – Syria and, more broadly, the Arab East? Did this adoption signify a kind of threat to the mother tongue, not because the latter was replaced, but because it was repressed and thereby perhaps culturally mis-translated, as the text of the adopted language becomes identified with the vague 'civilisational' Other, the Orient, that the repressed mother tongue represents? Or was this adoption a betrayal – in the double sense of the word – of his origin, his being an Arab and an Oriental, that is, no longer Arab but mainly an Oriental, when writing in English?

'The irreplaceable uniqueness of the mother tongue',[73] its untranslatability, to summon Derrida again, is precisely what renders it replaceable. It is replaceable because it is untranslatable; untranslatable, incomprehensible, in the host(ile) country, translatable only by way of replacement, which would not completely replace it in Gibran's case – the mother, the unique, the 'place of madness itself'.[74] Rather, English would repress and displace his mother tongue, as I show below; it would not replace it. And, as it must be remembered, it was Gibran's own displacement that entailed the adoption of the second language, the language of the host country, as a language of writing poetry. His poetic style in the adopted language, however, is one which is conspicuously biblical and parabolic. As such, it seems out of touch with the radical transformation of poetic sensibility in the US in the first two decades of the twentieth century. Yet this style is not merely a 'belated' one – a belatedness that nevertheless attests to its exilic nature, as discussed in the context of *The*

Prophet in Chapter One. The Bible, for Gibran, 'is Syriac literature in English words [. . .] the child of a sort of marriage'.[75] Adopting the biblical style in English is an assertion, in other words, that his writings bear the trace of 'Syriac literature', that what he writes in English remains 'Syriac', a trace of identity. 'There is nothing in any other tongue to correspond to the English Bible. And the Chaldo-Syriac is the most beautiful language that man has made – though it is no longer used'.[76] English has repressed his mother tongue because the style that he would adopt in it is invocative of the Bible, of Syriac literature in English, which is to say that English is secondarily important here, that it does not have the power, because of its secondary importance, to replace. It can only repress his first language because it bears the trace of Syriac literature, the literature of the dead mother tongue[77] – can one have two mothers, two 'mother tongues', one dead, but not forgotten, the other alive, but repressed? English, thus, by being associated with a dead mother tongue, would not be entirely alien to him. Nevertheless, this dead mother tongue, 'Syriac', remains dead, invoked only as an old source of identity that is retained, by way of translation, in the English Bible.

Hence, what is forgotten here is not Syriac but translation; what is lost, forgotten, eclipsed, buried or unnoticed is not that which is translated, but translation itself. Gibran's adoption of the parable and the biblical style is therefore a self-translation that invokes what is dead by forgetting itself, by forgetting the movement from Arabic into English and what this movement entails. I should highlight, in this respect, two essential things. The first is that some of the texts he published in *The Madman* were written and published in Arabic first,[78] and he even confesses to Mary Haskell that '"The Perfect World"', the last poem in *The Madman*, is the first poem he wrote from scratch in English; namely, without translating anything from Arabic.[79] And the second is the paramount role that Mary Haskell, the woman who was his close friend and financial supporter for a great number of years, played in editing his English work before publication – and the evidence suggests that she was a consistent and meticulous editor.[80] We should not forget, furthermore, that his adoption of the parable and the biblical style also boils down to the post-religious nature of his literary enterprise: one reinvents the religious by adopting a somewhat religious language; and, after all, the style of his early Arabic writings was partly developed thanks to the well-known

1865 Protestant translation of the Bible into Arabic.[81] Nor should we deem language only a means, a tool of expression, severed from the culture that appropriates it and that it, in turn, articulates. This would lead me to foreground the question of hospitality, of the *hospes* (the host, the master, the guest and the stranger) and a whole 'chain of significations' that links hospitality to hostility in relation to language.

Bilingualism between Hospitality and Hostility

I wish, once again, to discuss the important question raised by the above-mentioned biographers: What led Gibran to compose in English? What drove him to write in English in the first place? This requires that the question be tackled phenomenologically, but within the worldly context of immigration and foreignness. Drawing on Derrida's reading of Levinas, I address the question of language and bilingualism through the prism of hospitality and hostility. By way of ethicising phenomenology, so to speak, Emmanuel Levinas postulates that the Other is always already hospitable, *passively* hospitable, because the face of the Other always already signals a *yes*: 'there is no face without a welcome'.[82] The originary *yes* of the Other is therefore necessarily a welcoming; the face, in its intentionality, receives and welcomes the Other, and hence it is essentially hospitable. If the face of the Other is inherently hospitable, then so, as I would suggest, is the language of the Other, which does not belong to him/her. Writing in the language of the Other is a 'yes *to* the Other', the responsible *yes* that not only 'precedes the *yes of* the Other',[83] as is the case with the face, but does not even depend on it. The language of the Other, like the face of the Other, is inherently hospitable; yet language, unlike the face, does not belong to the Other, or to anyone for that matter. As the Other which does not belong, language does not lend itself to possession. Rather, language is appropriated, not possessed, as native. Hence its foreignness, and openness, to those for whom it is not native. The openness of the host – the face of the Other, the language *as* Other – necessitates the openness of the guest, and this (double) openness is perhaps what the French word *hôte* seems to encapsulate, as it is the word for both the host and the guest. This originary linguistic hospitality, however, does not always lead to cultural hospitality; in fact, it may produce the opposite: cultural hostility. Language, albeit essentially hospitable – that is, inherently open to the Other

– is necessarily appropriated in and by (a certain) culture. The foreigner, as a result, would be subject(ed) at once to hospitality and hostility, for the foreigner is not only foreign to the Other's language, but also to the culture in which this language is appropriated as the culture's 'own' language.

I am here thinking about hospitality, openness, foreignness and hostility in relation to language and the experience of writing in a language which is not 'maternal' as a foreigner, a *xenos*, an outsider; this 'house of Being'[84] that one inhabits but never possesses, a house for all, by nativity or adoption, a house that receives and hosts its guests in a hospitality offered by language, language as such. And since in every hospitality lies an addition, a contribution of some sort, writing in the adopted language bespeaks that which lies in every hospitality – namely, that the guest is fundamentally (bringing) an addition to the host language, country, culture and so on, a contribution captured by the lexical/etymological proximity between the two Arabic words *ḍiyāfa* (hospitality) and *iḍāfa* (addition), and even between the latter and *istiḍāfa* (hosting, receiving).[85] 'What is added to Being is that which is hosted from addition itself [*mā yuḍāf fil-wujūd huwa mā yustaḍāf mina al-iḍāfa nafsihā*]',[86] writes Muhammad Chaouki Zine. He goes on to note that 'immigration, translation and language are the manifestations that attest to hospitality as addition [*ḍiyāfa* as *iḍāfa*]'.[87] It follows that writing in the adopted language is not an act of (self-)betrayal, because one is inherently and unwittingly hospitable and open to the Other. This is the case even if one betrays hostility to the guest, since what preconditions hostility is 'intentionality', a movement towards the Other that is essentially hospitable as it moves to, receives and hosts the Other. For Gibran – and many other *émigré* bilingual writers – writing in two languages reflects and materialises, as it were, the welcoming response to the welcoming *yes* of language that 'begins' and 'commands'.[88]

This might explain why Gibran was so insistently keen on writing in English, his self-awareness of his status as *xenos* notwithstanding. Did he feel bound to answer to the hospitality of the host country and its language by writing – and insisting to do so – in that very language, the strenuous endeavour that might have led him to capitalise on his status of an Oriental *xenos* as a strategy of appeal, even of 'survival', as Richard E. Hishmeh argues?[89] One is indeed reminded of his struggle to gain literary recognition in the US and his decision to write parables in English, despite his belief that 'English is not the language for parables'[90] – an otherwise questionable statement. This decision could be seen as a 'foreignisation' of English, as that which testifies to *ḍiyāfa* as *iḍāfa* (hospitality as that which entails addition). In other words, unable to write in English as a native could, he would nevertheless write in it as an Arab Syrian for whom English still carried a 'Syriac' trace, an English tinged with an imagined trace of the old sources of one's identity. His shift into English would therefore efface the aesthetic particularity of his Arabic mode of writing, for he could not be as linguistically inventive in English as he was in Arabic. In other words, he could not effect a change in literary writing in English in the same way as he did in Arabic. This does not mean that his English work is not creative; it just means that he was not able, in the second language, to be as stylistically inventive as he was in the first.

His literary contribution in English, thus, would not be evaluated on its own terms – that is, by considering both its limitations and merits in a manner that does not allow the former to eclipse the latter. His English mode of writing, prophetically staged and ethically and universally oriented, would be deemed 'belated' and 'Oriental',[91] for better or worse, in the imaginary and discursive universe of the metropolitan culture. Hospitality becomes entwined with hostility, a rather subtle and invisible one, and therein lies its discursive potency. This subtle hostility forces the foreign, Arab writer and his English text into the identitarian category imposed on him in the host(ile) culture. It forces the foreign, Arab writer to be a representative of the Orient in the Occident, and as a representative of the Orient, his text would become nothing more than an emanation of that Oriental essence, which he and his text thereby cannot escape.

The originary hospitality of language, this universal hospitality of language as a house of Being, is that which conditions, in Gibran's case, both the contribution (*al-iḍāfa*) and its hostile, albeit subtle, domestication in the host culture, the appropriative culture that separates the same and the Other, that identifies, by way of discursive strategies and rules, what falls within and without.[92] To be more specific, by writing in the second language, the language of the host culture, Gibran's English text is identified as essentially 'Oriental', and this identification is one that Gibran took for granted because the civilisational separation of the world into Orient and Occident had been discursively ossified in modernity and the *Nahḍa*. But as to what the signifier 'Oriental' – or, for that matter, 'Occidental' – signifies, the signified becomes so many things at once. I deliberately avoid, therefore, using the term 'self-Orientalisation' in this specific context, because it presupposes, on the one side, an agential condition, or a set of conditions, where the Oriental *can* evade being an Oriental in that cultural location at that specific point in history but chooses not to – which was *not* the case.[93] It also presupposes, on the other side, that 'Oriental' can refer to one and only one thing, an essentialist Orient that is ontologically distinct from and inferior to the Occident – which was *not* the case either. Self-Orientalisation, in this respect, becomes nothing more than a political judgement or a culturalist assumption based on a monosemic and unchanging notion of symbolic geography, which forgets the discursive and historical conditions in which 'Orient' and 'Occident', as entrenched identitarian categories that often went unquestioned in the modern imperial period, held specific and varied designations and generated different performative acts depending on who uses them, where and for what purpose.

In this context, Gibran speaks Abrahamically but as an Oriental, and the Abrahamic – more specifically, the prophetic – cannot be reduced to the Oriental. The poetic impulse of his Anglophone text, and the fact that he was deeply concerned with 'life-thinking' and not with 'self-thinking', attest to the fact that what mattered for him was neither Orient nor Occident – nor, for that matter, the 'bridging' of the two – but the identitarian veils that mask our faces everywhere, which was one of my concerns in Chapter One. But because he speaks as an Oriental, because of that pervasive identitarian reason, the literary thrust of his writings is filtered through that discursive prism of identity. The agential space within which he could act as an Arab writer in English was therefore very limited. In other words, he could only speak as an Oriental, as an outsider, and this Orient as Outside would supplement and, alas, sometimes supplant the prophetic as Outside – the poetic that offers an alternative horizon of being and dwelling in the world.

The chasm that Gibran wanted to cross between his Syrian and English work is perhaps unbridgeable. But this chasm goes beyond his own writings, which, as Chapter One has shown, disrupt and transcend identitarian reason by virtue of the poetic. This gulf is therefore the by-product of his bifurcating experience as an *émigré* bilingual writer in the worldly and cultural context in which he lived. Both here and there, neither here nor there, but seeking no 'third space', his bilingual experience is one in which the two languages in question depend on one another (as shown below), but in such a way that one, Arabic, overwhelms the other, English. Ironically for him, this resulted in continuing to write poetry in the second, despite the entrenched and overwhelming presence of the first. His attachment to Arabic therefore never withered, and it manifested itself, not in his English work – which supplied him with the possibility of literary recognition as an Arab cosmopolitan writer in the US – but in his engagement with debates concerning Arab literary and cultural modernity, the Arab *Nahḍa* and, more specifically, the Arabic language.

Arabic, Bilingualism and the Orient as Identitarian Veil

Gibran's attachment to Greater Syria – the geographical space that includes, nowadays, Syria, Lebanon, Jordan and Palestine/Israel – was unwavering, even though he lived in the US for almost thirty years.[94] English never outweighed his profound intellectual and cultural attachment to the Arabic language. The alien tongue, to put it otherwise, was not tempting enough for him, but was tempting all the same, strongly and persistently preoccupied as he was with the linguistic, cultural and civilisational status of Syria and the Arab East at the time. Not only is this evinced in his literary and poetic writings, but it is voiced, most importantly, in the numerous articles and one-act plays that he wrote for the active Arab press in the *Mahjar* over the years. I will examine the national and *Nahḍawī* tenor of his literary and intellectual enterprise at length in the next chapter. Since in this chapter I am interested in Gibran as a bilingual writer, I now turn to his late Arabic writings, and particularly to his essay 'Mustaqbal al-lugha al-ʿarabiyya' (The Future of the Arabic Language). This essay testifies to and exemplifies his relentless preoccupation with the Arab East as a civilisational space, even when he was writing poetry exclusively in English in the 1920s. I underscore this aspect in relation to his bilingualism: namely, to what each language represented and meant for him as a bilingual writer.

In 'The Future of the Arabic Language' – first published in 1920 in the periodical *al-Hilāl* as an interview and republished as an essay in *al-Badāʾiʿ wa al-ṭarāʾif* – Gibran lends utmost significance to what he calls the 'the power of invention',[95] which for him stands as the basis upon which the future of the

Arabic language is ultimately contingent. 'Language is one manifestation of the power of invention in a nation's totality or collective self', he writes. 'But if this power were to subside', he goes on, 'language would halt in its progress. In such a halt lies regression, and in regression lies death and extinction'.[96] The notion that language is a collective manifestation of national progress and moral health, and therefore in need of reform and rejuvenation, was widespread in the *Nahḍa*. It is reflected, for instance, in 'Abd al-Qadir Maghribi's *Kitāb al-ishtiqāq wa-l-ta'rīb* (The Book of Derivation and Arabicisation, 1908) and Jurji Zaydan's *al-Lugha al-'arabiyya kā'in ḥayy* (The Arabic Language is a Living Being, 1904), both of whom, like Gibran, postulate this conception of language by invoking the evolutionary principle of survival of the fittest.[97] What is this 'power of invention'? 'It is genius individually and vigour collectively. And individual genius is nothing other than the ability to transform the people's latent dispositions into visible and perceptible forms'.[98] It is not difficult to discern in this statement the idea of national spirit or *Volksgeist*, predominant in post-Enlightenment Romanticism, which shaped – among other factors – the emergence of modern nation-states.[99] Yet, what is peculiar here is that individual genius, albeit universal, becomes the expression of collective or national life.[100] That is, the collective power of *al-umma* can be only expressed through, and embodied in, individual genius, so that the particularity of the nation/civilisation becomes simultaneously universal, with poetry taking on a new meaning and function in this equation.

Gibran warns that, unless invention is present 'in all the nations that speak Arabic, the future [of Arabic] will be like the present of its two sisters – Syriac and Classical Hebrew'.[101] He predicates his argument, unsurprisingly, on the poet as at once an epitome and a metaphor for *ibtikār* (invention), such that the figure of the poet becomes everything which an imitator is not. The poet, for him, is 'the language's father and mother', and if so, he argues, 'the imitator is its shroud weaver and gravedigger'.[102] The poet is, by definition, 'every inventor, major or minor, every discoverer, strong or weak, every creator, great or lowly, every lover of pure life, priestly or wretched, and everyone who stands in awe before the days and nights, philosopher or vineyard keeper'.[103] The life and revival of the language and, by extension, the countries in which this language is spoken,[104] are contingent on the poetic – that is, in Gibran's logic, the inventive as opposed to the imitative – energy and rigour of its speakers, not solely in poetry or writing but, as Gibran's stretched metaphor of the poet indicates, in every domain of life. What this means is that poetry becomes more than the act of producing poems: poetry now manifests and attests to the power of turning the invisible spirit of the people into 'visible and perceptible forms'. This Romantic conception of poetry – which exceeds Romanticism as a 'movement' in its transformation of the very concept and function of literature in modernity[105] – means that language now is understood as the expression of the life or being of its speakers, the language that survives and thrives by virtue of expressing, through individual genius, the collective spirit of *al-umma*. This is why the absence of invention in this particular sense results in imitation; that is, the regression of a language incapable of transforming and embodying *al-umma*'s latent spirit. What is more, the 'power of invention', as 'hunger, thirst, and a desire for the unknown',[106] is that which would liberate the Arab self from being hostage to its own identitarian closure – namely, to its past as the sole horizon for its *raison d'être*. Language should never cease to be regenerated by the individual creativity of its speakers, upon whom now is incumbent the task of opening up language to its potentiality of *ibtikār* and *iḥdāth*. This is because, to quote Yacine Nourani in his analysis of the national ideology of language as self-generating in the reformist project of the *Nahḍa*, 'if the language fails to grow, it reflects the passivity, the internal moral failure of its speakers'.[107]

Gibran employs the image of the poet, so steeped in Arab culture, by extending it to encompass every domain of social, cultural and economic life, with the underlying aim of 'reviving' the Arab civilisation. In this regard, Gibran must be seen as pursuing the Arab *Nahḍa*'s intellectual trajectory. Although he does not embrace the rationalist paradigm that some of the prominent *Nahḍa* intellectuals and reformers espoused,[108] he cannot but consider the West, as did the *Nahḍa* reformers, to be leading the 'procession' of history which the Arabs had led in the past, and in whose 'rear' they now 'march'. Unlike some of the *Nahḍa* reformers, however, Gibran does not regard the West as *the* model of civilisation and progress. In other words, the civilisational trajectory that the Arabs would carve out for themselves, so Gibran argues, should not take as its model that of the West. The revival of this civilisation should rather spring from within, from the Arabic language itself as the locus of its speakers' 'power of invention'. Any borrowing from the West or the Arabo-Islamic past is inevitable, but this inevitability entails an alert, critical attitude. This Gibranian stance is at odds with the *Nahḍa*'s positivist and rationalist epistemology of 'civilisation and progress', which embroiled modern Arab subjectivity in a strained Hegelian interaction with the West and its colonial modernity.[109] Yet Gibran's essay, it must be remembered, was written when Greater Syria fell into the hands of colonial France and Britain, resulting in the well-known partition of the area whose effects are still felt today. His concern for the future of the Arabic language is therefore not only reflective of the primacy of Arabic for him. It is, most importantly, part of a resistance movement that sought to ward off the colonial and cultural influence of the West on the Arabs, who must preserve their particularity by generating the power of invention necessary for their civilisational survival – that is to say, by realising through individual genius the universal potentiality that this Arab particularity still possesses.

Gibran goes as far as defending the dialects and foresees, albeit soberly, their integration into the 'body of *al-fusḥa* [the standard]' by drawing on the example of the creative use of Italian by Dante, Petrarch and St Francis of Assisi, as well as its decisive role, as he sees it, in transforming Italian from a vernacular into a standard language. Towards the end of the essay, Gibran makes a plea for an Eastern originality in Arabic literature which breaks with the outdated modes of poetics that are no longer able to answer to the (then) Arab social, political and cultural *status quo*:

> If you take pride in your aversion to writing in traditional poetic forms – like the praise poem, eulogy, and felicitation – it is better for you and for the language to die shunned and despised than to give up your hearts as burnt offerings to icons and idols. If you have a nationalist passion for portraying Eastern life in a way that reveals its marvels of pain and joy alike, it is better for you and for the language to take as your subject the simplest phenomenon in your native surroundings than to Arabize the grandest and most magnificent of what Westerners have written.[110]

I wish to stress two points here. First, 'nationalist passion' for Gibran becomes a strategic incentive for rejuvenating Arabic literature in that its subject-matter should derive from the local life and surroundings of the Arab subject. To put it differently, 'nationalist passion' should encourage an *ibtikār* of national language rooted in the local imagination, itself contingent on the material conditions of the present and detached from the past; that is, from traditionalism insofar as it perpetuates modes of expression that are unable to articulate the present of the Arab subject in its yearning for a better future. Second, this national literature, however modest, becomes, according to Gibran, better than any translation of Western literature, however great. Gibran might be alluding to Lutfi al-Manfaluti, whose rather 'unfaithful' and 'domesticating' adaptations of French literature[111] marked the Arab literary scene at the time. But why is Gibran, arguably one of the pioneers of Arab literary modernity whose work in Arabic exhibits many 'Western' influences, dismissive of translation and supportive of a notion of Arabic literature that is premised, albeit strategically, on an Arab national spirit? Was the kind of literature that he wrote possible at all without the influence of modern Western literature? Gibran is not referring to modern forms of literature whose provenance is undeniably European, but to literature's capacity to articulate the local reality and imagination of the Arab subject and, more importantly, to express the spirit of a people through individual genius. And this feeds into his emphasis, as discussed at length in Chapter Three, on moral autonomy (*al-istiqlāl al-maʿnawī*) as the requisite foundation of an original *Nahḍa* in both poetics and politics. The autonomous realisation of this creative capacity would thereby preserve the Arab cultural and social particularity but in a literary form whose 'universality' is taken for granted. In response to a question regarding the influence of Western civilisation on the Arabic language, Gibran writes:

> The spirit of the West is both our friend and enemy: a friend if we subdue it, and an enemy if it subdues us. A friend if we open our hearts to it, and an enemy if we surrender our hearts to it. A friend if we take from it what agrees with us, and an enemy if we put ourselves in a position to agree with it.[112]

This passage should be read in its proper colonial historical context.[113] Gibran espouses a critical version of nationalism and a poetics of language whose inventiveness should come exclusively from within the (re)sources of the Arab self. Translation without innovation is undesirable and must be avoided. Cautious and critical borrowing, however, is preferable – indeed recommended – because the 'ingenuous' Western civilisation, 'marching on its [life's] frontline', necessarily exerts influence on the nations 'walking at the procession's end', the inevitable imitators.[114] Is not this cautious borrowing of 'what agrees with us' an instrumentalisation? Since the Arabs are no longer at the forefront of the civilisational procession, dispossessed of the agential and civilisational capacity to influence the Other, the sole means for their language and literature to thrive is through an inventive borrowing that would not eclipse their own particularity. Otherwise, the 'enemy' would simply 'subdue' them. Put succinctly, cautious borrowing in this Western age is ineluctable, yet a critical and autonomous spirit must accompany it.

The bilingual Gibran, who in the same year published *The Forerunner* in English, is a staunch defender of the Arabic language. Its survival, as he sees it, depends on 'the power of invention' as the individual expression of the Arab *umma*. Imitation, of the past or the West, would cause the regression and death of the language and, for that matter, of its speakers. This would be understandable if Gibran were a monolingual writer. His bilingualism, however, means that English for him – the second acquired language – is necessarily and unsurprisingly secondary in its cultural and civilisational importance. But if it holds this secondary importance, which does not mean that it is unimportant, then this is because it is simply not 'the language of the mother'. So, what happens to the latter when one writes in the adopted language? Does writing in the second language necessarily entail or presuppose the forgetting of the first? Gibran writes in the second language, the language of the civilisation that 'adopted' him,[115] only by remembering the mother, by returning to the mother, by perpetuating the mother. The language of the mother must be maintained, and this maintenance is the condition of writing in the second language. In other words, writing in the adopted language depends on the active remembrance and maintenance of the first. Thus, to write as a poet in English, for Gibran, requires the active preservation of Arabic, the tongue that lost its universal force but that nevertheless still retains, and is able to realise, its potential for universality – which hinges on the inventive spirit of its speakers insofar as it expresses their moral autonomy.

Yet, to write as an Arab writer in English, to express the universality of the prophetic in a Western language as an Arab writer, requires at once an assiduous effort of self-translation – translation in the sense of carrying oneself across from one language to another,[116] a transformation whose outcomes would go beyond the 'intentions' of the self-translated writer – and a struggle for recognition in the cultural space that 'adopted' him. This recognition would assuage the anxiety and affliction of living in a country which is not his own and writing in a language which is not his native, and it would further mitigate those adverse aspects of exile that are deliberately marginalised in the liberal cosmopolitan imagination of the metropolis,[117] but only at the cost of cultural translation. As an Arab, Oriental immigrant in that linguistic and cultural location, Gibran faced the double challenge of writing well in the adopted language and gaining the cosmopolitan recognition of the culture that adopted him. To adopt, therefore, a language whose 'civilisation' is leading the procession of history is to be willy-nilly adopted by its culture. How would this culture adopt him then, he who writes in the name of the madman, the forerunner and the prophet, those prophetic, post-religious poets who set out to demolish the new gods of modernity by announcing a poetic – anti-positivist and irreducible – dwelling in the world? I will address this question in detail in Chapter Four; suffice it for now to point out that this culture would essentially adopt him as an Oriental, as an outsider who speaks in the name of (who speaks, as it were) the Orient, in an Occidental cultural sphere. I am here speaking of the Orient as fashioned in the imperial imagination of the Occident: essentially mystical, mysterious and strange, the simultaneously threatening and desirable Outside that is constitutive, by virtue of its domesticated distance, of the self-definition of the Occident itself.

Thus, by writing in the adopted language Gibran is not so much seen as linguistically and culturally different as ontologically distinct, because 'Oriental', from the Occidental culture. Filtered through the discursive prism of the host(ile) culture, he becomes the incarnation of the Oriental as an essentially different Other. In other words, far from being the universally equal Other whose essence remains inaccessible and unamenable to the appropriation of the same, he is automatically categorised and appropriated as a cultural Other. This means that his text would be culturally mis-translated – that is, understood and interpreted in culturalist and reductionist terms, not in universal, literary terms (for a detailed analysis, see Chapter Four). Yet his text, as a self-translated text, as a bilingual offspring, cannot be reduced to an Oriental, identitarian designation. The Orient, rather, functions as an identitarian entity that veils the text itself and haunts it, so to speak, that predetermines the understanding and interpretation of the text by reducing it to an imagined essence and genealogy: the Orient itself; while the latter remains one discursive element, among others, in the multi-layered act of reading, understanding and interpretation. This means that, in a Euro-American cultural context, both the specificity and universality of his prophetic vision as a poet *and* the Orient as identitarian veil would simultaneously and paradoxically inhabit his English text, two elements that should *not* be confused with one another, but that ought to be hermeneutically uncovered and critically unveiled, respectively.

I wish to finish this section by discussing one of Gibran's powerful prose poems in English, 'My Friend', published in *The Madman*. This is a text that offers us the possibility of closely reading it in relation to what I have been discussing so far: namely, the questions of the literary text, identity as a mask or veil and what lies beneath or beyond any bilingual or bicultural chasm. I am, in a manner of speaking, thinking with literature – with Gibran's texts *as* literature – about his own enterprise as a bilingual writer. Who is this friend that the Anglophone Gibran is addressing in the prose poem? And why friendship? We should, perhaps, not so much inquire about 'who' the friend is – that is, his 'identity' – as about what the madman is saying to this hypothetical friend:

> My friend, I am not what I seem. Seeming is but a garment I wear – a care-woven garment that protects me from thy questionings and thee from my negligence.
>
> The 'I' in me, my friend, dwells in the house of silence, and therein it shall remain for ever more, unperceived, unapproachable.[118]

Seeming and being, the madman is saying, are two different things. We may conjecture that this friend has mistaken the madman's 'garment' for his being. The madman therefore responds by revealing in a prose poem addressed to this friend, that his being, his 'I', remains 'unperceived' and 'unapproachable', irrespective of his 'garment'. But the garment protects the madman from the friend's questionings and protects the friend from the madman's negligence. Does this mean that without the garment the madman would neglect the curiosity of the friend, that the 'care-woven' garment – that is, identity – is a necessary tool of protecting the self from the Other and the Other from the self? The madman goes as far as telling the friend that he would not have him understand his 'seafaring thoughts', visit him in his Hell, 'hear the songs of [his] darkness nor see [his] wings beating against the stars'[119] at night. The prose poem, paradoxically, discloses all this to the friend. It informs him that not only is he unable to perceive and approach the essence of the madman, but also that he is everything the madman is not, although even when the friend calls him 'across the unbridgeable gulf, "My companion, my comrade"', the madman would call back 'My friend, my comrade'.[120] We may infer that the friend is the hypothetical Other, perhaps his American reader – since the poem is written in English and published in the US – but also the human Other in general. What Gibran is saying is that the 'I' remains essentially inaccessible to the Other, irrespective of the cultural and social garments that we wear, irrespective of the language that we use or inhabit. In other words, ipseity – the 'I' – precedes identity and remains 'unperceived' and 'unapproachable', regardless of the identity of the friend and whether one shares it with her or not. Nevertheless, identity remains a necessary protective 'garment', but nothing more than a garment. We should therefore ask: Why would the madman reveal that which he does not want the friend to see, hear, visit or understand? Why would he say to his friend, 'thou art good and cautious and wise; thou art perfect – and I too, speak with thee wisely and cautiously. And yet I am mad. *But I mask my madness.* I would be mad alone'?[121] Can we reveal, in writing, that which we mask because, paradoxically, we do not want it to be seen? The mask, thus, does not mask the 'I' but the 'madness' of the 'I' – that is, its different mode of reason. After all, the madman is he who lost his masks, who belongs to himself without pre-fashioned masks, but when he is with his friend, he has to mask his madness again and announce, paradoxically, that he would mask it; that is to say, that he 'would be mad alone'[122] to protect the friend from his negligence. The madman, however, does not seem to care about the way in which the friend perceives and approaches, not his 'I', but his garment. Is this because 'seeming' is inessential, secondary and only necessary because protective? If 'seeming' is inessential but necessary, does this also apply to the identity of Gibran as an Arab, 'Oriental' writer in English?

What I wish to emphasise, before I address this question, is that writing becomes both the mask and that which the mask is masking. That is, writing reveals, not the madness behind the mask, but the mask in its masking of the madness: 'I am not what I seem', but I mask it nonetheless! It is the text that reveals what it simultaneously conceals, that which, in its essence, cannot be revealed: the inaccessibility of the 'I'. But this text is written in English, in Gibran's adopted language, which masks both his native language and his individual style in that native language. The point is that the language in which the text is written is not reducible to the 'culture' that appropriates it as its 'own', that adopts the foreign writer who adopts this language as a language of writing, and that close attention to the text and what it reveals and conceals would 'protect' it from being reduced to its own 'garment', from the reader who would mistake seeming for being. And because we cannot approach and perceive being as such, we can nevertheless approach that which lies between seeming and being – across one language and another, one culture and another – both of which, like form and content, or identity and ipseity, remain indissociable. Thus, the chasm becomes primarily interpretative, not culturalist or identitarian. The chasm would cease to be an essentially bilingual one: 'My friend, thou are not my friend, but how shall I make thee understand? My path is not thy path, yet together we walk, hand in hand'.[123]

Gibran's 'path', as a versatile bilingual writer, is thus necessarily multiplied. In the creative multiplicity of Gibran's path, I have ferried from the aesthetics of his early Arabic text to its poetics of the universal, from the uneasy decision to write in English to the challenging double enterprise of being a poet in English and committing to the national and civilisational cause of Syria and the Arab East, respectively, in Arabic. The latter, as a crucial facet of his literary and intellectual enterprise, will attract my focused attention in the next chapter. What this chapter has meant to show is that the universal and the particular in Gibran's bilingual enterprise coexist and depend on one another in ways that are not readily perceptible, albeit not without inevitable tensions. What I have been calling the bilingual chasm is that space between one language and another which simultaneously allows for the creativity of the 'foreigner' and subjects her to the identitarian reason of the host(ile) culture. Gibran's case is illustrative of this tension, yet his text, as a literary text, betrays that what is at stake here is as much about bilingualism – dwelling in two divergent linguistic and cultural spheres – as it is about hermeneutics: the subtle hostility of culture can be countered with a critical hospitality of reading.

Notes

1 Gibran, *Iqlib al-ṣafḥa yā fatā: Makhṭūṭāt lam tunshar* (Turn the Page: Hitherto Unpublished Manuscripts), ed. Wahib Kayruz and Antoine Khuri Tuq (Lebanon: Gibran's National Committee, 2010), 20 [emphasis mine]. The friend to whom Gibran is speaking here is not specified.

2 Jacques Derrida, *Monolingualism of the Other, or the Prosthesis of Origin*, trans. Patrick Mensah (Palo Alto: Stanford University Press, 1998), 40 [emphasis in the original].

3 KG to MH, 21 June 1918.

4 See Sabry Hafez, *The Genesis of Arabic Narrative Discourse: A Study in the Sociology of Modern Arabic Literature* (London: Saqi Books, 1993), 170.

5 Derrida, *Monolingualism*, 58.

6 This is one of his most valuable and enduring contributions to modern Arabic Literature. See Salma Khadra Jayyusi (ed.), *Modern Arabic Poetry: An Anthology* (New York: Columbia University Press, 1987), 4–5. For more on the particularities of this style, see Khalil Hawi, 'Analysis of his Form and Style', in *Kahlil Gibran: His Background, Character and Works* (Beirut: The Arab Institute for Research and Publishing, 1972), 244–77.

7 Derrida has famously coined the term *différance,* which 'is not a word or concept', but the 'the possibility of conceptuality', the difference and deferral of signification that disrupts the signifier/signified duality, whereby the signifier is secondary to the signified (the referent, the concept), and erupts writing or *écriture* – the Latin verb *differre,* in French *différer,* has two distinct words in English, *to defer* and *to differ*. It is here understood as embedded in Gibran's literary text by way of metaphor; that is, the signifiers in this text are made different and deferred by means of an excess of metaphor and imagery. See Jacques Derrida, 'Différance', in *The Margins of Philosophy*, trans. Alan Bass (Brighton: Harvester Press, 1982), 1–29.

8 There is no need for 'deconstructing' the text here, since the literary text – the narrative one in particular – already incorporates the problematic of writing into its very structure, as Edward Said has shown in another context. See Said, *The World*, 192–94.

9 This essay was originally written in 1907, the first essay that Gibran wrote for a newspaper. See Mas'ud Habib, *Jubrān ḥayyan wa mayyitan* (Gibran in his Life and Death) (Beirut: Dār al-Rihāni, 1966), 31.

10 *CWs in Arabic*, 141 [emphasis mine]. I sometimes rely on H. M. Nahmad's translation of *Dam'a wa ibtisāma* into English, only to adjust and refine it, a translation in which the Arabic is made to resemble, as much as possible, Gibran's style in English. This is an approach with which I take issue because the poetic nature of Gibran's Arabic prose, which remains untranslatable, is often replaced, in translation, by a prose poetry whose English is made to sound like Gibran's other English writings. This is an attempt to be 'faithful' to Gibran's English texts and readers by being 'unfaithful' to the particularity of his Arabic mode of writing.

11 Ibid.

12 Ibid.

13 I am not arguing for the 'purity' and 'exceptionality' of the original in the context of translation, but one should be aware of Abdelfattah Kilito's injunction 'Thou Shalt Not Translate Me' – that is, that the untranslatable is that which, defying translation, demands an inexhaustible translational effort. See Abdelfattah Kilito, *Je parle toutes les langues, mais en arabe* (I Speak all Languages, but in Arabic) (Arles: Sindbad-Actes Sud, 2013), 53–55.

14 *CWs in Arabic*, 141 [emphasis mine].

15 See Muhammad Chaouki Zine, 'Tafkīkiyyat Ibn 'Arabi: al-ta'wīl, al-ikhtilāf, al-kitāba' (Ibn Arabi's Deconstruction: Hermeneutics, Difference, Writing), *Kitābāt Mu'āṣira* (Contemporary Writings) 36, no. 9 (March 1999): 53–59.

16 Gibran, writing about music as seen in Greek and Roman mythology, recognises that what had been said and believed about music in ancient times is now deemed 'myths created by illusions'. Yet, in a patently Romantic gesture, he wonders rhetorically: 'what would harm us if we called those [ancient] stories a *poetic exaggeration* created by the subtlety of emotions and the love of beauty. Is this not, in the custom [*'urf*] of poets, poetry itself?' *CWs in Arabic*, 12 [emphasis mine].

17 Ibid., 10 [emphasis mine].

18 Ibid.

19 See Fatima Qandil, *al-Rāwī al-shabaḥ: Shi'riyyat al-kitāba fī nuṣūs Jubrān Khalīl Jubrān* (The Spectral Narrator: The Poetics of Writing in the Texts of Gibran Khalil Gibran) (Cairo: Dār al-'Ayn li al-Nashr, 2015), 13.

20 *CWs in Arabic*, 10.

21 Jacques Derrida, *Dissemination*, trans. Barbara Johnson (London: The Athlone Press: 1981), especially 53.

22 *CWs in Arabic*, 12.

23 On the ambiguity of what the tongue of Adam means, see Abdelfattah Kilito, *The Tongue of Adam*, trans. Robyn Creswell (New York: New Directions Paperwork: 2016), 3–6.

24 Ibid., 53.

25 Muhammad Jamal Barut, 'al-Ḥadātha al-'ūla: Mushkilāt qaṣīdat al-nathr min Jubrān ilā majallat *Shi'r*, al-juz' al-'awwal' (The First Modernity: The Problem of the Prose Poem from Gibran to the Journal of *Shi'r*, Part I), *al-Ma'rifa* no. 283–84 (1 September 1985), 128. Barut sees in Gibran 'the first enzyme of the meaning of poetic modernism', which matured with the well-known movement of the journal of *Shi'r* that was led by such important poets as Yusuf al-Khal, Adonis, Unsi al-Haj and others.

26 See Salma Khadra Jayyusi, 'Modernist Poetry in Arabic', in *Modern Arabic Literature*, ed. by M. M. Badawi (Cambridge: Cambridge University Press: 1992), 143.

27 Ibid.

28 Ibid.

29 See Adonis, 'Jubrān Khalīl Jubrān', 156.

30 Gibran celebrates in some of his short essays what he deems 'rebellious' figures in the history of Arabic poetry and thought, such as al-Maʿarri, the author of *Risālat al-ghufrān* (The Epistle of Forgiveness), and Abu Nuwas, the poet who is often described as 'decadent' (*mājin*). See *al-Majmū'a al-kāmila: Nuṣūs khārij al-majmū'a*, 40–45 and 66–68.

31 Adonis does not posit the 'modern' against the 'ancient'. For him, 'modern' poets such as Gibran and al-Sayyab (1926–64) 'share a poetic house with the "ancients" Imru'l-Qays and Tarafa Ibn al-ʿAbd (538–64), and with Abu Nawas and Abu Tamam who were "modern" in relation to the pre-Islamic poets but are today considered "ancients" when judged in terms of chronological time. All of these poets come together, beyond the simple categories of modern and ancient, in the single melting pot of poetic creativity, to form what I call the entirety of authentic Arabic poetry, or, from a historical point of view, "the second modernity"'. In other words, the modern, within a particular literary tradition, is essentially creative, irrespective of chronological time. See Adonis, *An Introduction to Arab Poetics* (London: Saqi Books, 1999), 98–102.

32 For a conceptual elaboration on the possible complementariness of patriotism and cosmopolitanism, see Pauline Kleingeld, *Kant and Cosmopolitanism: The Philosophical Ideal of a World Citizenship* (Cambridge: Cambridge University Press, 2012), 26.

33 *CWs in Arabic*, 192 [emphasis mine].

34 There is no English equivalent to the Arabic word *al-bashar*, whose etymology – it is derived from *bashara* (skin) – suggests those whose skin is visible; that is, human beings.

35 Ibid. [emphasis mine].

36 Ibid., 192–93.

37 Kleingeld, *Kant and Cosmopolitanism*, 26.

38 *CWs in Arabic*, 193.

39 Ibid., 193 [emphasis mine].

40 Quoted in Seyla Benhabib, *The Rights of Others: Aliens, Residents and Citizens* (Cambridge: Cambridge University Press, 2005), 27.

41 I am here referring to Derrida's reading of Levinas regarding hospitality: 'The implacable law of hospitality: the hôte who receives (the host), the one who welcomes the invited or the received hôte (the guest), the welcoming hôte who considers himself the owner of the place, is in truth a hôte received in his own home. He receives the hospitality that he offers in his home; he receives it from his own home – which, in the end, does not belong to him. The hôte as host is a guest. The dwelling opens itself to itself, to its "essence" without essence, as a "land of asylum or refuge"'. Jacques Derrida, *Adieu to Emmanuel Levinas*, trans. Pascale-Anne Brault and Michel Naas (Palo Alto: Stanford University Press, 1999), 41.

42 Ibid. [emphasis in the original]. The French *hôte* is the word for both host and guest.

43 I must note that the imperative of hospitality towards the guest as traveller is steeped in Islam as religion, tradition and culture, and Gibran must have been aware of that. As Mona Siddiqui points out, 'Islam holds hospitality as a virtue that lies at the very basis of the Islamic ethical system, a concept rooted in the pre-Islamic Bedouin virtues of welcome and generosity in the harsh desert environment. The concept can be found in the Arabic root *ḍayāfa*. The Prophet is reported to have said, "There is no good in the one who is not hospitable"'. Mona Siddiqui, *Hospitality and Islam: Welcoming in God's Name* (New Haven; London: Yale University Press, 2015), 10–11.

44 Paul De Man, *Blindness and Insight: Essays in the Rhetoric of Contemporary Criticism* (New York: Oxford University Press, 1976).

45 *CWs in Arabic*, 193.

46 Ibid.

47 Ibid.

48 Here is where the influence of the Bible on Gibran is quite manifest, a humanistic understanding of Christianity that goes back to such influential Lebanese reformers in the *Nahḍa* as Butrus al-Bustani and especially Ahmad Faris al-Shidyaq. See Hawi, *Kahlil Gibran*, 46–47.

49 *CWs in Arabic*, 194.

50 Ibid.

51 Ibid., 195 [emphasis added].

52 Ibid.

53 Ibid.

54 For more on Gibran's enormous influence on modern Arabic literature and poetry, see Jayyusi, *Trends and Movements*, 91–107.

55 Gibran and Gibran, *Khalil Gibran: His Life and World*, 313 [emphasis added].

56 Quoted in Steven G. Kellman, *The Translingual Imagination* (Lincoln: University of Nebraska Press, 2000), x.

57 Ibid.

58 Ibid., 16.

59 Gibran and Gibran, *Kahlil Gibran: His Life and World*, 370.

60 Ibid.

61 For a very brief survey of the early criticism and interpretation that the poem invited, as well as a critical reading of it, see Hawi, *Kahlil Gibran*, 219–22.

62 'Abbas Mahmud al-ʿAqqad, '*al-Mawākib*', in *al-Fuṣūl* (Cairo: Hindāwi, 2014 [1922]), 50.

63 Hawi, *Kahlil Gibran*, 220–22.

64 *CWs in Arabic*, 205. Some of the final lines of the poem, including the above, were famously turned into a song by the legendary Lebanese singer Feiruz.

65 No wonder that it is music that celebrates nature here – *al-Mūsīqa* was Gibran's first published work – in that in music the form itself is the content, the idea its expression, the soul its body: no gulf between sense and meaning; no dualism. For an insightful analysis of the poem in the context of Arab Romanticism, see Ihsan ʿAbbas and Muhammad Yusuf Najm, *al-Shiʿr al-ʿarabī fi-l-mahjar: Amīrca al-shamāliyya*, 3rd edition (Beirut: Dār Ṣādir, 1982), 41–49.

66 I touch upon this issue in section two of Chapter Four.

67 MH Journal, 6 May 1918 [emphasis mine].

68 Kilito, *Je parle toutes les langues*, 50.

69 Gibran and Gibran, *Kahlil Gibran: His Life and World*, 363–64 [emphasis added].

70 Abdelfattah Kilito, *The Author and His Doubles*, trans. Michael Cooperson (Syracuse: Syracuse University Press, 2001), 108.

71 See Waïl S. Hassan, 'Introduction', in Abdelfattah Kilito, *Thou Shalt Not Speak My Language*, trans. Waïl S. Hassan (Syracuse: Syracuse University Press, 2017), xiv, xviii, xix.

72 Derrida, *Monolingualism*, 21–22.

73 Ibid., 86–88.

74 Ibid., 87.

75 Gibran and Gibran, *Kahlil Gibran: His Life and World*, 313.

76 Ibid.

77 If Syriac is dead in Lebanon as a spoken everyday language, it remains the Maronite Church's main liturgical language; see Hawi, *Kahlil Gibran*, 34–35. Gibran is unlikely to have acquired it, but he must have been exposed to it in his childhood. It is worth noting that Syriac had been replaced by Arabic as a literary language in Lebanon since the fifteenth century. The Christian literary revival in the nineteenth century, which deeply influenced Gibran, was an Arabic revival against the generally poor or ineloquent usage of Arabic by Maronite Christians prior to the *Nahḍa*. See Marun 'Abbud, *Saqr Lubnān: Baḥth fi-l-nahḍa al-'adabiyya al-ḥadītha wa rajulihā al-awwal Aḥmad Fāris al-Shidyāq* (Lebanon's Falcon: A Study of the Modern Arab Renaissance and its First Man: Ahmad Faris al-Shidyaq) (Beirut: Dār al-Makshūf, 1950), 47–48. Many of the *Nahḍa*'s early pioneers were proficient in Syriac, Arabic and at least two European languages. See Marun 'Abbud, *Ruwwād al-nahḍa al-ḥadītha* (The Pioneers of the Modern Renaissance) (Qairo: Hindawi, 2015 [1952]), 22.

78 These texts, which were published in *al-Funūn*, include: 'al-Layl wa al-majnūn' (Night and the Madman) (July 1916, 97), 'al-Falakī' (The Astronomer) (December 1917, 673), 'al-Namlāt al-thalāth' (The Three Ants) (February 1917, 781), 'al-Ḥakīmān' (The Two Learned Men) (November 1917, 275) and 'Bayna faṣl wa faṣl' (Said a Blade of Grass) (November 1917, 275). See Hawi, *Kahlil Gibran*, 179.

79 Gibran and Gibran, *Kahlil Gibran: His Life and World*, 242.

80 See, for instance, MH to KG, 20 October 1917; KG to MH, 5 February 1918; MH to KG, 10 February 1918; KG to MH, 29 May 1918; MH to KG, 31 May

1918; KG to MH, 5 June 1918; MH to KG, 9 June 1918; KG to MH, 11 June 1918; and KG to MH, 11 July 1918. Gibran famously dedicated his *al-Ajniḥa al-mutakassira* to Mary Haskell: 'TO THE ONE who stares at the sun with glazed eyes and grasps the fire with untrembling fingers and hears the spiritual time of Eternity I dedicate this book. – Gibran'. Kahlil Gibran, *The Broken Wings*, trans. A. R. Ferris (London: Heinemann, 1959).

81 Hawi, *Kahlil Gibran*, 35.

82 Derrida, *Adieu*, 24.

83 Ibid. [emphasis in the original].

84 See Heidegger, 'Letter on Humanism', in *Basic Writings*, ed. D. F. Krell (London: Routledge: 1978), 217.

85 See Muhammad Chaouki Zine, 'al-Hijra, al-maskūniyya, al-manzil al-mafqūd: 'Anāṣir fī hājis al-gharāba' (Migration, Habitability and the Lost Home: Elements in the Apprehension of *Heimlich*), *Majallat Yatafakkarūn* no. 11 (2017): 14–31.

86 Ibid., 20.

87 Ibid.

88 'But since everything must begin by some *yes,* the response begins, the response commands'. Derrida, *Adieu*, 240 [emphasis in the original].

89 Richard E. Hishmeh, 'Strategic Genius, Disidentification, and the Burden of *The Prophet* in Arab-American Poetry', in *Arab Voices in Diaspora: Critical Perspectives on Anglophone Arab Literature*, ed. Layla Al Maleh (Amsterdam; New York: Rodopi, 2009), 65–92.

90 Gibran once wrote to Mary Haskell: 'English is not the language for parables, but one is apt to find faults with his tools when he cannot use them well. The fault lies within me. But I *will* learn how write in English'. KG to MH, 16 May 1916 [emphasis in the original].

91 The Orient as an identitarian category here precedes and predetermines the literary value of the text. See my analysis, in Chapter Four, of the early reception of Gibran's works in the US; in particular, *The Nation*'s review of *The Madman* and *Poetry*'s reviews of *The Forerunner* and *The Prophet.* See also, Waterfield, *Prophet*, 216.

92 Every culture, *as* culture, does that, but it becomes problematic when it is carried out in essentialist, racialist and hierarchical terms.

93 Which does not mean, crucially, that the Oriental was not able to question it. The point is that the identification, because ubiquitous, was almost impossible to avoid.

94 Gibran emigrated to the United States in 1895, returned to Lebanon in 1898 to study Arabic, and in 1902 went back to America where he lived – apart from an interval of two years in Paris – until his demise in 1931.

95 *CWs in Arabic*, 317. I rely, with some necessary alterations, on Angela Giordani's translation of the essay in El-Aris (ed.), *The Arab Renaissance*, 50–67. I will cite the Arabic text when I depend on my own translation.

96 *CWs in Arabic*, 317.

97 See Yaseen Noorani, 'Hard and Soft Multilingualism', *Critical Multilingualism Studies* 1, no. 2 (2013): 20–21.

98 Ibid.

99 See Aziz Al-Azmeh, *Islams and Modernities* (London; New York: Verso, 2009), 31, 99–102.

100 This is something that Jacques Rancière also discerns in another modern context, that of France and Europe in the nineteenth century. Poetry, in the Romantic revolution of modernity, becomes a 'mode of language' that hinges on the principle of expression, not representation. This means that 'Romantic genius is that of an individual insofar as it is also that of a place, a time, a people, a history'. See Jacques Rancière, *Mute Speech: Literature, Critical Theory, and Politics*, trans. James Swenson (New York: Columbia University Press: 2011), 69.

101 *CWs in Arabic*, 317.

102 Gibran, 'The Future of the Arabic Language', 58.

103 Ibid.

104 As far as Arabic is concerned, we cannot speak, *stricto senso*, of 'national' literature in the modern European sense of the term. Arabic literature (*adab*), which predates modernity – Arabic as a language has not witnessed a dramatic transformation in and after modernity; the Qur'ān or any premodern text in Arabic is legible and comprehensible to the modern Arabic reader, albeit with some difficulty – cannot be understood as strictly confined to one particular national state. It is, in a sense, already transnational; or, perhaps more accurately, the 'colonial' birth of the modern nation-state in the 'Arab world' has transformed Arabic from a pre-national cosmopolitan language into a trans-national one.

105 Rancière, *Mute Speech*, 68–70.

106 Gibran, 'The Future of the Arabic Language', 52.

107 See Noorani. 'Hard and Soft Multilingualism', 24.

108 See Sheehi, *Foundations*, 24–25.

109 Ibid., 33–36.

110 Gibran, 'The Future of the Arabic Language', 11 [emphasis added].

111 Most of the works of Mustafa Lutfi al-Manfaluti (1876–1924), except *al-Naẓarāt*, are Arabised or adapted, rather than translated, versions of French texts, which render them 'faithful' to the Arabic literary tradition by being 'unfaithful' to the original French language and cultural, literary context. al-Manfaluti, after all, did not speak any European language. On the impact of al-Manfaluti's work on modern Arabic literature, see Kilito, *Thou Shalt Not Speak My Language*, 3–5.

112 Gibran, 'The Future of the Arabic Language', 8.

113 The essay is based on *al-Hilāl*'s interview with Gibran in 1920, that is, after the end of World War I and the enactment of the colonial ambitions of France and Britain, concocted in the (in)famous Sykes-Picot Agreement (1916), the content of which had remained secret until after the war. See T. G. Frazer, *The First World War and its Aftermath: The Reshaping of the Middle East* (London: Gingo Library, 2015), 6.

114 In his one-act play, 'al-Ṣilbān', published in *al-'Awāṣif*, the preservation of the supposed 'purity' of Arabic literatures – according to one of the characters, Yusuf Masarrah, a writer and litterateur – would bring about the death of the language and its literatures. 'The old nations which do not benefit from what the new nations produce run the risk of literary death and spiritual extinction', Yusuf responds to Khalil Bik, a government employee who believes that 'the influence of the Western literatures on our language is a pernicious thing'. Gibran, 'al-Ṣilbān', *CWs in Arabic*, 270.

115 See the first epigraph of this chapter.

116 I am drawing on the Latin root *translatio*, which combines *trans* (across) and the past participle of *ferre*, *latio*, meaning 'to carry' or 'to bring'. *Translat* (that is, 'carried across') is the past participle of *transferre*.

117 'Conceiving of exile solely as an engine for the production of cosmopolitan attitudes can, and often does, leave out its other essential aspects: the need to circumscribe one's experience in the constraints of a new cultural framework, the imperative to begin to translate that experience in languages that are often not yet one's own, and to grope one's way through the loss and trauma intrinsic in this process of transition'. See Galin Tihanov, 'Narratives of Exile: Cosmopolitanism Beyond the Liberal Imagination', in *Whose Cosmopolitanism? Critical Perspectives, Relationalities and Discontents*, ed. N. Glick Schiller and A. Irving (New York and Oxford: Berghahn, 2015), 141–59.

118 *CWs*, 7.

119 Ibid.

120 Ibid.

121 Ibid., 8 [emphasis added].

122 Ibid.

123 *CWs*, 8.

3

Gibran as Nationalist and *Nahḍawī*

He who empties his heart from the illusions and false dreams of the Ottoman state only to fill it with the promises and ambitions of the foreign states resembles one who runs from fire to hell. The Syrian has only his self-reliance and his talents, intelligence and excellence to rely on.

Kahlil Gibran[1]

I am a Lebanese and I'm proud of that,
And I'm not an Ottoman and I'm also proud of that.
I have a beautiful homeland of which I'm proud,
And I have a nation with a past –
But there is no state which protects me.
No matter how many days I stay away
I shall remain an Easterner – Easterner in my manners,
Syrian in my desires, Lebanese in my feelings –
No matter how much I admire Western progress.

Kahlil Gibran, 'To the Muslims from a Christian Poet'[2]

By the end of World War I, the Ottoman Empire had fallen and the map of what we today call 'the Middle East' was fundamentally reshaped in accordance with the colonial interests of the then Great Powers, Britain and France. The victory of the Allies left its indelible stamp on the modern history of the area. My interest in this chapter, in relation to Gibran, lies in 'Greater Syria', in the sense of 'geographical Syria' or 'natural Syria', the many names of what has been historically recognised, especially after the dawn of Islam, as *Bilād al-Shām.*[3] This is the geographical space 'stretching from the Taurus

Mountains in the north to the Sinai Peninsula in the south, and from the Mediterranean in the west to the Syrian desert in the east'.[4] It should not be construed, nevertheless, that Syria as a nation in the modern sense has always existed, in a Primordialist or Perennialist sense,[5] although the usage of the name 'Syria', Greek in its form and etymology, can be traced back to the late fifth and early sixth century BC.[6] The emergence of a Syrian national, self-conscious discourse can be discerned in the writings of the *Nahḍa*'s intellectuals, reformers and literati in the latter half of the nineteenth and the early twentieth century; chief among whom, to name but two towering and influential figures, are Butrus al-Bustani and Jurji Zaydan, whose work was paramount in constructing notions of Arab historical consciousness,[7] Arabism and Syrianness.[8] This discourse of 'Awakening' emerged against the background of a politically contentious and turbulent period, marked by European colonial interest and imperial, capitalist expansion, initiated by Napoleon's 1798 invasion of Egypt and the Ottoman struggle to maintain its political and economic control over the area – by introducing and enacting reforms – in the face of a medley of local and foreign challenges. It is this *Nahḍa* discourse that, whether consciously or not, occasions, informs and allows for the emergence of Gibran's nationalist writings. His nationalist engagement cannot be probed, therefore, in isolation from the discursive field that enables its emergence.

This chapter examines Gibran as a nationalist and *Nahḍawī* writer by looking, mostly but not exclusively, at some of the essays, articles and plays that he published in the active early-twentieth-century *Mahjar* press in the United States.[9] These pieces, written in Arabic, display and testify to Gibran's relentless commitment to the Syrian national cause and to the Arab East as a civilisational horizon. The chapter thoroughly examines the politics and ethics of the nation in Gibran. It demonstrates that Gibran's nationalism is imagined and defined *territorially*, in that it is the territory of geographical Syria as a pre-national, pre-state *waṭan* – homeland or dwelling[10] – that grounds this nationalism, not sect, religion or what Anthony Smith calls '*ethnie*'.[11] The question of Syria – its formation as a nation – is entwined with the question of the *Nahḍa* in Gibran. This formation is inextricably linked with liberation – from the Ottoman Empire until its collapse, from Western colonialism, but also from what Gibran refers to as the 'maladies of *taqālid* [old customs and traditions] and *taqlīd* [imitation, of the past or the West]'[12] which, for him, plagued Syria and the Arab East. While I highlight the textual intricacies, the recurrent motifs and the significatory paradoxes that mark this discourse, I situate it within its historical and discursive context. Gibran's specificity, so this chapter argues, lies in his constant emphasis on moral independence (*al-istiqlāl al-maʿnawī*) as the universal condition for the hoped historical ascendancy of Syria and the Arab East as national and civilisational entities, respectively. This emphasis on moral independence explains his wariness of assimilationism into Euro-America as the civilisational telos of history, while stressing the Eastern originality[13] of *ibtikār* or innovation, framed at times in essentialist and social Darwinist terms, seen as *the* prerequisite of a true *Nahḍa*.

In laying bare and discussing this crucial facet of Gibran's work as intellectual, this chapter has the double aim of highlighting that the nation, in the wider sense of Syria and the Arab East, was a fundamental concern for the bilingual writer – as indicated in the previous chapter – and that this concern, insofar as it is essentially ethical, is reconcilable with the universal vision that animates his poetic writings. This is best demonstrated, as my overall argument in this book insists, by paying close attention to his writings as they intervene in their political, cultural and social context without, crucially, reducing them to it.

A caveat should be stressed here. Gibran firmly and consistently believed in the geographical unity of Greater Syria, while remaining sceptical and suspicious of appeals and endeavours aiming to divide the area, even *after* the colonial partition. His well-known essay 'Lakum Lubnānukum wa lia Lubnānī' (You Have Your Lebanon and I Have Mine), published in 1923 (under the French mandate), reflects his acute dismay and disappointment at the kind of politics in which Lebanon was mired in the aftermath of the Mandate and the creation of Greater Lebanon in 1920.[14] The demonstrable idealisation of Lebanon in that essay, rather than being a mere sentimentalising of homeland as is mostly claimed, testifies to his disposition that consists in regarding Lebanon as a *mawṭin* – a homeland in the ideal sense of the term, the attachment to which is spiritual and apolitical, rather than a *patrie* or a nation in the modern, European sense of the term.[15] The potentiality of nation-state realisation for Gibran had been envisioned in Greater Syria before the partition, of which Lebanon was part.[16] This position is pronounced in most of the essays and plays analysed or referred to in this chapter.

'Mother Syria' and the Emergent 'Syrian Idea'

The 'Syrian idea' emerges in Gibran's writings in 1914, particularly in his short play *Bad' thawra* (The Beginning of a Revolution),[17] edited and published by John Daye in 1988.[18] The year 1914 marks the beginning of World War I, and the title reflects that the war was considered an opportunity to liberate Syria from the Ottoman Empire. The two characters of the play, one identified as a Muslim, Ahmad, the other as a Christian, Farid, are engaged in an intense conversation at the Café of the Sea in Beirut on a rainy day in February 1914, over the present and future of Syria as a nation. Farid contends that 'the Syrian idea' has been crystallising for two years, 'expanding against the backdrop of freedom, reform and the noble principles that produced Jean-Jacques Rousseau, Voltaire, Patrick Henry, Garibaldi and several others who lifted freedom as monuments in the heart of the Westerners', only to be thwarted by the 'magical anaesthetic that was concocted by the brains of the Ottoman politicians since the beginning of the nineteenth century'.[19] He goes on to maintain that it is the cunning of the Turks and their acute knowledge of 'the Syrians' acumen and the Arab character' that enables them 'to determine the spot in the Syrian body where the ailment exists, spilling their extracts of deception over it'.[20] Ahmad, however, repudiating this argument, vents his criticism at the Syrians' idiocy, confusion and blindness, because of which the Turks appear to the Syrians in the guise of a cunning plotter. That Farid is using the phrase 'the Syrian idea', and not nationalism (which Gibran elaborately invokes in a later essay), is not surprising: the *emergent* idea denotes the first stage of national consciousness, not identity,[21] necessary for the liberation of Syria from the Ottoman Empire. The idea is still taking shape, because Syria was still part of the empire and because those who advocated liberation from the Ottomans were a minority in comparison with the majority, who were either hesitant or in favour of staying under the protection of the Ottomans, given the burgeoning threat posed by the Western colonial powers at the time.[22]

What is furthermore interesting in the dialogue is that Ahmad's diagnosis of the *status quo* – in which he ascribes idiocy to both sides – lays importance on 'Islam', to the extent that it constitutes the 'body' in which the 'heart' of 'the Arab powers' reside.[23] Castigating and ridiculing both the Turks and the Arabs in bestial terms – he uses the pejorative word '*baghlana*' which, derived from 'mule' or 'donkey', connotes idiocy, mindlessness and stupidity – he asserts that he knew 'the greatness of Islam' when he lived in 'Europe', yet upon returning to his homeland he found himself a stranger among his own people. That, he goes on, has not blinded him, being amongst 'blind Muslims' notwithstanding, to what he describes as 'the glory of Islam'.[24] Islam, for Ahmad, who is in agreement with his friend Farid, is 'an absolute, abstract reality' – that is, one 'that should remain abstracted [*mujarrad*] of the excrescences [*al-zawā'id*] that purge it of determination and life',[25] in the words of the Christian character. Ahmad proceeds to proclaim that, if these 'excrescences' preoccupy the contemporary Muslims, it should not follow that the malady resides in Islam, 'as some Westerners wrongly assume', but precisely in the Muslims:

> Do not forget that Islam is not solely a religion, as English Orientalists like to think, but a religion and a civic law [*sharīʿa madaniyya*] or way of life whose enormous wings encompass all the needs of humankind in every age. The true Muslim, albeit following a spiritual emotion [*ʿāṭifa rūḥiyya*], is an individual in and a member of a civic collectivity and a grand civilisation.[26]

I construe this discourse as a performative one; that is, as an attempt to perform or produce a Syrian, Muslim subject, in agreement with a Syrian, Christian one, on the nature of religion beyond the Orientalist, colonial outlook on Islam as merely a 'religion', and therefore as 'un-culture'.[27] Yet, in the play, Islam is simultaneously posited as trans-historical – namely, abstracted as a metaphysical essence – and civilisational – namely, grounded in and manifesting itself in history – with Muslims, not Islam, seen as the sole cause of their own 'decadence'. This metaphysical binary of trans-historical *essence* and historical *manifestation* permeates Gibran's nationalist and civilisational discourse,[28] partly because it was prevalent at the time.[29] More pertinent to my discussion is the attempt to enact a Syrian sceptical subject who is not only suspicious of the association between Islam and Muslim 'decadence', but also of that established between 'Western civilisation' (*al-madaniyya al-gharbiyya*) and Christianity. When Farid deems Christianity 'a basis for the European and American civilisation',[30] Ahmed demurs, invoking the irreconcilability between the moral teachings of Christianity and the actions of the modern Christians: 'The Christian loves his enemies in the Church, yet outside the Church he is preoccupied with the effective means that would annihilate his enemies', something that stands in stark opposition to 'Islam' that 'teaches and acts in accordance to its teachings'.[31] This should not be read at face-value, as a preference for Islam over Christianity, because it is not religion *per se* that is at stake here. The moral domain was central in pre-modern Islam (as a historical and civilisational reality), whereas in modernity, a historical transformation that witnessed the secularising of Christianity, the moral domain was marginalised, particularly with the rise of the nation-state, the capitalist system and the modern interdependence of knowledge and power.[32] This backdrop helps us understand Ahmad's distinction between Euro-America as a civilisational power that separates the moral and the political, on the one hand, and Islam in its ideal version to which that separation is not constitutive, on the other. In other words, his criticism is an ethical one, however uncritical his invocation of an ideal Islam or a Christian West. Nevertheless, he stresses towards the end of the dialogue his respect for Christianity insofar as it is divorced from the actions of the Western Christians. For 'there was only one Christian [intriguingly invoking Nietzsche] and he died on the cross', adding: 'If Jesus of Nazarene was back to this world [referencing, interestingly, 'Jubrān Khalīl Jubrān'], he would die a stranger, in hunger and solitude'.[33]

Christianity, which Farid deems not solely the basis but the equivalent of Euro-American civilisation, is put into question through the lens of a Muslim character. The latter himself is very critical of Muslims, yet not of Islam as such, which is abstracted as a force that precedes, exceeds and transcends Muslim decadence. In other words, if Islam is severed from the 'decadence' that European Orientalism has 'discovered' in it,[34] it is nevertheless abstracted as an 'essence' irreducible to the 'dormant' Muslims, who are unaware of its enormity. Similarly, Ahmad's anger is vented less on Christianity *per se* than on the colonial wars and looting done in the name of 'the Christian West', on the double standards of this Western Christianity. It is useful to note, in this regard, that the early Gibran considers *al-kulliyya* or universality to be 'a general Christianity',[35] a term – *al-kulliyya* – which he uses to denote cosmopolitanism in the sense of citizens of the earth and which he defines as 'the preservation of the just rights of the self as well as the sacred rights of the Other'.[36] This might explain why Ahmed is averse to the Christian West that does not preserve these 'sacred rights of the Other', this Other who became an object over which European sovereignty presided in colonial modernity. What we observe in the play, thus, is a discursive endeavour to rescue Islam from (Eastern) Muslims and Christianity from (Western) Christians, and to sever 'religion' from (indeed to reimagine an 'essence' of religion beyond) Orientalism and imperialism. In other words, the version of religion proposed here is one that seeks to transcend its historical and political configuration or 'deformation' in modernity. It is one that aims to rescue what it takes to be the nature of religion, whose essence is irreducible to its manifestation in history, but whose civilisational worldliness, in the case of Islam, is yet to be reactualised.[37]

The occasional essentialism of this discourse aside, what is intriguing in the play is that twice do the characters refer to Gibran in the text. Ahmad regards him as an exaggerator who 'gazes at the Eastern condition from behind a black cloud',[38] while appealing to Farid who, in turn, declares that he used to deem him a pessimist. The self-referentiality of the play is not coincidental. The play serves as a platform on which ideas of reform, channelled through critique and debate between Syrian 'Muslims' and 'Christians', take shape. It is a space that allows for reform ideas and scepticism to emerge in conversational or dialogical terms across confessional boundaries, where the Muslim and Christian characters, both Syrians, are represented in a way that disrupts and invalidates any religious divisions inside Syria. These characters are the ideal subjects that Gibran's national discourse seeks to produce – that is, the Syrian subjects whose agency manifests itself in a spirit of interrogation and (self-)criticism across and beyond religious differences, contesting and/or affirming Gibran's own dispositions; these characters, unlike Gibran, are optimistic about the 'future of the East'.[39] In other words, the play as a form is deployed to create an atmosphere of conversation and debate across religious boundaries in Syria, where certain identifications and associations such as 'Christianity' and 'the West' or 'Islam' and 'the Turks' are destabilised, albeit by occasionally resorting to abstraction and essentialisation, and where self-referentiality serves as a tool of self-reflexivity that interrupts or contests the authority of 'the author' which lurks behind his text, foregrounding his 'Syrian', indeed 'Eastern' (not religious or confessional) identification.

Ultimately, 'the Syrian idea', as this play demonstrates, is inextricably linked with the wider East–West civilisational context, such that its potential realisation is indissociable from 'the Eastern question'.[40]

It should be remembered that the above-discussed play, published posthumously, was written in 1914, at least as far as the setting suggests, and the year, as we know, marks the beginning of World War I. At the time, some Arab nationalists, particularly those who advocated independence from the Ottoman Empire, saw the war as the event that would bring the Ottomans down and grant Syria its longed-for independence. Hence the title of the play, 'A Beginning of a Revolution', a revolution of thought that would bring about a revolution of action.[41] The war, however, was not conducive to the Syrians. In addition to the tragic famine during the war, the complex web of colonial interests in the area put the victorious Allied and Associated Powers in a position of unprecedented dominance and control over the region in 1919. The map of the modern Middle East, and particularly that of Greater Syria, was reshaped, mostly by France and Britain. The (in)famous Sykes-Picot Agreement, the results of secret negotiations between the French and the British in 1916, was instrumental in foreshadowing the partition of the region amongst France and Britain after the war.[42] By the time the war broke out, however, the Syrian nationalist activists, especially those in the *Mahjar*, placed some of their hopes in France and, much less, in Britain, while aware of the colonial interests driving the actions of those powers – interests that would jeopardise any sovereignty of a state to be potentially liberated from the Ottoman Empire. The situation was indeed very complex, and it is not my concern in this chapter to discuss it in detail (politically and historically speaking). What I am rather concerned with here is how Gibran's writings at the time reflect and approach this complexity of events and interests, in light of the horizons of actions and expectations permitting or hampering the realisation of Syrian nationhood.

One should be aware, therefore, of the intricacy of this situation, the paucity of options available, as well as the risk that accompanied the decisions that Gibran or the committees and organisations under which he worked were to take, especially during the war. The twists and shifts in perspective, expectation and direction of the struggle for the national cause should not surprise us, the persistence of the commitment to the cause notwithstanding. John Daye has delineated three phases in Gibran's political activism: the first starts in 1910 and ends by mid-World War I, where Gibran's disposition is revolutionary but less 'practical' than 'theoretical'; the second, characterised by reformism and partisan activism, begins with the foundation of the Syria Mount Lebanon Liberation Committee (1917) and terminates with the end of the war; the third and the last, marked by 'revolutionary theorising', begins in the early 1920s and gradually wanes in the years approaching Gibran's demise (1931).[43] This delineation, carefully outlined and chronicled by Daye, is useful to understand the proper historical and discursive context that informs and occasions what he calls Gibran's 'political literature', although I insist that the latter, as literature *explicitly* engaging in political matters, should not be read in isolation from his other work, which is *not explicitly* political.

In an article published in 1916 in the periodical *al-Mir'āt*, titled 'Ḥaffār al-qubūr wa-l-mubakhkhirūn' (The Grave Digger and the Vaporisers), Gibran performs and vehemently defends his 'grave-digging' enterprise – laying bare and burying all the forms, illusions and relics of servitude and blind submission to religious, political and social authorities, all of which are deterrents to a true *Nahḍa* – which is central to his call for reform and Awakening. While 'Ḥaffār al-qubūr', the short story published in *al-ʿAwāṣif*, is poetically and philosophically oriented, as discussed in Chapter One, this one is addressed to the Syrian people in a straightforward manner, with a markedly critical and satirical tone and style (the Syrians are addressed in the plural 'you'), and much less abstract and allegorical in its content. 'What did the Syrian people achieve in the last millennia?'[44] wonders Gibran, the first of several rhetorical questions that concern Syria's political, social and cultural situation, whose deplorable conditions he flagrantly lays bare. He goes on to ridicule the Syrian – and, by implication, Arab – Awakening [*al-yaqaẓa*], deeming it no more than 'dull translations of European books [*kutub al-ifranj*] and some volumes of sterile, ancient poetry that do not exceed, in form and content, the boundaries of salutation, praise and eulogy'.[45] 'Do you take pride in your patriotism,' he continues, 'yet if the Turks confer a medal upon one of you, he becomes a Turk?' Unapologetically polemical, the article illustrates the primacy that Gibran, particularly in the second half of the 1910s and the first half of the 1920s, accords to collective self-criticism as a stance of civilisational survival and cultural and social revival by means of 'grave-digging'. The Syrians, to whom this particular article is addressed, are subject to reproach, scorn and derision; the aim of their *rhetorical* deployment is none other than what Gibran conceives of as a 'true Awakening', and not 'a faint echo of modern Western civilisation', as he declares in a later essay.[46] 'There are those amongst you who know that the deepest sense in my being is the embodiment of saying "my country has the right and capacity to exist" [*bilādi muḥiqqa wa maḥqūqa*], but I have realised that the emotions attendant on patriotism [*al-ʿaṣabiyya*[47]] have blinded our literati and thinkers and halted our advancement and progress',[48] he asserts towards the end of the article.

This critical and cautious nationalism is voiced in another article published later in the same year under the title 'Uḥibbu bilādī' (I Love My Country), where Gibran is adamant to assert that one should only love one's country with insight – that is, without falling prey to the 'blindness' that patriotism (in the sense of *ʿaṣabiyya*) induces. Loving one's country and the people of one's country 'thoughtfully', 'insightfully' and 'wakefully'[49] stands in opposition to lame 'praise' and 'infatuation', he avers. For this love – one that takes precedence over, and assumes a more important status than the country, the object of love – is 'an agreeable, simple force that neither undergoes change or transformation nor does it ask anything for itself'.[50] But, interestingly, what propels and lends ethical justification and weight to his national commitment, and what furthermore profoundly binds him to his fellow Syrians and compels him to engage, at times reluctantly, in the Syrian nationalist cause, is the catastrophic. That is to say, the catastrophic is that which entails and amplifies the ethical necessity, urgency and immediacy of the national and the political. Before the war, it was the subjugation of Syria by the Ottomans and the ensuing suffering of the Syrians that, so he asserts, forced him to commit himself to the Syrian cause, because . . .

> I am an Absolutist, Mary, and Absolutism has no country – but my heart burns for Syria. Fate has been cruel to her – much more than cruel. Her gods are dead, her children abandoned her to seek bread in faraway lands, her daughters are dumb and blind, and yet she is still alive – alive – and that is the most painful thing. She is alive in the midst of her miseries.[51]

By the catastrophic, I am more specifically referring to the tragic famine in Greater Syria during the war. This tragedy, which is often overlooked in modern world history, is one of the reasons that led historian Leyla Fawaz to describe the area that witnessed it as 'a land of aching hearts'.[52] This tragedy deeply affected the Syrian and Lebanese *émigré* writers in the US. Their humanitarian activism during the war – the foundation and activity of The Syria Mount Lebanon Relief Committee,[53] to which Gibran's efforts and time were devoted – testifies to the fact that their homeland, as *émigrés* and exiles in the US, remained a foremost priority for them. Of notable importance here is Gibran's piece of poetic prose 'Māta ahlī' (Dead are My People) which, despite its prevailing mood of bitterness and powerlessness – the war as experienced by a Syrian *émigré* in America – places faith in, and draws optimism from, the generosity and solidarity that is required from the Syrians to build a new future.[54] He writes:

> The tempest that compels you, my Syrian brother, to give something of your life to those who are on the verge of losing theirs is the only thing that makes you worthy of the day's light and the night's quietude.
>
> And the penny that you put into the empty hand stretching towards you is the golden link in a chain that binds what is human in you to that which is over-human.[55]

The catastrophic fuelled Gibran's national sentiment and deepened his attachment to his homeland, which emerged as an ethical imperative. And this would manifest itself more visibly in his critically ethical nationalism.

The End of the War: Nationalism and the Unfulfilled Quest for Nationhood

By the end of World War I, and before the official partition of the area, Gibran published a short play, *Bayna layl wa ṣabāḥ* (Between Night and Morn), and an essay, 'Sūria 'alā fajr al-mustaqbal' (Syria on the Dawn of the Future), in the periodical *al-Sā'iḥ*, both of which highlight, denounce and lament, among other things, the divisions of the Syrians into religious or ethnic sects, each loyal to an external power. In this interregnum, so to speak, there was a sense of hope in Gibran, bespoken at least in the above-mentioned titles, of establishing a Syrian nation-state that is liberated from the Ottoman Empire and self-dependent in its formation, 'a Syria for Syrians only'.[56]

The play's tenor is less ideological and subtler than the essay, whose form does not permit the literary subtlety of the play in capturing this moment: namely, the fall of the Ottoman Empire and the end of the war. It is set in a dark prison on the outskirts of Beirut at the midnight of 9 January (in 1919 presumably, as it was published on 16 January of the same year). The play's characterisation and dialogue reflect the disunion of the Syrians, each sect or confession of which – a Muslim, a Christian, a Druze, a Jew and a poet (the adjectives are used to identify the characters' backgrounds) – pledges loyalty to and places faith in an external power, in the hope of erecting a new future for Syria. This is the case for all the characters in the play, except for the poet, Yusuf Karama, whose allegiance is vowed to Syria alone.

'O Syria! Mother without children!' Yusuf cries out, addressing his fellow Syrians in the prison during a heated conversation marked by sectarian divisions over Syria's future:

> O Syria, how great is your affliction! The souls of your children do not pulsate in your fragile and wasted body, but, alas, they pulsate in the bodies of foreign countries. For their hearts have forgotten you and their thoughts have abandoned you [. . .] O Syria, O nation of tragedies! While in your arms the bodies of your children dwell, their souls have run away from you, one strolling in the Arab peninsula [the Muslim 'Ali Rahman], another sauntering in the streets of London [the Druze Sharaf al-Din al-Huruni], another soaring above the palaces of Paris [the Christian Salim Balan] and yet another counting money while asleep [the Jewish Musa Haim]. O Syria, my childless mother![57]

In response to this long lamentation, 'Ali and Sharaf dismissingly describe Yusuf as a poet who adorns his imagination with beautiful words – that is, as someone who is cut off from *realpolitik*, a view against which Yusuf defensively retorts: 'Yes! I am a poet and not a politician. I love my country and the people of my country, and this is all I wish to know about politics'.[58] He proceeds to declare that it is his country's powerlessness and the injustice to which it has been subjected, as well as the fragmentation and confusion of its people, that drove him to devote his love to it; a disposition that Gibran proclaims elsewhere, as we have seen. The dialogue continues with each character insistently clinging to a foreign power, under whose leadership and guardianship each envision the future of Syria to be, except for Musa, who is portrayed as a money-worshipper (mumbling of money while asleep), a stereotypical depiction that Gibran astonishingly employs in the play. The mere presence of a Jewish character, however, suggests that Arab (Syrian) Jews for Gibran were regarded as an integral part of the future nation-state, by virtue of their dwelling in the Syrian territory for centuries before the war.

The heated discussion ends up with another long lamentation of Yusuf, whose anguish leads him to discern the predicament of Syria as one identical to, or analogous with, the fall of Babel, an invocation that is at once metaphorical and mythological:

> O Babel, O city of dispersion! Has God's shadow abandoned you, like ruins standing alone in the desert? O Babel, O nation of conflicts and grudges! Did you, in your dreams, build a tower whose head reaches out to the sky, outraging the Lord and driving Him to confuse your tongues and scatter your people upon the face of the earth? O Babel, O city of no dwellers! Will your people return to construct your walls and temples? Will God visit you a second time to lift you out of disgrace? O Babel, O city whose houses are pain, whose streets are wounds and whose rivers are tears! O Babel, city of my heart![59]

This metaphorical and mythological reference to Babel in this context should be understood as an invocation of the past that not only seeks to reconnect or construct a connection with it. It is one that aims to reckon with the chattered present in the light of this invoked reconnection. In other words, the (nascent) nation is imagined in the present, by reconnecting it with a past whose mythological invocation serves as a validation of its presence in the present, as a way of coming to terms with the fragmentation and disunion of the Syrians, and as one possibility of reconstructing Syria in the future ('Will your people return to construct your walls and temples?'). That is, in the mythological destruction of Babel lies its potential historical reemergence in the present, in that the destruction of the homogenous One should entail the construction of a unified multiplicity: Syria as an idea and a nation to which the different ethnic and religious groups who inhabit its land are faithful, without negating their differences. The summoning of a mythological past, thus, enables the horizon of a future nation whose material construction is, in one sense, a reconstruction of a past with which it is (imagined to be) territorially connected.

Later in the play, a woman is heard talking to her son, who is very hungry and wants some bread. 'Sleep, my child, sleep until morning', his mother tells him, 'God will send us bread tomorrow and we shall all eat'.[60] But her son dies of hunger moments later, whereupon someone is heard saying: 'Your son has died, and you are still calling unto God?! I told you that God Himself has died of hunger!'[61] This is, of course, a scene that alludes to the great famine that swept over Syria during the war, an event that poignantly affects Yusuf who, in a moment of desperation that epitomises Syria's predicament at the time, cries out:

> O Syria, crossroad of conquerors, will I live to see a new conqueror? Let it be should the pockets of its troops be full of bread. Let it be should there remain a brother to shield me and a sister whose voice I could hear. . . But, alas, how selfish am I, pleading to remain alive to see the faces of my brothers and sisters, while my life, had it been of any value, would have been taken by now![62]

The play closes with the liberation of the prisoners and the entrance of the Allied troops into the city of Beirut on the following morning, announcing the defeat of the Ottomans. Yet Yusuf, unlike the other jubilant prisoners, remains sober and sceptical, albeit not without an inevitable sense of hope for a 'true freedom' outside the prison.

The significance of the play lies in its capacity, its shortness notwithstanding, to register the disunited and conflicting voices and political interests of Syrians from divergent backgrounds over the best future that they each envision for their country. The appeal of these groups to the external powers to intervene in Syria is premised on the politicised ethnic or religious proximity/affinity that they believe to exist between them and those powers (Islam in the case of the Arab ʿAli and Catholicism in the case of the Maronite Salim, for instance). Equally important here is the setting of the play, the prison, for it is precisely inside the prison, simultaneously real and figural, that those 'prisoners' place their hope in countries other than Syria to liberate it from the Ottomans, who are thought to have imprisoned them in their own country. The intimation here is that the *moral prison* into which the Syrians are *willingly* caught – their faith in, and the loyalty that they pledge to, political entities whose economic, political or symbolic strength is believed to be of advantage to Syria, should they resort to them – is as pernicious as the Ottoman oppression to which they were subjected. 'Listen to me', Yusuf cries out angrily, 'you who are imprisoned in a prison within a prison within a prison: Syria belongs neither to the Arabs, nor to the British, the French or the Jews. Syria is yours and mine alone'.[63] The ending of the play confirms and sustains this double signification – at once real and metaphorical – of the prison, as 'true freedom' is all that Yusuf pines for, albeit without enthusiasm. Therein lies the power of the play as it captures the historical and political dilemma into which Syria was thrown by the end of the war, a conundrum from which Gibran envisioned no other way out but the realisation of a Syrian nationhood whose legitimacy is grounded in the sense of a shared and unified Syrian *waṭan*, not in religion, sect or ethnicity.

In this context, it should be remembered that Gibran reiterates that since Antiquity Syria had been invariably susceptible and subjected to foreign conquests, and that it survived despite being repeatedly invaded by Others, a sign of its eligibility for nationhood in the age of nation-states.[64] One can discern the social and historical Darwinism that, because it has survived, renders Syria as *waṭan* eligible to join the modern order of nations. This social Darwinism was part of the *Zeitgeist* of the period, and Gibran was no exception. What remains essential here is that the geographical unity of Greater Syria stands as that which grounds and justifies this nationalism, a discourse on which hinges the formation and realisation of the nation, as I shall now demonstrate in an essay published shortly after the play.

This essay, given the context, is unsurprisingly titled 'Sūria ʿalā fajr al-mustaqbal' (Syria on the Dawn of the Future). Explicitly ideological and political in its content and message, it sets out to analyse the factors that are believed to have deterred national unity in Syria. Gibran begins the essay by invoking, once again, the metaphor of 'the prisoner': 'Like a prisoner going out of his dark prison, vacillating between certainty and doubt as to his salvation, stands Syria today on the dawn of the future to proceed with the living nations in the procession of Life that is teeming with walkers and spectators'.[65] He then goes on to foreground that 'the spirit of the age into which Syria is entering will despatch the Muslim Syria, the Christian Syria and the Druze

Syria. Religious fanaticism will be erased out of its heart, and the long-awaited tolerance will supersede it'.[66] 'The age', in this context, does not connote a strictly temporal dimension, a new phase in the history of Syria. It is a 'liberal' age to whose 'spirit' Syria is entering or is hoped to enter: one that has already taken place – modernity in its political and civic configuration – whose mode of existence is nothing else but 'time'. As Fethi Meskini postulates, '[w]e are "our" time every time, that is, we are our mode of existence in a certain age as being the ultimate sense of the dwelling [*al-waṭan*] that *concerns us*'.[67] I should stress that this is the main dimension of the age – modernity's political transformation and the emergence of the nation-state as the sole horizon of a 'people' to exist in the form of a recognizable polity in the nineteenth century – to which Gibran subscribes in his own *Nahḍa* discourse (anti-Ottoman and anti-colonial nationalism). 'The spirit of the age', thus, is hoped to provide a new home – that is, a new mode of existence in which religious tolerance as a supposedly modern civic achievement is actualised within the secular nation – to which Syria, as a potential nation-state, will enter, optimistically precipitating the end of any definition of Syria in religious or confessional terms.

Gibran, however, admits the optimism of this prospect in which 'Syria is portrayed as it should be, not as it is' and addresses his 'Syrian brother' only insofar as he is a 'patriot':

> My Syrian brother, whether you are a Muslim, a Christian, a Druze or an Israeli, whether you are aligned with the Ottoman state, France, Britain or Russia, whether you are in agreement with me as to our eligibility for self-rule or not, there is an essential point at which we should stop: it is patriotism [*al-waṭaniyya*].[68]

Only those who are identified as 'patriots', in the sense of longing for and having the readiness to sacrifice oneself for the Syrian nation, are concerned with what Gibran has to say in the article. He then proceeds to reflect on what he deems the four factors that have torn asunder the 'national collectivity' of the Syrians: religious fanaticism, ignorance, lack of self-reliance and despotism. What is remarkable about the article is its lucid and down-to-earth (albeit at times problematic) analysis of the social and political conditions that have impeded the realisation – that is, the liberation and formation – of the Syrian nation-state. This is an analysis whose impetus lies in the force of nationalism as an ideology capable of directing intellectual and activist energies towards the aim of realising that which the ideology attempts to articulate and precipitate – namely, the construction of the nation as a realisable idea and the embodiment of the idea in the establishment of an autonomous and unified nation-state.

To that end, Gibran conceives of what he calls 'national life' (*al-ḥayāt al-qawmiyya*) as a natural, inherent human property. The naturalisation of nationalism, in the Arab context, should be comprehended in relation to the notion of *ḥubb al-waṭan*[69] (love of homeland) that found articulation in the revival of Arabism and the construction of modern Arab subjectivity – occasioned by the domestication of nationalism in the Arab world – in the *Nahḍa*'s nineteenth-century discourse,[70] leading to a confusion that is often made between *homeland* (place of birth and up-bringing) and *nation* (in the modern sense of the word), to both of which the sense of the term *waṭan* readily lends itself. This is evinced in the following passage towards the end of the essay:

> National life [*al-hayāt al-qawmiyya*] is a powerful spirit that emerges from the general interest of the nation and propels it toward a single Aim regardless of the preferences and inclinations of its individual members. It is a genuine and deeply penetrating psychological sentiment of love for the land in which man was born and reared, for the people to whom he belongs, for the customs to which he had become adapted, and for the language that he speaks. It is a patriotic sentiment in the path of which [or, for the sake of which] man sacrifices his wealth and life.[71]

I must note, first, that Gibran, speaking of 'national life', uses the term *qawmiyya*, not *waṭaniyya*, with the former usually translated as 'nationalism' and the latter as 'patriotism', although at times confusion arises. *Qawmiyya* is derived from *qawm*, meaning kinsfolk, tribe or clan in the strict sense of the word and, in its general and frequently invoked sense, a community with which one identifies. It is this fact of being born in and raised within the circle of a certain *qawm* (people) with shared language, customs and traditions that leads Gibran – of course, in addition to the ethical and ideological drive of his message (the realisation of the Syrian nation-state) – to perceive nationalism in natural or organic terms. For Gibran, love of one's country (*maḥabbat al-waṭan*) necessarily connotes love of one's birthplace. This love of homeland, the land into which one is rooted, is perceived by Gibran as an inherent human sentiment whose goodness is realisable only if this sentiment 'is engulfed and propelled by wisdom';[72] for it readily lapses into a 'vice', pernicious and detrimental individually and collectively, if it is infused with 'pretence' and 'vanity'.[73] This universal sentiment, in its insightful embodiment, is thus transformed into a driving force in the nationalist quest for nationhood.

We discern, furthermore, that nationalism has a specific 'aim' in this discourse, rendering it at once an intrinsic human sentiment and an instrument for the formation of a national education necessary for the independence of the nation, as I shall later demonstrate. The 'general interest of the nation', moreover, is taken as that which 'generates' this nationalism, identified here, unsurprisingly, as 'national *life*'. In other words, love of homeland, which precedes and exceeds nationalism as an ideology, becomes that which justifies nationalism itself – the use of the word 'life' is not arbitrary. Thus, the nation (*al-umma*) in the modern sense emerges from the deeply rooted love (literal translation of *hub muta'aṣṣil*) for the homeland. What emerges as problematic, which often passes as unproblematic in modern Arab discourse, is the use of the term '*al-umma*' as an equivalent of 'the nation'. One must note, here, that it is the (enduring) religious connotation of *al-umma* as a community of people who share a common religious belief (Islam) that allows for the domestication of the (Western) category of 'the nation' or '*la patrie*' in the Arab context. This domestication has confused its meaning by at once aligning it with Islam and the modern nation in the Arab discursive landscape to which it has travelled.[74]

The ideological force of this nationalism, which takes as its premise the natural love of *waṭan*, conditions and frames Gibran's scrutiny of that which hampers the concrete realisation of what he calls 'national life'. It is crucial to remember that Gibran does not posit a coherent theory or vision of nationalism; rather, his nationalist reflections are fragmentarily sketched out, warranted by specific historical moments or events within a certain field of discourse. A pattern, however, can be discerned: Gibran posits the inter-relatedness of national independence, self-reliance and Awakening, held together in a causal relationship. While national independence is dependent on the self-reliance of the Syrians in their quest for nationhood, self-reliance is predicated on 'moral independence', a foundational notion upon which Gibran lays a huge emphasis. And without moral independence neither is the enactment of an original Eastern Awakening possible, nor is self-reliance – and, by necessity, national independence – realisable. In other words, the Awakening, which is premised on moral independence and self-reliance, needs to take place for the nation to emerge, and the nation-state is the logical (institutional) result of the Awakening of Syria as an Arab, Eastern entity. Yet, this 'moral independence' should not preclude the Syrians, as revealed in his letters to Emile Zaydan between 1919 and 1922, from seeking out foreign (Western) 'tutelage' in 'scientific, economic and agricultural' matters, provided that the Syrian 'national character' (*al-ṣibgha al-sūriyya*) is upheld.[75] Following the passage on national life quoted above, Gibran identifies the necessary, lacking elements for Syria to become a recognizable nation:

> Tolerance, knowledge, independence and courage [*al-iqdām*] are the elements we lack to become a significant nation whose word is recognised in the international arena. Creating a scientific Awakening [*nahḍa 'ilmiyya*] that educates our men[76] in every science and art is the foremost of our priorities. For when these educated men are present amongst us, having created a *national literature, a national philosophy, a national music and a national industry and commerce*, once we realise this aim in the course of progress, there will be no power under the sun that would forestall our independence. And to the Syrian people, who are known for their intelligence and adaptability, this aim is not unrealisable.[77]

This is a discourse on national independence that is predicated on the formation of 'a national literature, a national philosophy, a national music, and national industry and commerce', all of which are requisite for the establishment of an independent nation-state; an independence that derives, essentially, from the self-dependence of the Syrian people in whom Gibran's faith and hope for an Awakening are placed, precisely because of his critical account of the conditions which he thinks are a deterrent to national unity inside Syria. This is a healthy move, in my view, for it takes as its point of departure a collective self-criticism, an agential self-affirmation that must not be confused with collective self-loathing, before highlighting the essential ingredients necessary for collective unity and self-transformation – for which nationalism acts as a robust ethical and ideological impetus and guarantor. I emphasise Gibran's concern for collectivity and collective action because it constitutes that which he deemed lamentably and gravely wanting in the Syrians, that which would affirm and sustain their country as a recognizable nation, hence nationalism as an ideology that manifests itself in the form of collective identification and solidarity.[78]

What is striking, however, is that Gibran's discourse reveals (or conceals) an incognizance – one might say an under-estimation – of the British and French colonial interest in the area, addressing the issue as though Syria had been immune from foreign, colonial intervention. This may boil down to the facts that the region had not been officially parcelled out until 1920, one year following the publication of the essay, and that the results of the Sykes-Picot Agreement had remained secret until 1919.[79] Also, the manifesto of The Syria and Mount Lebanon Liberation Committee, of which Gibran was Secretary of Foreign Correspondence, published in 14 June 1917 in *al-Sā'iḥ*, reflects the committee's unawareness of the true motives of the Allies. The manifesto announces that the committee's strategy for the liberation and independence of Syria from the Ottoman Empire, advocated by Gibran, consists in the enlisting of Syrians of all backgrounds (but especially those in America) in an Eastern military campaign to fight with the Allies, France in particular, against the Ottoman Empire. This agenda mirrors the military orientation of the committee, which, as John Daye points out, saw the war as an opportunity to gain military and political victories for Syria.[80] This is despite its caution and awareness, in the words of Ameen Rihani, another influential *Mahjari* writer and nationalist, that 'the salvation of one nation by another is one that necessarily entails foreign sovereignty over one's nation, and [that] any foreign sovereignty, however just and beneficial it could be, is an option that we would never be content with'.[81] We should not forget, furthermore, the wide appeal to Woodrow Wilson's endorsement of the right to 'national self-determination' that was announced in 1918, regarded by the committee (based in the US) as an immense political support to their cause.[82] Yet, this strategy of fighting with the side of the Allies was neither effective on the ground, nor did it bear political fruit for Syria after the war. It was, in short, miscalculated but understandable given the scarcity of options conducive to their struggle at that juncture in history, and not as simply naïve as some have argued from today's privileged standpoint.[83]

Apart from this crucial political context, Gibran insists that the realisation of national collectivity must be premised on the Syrians' (awakening of their) moral independence, hence his essential reconfiguration of independence as an intrinsic property of being whose actualisation warrants one's self-consciousness of its existence *within*. This self-consciousness, then, must precede and predicate an independence *from* (any encroaching or colonising Other). 'The Westerners', he wrote to Emile Zaydan after World War I, 'might be able to help us scientifically, economically and agriculturally, but they cannot grant us moral independence [*al-istiqlāl al-maʿnawī*], without which we cannot emerge as a living nation'.[84] This independence is moral insofar as it is radically and universally human, but it can solely take the form of a unique 'national character' by virtue of which one's *difference* is articulated and preserved. In other words, Gibran is positing moral independence as a universal category whose embodiment manifests itself (only) within the spectrum of national difference, with each nation having its own distinct character but within a *similar* spectrum of difference (the modern, universalised category of the nation). The 'Syrian character', the adherence to which is necessary for moral independence to crystallise, is that which would preclude the Syrians from being 'shewn, ingested and digested' by the 'tutelage' of a foreign, 'developed' country.[85] It is this emphatic and adamant concern for Awakening (incumbent on the 'slumberous' Syrian subject) that may have blinded Gibran to the logic of *realpolitik*, to the gulf between Enlightenment ideals and colonialist politics. His cautious belief in France or Britain as a 'tutor' for the Syrians – a transitory tutelage – is nevertheless revoked in his recently published manuscripts.[86] In one of them, unfortunately undated, he writes that 'the Westerner' is an 'enemy' who is driven by his own interests when he turns his face to the East, and that 'his virtue resides only in the West'.[87] In another, he avers that there is no distinction between a mandate and an occupation, urging the Syrians to ground any action they set out to undertake for Syria or in their struggle against France on wisdom, caution and thoughtfulness (and one can readily infer that the French Mandate was the context in which this statement was written).[88]

These manuscripts reveal a profound disappointment with the post-war turn of events in the region – namely, the partition of Greater Syria and the demonstrably colonialist nature of the French Mandate. For Gibran's strong commitment to 'the maintenance of the unity of geographical Syria and the independence of the country under a national, representative system'[89] was not fulfilled, and neither was his (somewhat far-fetched) call for the provisional and conditional placement of Syria under foreign 'tutelage' after the war.[90] Notwithstanding the failure of this political activism and vision, which he shared with other notable Syrian writers, activists and reformers in the US, what is remarkable and worthy of critical attention is his unwavering belief in the dire necessity and potentiality of enacting an original Syrian and Arab Eastern *Nahḍa*, as well as in the urgent need for a collective Syrian unity that was hoped to ward off any Western colonial infringement.

In 'Syria on the Dawn of the Future', he warns against the dangers of falling prey to 'religious fanaticism', one deterrent to national unity and Awakening, ridiculing any reduction of nationalism to it. Addressing the leaders of the Syrian parties towards the end of the essay, Gibran reiterates his demand for national collective unity:

> If your patriotism does not triumph over every emotion of zealotry in your being, and if you do not unite your demands before it is too late, there will come the day where you look at the map of Syria being tinged with different colours as is the case in black Africa, colours indicative of its division into spheres of influence and foreign colonies.[91]

Syria was indeed divided, as Gibran had anticipated, yet the main cause of its division was not the disunion of its political parties, but the decision of the victorious Allies, France and Britain in particular, to partition the region that had formerly been part of the Ottoman Empire in line with their colonial interests and in complete indifference to the people who inhabited it.[92] As far as Gibran is concerned, it is the position from which he spoke – that of the Syrian, Eastern subject concerned as a writer and intellectual committed to Syria and the Arab East – that led him to *over-emphasise* the role and responsibility incumbent on the Syrians in the making of their own history, especially after what became known as centuries of 'decadence' or *inḥiṭāṭ*[93] under Ottoman governance, and to regard as secondary any foreign, colonial role in the potential reshaping and remaking of the area.

In the same essay, Gibran attributes the deplorable political and social conditions in Syria, among other factors, to 'Eastern despotism'. Gibran proclaims that the 'Syrian' lacks, 'as an Easterner',[94] an awareness of his own 'rights' and 'duties': the right to social welfare and the right to criticise the governor or the clerk, on the one hand, and the duty of the individual, on the other hand, *vis-à-vis* the community (*al-jamāʿa*) as a collectivity within which the individual exists and operates as a social agent. Here, it is not initially clear whether Gibran considers docility, lack of individual autonomy and susceptibility to despotism inherent to the 'the Easterner', or whether these elements are merely historical, and therefore changing or changeable. However, since the aim of his critical engagement in the national cause lies in contributing to the construction of a democratic state for whose functioning notions of individual autonomy and collective good are central, then it becomes clear that this so-called Eastern despotism is eradicable, and therefore not a stable, ahistorical element that is intrinsic to the Syrian *qua* Easterner. 'When the social collectivity neglects its duties towards the individual', he writes, 'the latter will absolve himself of his responsibilities towards it, and therein lies the defect that would take the form of disorder and despotism'.[95]

In the same passage, Gibran abruptly shifts attention to 'the massive gulf that exists between us and the nations that are civilisationally advanced' and endeavours to bridge it – a bridging that aims to invalidate the dichotomy of inherent backwardness or advancement – by suggesting that 'progress' is a project that could be carried out in a short temporal span, citing the US as an evidence of its realisability within a period of fifty years.[96] His premise consists in the fact that 'it was science [in the last fifty years] that made possible all these astonishing miracles [all the material and technological advancements of modern life in the US]', and science, so he avers, is a universal 'light' that shines not on one part but on the whole of the Earth: 'Do we remain asleep, then', he wonders rhetorically, 'or shall we awaken to move in its light?'[97] Thus, what emerges as 'lacking' in the Syrian subject is not a modern scientific backdrop against which 'progress' is actualised *a la Européenne*, but 'a will to work' and 'a persistence in work',[98] a diagnosis that locates the civilisational slumber within the Syrian subject as a historical agent, albeit one that cannot be dissociated from the Euro-American civilisational challenge. In other words, the lack is not a lack of 'civilisation and progress' materially realised in the Western Other (one that defines the self as 'backward' *vis-à-vis* the 'civilised' Other), but a lack of the will to work and the persistence in work within the subject itself at that historical juncture, having once led the (historical) 'procession of life', as he puts it. In this way, Gibran inscribes the collective self in a historical universalism in which history is divided into chapters, with one distinct civilisation as the protagonist of a chapter, as it were, leading the procession of life at a specific epoch in history, yet with no clear teleology. Euro-America is not *the* civilisational telos for Gibran, but the one leading the procession of life in modern times. This will lead me to touch more closely on the Eastern civilisational question and on the way in which Gibran approaches the predicament of the *Nahḍa*.

Syria and the Arab East: Civilisational Anxiety and Gibran's Vision of the *Nahḍa*

In an undated short text titled 'Ilā al-sharqiyyīn' (To the Easterners), found in the manuscripts that John Daye published in 1988, Gibran draws an important distinction between 'his Eastern conscience' (*wujdān*), which he invokes to address those to whom the short article is written, and his 'everywhere alienated soul': 'I address you now as a man and not as a poet, and I appeal to your Eastern conscience with my own Eastern conscience, not with my soul that is everywhere alienated from your souls that are everywhere alienated'.[99] Of notable significance here is Gibran's statement at the outset – 'I now address you as a man and not as a poet' – which echoes his self-consciousness of a certain poetic identity, voiced in his short play *Between Night and Morn* and elsewhere,[100] that is purportedly at odds with 'politics' as a practise of power and vying interests, yet inevitably entrenched in 'the political', or, as Jacques Rancière puts it, literature 'doing' politics *as* literature (albeit in another context).[101] Thus, Gibran provisionally suspends his being a poet in his endeavour to engender and revive the Syrian will to the work necessary for the realisation of the *Nahḍa*, the intimation here being that poetry addresses the universal, the soul that is *everywhere* alienated. In other words, poetry as such cannot be national or identitarian. Rather, it speaks to the human as such, even if it is articulated in a certain language and within a certain tradition or culture.

Yet, why the 'Eastern conscience' in this context? 'Eastern' here, as a label of 'imaginative geography',[102] to use Said's phrase, at once stands for and encompasses the Syrian. The use of this qualifier should not be readily construed as an instance of essentialisation, precisely because of the above-mentioned distinction. Gibran is addressing his fellow Syrians as Easterners insofar as they are aware, or *made* aware, of their own cultural and imaginative identity – in the anthropological sense – in a specific historical moment.

Addressing the Eastern conscience of the Syrians with his, Gibran writes:

> You are seeking freedom and yearning for independence; you are aspiring for an Eastern civilisation that rivals the Western one; and you wish to dispense with the foreigners, nay you want the foreigners to come to you asking for your friendship instead of you asking for theirs. I address now as a man and not as a poet, and I appeal to your everywhere alienated souls, so listen. . . [103]

Gibran, in other words, is addressing the identitarian layer of their being, insofar as 'identitarian' denotes the cultural and anthropological identification of the self,[104] located in a specific geographical and symbolic space demarcated – imagined, constructed and entrenched – as the East. Yet, he is invoking this layer in the specific context of 'civilisational' rivalry and survival, where the West as the civilisational, identitarian Other is not solely a challenge and a threat, but that which instigates, occasions and sets the terms of the 'Eastern' quest for a 'civilisation' of its own. Interestingly enough, however, one discerns that Gibran towards the end of the above-cited passage is not addressing this layer, but appealing 'as a man and not as a poet' to the Syrians' 'everywhere alienated souls'. This should not be taken for granted, for in this discursive shift Gibran is addressing what he takes to be the human as such in his fellow Easterners/Syrians – that is, the originary ontological structure of being human in the world as he understands it. For the self as an 'everywhere alienated soul', if one apprehends it in the light of Gibran's thought, is the existentially alienated self by dint of being in the world, *anywhere* in the world; hence, its alienation, not conditioned by lack, is constitutive. More specifically, he is addressing the originary layer of the self that lurks behind the 'veils' of national, cultural and imaginative identity. No wonder that he is using the word 'alienated' here (*gharīb*, meaning 'estranged', takes up the connotation of 'alienation' in the existential sense that the word *ghurba* denotes).

This word designates the primordial, displaced sense of the self that comes before or despite any cultural, social, national (in short, identitarian) veiling. I should note that I am not so much concerned with alienation *per se* in my analysis here as with this 'universal' underlying structure – for Gibran – at the core of being human in the world irrespective of, or in tandem with, its identitarian layer. By appealing to this originary and universal self, Gibran attempts to (re)invigorate the will to work requisite for the Awakening of women, the plantation of the fields (on which great emphasis is placed) and the education of the youth, all of which the Syrians are keen on realising, yet only, as he asserts, 'with [their] silent will'.[105] The ambivalence of the Syrians, as he diagnoses it – willing to work but working in words, to paraphrase him – is the sign of a double, conflicting personality: 'one liberating itself [*tataḥarrar*] in secret, the other submitting (itself) [*tamtathil*] in public'.[106] This is an Awakening that is solely possible if the self is understood and addressed – the addressing and addressed self – beyond or beneath its identitarian surface, albeit an Awakening that inevitably manifests itself in identitarian terms; that is, as an Eastern one.

Along with his emphasis on the will to work and the embodiment of the will to work or lack thereof in the Syrian, Eastern subject, it is crucial to accentuate the foundational weight that Gibran lends to moral independence as the condition of *ibtikār* (innovation or inventiveness) and of fostering an original Arab Eastern *Nahḍa*, be it in poetics or politics. This is not only manifested in his concern for the future of the Arabic language, which is contingent on the poetic 'power of invention' in the collective body of its speakers, as discussed in Chapter Two, but also in his scepticism *vis-à-vis* the Arab *Nahḍa* itself, one that tormented him a great deal, as revealed in his posthumously published manuscripts. Dawud, a character in one his unpublished plays, castigates the imitative and uncritical reliance of Arab writers and intellectuals of the *Nahḍa* on classical poetry and *adab*, on the one hand, and on Western literature and thought, on the other. In a powerful passage, he says that he does not deny the existence of a literary *Nahḍa* in Egypt and *al-shām* (the Levant); yet, 'if by *Nahḍa*', he avers, 'you mean the existence of foreign schools and the abundance of Western newspapers and journals as well as physicians and lawyers', then 'this is a movement, not a wakefulness or a renaissance'.[107] His reasoning is that 'literary and intellectual revolutions are born in the aftermath of military conquests or after the emergence of great geniuses [*nawābigh ʿiẓām*], with new and innovative ideas that command the attention of people and entail their awakening'.[108] The idea of a great genius, prevalent since the Enlightenment, functions as the catalyst of massive civilisational transformations in history: 'If we look at the parades of bygone generations, we find that every civilisation had an existing intellectual youth as well as teeming ideas in the mind of a determined prophet or a great leader, or in the swaying emotions at the heart of a great poet'.[109] For Gibran, what counts most as far as intellectual and literary awakenings are concerned is what he calls 'the power of invention', the lack of which led to, or was caused by, the prevalence of two camps of writers in the *Nahḍa*, according to him: those who attempt to 'revive' tradition and stick to its *modi operandi*, thereby obfuscating their own *modus vivendi*, and those who are taken with Western intellectual and literary production, thereby wanting in moral and cultural autonomy. In both cases, a genuine sense of individual and collective selfhood is either obscured or lacking.

In another posthumously published manuscript, he wonders: 'Is it a *Nahḍa* or a short wakefulness that precedes death? Are we determined to recover a lost glory, or is it just a host of dreams that invocations of the past create, and we've taken them for facts?'[110] This scepticism, which he admits to be torturing him,[111] arises from a certain diagnosis that attributes imitation of the past ('traditionalism'[112]) or the West (westernisation) to the shrinking 'capacity to innovate and create in the nation's spirit [*nafs al-umma*]'.[113] The result of this decline is either the inevitable reproduction of 'what other nations innovate',[114] or, if one is not an imitator of the West, an 'enchantment' with ancient, glorified 'effects' and a submission to 'the power of continuity' (*quwwat al-istimrār*) from the past, of which Gibran speaks so robustly in his poetic essay 'al-ʿUbūdiyya' (Slavery, 1920).[115]

In 'Nahḍat al-sharq al-ʿarabī' (The Awakening of the Arab East), an interview conducted with Gibran in the periodical *al-Hilāl* in 1923 and later turned into an essay, Gibran spells out his take on the Arab *Nahḍa*, which he deems 'no more than a faint echo of modern Western civilisation [*al-madaniyya al-gharbiyya al-ḥadītha*]'.[116] This is because 'this blessed *Nahḍa*', according to him, 'has created nothing out of itself, and what it has hitherto produced lacks the stamp of its unique character, the colour of its own imprint'.[117] He then goes on to lament, after asserting that 'the East, in its entirety [. . .] has become a huge Western colony', the fact that 'the Easterners, those who take pride in their past and boast of their traditions and their ancestors' achievements, have become slaves, with their thoughts, preferences and leanings, to the Western idea [*al-fikra al-gharbiyya*]'.[118] He is quick to maintain, however, that what concerns him is not 'whether the Western civilisation is, in itself, good or not' – it is still alive after and despite World War I, he asserts, a sign of its survival and persistence. He is, rather, dwelling on the question of whether the Arab nations are wakeful (*nāhiḍa*) or not, and to that end, he suggests looking into the various connotations of the word *nuhūḍ* (Awakening) and what each connotation entails in the then Arab context. Thus, should we take the word in the sense of 'apprenticeship' – that is, importing, adopting, appropriating and superficially imitating the (material) manifestations of Western civilisation (*madaniyya*) – in order to 'amend' the ruinous and dilapidated social, economic and cultural reality of the Arab nations, then the latter, so asserts Gibran with irony, 'have awakened to the point of reaching out to the galaxy'.[119] Gibran's use of the word *madaniyya* is not arbitrary, it seems to me, for in this context *madaniyya* connotes that which is *materially visible* in the modern West, embodied in its metropolitan centres (the word shares its root with *madīna*, city; therefore, it can be also understood as *urbanity*), which explains his ridiculing of any unquestioned imitation or appropriation of it. 'If the Awakening, however, manifests itself by way of inventing and innovating, then the Arab nations are still in slumber', he states. Yet, interestingly, 'this is indeed the case if we look at invention and innovation with eyes captivated by Western civilisation and its mechanical novelties'.[120] What Gibran is staunchly at odds with here is any instrumentalist appropriation of Western modernity in its technological facet and, more precisely, its reappropriation *as* an Arab *Nahḍa*. Any technological infatuation with the West is therefore scorned and dismissed as mere imitation that results from a dwindling and dying capacity to innovate in the Arab, Eastern subject. This stance is not simply a Romantic backlash against the epistemological nomenclature of the *Nahḍa*'s 'reform-rationalist paradigms',[121] as Stephen Sheehi contends. It is a position that seeks to dispense with both traditionalism and westernisation – both of which Gibran understood rather schematically – by carving out an original Awakening that is predicated on the force of invention, insofar as it invests in the Eastern yet-to-be excavated 'treasures', the unstirred (re)sources of the Arab Eastern self, so to speak.[122] Paying attention to Gibran's fiction alone is what prompted Sheehi to conceive of Gibran's ideal fictional subject as a Romantic one who does away with 'civilisation as urbanity'.

Gibran, I argue, is wrongly understood as being averse to civilisation *per se*, a reputation he acquired based on his early fiction and especially his long poem *al-Mawākib* (The Processions, 1919), in which he contrasts the idyllic, monist world of *al-ghāb* (the woods) with the corrupt and dualist world of the modern city – a juxtaposition, as discussed in Chapter Two, that is irreducible and unresolved, structuring the form and meaning of the poem. In his short story 'al-ʿĀṣifa' (The Tempest, 1916), one is bewildered by the renunciation and isolation – not the asceticism, as it first appeared to the narrator[123] – of Yusuf Fakhri, the principal character of the short story who has decided to live in a hut far away from the city, the emblem of 'civilisation as urbanity', and who delights in walking amidst 'the storms' in the mountains of north Lebanon. The narrator, trying to find a safe refuge from a howling storm that has taken him aback, tells us that he chanced upon Yusuf's hut, where he was indeed admitted and hosted. The long dialogue that unfolds between the narrator and Yusuf is an intriguing case of discussing and contesting the value of modern civilisation. Yusuf, to the narrator's surprise and admiration, evinces a critical awareness of all the 'maladies' that have swept over society, as he explains why he forsook the city, having chosen to distance himself altogether from what he deems the very source of those maladies, 'the city' itself. This is to the dismay and bafflement of the narrator who finds in him, having diagnosed those 'ills', a 'physician' who would have contributed to the 'healing' of society – a prevalent trope in the *Nahḍa*. What is notable is that Yusuf, his cynicism notwithstanding, regards the 'wretchedness of the East' as 'the wretchedness of the whole Earth', because 'human nature is the same and people differ from each other only in extraneous features, which should not be taken seriously'.[124] He goes on to express his profound scepticism *vis-à-vis* the advancement of the West in that 'slavery – slavery to life, slavery to the past, slavery to teachings, customs and fashions, and slavery to the dead – remains slavery even if its face is painted and its dress is changed, even if it calls itself freedom'.[125] This is how he shuns the idea of a 'backward East' and an 'advanced West', ending up by dismissing civilisation altogether as 'a vanity'. All that he yearns for and venerates now is a 'wakefulness [*yaqaẓa*] in the depths of the self; he who has witnessed it cannot disclose it in words, whereas he who has not does not and will not attain its secrets',[126] a notion drawn, unsurprisingly, from Sufism. While this can be readily construed as a Gibranian Romantic aversion to 'civilisation', the narrator's reflection reveals not so much a concurrence with Yusuf but a contesting rumination. He does not dismiss civilisation/urbanity in favour of a 'spiritual wakefulness', which is nevertheless hailed as 'the aim of Being', but sees the former, 'with all its obscurities and ambiguities', as being 'one of the causes' of the latter. 'How is it possible to deny an existent thing when its very existence is evidence for the truth of its right?' he wonders.[127] Even if 'modern civilisation is a passing accident', the narrator believes that 'eternal Law' (*al-nāmūs al-abadī*) will have made of it a step in the 'staircase [. . .] that reaches to the absolute substance'.[128] The metaphysics that informs the narrator's judgement aside, his contestation suggests that Gibran is not against civilisation as such, that 'modern civilisation' for him is a cause of ambivalence and perplexity as much as it is a phenomenon that should not serve as a yardstick to gauge 'progress' and 'backwardness'.

As for his later non-fiction work, exemplified by his essay 'The Awakening of the Arab East', it discloses an understanding of a *Nahḍa* whose trajectory must be radically different from the one taken by Western civilisation. The renaissance must derive its urge and 'moral wakefulness'[129] (*yaqaẓa ma'nawiyya*) as well as its independence from the 'essence' and 'spirit' of the Arab East.[130] Thus the *Nahḍa*, in the genuine sense of the term, should embrace an Eastern spirit of *ibtikār* unmediated by the West – except, perhaps, in understanding Western civilisation itself as an offspring of an autonomous spirit of innovation. Miss Wardah, one of the main characters of his short play 'al-Wujūh al-mulawwana' (The Chameleonic Faces, 1916), echoes this point. She hopes for the awakening in the young Syrians of 'those elements that brought about the awakening of the Western nations', by which she means a '*moral awakening* that made of their lives a continuous ceremony on the stage of Being'.[131] This is why in a posthumously published polemical essay Gibran heaps his criticism on Kemal Ataturk for failing to realise that reform should not be enacted by 'importing the modern glittering shells' of Western civilisation (*qushūriha al-barrāqa al-ḥadītha*) while being oblivious to its 'essence' or 'kernel' (*lubāb*), where its true meaning resides (for him).[132]

Gibran, however, is not unaware of the inevitability of influence, as revealed in his play 'al-Ṣilbān', for instance.[133] Yet, his suspicion of 'borrowing' and 'emulation' stems from their potential transformation into a 'lethal venom' and a 'grave' for the borrowing Easterner;[134] he is wary of the extent to which what is borrowed might erase 'the character' of the borrower and efface their particularity. 'The matter', he writes, 'does not concern what the East ought or ought not to borrow from the elements of Western civilisation. Rather, the crux of the matter lies in what the East can do with those elements after eating them'.[135] This explains his use of the metaphor of 'digestion' in this context: rather than swallowing influence in a single gulp, digestion emphasises the 'Eastern being's' transformation and domestication of that which is borrowed from 'the West' while also belying a fear of becoming 'quasi-Western', a state about which Gibran is deeply anxious.[136] What is the ontological underpinning, one wonders, of Gibran's line of thinking here? 'The creative nature (*al-fiṭra al-mubdiʿa*) of the Eastern self is akin to a harp's strings whose notes', he maintains, 'are divergent by their nature from every note of every string in a Western harp. The Easterner cannot bring together the tones and silences of two distinctive notes without corrupting one or both'.[137] Gibran here is underscoring the creative nature, not human nature. And what matters in creativity is originality and particularity, which for Gibran cannot be sacrificed. Thus, while the opposition between the East and the West may be construed as an essentialist one, Gibran's focus on the nature of creativity means that this divergence is to do with the creative nature, not with the East and the West as such. For, to reiterate what I have discussed earlier, creative originality must stem from an originary sense of moral independence, which manifests itself in national and civilisational difference.

Thus, Gibran's *Nahḍawī* vision is not simply a Romantic backlash against the principle of civilisation as urbanity. Rather, it is a self-conscious critical position that takes moral independence individually and collectively as the predicate of a true renaissance, an independence that conditions the acquisition and production of knowledge as much as it frames its social and material embodiment. The Romantic disposition may occasion and reflect this critical position, but it does not account for and exhaust it. For what is at stake here is a profoundly ethical (read: universal) condition that precedes and enables particular epistemological, literary, identitarian and ideological configurations. And the tension between the universal condition and the particular manifestation – as in the way in which identity is imagined and articulated in a Romantic vein reflecting the spirit of the time[138] – remains unresolved. This critical stance towards the renaissance is what distinguishes Gibran from Butrus al-Bustani and the nineteenth-century reform-minded humanists, as well as from late influential figures like Salama Musa,[139] whose fascination with the West's advancement and progress he did not share. Although the spirit of national independence and scepticism towards 'superficial' westernisation[140] was ever-present in the rich and diverse work of the renaissance thinkers and reformers, its function in their *Nahḍawī* vision of reform was not as morally foundational as in Gibran's.

Gibran's constant emphasis on moral autonomy should therefore be understood less as a plea for authenticity than a call for originality. In its culturalist connotation of maintaining a pure, albeit distorted, transhistorical notion of the same, authenticity does not quite capture the moral autonomy that Gibran sees as the condition of ingenuity. Rather, the independent spirit of *ibtikār* is what is necessary to reinvent the self. With a prospective view of the future as the horizon of its becoming, *ibtikār* accomplishes a sort of authenticity without negating identitarian and cultural particularity. Retooled in this way, particularity can subsist if it reinvents itself independently and universally, not in isolation from the Western Other and the ancient eras that preceded it, but in a cautious and critical interaction with the two. Gibran, however, never paid attention to the role of modernity and colonial capitalism in the reshaping and destabilisation of the region since Napoleon's invasion of Egypt in 1798[141] – that is, to the extent to which Western imperialism was instrumental in the restructuring of the area despite local resistance (the asymmetrical power relation need not be overstated here). He was, nevertheless, mindful of what he deemed the Western colonialist logic of power, driven by imperialist, economic interest, that would hamper any possibility of Arab unity.[142]

The foregoing discussion has demonstrated that Gibran's intellectual commitment to the Syrian national cause is concomitant with his concern for the *Nahḍa* – the one entails and reinforces the other. Gibran's nationalism, albeit inevitably ideological, is fundamentally ethical. This is not only attested by the idea that the Syrian *waṭan* or homeland is the sole unifier of its inhabitants. It is also evinced in the vision that the liberation/formation of a nation-state in Syria and the Awakening of the Arab East must stem from 'moral independence', the foundational condition for any original Awakening to emerge and subsist. Ultimately, however, the modern/colonial logic of power reigned supreme. The colonial partition of Greater Syria by the end of the war meant the impossibility of realising the quest for nationhood and the *Nahḍa*. Yet, Gibran's diasporic voice and its persistent echoes attest to an early 'decolonial' intellectual vision whose realisability was impeded by the colonial conditions of impossibility. This intellectual, national commitment notwithstanding, Gibran never ceased conceiving of himself as essentially a poet – poetry being that which, however linguistically and culturally situated, is concerned with the universal as such. Thus, the local and the universal in Gibran are, as I have argued throughout, complementary, or at least located on different planes of experience and discourse. Yet this singular versatility has been lost on the mixed reception that his Anglophone work has elicited in its linguistic and cultural travelling beyond the nation and back to it, which is the subject of my next and final chapter.

Notes

1 This is from a speech that Gibran gave at a gathering in 1911 of *Jam'iyyat al-Ḥalaqāt al-Dhahabiyya* (Society of Golden Circles, whose aim was social and political reform in Syria) in Boston. See Hani J. Bawardi, *The Making of Arab Americans* (Austin: University of Texas Press, 2014), 67. For a historical account of the society and Gibran's role in it, see Daye, *'Aqīdat Jubrān*, 21–33.

2 This is taken from an open letter to Islam that Gibran published in *al-Funūn* in 1913. This translation is cited in Gibran and Gibran, *Kahlil Gibran: Beyond Borders*, 257 [emphasis added].

3 'Gibran's Syria is equivalent to Bilad al-Sham, a name devised by the Arabs after the Muslim Rashidun victory over the Byzantine Empire at the Battle of Yarmouk (AD 636). Meaning left or north, Bilad al-Sham is so called because it is left of the holy Kaaba in Mecca'. See Adel Beshara, 'A Rebel Syrian: Gibran Kahlil Gibran', in *The Origins of Syrian Nationhood: Histories, Pioneers, Identity*, ed. Adel Beshara (London; New York: Routledge, 2011), 149–50.

4 Leila Tarazi Fawaz, *A Land of Aching Hearts: The Middle East in the Great War* (Cambridge, MA: Harvard University Press, 2014), x.

5 For a short account of the paradigms of Perennialism and Primordialism in relation to the ideology of nationalism, see Anthony D. Smith, *Nationalism: Theory, Ideology, History* (Cambridge: Polity, 2010), 53–60.

6 For an account of the history of the word Syria, see Lamia Rustum Shehadeh, 'The Name of Syria in Ancient and Modern Usage', in *The Origins of Syrian Nationhood: Histories, Pioneers and Identity*, ed. Adel Beshara (London; New York: Routledge, 2011), 17–29.

7 Zaydan's historical novels are a case in point.

8 See Hourani, *Arabic Thought*, especially in the chapter 'Arab Nationalism', 275–77; Hisham Sharabi, *Arab Intellectuals and the West* (Baltimore: The Johns Hopkins Press, 1970), 64–65; and Thomas Phillip, 'Jurji Zaydan's Role in the Syro-Arab Nahda: A Re-evaluation', in *The Origins of Syrian Nationhood*, 79–90.

9 For an account of the Syrian *Mahjar* press in the US, see Bawardi, 'The Syrian Nationalism of the *Mahjar* Press', in *The Making of Arab Americans*, 54–80.

10 This is indeed one of the essential connotations of the word *waṭan* before the advent of Arabism, Arab nationalism and the modern nation-state. In Gibran's nationalist discourse, the nation, to draw on Anthony Smith, becomes 'a *felt* and lived community, a category of behaviour as much as imagination, and one that requires of the members certain kind of action'. Smith, *Nationalism*, 11 [emphasis mine].

11 Ibid., 13–15.

12 This is quoted from a letter that Gibran wrote to al-Khoury al-Kufuri in 1913, in which he calls for 'an enormous intellectual tornado' as the sole remedy to those maladies. See Daye, *'Aqīdat Jubrān*, 367.

13 Here, I deliberately avoid the term 'authenticity', used mostly to translate the word and concept of *aṣāla*, which Gibran never used in its contemporary sense in Arab intellectual discourse, that of clinging to a supposedly uncontaminated and continuous notion of the same. What is at stake here is an Eastern *originality* of invention or innovation, albeit not without essentialist overtones, and not a culturalist identitarian authenticity that the term *aṣāla* has come to designate.

14 For an account of the historical circumstances leading to the partition, see Frazer, *The First World War*, 10–11.

15 The first half of the essay creates and invokes a Romantic and idyllic version of Lebanon, hence my contention that Lebanon for Gibran is more of a *mawṭin* (in the spiritual or spatial sense) than a *waṭan* (in the politicised sense that impregnated the term in the *Nahḍa* discourse). The post-Partition Lebanon, which for Gibran is 'your Lebanon' or the bad Lebanon, is the subject of his scathing

criticism in the essay (levelled over the 'westernisation' of the area and the lack of ethical, national commitment). He writes, for instance: 'Your Lebanon is at times attached to Syria and at times detached from it, then it contrives against both positions to become at once knotted and unfastened; while my Lebanon is neither attached nor detached, nor does it magnify or belittle itself'. See *CWs in Arabic*, 305.

16 This is, it must be stressed, the stance *of* Gibran, who was not, of course, alone in his political orientation. The idea of an autonomous state in the whole of 'geographical Syria' dates back to the second half of the nineteenth century, with its roots in Butrus al-Bustani's periodical *al-Jinān*, in which he speaks of the Ottoman Empire as our *waṭan* and Syria as our country or *bilād*. It is important to remember that there were calls for an autonomous state in Mount Lebanon during the same period. See Hourani, *Arabic Thought*, 274–76.

17 It is significant to stress that Gibran was not pleased with the Syrian Arab Congress that was held in Paris in 1913, to which he declined an invitation to give a speech on the grounds that it did not reflect his own disposition. Mary Haskell notes in her journal that 'Gibran wants revolution [. . .] It need not be planned. Revolution even failing will be met with Home Rule, succeeding, will free Syria and Arabia'. MH Journal, 22 June 1913.

18 Daye, *'Aqīdat Jubrān*, 249.

19 Ibid.

20 Ibid.

21 National consciousness precedes and grounds, although it does not necessarily lead to, a nationalist movement or ideology necessary for the formation of a nation-state, which consolidates this sentiment in terms of national identity. On the distinction between national consciousness and nationalism, see Smith, *Nationalism*, 6.

22 It is important to draw a distinction between Arabism as a potent notion that emerged in the intellectual discourse of the *Nahḍa* and Arab nationalism as a political movement with clear ideological goals, which, as Ernest Dawn points out, was not a palpable political force until after 1914. Arab nationalism, however, is premised on and indissociable from Arabism. Syrian nationalists who opposed Ottoman governance and Ottomanism remained a minority until 1918, so Dawn notes. Of the *émigré* nationalists, Dawn only mentions Ameen Rihani. See Ernest C. Dawn, 'The Origins of Arab Nationalism', in *The Origins of Arab Nationalism*, ed. Rachid Khalidi et al. (New York: Columbia University Press, 1991), 11–12.

23 Daye, *ʿAqīdat Jubrān*, 250.

24 Ibid.

25 Ibid.

26 Ibid.

27 Here, I am relying on Reinhard Schulze who argues that, since 'decadence' was attributed to Islam at the birth of the colonial *mission civilisatrice*, Islam acquired the status of 'un-culture' for 'the Europeans spectators of the Orient', because 'culture was used as a synonym of humanity, reason and freedom', only to obtain, after the colonial encounter, a 'traditional' sense of culture deemed the antithesis of 'modernity'. See Reinhard Schulze, 'Mass Culture and Islamic Cultural Production in the Nineteenth Century Middle East', in *Mass Culture, Popular Culture and Social Life in the Middle East*, ed. George Stauth and Sami Zubaida (Frankfurt; Boulder: Westview Press, 1987), 190.

28 In his essay 'al-Umam wa dhawātuha' (Nations and the Selves of Nations), Gibran postulates that 'every people [*shaʿb*] has a Collective Self [*dhāt*], analogous in its essence and nature to the individual self. Although this Collective Self derives its being from the individuals of a nation [. . .] it is nevertheless independent from the people in that it possesses a particular life and a unique will'. *CWs in Arabic*, 251–53. This postulation is reminiscent of the Romantic notion of the nation's spirit or *Volksgeist*, especially that of Herder or Renan.

29 This notion of an essence that defines the historical subject in terms of 'an alternance in a continuity of decadence and health' was pervasive in many revivalist projects in modernity, of which the *Nahḍa* is one example. See Al-Azmeh, *Islams and Modernities*, 97–100.

30 Daye, *ʿAqīdat Jubrān*, 250.

31 Ibid., 251.

32 I am drawing on Wael Hallaq who, relying on Carl Schmitt, Thomas Kuhn and Michel Foucault in his use of such concepts as 'paradigms' and central of peripheral 'domains', argues that the moral was the central domain in premodern Islamic governance or *Sharīʿa*, while in modernity the moral has become a peripheral domain, subject to the legal mechanisms of the modern nation-state. For more on this, see Wael Hallaq, *The Impossible State: Islam, Politics and Modernity's Moral Predicament* (New York: Columbia University Press, 2012), 6–13.

33 Daye, *ʿAqīdat Jubrān*, 251

34 See Schulze, 'Mass Culture', 189.

35 This is taken from a short essay that Gibran wrote in response to Jamil Maalouf's criticism of his essay 'Ṣawt al-shāʿir', which I have analysed in the previous chapter, where Gibran posits *al-kulliyya* against *al-ʿaṣabiyya*. See Daye, *Lakum Jubrānukum*, 274.

36 Ibid., 274. See my discussion of Gibran's cosmopolitan poetics of hospitality and Love *qua* justice in Chapter Two.

37 Gibran, in an interview conducted with him in 1915 (*al-Sā'iḥ*, issue 240), maintains that 'reclaiming the glory of Islam is a beautiful dream, yet the power of Islam has waned, and almost nothing has remained of the Islam that various nations in the past, different in their religious and worldly aspects, had adopted, except for withered emotions which are unable to unify these divided nations today'. Daye, *ʿAqīdat Jubrān*, 330.

38 Ibid., 249.

39 Ahmad declares: 'I am not, albeit living amongst idle [*moqʿadīn*] Easterners, desperate about the future of the East'. Ibid., 250.

40 Ahmad's views are not so different from Gibran's. An article in the periodical *al-Sā'iḥ*, 'Gibran and Islam' (25 May 1916), reports a speech that Gibran gave at a ceremony organised by the American Association of Religions, where he stressed the influence that the Arabs of Andalusia had exerted on European art and science, while attributing the modern degradation and decadence (*inḥiṭāṭ*) in the Muslim countries mainly to the conquests of the Ottomans and their lack of the elements of creativity and innovation. The writer of the article goes on to foreground, in a laudatory manner, that Gibran talks about the merits of Islam in the West as a Christian Arab, quoting his words 'Jesus resides in half of my heart and Muhammad resides in the other' and pointing out, following Gibran, that if Islam does not triumph over the Ottoman state, the East will fall into hands of the West. See Daye, *Lakum Jubrānukum*, 296–98.

41 Mary Haskell records in her journals that, for Gibran, neither the diplomatic appeal to the Powers of Europe nor Turkey's diplomatic consent would give the Syrians Home Rule. Only a revolution could make this possible. MH Journal, 22 June 1913.

42 The title of the Agreement refers to the two men who carried out the secret deliberations, Charles Francois Georges-Picot, the French consul-general in Beirut before the war, and Sir Mark Sykes, a British conservative member of Parliament, who authored two books on the Ottoman Empire. The French had their eyes on Syria, while the British were seeking to control Mesopotamia, and the agreement was crucial to the partition of the Arab territories by the end of the war. 'This

projected division of these territories', writes T. G Frazer, 'as yet theoretical and negotiated away from the public eye [in 1916], took no account whatsoever of the possible wishes of the people who lived there, but simply reflected the priorities which London and Paris had at the time'. Frazer, *The First World War*, 6.

43 Daye, *'Aqīdat Jubrān*, 15–16.

44 Ibid., 252.

45 Ibid., 253.

46 Ibid., 345. See the last section of this chapter.

47 *'Aṣabiyya*, in Ibn Khaldun's sense, means 'mutual affection and willingness to fight and die for each other'. In the educational discourse of the *Nahḍa*, however, and especially in regard to Rifa'a Rafi' al-Tahtawi, Hourani points out that the term takes up the meaning of *ḥubb al-waṭan* (love of homeland or country) – that is, that 'of solidarity which binds together those who live in the same community and is the basis of social strength'. See Hourani, *Arabic Thought*, 23, 78–79.

48 Daye, *'Aqīdat Jubrān*, 255.

49 Ibid., 260.

50 Ibid.

51 KG to MH, 22 October 1912. For Gibran, the universal, or what he considers 'world-consciousness' or 'life-thinking', should be the locus of aesthetic and ethical engagement, not the national, which for him stands for parochialism. But because it is precisely the ethical that calls for the national – the aching and suffering of Syria – he had no choice but to be nationally committed, as revealed in many of his letters to Mary Haskell and her journals. See Sayigh, *Aḍwā' jadīda 'alā Jubrān*, 141–43.

52 For more on the social history of the great famine and its unspeakable consequences (over half a million people were reported to have died in Great Syria alone during World War I), see Fawaz, *A Land of Aching Hearts*, 99–110, 277.

53 For more on this see Daye, *'Aqīdat Jubrān*, 69–80.

54 Fawaz, *A Land of Aching Hearts*, 284.

55 *CWs in Arabic*, 249–51.

56 Daye, *'Aqīdat Jubrān*, 294.

57 Ibid.

58 Ibid., 295.

59 Ibid., 295–96.

60 Ibid., 296.

61 Ibid.

62 Ibid.

63 Ibid., 294.

64 See Gibran, 'al-Hijra wa futūḥ sūria' (Immigration and Syria's Subjection to Foreign Conquests), in *Iqlib al-ṣafḥa*, 119–20. As for Syria's nationhood, in an interview conducted with Gibran in 1915 for the periodical *al-Sā'iḥ*, Gibran asserts that 'the glorious future that I envision for Syria is for it to become a republic', going on to maintain that all the pre-modern kingdoms should now turn into republics, for 'the republic is the sole track upon which a country proceeds towards prosperity'. Daye, *Lakum Jubrānukum*, 300.

65 Daye, *'Aqīdat Jubrān*, 298.

66 Ibid.

67 See Meskini, *al-Huwiyya wa al-zamān*, 36. Meskini posits the 'contemporaneity' (*mu'āṣara*) of the Arabs to the modern, 'Western' age (*al-'aṣr*) as the efficient, non-identitarian mode of resistance against the metaphysical dominance of the West over the rest of the world (the objectification of non-European humanity).

68 Daye, *'Aqīdat Jubrān*, 298.

69 Hourani points out that in the *Nahḍa* the term has acquired 'the specific meaning of territorial patriotism in the modern sense'. Hourani, *Arabic Thought*, 79.

70 Sheehi, *Foundations*, 9–10.

71 This passage is cited in translation by Adel Beshara in 'A Rebel Syrian', 151.

72 Gibran maintains this in his short article 'Uḥibbu bilādī', in Daye, *'Aqīdat Jubrān*, 260–61.

73 Ibid., 260.

74 The point here is not to foreground the 'origin' of the concept and therefore (de-)legitimise its appropriation, but to account for the conditions and consequences of its appropriation, universalisation and naturalisation – which nonetheless should be questioned – as it travels and embodies itself in non-Western forms of life. Talal Asad, relying on Benedict Anderson's concept of the nation as inherently limited and sovereign, has maintained that the term *umma*, being used today to denote the Arab nation (*al-umma 'al-'arabiyya*), 'is cut off from the theological predicates that gave it its universalizing power, and is made to stand for an imagined community that is equivalent to a total political society [. . .] in a secular (social) world'. Asad, *Formations of the Secular*, 197–98. My point, however, is that the entrenched religious sense of the word *umma* is that which had occasioned the domestication of the modern concept of the nation, a domestication that has nevertheless regionalised and de-universalised its

original sense (that is, one that has confined it to the Arab and, in this case, Syrian nation), all the while retaining its religious connotation, making it readily prone to a (Derridean) 'undecidability'.

75 Daye, *'Aqīdat Jubrān*, 369–70.

76 It is astonishing, one must remark, that Gibran speaks only of 'men' when it comes to education and Awakening, all the more so because he was a staunch advocator of women's rights in Syria, as many of his early short stories attest.

77 Ibid., 303 [emphasis added].

78 In 'Ḥaffār al-qubūr wa al-aḥyā'' (Grave Digger and the Living), Gibran stresses the existence of 'living seeds' suitable for growth in the Syrian as an individual and the absence thereof in the Syrians as a collective whole; hence his emphasis on *al-ḥayāt al-qawmiyya*, national or collective life. Ibid., 256–57.

79 Frazer, *The First World War*, 10.

80 For a short historical account of the committee's foundation and activity, see Daye, *'Aqīdat Jubrān*, 81–90.

81 Ibid., 82.

82 'Wilson was talking in the context of Europe, and national self-determination came to be a major feature of how the continent emerged from the Paris Peace conference, but the idea was understandably taken up with alacrity in other parts of the world, including the Middle East'. Frazer, *The First World War*, 8.

83 Adel Beshara contends that Gibran was not unaware of 'international diplomacy and Western colonial interest in Syria', but he 'never imagined the Allies, brought up in the spirit of democracy and liberal morality, would allow their imperial interests to completely eclipse their war-time pledges to the newly-liberated people of the world and trample all over them as though they had no intrinsic human value'. Beshara, 'A Rebel Syrian', 154. The point is indeed well-taken, but the situation was far more complex than Beshara put it. Gibran was cognizant of the dangers and repercussions of colonialism, voiced before and after the war in his 1916 article 'Ḥaffār al-qubūr wa al-aḥyā'', in his letters to Emile Zaydan (1919–22) and in his recently published manuscripts, but saw foreign 'tutelage' as inevitable and necessary. This is due to his firm belief in a (national) social, cultural and economic Awakening as a precondition for the foundation of the nation. What is intriguing here is that Gibran, before the official partition of the area, considered foreign 'tutelage' to be separable from colonialism. Whether this was naïve or strategic is hard to tell.

84 Daye, *'Aqīdat Jubrān*, 370.

85 Ibid.

86 Some of these manuscripts have been published by John Daye (1988) and others transcribed and assembled in an edited collection published in Lebanon in 2010, available in Gibran's Museum (Bsharri, north Lebanon).

87 Daye, *'Aqīdat Jubrān*, 374.

88 Ibid., 375.

89 Ibid., 369–70. For a translation of one of the letters he sent to Emile Zaydan, see Beshara, 'A Rebel Syrian', 154.

90 Gibran asserts that, '[i]f Syria is placed under the tutelage of America, France or England – or all of them as some Syrians are calling for – there are fundamental things that we must insistently and persistently adhere to, namely, the geographical unity of Syria, national, participatory governance, compulsory education and the permanent priority and official status that should be accorded to the Arabic language'. Daye, *'Aqīdat Jubrān*, 370.

91 Daye, *'Aqīdat Jubrān*, 303.

92 An Allied commission, proposed by President Woodrow Wilson, was sent to Syria 'to ascertain the views of the population' as to their future following the war. The findings of the 'shelved' report reflected that 'the overwhelming opinion in Syria was against a French Mandate and that nine-tenths of the population was opposed to Zionism'. See Frazer, *The First World War*, 10–12.

93 Recent scholarship has moved away from the 'decadence paradigm' in their approach to the *Nahḍa*'s intellectual enterprise. See, for instance, Stephen Sheehi, 'Towards a Critical Theory of *al-Nahḍah*: Epistemology, Ideology and Capital', *Journal of Arabic Literature* 43, 2/3 (2012): 269–98.

94 Daye, *'Aqīdat Jubrān*, 302.

95 Ibid.

96 'If you contrast the massive gulf that exists between us and the nations that are civilisationally advanced', he asserts, 'you would readily assume that our nature [*tīna*] is inferior to theirs'. He then goes on to refute this surface observation. Ibid., 302.

97 Ibid.

98 Ibid., 303.

99 Ibid., 374 [emphasis mine].

100 In his manuscripts, Gibran reiterates that he is not a politician and does not want to be a politician (in the context of nationalism). See Gibran, *Iqlib al-ṣafḥa*, 102.

101 See Jacques Rancière, 'The Politics of Literature', *SubStance 103* 33, no. 1 (2004), 10.

102 Said, *Orientalism*, 49–73.

103 Daye, *'Aqīdat Jubrān*, 374.

104 See Meskini, *al-Huwiyya wa al-zamān*, 7–8.

105 Daye, *'Aqīdat Jubrān*, 374.

106 Ibid.

107 Passages from this text, entitled 'al-Shā'ir', are published in Wahib Kayruz, *'Ālam Jubrān al-fikrī II* (Beirut: Basharīyā, 1983), 135.

108 Ibid.

109 Ibid [emphasis added]. It is not surprising that the Prophet Muhammad, for Gibran, is the hero of history *par excellence*. See Nasib 'Arida, 'Muqābala ma'a Jubrān' (Interview with Gibran, 1933), in Daye, *Lakum Jubrānukum*, 310. The idea of Muhammad as a great legislator who founded a great civilisation is also found in Voltaire, Rousseau and other Enlightenment thinkers. See Ziad Elmarsafy, *The Enlightenment Qur'an: The Politics of Translation and the Construction of Islam* (Oxford: OneWorld, 2009), Chapters Four and Five in particular.

110 Gibran, *Iqlib al-ṣafḥa*, 115.

111 Ibid.

112 I use this word in the sense that Abdallah Laroui lends to it: that is, as an ideological deployment of 'tradition', wrongly posited as 'the anti-thesis of progressive change', which usually intensifies when there is foreign pressure or threat. See Abdallah Laroui, *The Crisis of Arab Intellectuals: Traditionalism or Historicism?* trans. Diarmid Cammell (Berkley; London: University of California Press, 1976), 33, 42–43.

113 Gibran, *Iqlib al-ṣafḥa*, 105.

114 Ibid.

115 *CWs in Arabic*, 213–15.

116 Daye, *'Aqīdat Jubrān*, 345.

117 Ibid.

118 Ibid.

119 Ibid., 346.

120 Ibid.

121 'The romantic subject', argues Sheehi, 'distinguishes himself from the previously seen reform subject by finding his ontology in a criterion exterior to civilization understood as urbanity'. Sheehi, *Foundations*, 98–100.

122 Towards the end of the same essay, he asserts, '[i]n the East, our old house, there are countless treasures, riches and wonderful things, yet they are all confused,

amassed and veiled by a layer of dust. It is commonly known that the West has mastered the art of organisation [*tartīb*] to an extreme degree [. . .] If imitation is ineluctable, let us imitate this art provided that we imitate none other than it'. Daye, *'Aqīdat Jubrān*, 350.

123 The narrator is surprised to have found 'wine, tobacco, and coffee in his [Yusuf's] cell'. 'I do not blame you', Yusuf said, 'for you, like many, imagine that isolation from men means isolation from life and from the natural pleasures and the simple delights of life'. Kahlil Gibran, *The Storm*, transl. John Wallbridge (Santa Cruz, CA: White Cloud Press, 1993), 15.

124 *CWs in Arabic*, 260. I rely, in part, on John Wallbridge's brilliant translation, which is nevertheless not without inaccuracies.

125 Ibid., 261. See also my reading of Almustafa's passage on freedom in *The Prophet* in Chapter One.

126 Ibid., 262.

127 Ibid., 262; *The Storm*, 26.

128 *CWs in Arabic*, 262; *The Storm*, 27.

129 Daye, *'Aqīdat Jubrān*, 347.

130 Gibran's essentialist language here invokes the notion of national essence, prevalent in post-Enlightenment Romanticism in and outside Europe, and the *Nahḍa* is no exception. See Al-Azmeh, *Islams and Modernities*, 31, 99–102.

131 *CWs in Arabic*, 266 [emphasis mine].

132 See '"Amān Allah" Malik al-Afghān', in Daye, *'Aqīdat Jubrān*, 379–80.

133 This is mainly in relation to literature. See *CWs in Arabic*, 270.

134 Gibran, 'Nahḍat al-sharq al-'arabī', in Daye, *'Aqīdat Jubrān*, 349–50.

135 Ibid., 349.

136 Ibid.

137 Ibid., 350.

138 See Gibran, 'al-Umam wa dhawātuhā', in *CWs in Arabic*, 251–35.

139 In 'What is the Renaissance?' Salama Musa, a contemporary of Gibran, asserts that 'the spirit of the [European] Renaissance is the spirit of independence itself'. By reading the *Nahḍa* against the European Renaissance and modern history, he attempts to draw lessons from the latter that could bear on and further inspire the former. Yet, Europe for him, unlike Gibran, is the unquestioned model of civilisation and progress. Moreover, his view that cultures naturally borrow from one another, fertilising one another, despite colonisation (which he staunchly denounced in Egypt), differs from Gibran's stance that borrowing, albeit inevitable, must be carried out in a critical, autonomous spirit. See Salama

Musa, 'From *What is the Renaissance*?' trans. John Barskerville, in *The Arab Renaissance: A Bilingual Anthology of the Nahda*, ed. Tarek El-Aris (New York: The Modern Language Association of America, 2018), 32–49.

140 Salim al-Bustani's criticism of 'his urban compatriots for confusing materialism with true progress', which prefigured 'the romantic paradigm', is a case in point. See Sheehi, *Foundations*, 105–6.

141 Fawaz, *A Land of Aching Hearts*, 10, 11, 25, 33, 34.

142 Daye, *'Aqīdat Jubrān*, 374.

4

Multiple Horizons of Expectations, Multiple Gibrans: Or, Gibran as World Literature

*I am not aware of any other example, in the history of literature, of so renowned a book [*The Prophet*], which has become a small bible for countless readers, and which continues nevertheless to circulate on the margins, as if under the coat, under tens of millions of coats, one must say, but under the coat all the same, as if Gibran was always a sacred writer, a shameful writer, an accursed writer.*

Amin Maalouf[1]

The East is not a simple (dialectical, speculative, culturalist) movement toward the West. They are for themselves the beginning and the end. And we are trying to go toward a planetary and plural thought, this other-thought, that is built step by step and without a certain end.

Abdelkebir Khatibi[2]

Where and how do we locate Gibran in the world today? To locate a bilingual *émigré* writer such as Gibran somewhere is, of course, to place him in more than one geography. The question of location in this sense goes beyond geography in the territorial sense. It is cultural, imaginary and epistemic. And to tackle this question is to locate oneself in, and carry oneself across, these different geographies. In the case of Gibran, this would entail the encounter of many problems, not the least of which is the fact that Gibran is seen as a popular sage prophet in one location (the United States) and as a rebellious modernising poet and writer in another (the Arab world). To view Gibran in this manner, however, is to locate oneself in two different languages and cultures *separately*. Yet Gibran's bilingual chasm, upon which

I have dwelled in Chapter Two, is a chasm that simultaneously separates and connects. This chasm has produced different incarnations of Gibran that are sometimes irreconcilable, due mainly to what is masked and unmasked, what is lost and gained, in (cultural) translation. No wonder that this chasm is most apparent in the divergent modes of how his English work has been received in the US and in the Arab world. Tracing this chasm and the worldly conditions of its emergence and persistence – that is, tracing and interrogating specific modes of reception which vary in their influence on the perception of that which is received – is my concern in this chapter.

Gibran, so I argue, is a writer whose English work is bilingual, because it belongs at once to both Arabic and American literatures, despite the lack of critical recognition in the American literary field.[3] As such, it is an instance of 'world literature' *par excellence*, not only in the sense that his work, following David Damrosch,[4] travels in translation beyond the culture of origin, but insofar as it inhabits two literary systems to neither of which it *fully* belongs. Hence, any appraisal of it should simultaneously consider its reception in these two literary spheres. I demonstrate that Gibran's English text has often been received as essentially and monolithically 'Oriental' and 'spiritual' in the US, designations that saturate and flatten this text *within* that specific cultural and normative location. When the same text travels to the Arab world, it is given another literary and hermeneutic life in that context, compelling us to approach it as world literature beyond English – namely, as world literature in Arabic. The American reception will occupy my analytical attention in the first two sections of this chapter. Gibran's presence in American literature is vague and perplexing: on the one hand, *The Prophet* has enjoyed a massive popular appeal since its publication in 1923; on the other, Gibran sits outside the canon of American literature. What is more, his other English works and Arabic writings have been eclipsed by the phenomenon of *The Prophet*. This problem, therefore, warrants focused attention to the ways in which his books have been received in the US, as well as, more specifically, to the American conditions of reading and horizons of expectations that have shaped particular modes of reading, (e)valuation and categorisation. Yet, the American reception remains one side of the picture. Of no less importance is the 'Arabisation' and recontextualisation of Gibran's work in the Arab cultural geography, where he is subject to another regime of value and other conditions of reading and interpretation that often obscure the question of translation. The reclamation of Gibran as a modern poet of rupture and vision by Arab modernists, as well as examples of the creative and philosophical afterlife of his Anglophone work in Arabic, will be discussed in reference to those conditions and in a way that offers critical reflections on Gibran and 'world literature' today (see the third and fourth sections).

Theoretically, I adopt Pierre Bourdieu's sociological approach, because it has the capacity to elucidate some of the issues that pertain to Gibran's American reception. For Bourdieu, the cultural/symbolic and the economic are interrelated but irreducible to one another; both of them are ultimately crucial in the process of valuation and 'consecration' of a literary work within a particular literary/cultural field, which operates according to its own internal and often unrecognised regulations of value, but, crucially, in relation to the field of power.[5] Despite its silence on essential elements such as race and gender,[6] Bourdieu's sociology of art and literature is helpful to illuminate *some* of the conditions that left Gibran outside the canon of American literature. Along with Bourdieu, I use Hans Robert Jauss' concept of the 'horizon of expectations'.[7] Jauss' 'aesthetics of reception' does not pay attention to literary works that are constituted by and received in two different linguistic and cultural spheres. Nevertheless, I use his concept, expanding it beyond his model (as a criterion of a literary work's aesthetic worth), to designate the discursive conditions and backgrounds against which specific modalities of reading or (re-)appropriating Gibran are produced, cemented and/or disrupted, in both the American and the Arab contexts. I understand that Bourdieu's approach may not be reconcilable with hermeneutics, but I am not combining and using them uncritically. My approach, in effect, aims to fill the gap between sociology and literary textuality, between the historical and socio-cultural, on the one hand, and the aesthetic and textual, on the other.

The Early Reception of Gibran in the US

The importance of tracing this initial reception of Gibran's English works lies not only in revealing whether his works were positively or negatively received. It resides, most importantly, in exposing the historical as well as the normative and evaluative framework within which his works were placed and according to which they were assessed. Critics have so far only pointed out that *The Madman* and *Jesus the Son of Man* are the two books of Gibran that received positive critical reception in the US – two books that remain relatively unknown compared to *The Prophet*. But by whom and how and in which historical and cultural context is this judgment made, what Bourdieu calls 'the symbolic production of the work' and its value?[8] What is the regime of value that informs these evaluative judgments? What was highlighted in the reviews, and what was absent and why? These are the fundamental questions that my discussion in this section endeavours to address.

To speak about this reception is to situate Gibran within the American literary field at the time. There were crucial changes in terms of literary and aesthetic taste in the aftermath of World War I.[9] Before the war, 'American literature' had not yet acquired an institutional status that demarcated its boundaries and history, but the formation of its canon began in 1910s and 1920s.[10] Tradition had to be invented, and T. S. Eliot's well-known essay 'Tradition and the Individual Talent' altered the perception of tradition from something inherited to something obtained by assiduous labour. Eliot speaks about novelty in relation to an existing order of 'European, English literature',[11] in relation to 'the mind of Europe'.[12] The implicit and 'natural' assumption here is that to write poetry in English is to belong to a European tradition of writing, to be conscious of this tradition as it inhabits the present. Moreover, Eliot's concept of novelty, embodied in his impersonal theory of poetry, posits the depersonalisation of the poet in a way that transforms emotion into palpable feelings manifesting themselves detachedly and creatively in *form*.[13] Eliot attacks the 'metaphysics of mysticism'[14] and 'the metaphysical theory of the substantial unity of the soul'.[15] He leaves no place for a variety of mystical experiences in poetry, for instance, or for poetry that is ethically engaged. Thus, 'the generation of literary critics who, following T. S. Eliot, began to come to prominence in the 1920s, were doubtful – if not altogether suspicious – of the power of art to shape behaviour at all'.[16] The 'New Critics' diverted attention to a literary work's language and form, seen as that which represents human creativity, by bracketing, if not dismissing, its subject-matter or the values it promotes.[17] They were suspicious of 'mass society' and keen on protecting culture by stressing the value of art *per se*, not the way in which it shapes conduct. As Paul Lauter puts it, this 'formalist aesthetic played an implicit role in the narrowing of the canon', as these 'arbiters of taste' often excluded black and female writers whose mode of writing did not invite the then predominant approach of New Criticism. Instead, . . .

> . . . upper-class white Americans in the twenties acknowledged the lives of black people, and the work of black writers, only in 'their place' – as 'exotic', like a taste for Pernod or jazz, a quaint expression of the 'folk'. It was very well to visit Harlem, but decidedly inappropriate to include blacks in the anthology or the classroom, much less in the Modern Language Association.[18]

This account is of course schematic, but it illustrates the general literary and aesthetic climate of post-World War I America, which was crucial to the formation and consolidation of the American literary canon until the 1960s and 1970s. Locating Gibran – the writer of an invisible 'ethnic minority' in the US – within this context will help us understand the American reception of his work. Gibran's English-language writings, whose concern is mostly ethical, cannot be appreciated by looking at them through the lens of Eliot's impersonal theory of poetry, nor by casting them as 'exotic' in relation to the dominant European, white male norms of writing and thinking. That was explicitly or implicitly the case, however.

Gibran's first book in English, *The Madman*, was generally well-received; yet, as two of his biographers observed, he 'often was portrayed as a mysterious hero, ready-made genius, and Near Eastern counterpart of Indian poet Rabindranath Tagore. His impoverished origins in Bsharri, adolescent days in the South End, and cultural apprenticeship in Boston were overlooked'.[19] This comparison to Tagore, who was well-known in America at the time, placed Gibran in the vague category of 'Oriental' poetry, with the Orient understood as an essential, over-arching civilisational identity that precedes the text itself and determines, *a priori*, its value. This judgment was not without (weak) foundation, however, as Gibran adopts the parable form in his English writings, despite his own realisation, as noted in Chapter Two, that 'English is not the language for parables'[20] – that is, for his own parables which were first imagined or even written in Arabic. The parable, however, is not necessarily an Oriental form. What is at stake here is not the parable as such, but the identity of the writer in question, and how this identity informs the act of (e)valuation itself.

Joseph Gollomb, in his interview with Gibran for the *Evening Post* in 1919, following the publication of *The Madman*, observes that a formal similarity between Tagore and Gibran exists, but quickly stresses the contrast between the two:

> Roughly speaking, what Tagore is to the East, Kahlil Gibran is to the Near East [. . .] Both employ largely the parable. Both have written in English with as fine a command of the Western tongue as of their own. And each is an artist in other forms besides poetry. But there the resemblances end and the differences appear, the most striking being their physical appearance. Tagore, with his long, picturesque hair and beard and his flowing robe, is a figure from some canvas Sir Frederic Leighton might have painted of a religious mystic. Gibran is Broadway or Copley Square or the Strand, or the Avenue de l'Opera – a correctly dressed cosmopolitan of the Western World.[21]

Waïl Hassan is sceptical about this portrayal in his assessment of 'the Gibran phenomenon',[22] because for Gollomb there seemed to be 'a chameleon-like ease of adaptiveness about [Gibran]', an Oriental who is 'a correctly dressed cosmopolitan of the Western World'. At issue here is not Gibran but Gollomb's appraisal, because for the latter Gibran could either be an Oriental *à la* Tagore or an Occidentalised Oriental – that is, seeming here is mistaken for being, to invoke Gibran's poem 'My Friend', which we closely read in Chapter Two.

The *Evening Post*'s review, for its part, highlighted the Near Eastern creative source of Gibran's *The Madman*, especially in its capacity to accommodate diverse cultural sources, 'a blend of Tagore, La Fontaine, Nietzsche, and Dr. Sigmund Freud – a blend which, in *The Madman*, is surprisingly successful'.[23] This blend, albeit not qualified here, makes *The Madman* irreducible to Orientalist and culturalist readings. By contrast, *The Nation*'s review considered the book appealing only to 'disciples of the modern cult of things Eastern', because 'most Westerners will find the work repellent in its exotic perversity, and will lay it aside with an uncomprehending shake of head, for East is East and West is still West'.[24] Note here that 'West is *still* West', meaning that what is deemed exterior to the West, 'the East', has not been able to change what it takes to be 'the West', particularly if those 'Easterners' are culturally active inside this 'West'. For 'Tagore has not really succeeded in bridging the chasm between them, nor do we think Gibran will do'.[25] The Orientalist ontological distinction between (and the potential 'bridging' of) 'Orient' and 'Occident' is clearly at work here. In other words, this is not so much an issue reducible to authorial inception – of course, that remains significant as far as the historical and discursive conditions of writing are concerned – as it is a matter of a specific mode of reception informed by its Western-centredness in a historical period of high imperialism, in which the Occident ruled territorially, epistemologically and imaginatively over the Orient. The fact that the US was not involved in the territorial colonisation of the Orient does not mean that its *imaginary* was not informed by the conceived superiority – racial, cultural and civilisational – of the Occident.[26]

If culturalist reactions to Gibran's work such as the above prevailed, Marguerite Wilkinson, in her anthology *New Voices: An Introduction to Contemporary Poetry* (1919), had a different view:

> Kahlil Gibran is writing poems and parables that have an individual music, a naïve charm and distinction and a structural symmetry based on symbol, contrast, repetition and parallelism. [It] is almost entirely a poetry of symbolism. His poems are parables, not designs in rhyme, rhythm or imagery, although his rhythms are clear and pleasing. In [. . .] *The Madman*, we have the best parables that can be found in contemporary poetry.[27]

Wilkinson did not ground her brief examination on an East–West outlook on poetry and literature. What mattered for her was, first and foremost, the poetry itself, and she did not refer to the parables as 'Eastern'. Albeit brief, an interpretation of Gibran's text of this sort has rarely been registered. Although Wilkinson's approach detaches the text from its 'worldliness' and 'circumstantiality', to use Said's words,[28] her focus on the aesthetic as such is not without significance. An incorporation of Gibran in an anthology of American literature such as Wilkinson's is significant, precisely because it abstains from evaluative judgements based on an Occident–Orient culturalist dichotomy, which informs so much of the reviews and criticisms of Gibran's texts.[29]

Another point to accentuate here is that this incorporation occurred *before* the publication of *The Prophet* – that is, before the instant and spontaneous popular appeal that 'overshadow[ed] literary approval from postwar elite intellectual circles'.[30] I shall return to the problem of *The Prophet* and how its reception eclipsed Gibran's other important works later, yet it is important to note that aesthetic considerations are never divorced from, and neither are they reducible to, the social and cultural circumstances of reception. A horizon of expectations, therefore, cannot be solely understood in aesthetic terms – even though the aesthetic absorbs what is other than it – because what is at stake here is a bilingual writer whose shift from one language to another (and from one culture to another), whose mode of writing adopted in English (considered Romantic, belated, anachronistic, aphoristic and so on) and whose perceived cultural distance or foreignness at that specific historical juncture complicate any appraisal of his Anglophone writings. On the plane of form, Gibran did not create a 'horizontal change' in English in the way in which he did in Arabic, but his English texts are, as it were, constituted by translation,[31] which is to say that they are bilingual texts even if they do not exhibit that on the surface. What should be emphasised is his work's 'response to *questions of meaning* such as they could have posed themselves within the historical life-world of its first readers'.[32] Tracing this response, following Gadamer and Jauss, should be complemented by a hermeneutic 'application' – that is, by highlighting the work's relevance to the horizon of the present.[33] *The Madman* critically engages with many aspects of life in modernity, and not only with perennial human concerns such as God and friendship, for instance. And Gibran does just that, as discussed in Chapter One, in full awareness of the power of poetry and the parable in his specific historical and worldly context. Some of those modern aspects include calculative reason and the quest for 'perfection' in (late) modernity, and his powerful poem '"The Perfect World"' is a case in point:

> I dwell in the midst of a perfect race, I the most imperfect.
> I, a human chaos, a nebula of confused elements, I move amongst finished worlds – peoples of complete laws and pure order, whose thoughts are assorted, whose dreams are arranged, and whose visions are enrolled and registered.
> Their virtues, O God, are measured, their sins are weighed, and even the countless things that pass in the dim twilight of neither sin nor virtue are recorded and catalogued.
> [. . .]

> It is a perfect world, a world of consummate excellence, a world of supreme wonders, the ripest fruit in God's garden, the master-thought of the universe.
> But why should I be here, O God, I a green seed of unfulfilled passion, a mad tempest that seeketh neither east not west, a bewildered fragment from a burnt planet?
> Why am I here, O God of lost souls, thou who are lost among the gods?[34]

The poem, written in the second decade of the twentieth century, is an acute reflection on the maddening regulation of human life that turned bodies into commensurable and surveyed entities in the modern (and late modern) age. Its prescience, therefore, must be appreciated. The point here is that close attention to his texts, however rarefied they seem, with a simultaneous cognizance of their historical situatedness and their relevance to the contemporary situation, *eo ipso* nullifies the kind of judgements that prevail in most accounts of his work, be they laudatory or derogatory – is there, for instance, anything *intrinsically* Oriental or mystical in the poem that I cited?

The Forerunner, Gibran's second book in English, published in 1920, received less critical attention than *The Madman*. Most of the reviews were unkind,[35] but it is crucial to note that the East–West cultural identitarianism was the primary, if not sole, prism through which the book was assessed and valued. In his response to *The Bookman*'s review (December 1920) of the book, which found in it 'the exotic fancy and mysticism of the East', Robin Waterfield writes that 'this had become already a meaningless cliché from reviewers of Gibran's books: there is nothing peculiarly Eastern about *The Forerunner*'; he goes on to stress that 'Gibran's models might just as well have been Aesop's or some of the short allegorical prose pieces in Stephen Crane's *The Black Riders and Other Lines*'.[36] Again, the East as Gibran's civilisational or cultural genealogy predetermines and therefore produces the symbolic value of his own English text in the US. No wonder that the exotic – and there is, of course, nothing intrinsically exotic about *The Forerunner* – serves as a 'symbolic system'[37] that operates in the host(ile) culture by conferring a specific value on objects, in this case texts, deemed strange and culturally different; in short, non-Western, thereby assimilating and evaluating them in accordance with that system. Exoticism, by bridging the imagined distance of the East, obscures the text itself by subsuming it in its representational and assimilationist potency. There is no attempt, in this context, at attending to the difference of the Other without falling prey to an exoticising that eradicates its inexhaustible alterity. Other reviews, such as the one by Isidor Schneider in *Poetry*, did not welcome the didacticism of the book, nor its form, 'which a world grown sceptical is tempted to snub', judging it to be lacking 'the authenticity of prophecy' and leaving us merely with 'a pompous dramatization of only half-individualised platitudes'.[38]

What is at stake here is not simply a 'highbrow contempt'[39] that Gibran's non-elitist poetry evokes, but a certain implicit *expectation* of what a work of poetry should exhibit – in form and content – in an age which is increasingly becoming 'sceptical' from an American point of view, which is to say, in a 'Western' age. *The Forerunner* did not break a horizon of expectation to create another. Its use of the parable and of a language reminiscent of Victorian English is quickly deemed archaic, Eastern and (therefore) not in keeping with the 'spirit of the age', although the book, a collection of prose poems and parables, is not as didactic as *The Prophet.* Such a judgement, however, misses the power of the parable in its subtle reflection on the subject it ponders. The book neither satisfied nor broke an aesthetic horizon of expectation, because its own horizon of meaning demands an interpretative effort that does not shed its form *a priori*, but that rather engages closely with the text's specificity without losing sight of its situatedness and polysemy; and this polysemy is not accountable for by resorting to 'the East' or, for that matter, to 'Eastern mysticism'. It is important to remember, for instance, that the first poem in the collection invokes Nietzsche in a strikingly evident manner: 'You are your own forerunner, and the towers you have builded [*sic*] are but the foundation of your giant-self. And that self too shall be a foundation', going on to underline the idea of continuous 'beginning' as opposed to 'origin'.[40] What is neglected here is the text's own plane of meaning, a neglect that is prompted not only by the text's lack of formal innovation if judged within the Western poetic tradition, but also by the imagined cultural distance or strangeness attributed to its author. This mystified strangeness is one that obfuscates what lies beyond, beneath or before strangeness itself. The essential question therefore is not strangeness *per se*, but to whom one is a stranger.

To speak to *The Forerunner*, as it were, from our own inescapable present horizon of meaning – that is, to (try to) enact its singularity – let us look closely at one among its parables, 'God's Fool', precisely because it touches on this question of the stranger. We are told that a man, 'a dreamer from the desert', went to the city of Sharia, the language of whose inhabitants he cannot speak, nor can they speak his own language. He was served dinner at a vast inn, which he initially thought to be a shrine. Upon entering the inn, he reckoned a feast was given 'by the prince to the people, in celebration of a great event'.[41] When a large man whom he thought to be the prince himself asked him to pay for the dinner, he 'did not understand and thanked the man heartily'.[42] The large man called four watchmen from the city, which 'the stranger' thought to be 'men of distinction' due to 'the ceremoniousness of their dress and of their manner'.[43] The watchmen took him to the House of Judgment. There, he mistook the judge for the king, who appointed two advocates, 'one to present the charge and the other to defend it', but 'the dreamer thought himself to be listening to addresses of welcome'.[44] Unbeknownst to him, a sentence was passed, 'that upon a tablet hung about his neck his crime should be written, and that he should ride through the city on a naked horse, with a trumpeter and drummer before him'.[45] As the sentence was being carried out, people were running after the noise and laughing at him, and he became ecstatic, deeming the tablet the king's blessing and the procession an honour. Suddenly, he sees a man from the desert and cries out: 'Friend! Friend! Where are we? What city of the heart's desire is this? What race of lavish hosts? – who feast the chance guest in their palaces, whose princes companion him, whose king hangs a token upon his breast and opens to him the hospitality of a city descended from heaven'.[46] The man did not reply, but smiled and nodded, and the procession went on.

How does one read and engage with such a parable *now*? First, one must accentuate that it is the form itself – the parable – that enables this creative ambiguity of meaning: the metaphorical world, the reversal of expectation and the paradox built into it in such a way that language 'laughs at itself', producing a reading experience that puts the reader's world into question.[47] Second, one must emphasise the fundamental question of language in relation to the foreigner, to the *xenos* as an absolute stranger, to hostility and/as hospitality or *vice versa*.[48] Which is to say that the parable is an occasion for an interpretative reflection that should be nonetheless contextualised, for Gibran himself was a Syrian immigrant in the US (he spent his childhood in the poor South End district of Boston) at a time when racialist discourse determined immigration policy in the US – the immigrant Syrians were generically classified as Turks.[49] This context does not, of course, subsume the text, but it tells us something about Gibran's *Mahjari* or exilic imagination, which challenges received or unquestioned ideas about belonging and foreignness.

In the parable, the absolute stranger is a dreamer, and it is no coincidence that he is described as dreamer, one for whom every gesture from a hostile host is a gesture of lavish hospitality, not without a hint of irony, however, captured in the smile of the other man from the desert who does not reply but merely watches and shakes his head. By highlighting the stranger's attitude and the way in which he perceives the (for him) strange city, the city of Sharia, Gibran underscores the psychology of a particular kind of stranger, 'God's fool', who in his absolute distance from the host – that is, in his dwelling in a language which is absolutely Other – unwittingly subverts the very hostility of the host, who can only recognise this *surface* strangeness. One can only be 'God's fool' by not knowing the host's language – the host who does not know the stranger's language either – thereby radically misrecognising the signs of the host's culture and the host's law. That the city is called 'Sharia' is not coincidental either: transgressing the law is punishable, be the transgressor an insider or an outsider. In other words, the law in this city is applicable to everyone. But the stranger does not recognise the law or the language of the law. Thus, he exposes and pushes the law to its own limits. He misrecognises, unbeknownst to him and to his host, the law and the language of the law. This mutual misrecognition, occasioned by the absolute strangeness of both the stranger and the host (to each other), obscures the line between hospitality and hostility: the host becomes *at once* hostile and hospitable.[50] This is why 'the dreamer's face was uplifted and his eyes were overflowing with light': the irony is unmistakable, and the parable resists any reading that eliminates this inherent paradox of the situation – by invoking, as does Bushrui, for instance, the Sufi figure of the fool and the dreamer's 'purity of vision'.[51] This dreamer is a stranger to the city, and his naiveté as dreamer is conditioned by his absolute linguistic Otherness. The primary issue here is therefore not one of vision, but of the figure of the absolute stranger who could solely be God's fool by being and remaining *absolutely* foreign, thereby drastically misreading the cultural codes and the law of the host's city. And the host is also a stranger – perhaps even a fool – to the extent that he does not know the stranger's language and does not recognise the stranger's misrecognition of his hostility, to the extent that his law is recognisable as law only if inscribed in language, in his own language. Only a 'God's fool' can show and transgress, albeit unwittingly, the limits of the law.[52]

It bears repeating that this brief close reading of the parable is a reminder of the hermeneutic carefulness that should be adopted when engaging with Gibran's texts. This carefulness serves to avoid homogenising readings that veil its polysemic textuality. Exoticism here remains a para-textual and relational element. As such, it should not predefine the text but must be rather demarcated within a specific cultural field in which it operates. Otherwise, we run the risk of collapsing a potentially polysemic textuality into a culturalist notion of a text defined, approached and flattened by exoticism. Laying bare the discursive and cultural tools of exoticism is necessary but limited. What is critically needed is a hermeneutic movement that pays *close* attention to the text, that makes it *visible*, by inscribing rather than forgetting its worldliness: a care for the text – and its singularity – that is not preceded by the identity of its writer, but that nonetheless takes it – as a linguistic, cultural and discursive factor rather than a rigid identitarian element – into account as part of the hermeneutic movement itself.

I should now turn my attention to *The Prophet*. This 'strange little book'[53] received less critical attention than *The Madman* and *The Forerunner*.[54] Upon publication, however, the book generated a 'spontaneous popular appeal',[55] even though it was never advertised, let alone 'exoticised' so far as the book cover of its first edition is concerned.[56] It is this very popularity, coupled with its supposedly non-European mystical aesthetics, that thwarted serious critical engagement with the book since its publication, exceptions aside. *The Prophet* was not aimed at the high literary circles of the time – in Bourdieu's terms, it was not produced for other producers – but was self-consciously written in a simple style,[57] in such a way that the optimistic message of the book merges perfectly with its biblical, incantational rhythm. The issue here is not solely aesthetic. It is one of cultural and racial difference insofar as it relates to aesthetics. To demonstrate this, let us look at a review in *Poetry* by poet Marjorie

Allen Seiffert, as it exemplifies the lukewarm interest in Gibran within the New Work literary circles at the time. This tepidness towards his work is prompted, primarily, by the foreign, 'mystical' element that it represents, one that does not fall within the space of 'our' culture:

> Kahlil Gibran has written a third book, *The Prophet*, following two others of the same genre, a book that will have a deep appeal for some readers and leave many others cold. *It is a bit of Syrian philosophy, a mode alien to our culture* and yet one in which many restless and unsatisfied spirits of *our race* and generation find a curious release [. . .]
>
> The discourse on beauty ends with the following lines:
> Beauty is eternity gazing at itself in the mirror.
> But you are eternity, and you are mirror.
>
> This seems to relapse into the sheerly mystical, and as the poem curves on to its end, one feels that it could never be a satisfying interpretation of our world. Moreover, the book lacks vigor [. . .] One feels that the poem could be a sort of decoration for us, like a faded Buddhist painting, that it could hang on our walls, *but it would never be part and parcel of our house* [. . .] Doubtless this book will awake response in many readers, for it is not without beauty, and the essence of the book, which is its spiritual significance, *cannot satisfy the robust hunger of the occidental spirit.*[58]

Note the references to 'our culture' and 'our race' as *the* grid through which to judge the book. Again, the work's perceived foreignness and civilisational distance – that is, its *different* normative and imaginative source, which is imagined rather than grasped – preceded it and determined its literary and aesthetic value. Of course, one can dislike the book or may find it too vague and mystical, as she did, but what I am concerned with here is how and on what grounds such an evaluation is made, not the aesthetic judgment itself. What is problematic in Seiffert's assessment is a demarcation of 'our' culture in opposition to what is 'alien' to it, not the aesthetics and mysticism of the book as such. And since *The Prophet* 'is a bit of Syrian philosophy' (how so, we are not told), an 'alien' mode of thinking, its aesthetic worth could not escape this pigeon-holing; it is rather deemed a 'curious release' for certain 'restless and unsatisfied souls of our race'.[59] Nor could it be approached on its own terms – which is to say, taking seriously, aesthetically and hermeneutically speaking, this foreign element that makes it a 'mode alien to our culture'.[60] The end of the passage sums up Seiffert's point: the spiritual significance of the book 'cannot satisfy the robust hunger of the occidental spirit'. There is no room here for what Chaouki Zine calls *ḍiyāfa* (hospitality) as *iḍāfa* (addition) or, even more importantly, for evaluating this addition by going towards the Other in the attempt to understand what it has to say, not by falling back to the sphere of the same as the sole arbiter, the 'occidental spirit' whose Others can speak only to satisfy its 'robust hunger'. But, ironically, the increasing sales of the book since its publication and the global 'afterlife' of the book, to use Walter Benjamin's well-known description of translation,[61] indicate that it speaks to something in the human spirit, beyond the Orient–Occident divide.

The Irish poet George William Russell has praised the book for the same mystical element that Seiffert found alien and undeserving of 'high' literary and aesthetic worth. 'I do not think the East has spoken with so beautiful a voice since the *Gitanjali* of Rabindranath Tagore as in *The Prophet* of Kahlil Gibran, who is artist as well as poet',[62] writes Russell. Although Gibran here is still seen through the prism of the civilisational category of the East – that is, as a representative voice of the East in the West – the essential poetic character of *The Prophet* is nevertheless underscored: 'I have not seen for years a book more beautiful in its thought, and when reading it I understand better than ever before what Socrates meant in the *Banquet* when he spoke of the beauty of thought, which exercises a deeper enchantment than the beauty of form',[63] declares Russell, going on to quote the well-known passage on children in *The Prophet* and another on dwelling. What we see here is not merely an appreciation inspired by the Eastern spirit of the book, but an understanding of it that locates its aesthetic innovation and the 'enchantment' that it engenders in 'the beauty of thought' rather than in that of form. This brief appraisal should be read in the context of modernism, where so many *formal* transformations radically changed English poetic conventions – with the seminal work of T. S. Eliot, Ezra Pound, Gertrude Stein and others. In the US, this transformation was institutionally reinforced by the New Critics whose approach excluded other forms of writing that did not fit within this new aesthetic norm, as I explained earlier. Russell's emphasis on *The Prophet*'s beauty of thought, thus, betrays his awareness of its difference from contemporaneous English poetry. This appreciation can be also understood in light of Russell's life-long interest in Celtic mysticism and theosophy in general, as his acclaimed *The Candle of Vision* (1918) testifies. Beyond this element of mysticism, however, or maybe because of it, one can discern a genuine interest in the book and a cultural openness exemplified in the following passage:

> How profound is that irony of Gibran's about the lovers of freedom 'who wear their freedom as a yoke and a handcuff'. Have we not seen here souls more chained to their idea of freedom than a prisoner is limited in his cell? The most terrible chains are those that gnaw at the soul. I wonder has the East many more poets to reveal to us? If Europe is to have a *new renaissance* comparable with that which came from the wedding of Christianity with the Greek and Latin culture it must, I think, come from a second wedding of Christianity with the culture of the East. Our own words to each other bring us no surprise. It is only when a voice comes from India or China or Arabia that we get the thrill of strangeness from the beauty, and we feel that it might inspire another of the great cultural passions of humanity.[64]

Russell's reference to a 'new renaissance' that weds 'Christianity with the culture of the East' is reminiscent of Raymond Schwab's *La renaissance orientale* (1950). In this work, Schwab argues, in contrast to Russell who thinks that Europe is yet to have such a renaissance, that Europe had actually witnessed a second renaissance with the massive Orientalist discovery in the eighteenth and nineteenth centuries of the languages, literatures and philosophies of the East, whose enormous impact can be discerned in European thought itself.[65] Russell's comments, however, speak more of Gibran who actually weds Christianity – Gibran's Christianity[66] – with Sufism and Nietzscheism, a blend that resists, as I have argued throughout, a categorisation of the book as Eastern spirituality. Russell does not so much accentuate Gibran's mysticism here as he draws attention to important passages in *The Prophet* that reveal what he considers the 'beauty of thought'. Allowing difference to speak, thus, Russell listens to the East as it manifests itself in poets such as Gibran, an openness that nevertheless runs the risk of not recognising how the East itself received Western ideas and domesticated them in the Arab *Nahḍa*. For '[t]he East', as Abdelkebir Khatibi reminds us, 'is not a simple (dialectical, speculative, culturalist) movement toward the West. They are for themselves the beginning and the end'.[67]

It remains a fact, however, that *The Prophet* is one of the least reviewed books of Gibran upon publication.[68] It was privately well-received, nevertheless, as recorded by Gibran himself in Mary Haskell's journals: 'Yes – *The Prophet* has been more than well received. I have been overwhelmed by letters'.[69] Mary Haskell herself, in a prescient remark about the book's success, writes in a letter dating back to October 1923:

> The book will be held as one the treasures of English literature. And in our darkness we will open it to find ourselves again and the heaven and earth within ourselves. Generations will not exhaust it, but instead, generation after generation will find in the book what they would fain be – and it will be better loved as men grow riper and riper.[70]

It is no coincidence, to reiterate, that the book's appeal since its publication would hinder serious critical evaluation of it. Its perceived Eastern source, its 'spiritual' tenor and soft didactic tone, its Romantic elegance and simplicity of style, as well as its captivating beauty of rhythm, have contributed to make the book the popular phenomenon that it has become. All these elements, however, cannot exhaust the singularity of the text. Although simplicity runs the risk of falling into platitude,[71] the above-mentioned elements are essential to the message that Gibran wished to convey, but his vision in the book cannot be reduced to them.[72] This is an important point to underline. And I insist on it by way of resisting, in the words of Edward Said, 'a formidable mechanism of *omnipotent definitions* [that] would present itself as the only one having suitable validity for your discussion [about the Orient]'.[73] In other words, this is an insistence on the need to avoid systemic analyses whereby discursive overdeterminations and homogenising entities such as the Orient and the Occident are employed in a way that erases the multi-faceted nature of that which is analysed. Thus, one also avoids the rigid distinction between high and low literature, to neither of which a text such as *The Prophet* can be said to belong. This is because it destabilises the dichotomy and shows – in the contested way in which it has been received since its publication and in its travelling beyond the US, where it is accommodated and valued in a fundamentally different way – that its worldliness resists the specific symbolic production of its value in the American cultural geography. The paucity of reviews of *The Prophet*, therefore, has less to do with the work itself than with the dynamics of the American literary and cultural field within which it initially emerged. In this context, the book could not escape its imagined Oriental genealogy that for American readers determined and produced its aesthetic, cultural and symbolic value. In other words, it fell outside 'the mind of Europe' within whose contours T. S. Eliot posits his conception of poetic novelty and tradition, for *The Prophet* embodies the very mysticism that Eliot (and the New Critics after him) discarded. This symbolic value was also determined by the increasing sales of the book since its publication, and particularly in the New Age movement.[74]

Before tackling the problem of *The Prophet* in its later reception, I should draw attention to Gibran's longest book in English and the most important after *The Prophet* – *Jesus the Son of Man* (1928). In the years between the publication of these two books, Gibran published *Sand and Foam* (1926), a book of sayings and aphorisms that was not well-received.[75] For reasons of space, I briefly focus on *Jesus the Son of Man*, which expresses Gibran's fascination with Jesus in a remarkably poetic manner. It is the book that received the most favourable critical attention amongst his English works.[76] In it, Gibran recasts Jesus as an essentially powerful man and poet, 'the Master Poet'[77] who represents the ideal of the Greater Self – that is, one who realises the divinity within *as* a man and a poet. The book, written in a charming biblical style, is an imaginative collection of how certain historical and fictitious contemporaneous figures of Jesus thought of him. What is interesting about the book is that it gives an unconventionally diverse and rounded portrait of Jesus as reflected in the minds of those who speak about him, favourably or not. As such, it is a literary book, not a historical one, concerned with the humanness of Jesus and the potency of the symbolic prototype that he incarnates. This is what Gibran had to say about his vision of Jesus to his friend Naimy:

> Jesus has been haunting my heart and imagination for some time past. I am sick and tired [. . .] of people who profess to believe in him, yet always speak of him and paint him as if he were but a sweet lady with a beard. To them he is beautiful, but lowly, humble, weak and poor. I'm also weary of those that deny him, yet present him as a sorcerer or an imposter. Still more weary I am of 'the scholars' who are ever digging into antiquity to produce lengthy and

> stupid arguments *either for or against* the historicity of his personality which is the greatest and most real personality in human history. What shall I say of the senile juggleries of theologians which make of Jesus a sort of hybrid, half-God and half-man? My Jesus is human like you and me [. . .] To me he was a man of might and will as he was a man of charity and pity. Lowliness is something I detest; while meekness to me is but a phase of weakness.[78]

Indeed, Gibran's Jesus was born naturally in Nazareth, not miraculously in Bethlehem,[79] and he is described as 'the Mighty Hunter' and 'the mountainous spirit unconquerable',[80] a 'stranger', 'a madman'[81] and 'a man of Joy',[82] to mention but a few unorthodox descriptions the most recurrent of which is that of the mighty. The book was praised in *The New York Times* as a 'certainly unusual, possibly unique' adoption of this 'immortal theme', and Gibran was credited for 'his aptitude for simile'.[83] The different views about Jesus, as writes P. W. Wilson in the same review, 'are often brilliant in phrase and accurate in perception'.[84] The book, furthermore, was critically acclaimed in *The Springfield Union*, *Manchester Guardian* and *Herald Tribune*.[85] This positive critical reception boils down to the nature of the topic itself and Gibran's mastery of the English biblical style – his anxieties over English as a second language could be said to have been overcome at this stage – together with his capacity for reinventing Jesus in/for the twentieth century. This is a post-religious Jesus, to the extent that he represents a rupture with the orthodox conception of Christ in Christianity, transcending such rigid binaries as secular and religious. That the book is both literary (imaginary and fictitious) and religious, insofar as both reflect one another for Gibran, is therefore a response to a horizon of expectation silently waiting to be fulfilled, as it were. For what we have here is a hermeneutic of reinvention that breaks with what is perceived as tired religious – or, for that matter, anti-religious – narratives (whether scholarly or not) only to put forward its own. To transcend these narratives, it relies not so much on the historicity of Jesus or lack thereof – that is, its concern is not historicist, positivist or rationalist – as on the imaginative and interpretative force of reinvention to rejuvenate the figure for the twentieth century. Which is to say that a *modern* discursive terrain lays the ground for such a poetic reinvention to take place: the epistemological retreat of Christianity in modernity and the persistence of a certain imaginary of Christ led Gibran to adopt a poetic hermeneutic of reinvention that dislodges the figure from both traditionalist, lazy understandings of Jesus and modernist endeavours to rescue or deny his existence, because the figure *lives on* irrespective of such attempts. This reinvention derives its poetic force from the biblical style that Gibran consciously and beautifully deploys. What is important here, as far as the book's reception is concerned, is the following: because what Gibran embarked upon is a *re*invention of such a central figure in human history and not an invention of a post-religious poet-prophet – as is the case of Almustafa in *The Prophet* – *Jesus the Son Man* did not provoke the culturalist, sceptical responses[86] that *The Prophet* sometimes induced, nor did it generate the same popular appeal. Yet the book, despite the critical attention that it initially enjoyed, has been eclipsed by the phenomenon of *The Prophet*, whose Almustafa is nevertheless not so dissimilar from Gibran's Jesus.

The Problem of *The Prophet* in the American Cultural and Literary Field

As stated earlier, *The Prophet* is a problem insofar as its popularity and idiomaticity – its Romantic, mystical and abstract lexicon – are at once embraced and rejected in the American cultural and literary field: embraced by millions of readers and rejected by the mainstream institution of criticism, to put it somewhat schematically. Its initial reception in the US encapsulates this tension, one that would continue and intensify with the increasing sales of the book, which rocketed in the New Age movement, up until today. Moreover, *The Prophet* has been translated into 104 languages, according to recent research.[87] This is indeed a phenomenon, and it can be understood in the US by situating it within the dynamics of the American literary and cultural field.

The uncanonical status of Gibran in American literature, I argue, is due to the massive and continuous popular appeal of *The Prophet*, not despite it. This popularity, furthermore, boils down in part to Gibran's Romantic and biblical style and optimistic, post-religious message, which in the context of English poetic modernism would be shunned by critics, if not ridiculed. Irfan Shahid, in defending the case for the canonisation of Gibran, underlines his particularly Romantic idiom, the overlooked importance of his Arabic works and the Arab heritage – inaccessible to the American critic – that shaped both his Arabic and English writings.[88] He even contends that *The Prophet*, if judged by applying the American philosophy of pragmatism to it, is a success. Shahid's contextualisation of the problem is remarkable, yet his argument misses a crucial point: the American literary field does not abide by a pragmatist logic. It is the popular spiritualist appropriation of *The Prophet* in American culture, which turned it into a quotable text at weddings and social occasions, a sort of 'secular Bible'[89] or a spiritual fetish, that entailed the categorisation of the book as 'Eastern spirituality' or, more specifically, as 'mind, body, spirit' in Western bookstores,[90] leaving it therefore uncanonised. This is a mode of reception that has produced and reproduced the symbolic value of *The Prophet* as a religious work, not a literary one. Mediated by an exoticist discourse in terms of which cultural difference is approached and domesticated, this mechanism of value-coding has been one deterrent to *The Prophet*'s literary legitimation. In other words, the book, and by extension Gibran's English *oeuvre*, has not acquired enough symbolic capital in the US to be consecrated as high literature, which is a condition of canonicity.

This is all the more complicated by the imagined Eastern genealogy of Gibran and his work: 'entirely of the East, with no shading of Western thought and content', as mentioned in the blurb of the 2011 penguin edition of *The Madman*, for instance.[91] This Eastern spirit is seen as essentially constitutive of his work, believed to be an emanation of a cultural difference whose value and meaning are produced, in part, by 'an exotic system that domesticat[es] the foreign while retaining its otherness'.[92] These social and cultural conditions of reading are essential, not only to the shaping of the literary, cultural and symbolic value of *The Prophet*, but also, subsequently, to the manner in which it is read and hermeneutically approached. What is more, this has disadvantageously affected the way in which Gibran's other English works, overshadowed by *The Prophet*, are read, appraised and valued.

Another important point to underscore here is the vision that Gibran puts forward in *The Prophet* and its relation to the book's celebration in the New Age movement. As I argued in Chapter One, Gibran's prophetic vision, not solely in *The Prophet* but in his Arabic and English writings generally, is premised on a poetic reinvention of religion that de-theologises it. Reinventing Christian and Sufi concepts in an evolutionary and Nietzschean spirit, this post-religious vision as articulated in *The Prophet* dovetails with many intellectual and religious currents of New Age thought.[93] This affinity made the book prone to spiritualist appropriations which, in the American context, are inseparable from commodification. What is more, this American spiritual consumption is conditioned by an 'aesthetics of de-contextualization'[94] essential to the dynamics of the postmodern, late-capitalist market. Hence the exponential increase of *The Prophet*'s sales in the 1960s and 1970s and the concurrent inattention to Gibran's other English and Arabic works. The book has indeed become a kind of post-religious manifesto for an alternative spirituality, the need for which is specific to Euro-American socio-cultural conditions.

This brings us to the difficulty of categorising *The Prophet*. The book is first and foremost a work of prose poetry, however religiously, philosophically or spiritually it may be understood.[95] Drawing on John Guillory, we must distinguish between the *function* and the *use* of a literary work, between its aesthetic function as a work of art/literature and the uses to which it is or can be put.[96] I emphasise this distinction because it is *as* a work of prose poetry – its function – that *The Prophet* could be put to different uses by multiple readers or reading communities. This is not a negation of its post-religious poetics. Rather, it is precisely as post-religious poetry that its use as a popular inspirational or spiritual guide exceeds its aesthetic function in the US, considering the role of the institution of criticism in forming a relative or imagined unanimity about what counts as high aesthetics in a specific literary field. And since *The Prophet* in the US has come to be seen as a 'pioneer of the New Age',[97] it is readily and primarily regarded as a spiritual and not a literary book. In other words, its perceived non-aesthetic use – again, from an institutional point of view – has undermined its aesthetic value, since popular use here is conflated with, overshadows and denigrates its function.

The aesthetic and literary value of the book, however, is still a site of a continuous and profound contestation. Robin Waterfield, for instance, writes: '[T]hat *The Prophet* came into the world with a whimper, not a bang, must stand as one of the greatest ever underestimations by the literary community of the importance of a book to the reading public'.[98] The peculiarity of Gibran's status in American literature is a reminder of the contested and disputed nature of value itself, and of the role of different valuing communities – imagined rather than real, whether we are speaking of an 'interpretative community'[99] or a general reading community – in shaping literary and aesthetic value relationally. There is no pure value that transcends its social and cultural situatedness. Yet this does not mean that there is no aesthetic experience, nor does it suggest that aesthetic value is the same as economic value (that is, equally commensurable), nor does it further intimate that the aesthetic is only extrinsically imputed to a work of literature/art. Aesthetic experience, it must be emphasised, is *mixed rather than pure*,[100] and the aesthetic itself is experienced and valued differently across different cultural geographies and interpretative communities, as the next two sections of this chapter will also demonstrate.

In this context, it would be illuminating to look at the appeal of Gibran in conjunction with the popular reception of Rumi in the US. Known in the West as Rumi, Jalal ad-Din Muhammad al-Rumi was a Persian poet, mystic and theologian who lived in the thirteenth century, deemed sometimes the foremost Islamic Sufi poet of all time. Rumi's poems in the US have made quite a massive success over the past four or five decades. But this commercial success boils down, primarily, to the domesticating translations and adaptations of Rumi's poetry by Coleman Barks in the spirit of the New Age movement.[101] This appropriation of Rumi reveals the role of a certain modality of reception that refashions and reconfigures the value and cultural relevance of foreign literary works, such that their perceived difference is assimilated in ways that decontextualise their history and genealogy. Rumi's poetry is both Islamic and universal – that is, it articulates an Islamic universal vision – yet the New Age translations of his poems highlight the universal and forget the Islamic, assimilating and de-Islamising Rumi in the process.[102] The Rumi phenomenon is underlined here because it sheds an illuminating light on the Gibran phenomenon, in that the poetry of both has been *spiritually consumed* in the US. As the condition of a specific kind of reading, this spiritual consumption is the horizon of expectation that both Gibran and Rumi's poetry has served or, perhaps more accurately, has been used to fulfil.[103] Gibran, however, was not a Sufi poet whose Islamic background is obfuscated in favour of a 'syncretic' one, as is the case with Rumi. Yet both poets, because their universal visions bear an affinity with New Age thought, have been almost completely decontextualised in the American cultural sphere. Gibran's bilingualism, his background as immigrant, and the Arab and Sufi heritage in which he is steeped, not to mention his other English and Arabic works, have often gone unnoticed in the domestication of his work as essentially Eastern, spiritual and universalist in the US.

This spiritual appropriation and specific mode of valuation should be understood, therefore, within the larger context of translation and travelling ideas. Gibran's is a travelling vision that has been subject to translational reconfigurations, which is to say that translation, in the sense of self-translation and cultural translation (overlapping but not identical), has structured and accompanied this bilingual movement from Arabic into English, altering in the process the translated and the manner in which it is read, interpreted, evaluated, valued and appropriated. For that which travels is necessarily subject to new regimes of value and socio-cultural conditions of reading and consumption. This travelling, moreover, is not necessarily from one location to another, but from one point in time to another within the same location or beyond – which is to say that regimes of value are obviously not static but historically contingent, albeit with some elements or forces being more potent, persistent and impactful than others, and with some regimes, due to their imperial nature, evidently more influential than others. Translation in the case of Gibran acts as both hermeneutic and epistemic mediator. More specifically, cultural translation – that is, 'the superimposition of dominant ways of seeing, speaking and thinking onto the marginalized peoples and the cultural artefacts they produce'[104] – has been the most influential force in the production of the value and meaning of Gibran's work in the US. The production of a literary work, it is crucial to remember, involves many 'agents of legitimation' – writers/artists, publishers, reviewers, critics and institutions or, generally speaking, producers of meaning – who produce certain modes of reading and consumption entangled with certain practices of value-coding.[105] It would be erroneous, therefore, to project a specific history of reception onto the author-as-cause, since the author is the initial producer of meaning but by no means the determinant one. Following this logic, self-translation overlaps – because it takes place within a specific worldly context – with cultural translation, but is not identical with or reducible to it, simply because the text survives its author and is configured by practices of cultural translation that go beyond the initial historical moment of the text's emergence. This perspective allows us to understand exoticisation itself as a process that operates with varying degrees of intensity and influence at specific historical junctures and in *particular* geo-epistemic and cultural locations.[106] This also means that the text itself becomes a process rather than a given, subject to the reconstructive nature of open readings and appropriations, themselves socially mediated and culturally situated.

The issue, however, resides in the fact that the textuality of Gibran's English texts has been almost erased in the process, as his work becomes a phenomenon rather than a text. Of course, one does not negate the other, but in this case the former has eclipsed and flattened the latter, with *The Prophet as phenomenon* overshadowing not only *The Prophet as text* but also other significant works of Gibran in English and in Arabic. Which is to say that an instance of 'symbolic violence'[107] is at work here, functioning *implicitly but potently*, evidenced in the institutional inattention to which Gibran's English works have been subjected in the American academy. The symbolic nature of this violence, which has rendered Gibran's texts invisible, is precisely what renders *this violence itself* invisible. This should be understood as a *necessary* outcome, rather than an intentional act, of the dynamics of the American literary and cultural field. The conditions of canonicity and canon-formation within this field remain often ignored or unquestioned, and it is these historical, social and institutional conditions, rather than the canon itself and what it (unfairly) represents and should (therefore) represent or include, that must be the object of critique.[108] Pierre Bourdieu reminds us:

> To denounce hierarchy does not get us anywhere. What must be changed are the conditions that make the hierarchy exist, both in reality and in minds. We must – I have never stopped repeating it – work *to universalize in reality the conditions of access* to what the present offers us that is most universal.[109]

In this context, contending that Gibran's universal message precluded it from being admitted to the American 'multicultural' canon of literature[110] is a questionable gesture, to the extent that it does not question the canon's own conditions of canonicity. This contention presupposes that an Arab writer can only speak an ethnic, particularist idiom in America, that the Arab writer cannot speak universally, and if this writer does so in the manner of Gibran, they would not be heard by the academic institution of criticism but would instead be assimilated by – or seen as assimilating to – Orientalist discourse. Put differently, a preference for a literary expression that foregrounds the ethnic particularity and 'minoritarian' status of immigrants or people of non-white ethnicities and their social experiences in America becomes the norm rather than an option or a strategy. If an Arab writer such as Gibran speaks universally *and* mystically in English, Orientalist imagination is quickly summoned, and the complex texture of the text[111] itself and the history of its discursive production and reception are brushed aside by dint of its massive popular appeal. This reduction of mysticism to Orientalism in the case of Gibran, which finds its justification in the essentialist attribution of mysticism and irrationality to the Orient in classical Orientalist discourse, has obscured the complexity of his text in its specific lexicon and discursive context of enunciation. This specificity does not necessarily or solely elicit criticism whose main concern is the nexus of Orientalism, colonialism and capitalism, nor is it reducible to culturalist analyses of self-representation and identity politics. It rather demands a hermeneutical attention to the text that locates it, but does not subsume it, within its various discursive contexts. Reducing the Gibranian English text to a cultural object that exhibits an Oriental(ist) spirit is a gesture that runs the risk of falling into an Orientalism-in-reverse in its reliance on systemic analyses that do not pay attention to polysemia[112] and to how politics and aesthetics relate, as attested by the generalised comments on his work without quoting it and the persistent invisibility of works other than *The Prophet*. This gesture is also implicitly inclined to new canonical genres such as the novel or secular literary expressions of the non-Western self, which can be readily categorisable and decipherable in Euro-America. To highlight a trajectory of the Anglophone Gibran that would illuminate what is (rendered) invisible in the American context, let us turn to the translation of this text into Arabic and its recontextualisation in the Arab discursive universe. This is a significant trajectory that is completely forgotten in critical appraisals of Gibran in the Euro-American academy.

Gibran in Arab Modernism: A Modern Poet of Rupture and Vision

Enter the Arab or 'Arabised' Gibran, whose modernist reception – especially as represented by the journal *Shiʿr* – regards him as a poet whose work signals a rupture with the poetry of the *Nahḍa* and embodies a modern vision of transformation. Gibran, for such seminal modernist poets in Syria and Lebanon as Adonis and Yusuf al-Khal, is an innovative writer who produces a new conception of poetry as a destruction and creation of values, as prophetic and bearing – or giving birth to – a worldview, and as a new beginning in Arabic poetics and writing. The question of his bilingualism, however, and the fact that he wrote in English and for an American audience are curiously left unnoticed in this reception. Gibran is important, in this early modernist context, only insofar as Arabic literature and the questions that its own 'modernity' engenders and imposes on the modernist poet are concerned. Why is this the case, and why is it important to raise this question?

Before I address these questions, it bears stressing that, even when Gibran is the target of criticism by some Egyptian Romantics, be they conservative or liberal, he is essentially an Arabic writer, not a bilingual one. Apart from ʿAbbas Mahmud al-ʿAqqad's criticism of *al-Mawākib*'s language and vision, as discussed in Chapter Two, Mustafa Sadiq al-Rafiʿi took issue with Gibran because he dared announce the birth of his 'own' new language against the old 'conservative' language, in reference to his well-known essay 'Lakum lughatukum wa lia lughatī' (You Have Your Language, and I Have Mine).[113] In his criticism, al-Rafiʿi mistakes the creative use and reclamation of language with 'ownership' of the language as a whole, confusing *parole* with *langue* to use De Saussure's terms. For it is obvious that Gibran's rhetorical gesture, in its invocation of the Qurʾān, juxtaposes two ways of being in language: one that seeks a new mode of writing concomitant with the 'new age',[114] and another that revives and expands on an old mode of writing – rich and seen as unmatched – in fear of the sweeping avalanche of the new.[115] Another Egyptian Romantic who took issue with Gibran is Lutfi al-Manfaluti, whose criticism of Gibran's *al-Arwāḥ al-mutamarrida* is essentially moralist, not literary or aesthetic.[116] Much of this criticism, it bears emphasising, occurred before the modernist radical 'revolution' in the 1940s and 1950s – that is, in a literary and cultural environment that did not yet allow for a radical transformation of literary form, and liberals were no exception. Tharwat ʿOkasha, an important writer, critic and former minister of culture in Egypt, would later break with the early Egyptian lukewarm reception of Gibran, offering one of the best Arabic translations of *The Prophet*,[117] which will be briefly discussed in the next section.

How and why does Gibran, contrary to the early Egyptian reception of his work, assume such a paramount and foundational source for some Arab modernists, and particularly for Adonis and Yusuf al-Khal? These two poets are associated with the well-known journal *Shiʿr* (Poetry), a pioneering and influential platform for Arab poetic modernism. For Adonis, Gibran constitutes a fundamental break with the poetics of the *Nahḍa* and is, therefore, the first poet of 'modernity' as he sees it. In his seminal study on the fixed and the changing in the history of Arabic poetry, and particularly in the third volume, *Sadmat al-ḥadātha* (The Shock of Modernity), Adonis provides a powerful and penetrating reading of Gibran as a modern, visionary poet, one who broke with the *Nahḍa*'s reproduction of the poetics of form over meaning in pre-modern Arabic poetry.[118] For Adonis, Abbassid poets such as Abu Tammam and Abu Nuwas are the exception rather than the norm, because they dared to turn poetry into an arena of possibility, of potentiality and freedom rather than necessity and rhetorical predetermination. Theirs is a poetry that explores the vast and unknown space of inwardness rather than the known terrain of reality and history, in that it set out to create 'an identification between inwardness and nature, between subject and object, founding the sensuous on the non-sensuous, the visible on the invisible'.[119] This is poetry understood as an on-going search, and therein lies its 'modernity'. Gibran shares this essential concern with those poets. The poet, for Gibran, speaks a vision; in this sense, poetry reveals a new worldview, new relations between man and nature, between man and values, between man and God. The poet must have a 'message', for poetry is profoundly prophetic and visionary, in the sense that it stems from *ru'yā* as a constant possibility of meaning. And meaning here is wedded to the form it engenders or necessitates. 'Poetry in Gibran', writes Adonis, 'is a desire that remains a desire, a search that remains a search. For the world is not given *a priori*; it is rather open for discovery and disclosure'.[120] What is new with Gibran is that his prophecy is human: an *actively* human prophecy. Hence, his writings combine the madness of the social revolutionary with the dizzying yearning of the visionary to reach out beyond his territory of knowledge and experience.[121]

What is intriguing about Adonis' insightful reading of Gibran is that, while it reveals those creative and peculiar dimensions of Gibran's writings which are obscured by Romanticism as a movement, it takes Gibran's

Anglophone work as an extension of his Arabic-language writings. As my reading in Chapter One has tried to demonstrate, this is indeed the case on the level of worldview. This worldview is of course universal, but for Adonis its importance lies *within* the Arabic literary heritage. If poetic prophecy manifests itself in positing a new worldview and directing man towards a different kind of future, a future of infinite possibilities, then madness represents the expressive vehicle of that prophetic power. In *The Madman*, this power destroys values and turns them upside down. And, for Adonis, this is 'an intellectual image of what happens in the Arab world, for nihilism marks the contemporary Arab phase'.[122] That Gibran wrote this in English and that *The Prophet* – which Adonis sees as an affirmative expression of values – is also written in English does not pose any problem for Adonis. This is somewhat puzzling, considering that Adonis' book is about Arabic poetics. When we realise, however, that his main argument revolves around the conflict between a poetics that reproduces the past and a poetics that erects the future, we understand why Gibran acquires this central importance for him: Gibran is a poet of the future, of modernity as *ru'yā*, which Adonis gives the name of 'mystical realism' (*wāqiʿiyya ṣūfiyya*), in that Gibran's writing begins with observing reality critically but aims towards the future, the unknown, the infinite.[123] Further, and perhaps more importantly, Gibran's English-language writings are dominated by the parable and the prose poem, and the latter form is one that Adonis and the *Shiʿr* group adopted and vehemently championed in theory and practice.[124]

No wonder that for Adonis Gibran's Arabness overshadows the fact that he wrote in English. What is forgotten, more precisely, is not just English but translation. Gibran's English-language work is read and interpreted in Arabic in a way that obscures translation, since translation here is Arabisation as a return to the mother, not Arabisation as a translation of the Other. This translational movement, crucially, has hermeneutic and epistemic implications, for Gibran's work – Arabic or Anglophone – in the Arab context of modernity becomes imbued with meanings and values most of which the 'American' critic cannot even see, for reasons to do with the epistemic conditions of reading particular to that critic. And those meanings and values are tied to the Arabic literary field, which imposes its own questions and possibilities of reading. Now the question that begs itself is: Where is the particular here, and where is the universal? Is this Gibran universal or specific to the Arab literary field in the twentieth century? And if universality requires a movement beyond the particular, what do we make of Gibran's return to the mother, so to speak? This return, I argue, is not so much a return as it is movement that exposes what is lost and gained in (cultural) translation, that problematises the interplay of the particular and the universal in the uneven field of world literature. For it is precisely readings such as that of Adonis which simultaneously – and paradoxically – obscure and expose the invisible role of language and translation in the act of reading; that is, in the act of producing meaning and assigning value. Furthermore, if Gibran's meaning and value are specific to the Arabic literary field, this specificity does not mean that it is not universal. For Adonis stresses that 'poetry, in Gibran, is a primary activeness like love, like dream, like sex, and not simply a cultural habit'.[125] This focus on poetry as such, on Gibran as a poet for whom poetry is a mode of being, a mode of thinking, is precisely what problematises the question of the universal: the universal here reemerges from the particular, thanks to but beyond the question of form. Interestingly, Adonis reiterates his reading of Gibran as a visionary writer and a poet of the future in his preface to the 1992 French edition of *The Prophet*, published by Gallimard. Contrary to his status in the US, thus, where Gibran speaks universally mainly as an Oriental, as a 'spiritual guru' and not as a modern Arab poet, in French Gibran becomes a modern Arab representative of a universal poetic vision. Yet, the question of his writing in English – not in Arabic – is rendered irrelevant or secondary compared to the question of the poetic as such, and what is forgotten here is that the translation of Gibran into French was possible, at least in part, thanks to the 'success' of *The Prophet* in the US and elsewhere – that is, thanks to the Anglophone incarnation of the Arab Gibran.

For Yusuf al-Khal, another modernist poet who founded the journal of *Shiʿr*, Gibran is important beyond the labels of Romanticism and mysticism; that is, as a poet who radically rethought the existential role of poetry and opened up previously foreclosed avenues of writing and experimentation. In his essay 'Jubrān: Fikr munīr fī qālib fannī' (Gibran: Enlightened Thought in Artistic Form), which was written in celebration of al-Khal's own translation of Gibran's *The Prophet* (1965) into Arabic, al-Khal touches on some of the fundamental issues that concern the nature of poetry, locally and universally, except for translation. His main concern, in the heated literary background against which he wrote, is the distinction of poetry and prose. The journal *Shiʿr* was a major avant-garde platform of serious poetic experimentation and innovation beyond the classical Arabic poem, specifically in its advocating of *qaṣīdat al-nathr* (prose poem) – as opposed not just to the classical *qaṣīda* but also to *qaṣīdat al-tafʿīla* or *al-shiʿr al-ḥurr* (free verse) in Nazik al-Mala'ika's conception.[126] Within this context, Gibran is seen as the exemplary modern progenitor, in practice and criticism, of poetry as a liberating and authentic mode of creation, one that confounds the rigid distinction between poetry and prose, so that the form of any poem now springs from the poetic as a restless mode of creation, as a personal rebirth that compels the innovative use of form, that reinvents the connection between words, feeling and meaning. It is only in light of this understanding of poetry that al-Khal's translation of *The Prophet* is justified, for *The Prophet* is a book of prose poetry that creates a new connection between words, feeling and meaning, a new worldview in which love, friendship, marriage, giving, work, self-knowledge – and everything else Almustafa speaks about – are thought anew, precisely because of the poetic, understood as a deeply personal, tormenting and on-going mode of creation. And for Gibran, this mode of creation was torn 'between his earthly half and heavenly half', as al-Khal asserts, contrary to those who see Gibran simply as a mystic or Romantic poet.[127] This, of course, is a reclamation of Gibran as a modern poet who radically rethought what the poetic itself means, suggests and enables, thereby making possible further rethinking and experimenting with poetry in the heated twentieth-century scene of Arabic literature.

The question of language, however, is curiously absent here. If Gibran felt the need to write in English as an Arab writer, why did he do so? This is a question that al-Khal or Adonis do not address or even entertain. Yet, it is precisely this blindness to the question of linguistic choice that, in part, allows for their peculiar reading of Gibran in the context of Arab literary modernism. What we see here is a version of Gibran that is deeply at odds with the American one, and this divergence is a powerful example of the mutations of meaning and value in the field of world literature today. As my discussion has shown so far, these mutations occur because different conditions of reading and horizons of expectation – tied to language, culture, literary tradition and power – occasion different acts of reading and specific productions of symbolic value. In this travelling of texts, what is reconfigured is not just the text's meaning and its author's relevance and importance, but the very meaning and horizon of the universal and, by implication, the particular. And this reconfiguration is precisely what demands focused attention in the field of world literature today.

The Creative and Philosophical Afterlife of Gibran in Arabic

In Arabic, Gibran's Anglophone work is subject to reappropriative forces, de-exoticised in the process and situated within the Arabic literary context and its philosophical and spiritual heritage. This double translational movement is an illustrative example of 'world literature' in and beyond English, in that Gibran's Anglophone text moves back and forth between different worlds – that is, between different literary systems and regimes of value that are otherwise imperially and translationally related. This movement has produced different reading experiences that simultaneously veil and unveil its bilingualism; in other words, its situatedness in two linguistic and cultural worlds. Translation, in this respect, is not only constitutive of the work itself, but of how it is perceived, domesticated and valued; in short, of how it is experienced as a literary work in a certain language. Attending to the Arab literary and cultural world is not meant as a gesture that celebrates 'the authentic' or the same; it is an ethical stance that derives from the necessity of de-privileging certain epistemic geographies and evaluative regimes without falling prey to privileging others. In other words, the Arab world to which the Anglophone Gibran has travelled by way of translation is just *un*forgotten – and this gesture reveals difference within the Arab discursive and cultural universe itself. In so doing, I highlight the specificity of a different (e)valuation of Gibran from the vantage point of this 'significant geography'[128] that over the past two centuries has been deeply affected by the West's imperial and cultural infringement and domination and, at the same time, in constant interaction with it. As world literature in Arabic, Gibran's Anglophone work resists certain Euro-American modes of reading rooted in the hegemonic epistemic location within which they operate – that is, rooted in one particular imagining of the world.

Before discussing two creative engagements with Gibran in Arabic, it is crucial to remember that his English works, and particularly *The Prophet*, have been translated into Arabic many times, and this creative translational process, as noted earlier, is an 'Arabisation' in the specific sense of returning to the mother tongue. This Arabisation therefore implies a process of reappropriation. Even in interpretative engagements with Gibran in Arabic, this Arabisation is taken for granted, as these engagements often underscore the determining role of immigration in his literary and intellectual enterprise as an Arab writer, but not the fact that he also wrote in English as an Arab immigrant. In other words, the *Mahjari* element becomes important only as far as the Arabic literary field is concerned. This entrenched orientation has foreclosed the question of Gibran's status in the US from an Arab scholarly and critical perspective.[129] It has, however, produced a Gibran whose cultural and literary value is markedly different from the American one. Highlighting this side of the picture would help us illuminate what the other – the American – obfuscates, providing us with a more rounded picture of Gibran as a bilingual writer.

The multiple translations of *The Prophet* into Arabic were carried out by such acclaimed literary figures as Mikhail Naimy (1956); Yusuf al-Khal (1968); the Iraqi poet and translator Sargon Boulus (2008); the writer and former minister of culture in Egypt Tharwat ʿOkasha (1959); the Orthodox priest, translator and writer Antony Bashir (1923); the Lebanese writer and scholar Yuhanna Qomeir (1997); and the Syrian translator Jamil al-ʿAbed (2008).[130] Also, a new translation into Arabic of Gibran's English works by Nadeem Naimy was published in 2015.[131] This persistent translational interest bespeaks the enduring significance of Gibran for Arab poets, readers and critics. As such, it invalidates the misleading suggestion that his embrace of the prophet as a literary trope is either offensive to Arab Muslim readers or would make little sense to them, found in 'post-modernist' and 'post-colonialist' appraisals of Gibran in Euro-American scholarship. More specifically, Geoffrey Nash makes the generalised claim that 'Muslim Arabs might find the title of his most celebrated work [*The Prophet*] offensive from the beginning'.[132] Such assumptions not only betray unawareness of the reception of Gibran's English work in the Arab world, indicating that the dynamics of the Arabic literary field are deemed – whether consciously or not – unimportant and 'peripheral' by such scholars. They also run the risk of essentialising 'Muslim Arabs', a gesture that echoes old Orientalist clichés about Arabs and Muslims as static and intolerant. Waïl Hassan makes a similar contention: 'A title such as *The Prophet* would have been offensive to Arab readers', he writes, going as far as contending that 'even though the book was later translated into Arabic, it remains, together with his other books translated from English, far less known than his earlier, Arabic work'.[133] There are at least four elements to which Hassan's account fails to pay attention: Gibran's Arab Christian origins, the literary and fictional nature of his embrace of the poet-prophetic trope, the Arabic scholarship on and reception of Gibran's work, and the history and dynamics of modern Arabic literature and culture. Generalised comments about Arab Muslim readers and the intimation of their intolerance towards the different may paradoxically reproduce the very Orientalist stereotypes that such critical engagements set out to unravel. The number of *The Prophet*'s translations alone is proof enough that the book has never been perceived as 'offensive' by Arab Muslim readers. On the contrary, it is an indication of the heterogeneity and difference within the modern space of Arab society and culture.

The several translations of *The Prophet* are also important because they suggest, beyond the implication of Arabisation, that Gibran's Anglophone work is neither strictly American nor strictly Arab. As bilingual, *émigré* literature, it is both Arab and American. This is why its reception in these two literary worlds must be taken into account at once. Crucially, this Arab reception invites a different set of questions and concerns specific to that geography but ultimately central in any appraisal of Gibran's literary legacy: Why, one wonders, is there a host of Arabisations of Gibran's English-language work? Is this insistence on differently, and presumably better, translating Gibran into Arabic a sign that he has not been properly translated, or is it an endeavour to capture something elusively Arab in his English writings? And how does this reception bear on the status of Gibran from the perspective of world literature? While translation has constituted and configured Gibran's writings in the US in specific ways, as discussed earlier, it has also transformed these writings after their Arabisation, albeit invisibly so. The proliferation of these translations is emblematic of the symbolic and literary status of Gibran for the Arab 'interpretative community' and Arab readers in general. This status has been consolidated by Gibran's enormous influence on the course of modern Arabic literature, on the one hand, as the cases of Adonis and Yusuf al-Khal demonstrate, and by the world literary space which he is seen to have successfully entered, on the other, both of which have laid the ground for these translations to emerge and multiply. These conditions of reading and translation – that is, of interpretation in the broad sense of the term[134] – are rooted in a specific evaluative and normative framework that alters the translated text in that it produces a particular 'reading experience'.[135] Because translation here functions as a reappropriation, this experience is steeped in Arabic literary and cultural memory, a prism through which the text itself is read, evaluated and ultimately valued. Thus, the Arabisation of Gibran's English work is a recontextualisation in a double sense: an insertion of the translated text into the Arabic literary and philosophical context and a subsequent recuperation of the text in that specific context.[136]

Neither the scope nor the focus of this chapter allows for an extended reflection on the translations of *The Prophet* into Arabic, yet the sheer number of them requires some attention. Suffice it to look at Naimy's and 'Okasha's translations to understand why a text such as *The Prophet* has been translated into Arabic eight times. Naimy's translation reads like a faithful rendition of the source text that often undermines its poetic character in Arabic, albeit the poet in him does sometimes surface in the text. This hyper-faithfulness, so to speak, comes at the cost of idiomatic domestication and poetic creativity, which any translation of *The Prophet*, as a book of prose poetry by an Arab writer, necessarily demands. It is Naimy's approach to translating Gibran, which does not permit flexibility,[137] that restricts the creative potential of translating the text poetically. In contrast, 'Okasha's remarkable translation, being unfaithful to the literalness of the English text, has created an Arabic version whose rhetorical force and poetic energy attest to a poetics of translation that not only carries the text from one language to another, but that gives it a new life in the target language. More specifically, 'Okasha's translation allows for the rich idiomaticity of the Arabic language to translate into itself the source text, as it were, without sacrificing its meaning. What emerges is a translation that is faithful to the poetic heritage of the target language, without at the same time being unfaithful to the meaning of the source text, reminding us at times of the powerful and allusive terseness of classical Arabic poetry and prose.[138] The Arabic afterlife of *The Prophet*, thus, attests to its bilingual status, to the fact that it simultaneously belongs to American and

Arabic literatures. As such, it necessarily relativises the American (e)valuation of it.

If the translations of *The Prophet* and Gibran's Anglophone work into Arabic are numerous and different, so are the interpretative and creative engagements with it. The first example I wish to highlight here is Mansur Rahbani's play *Jubrān wa-l-nabiyy* (Gibran and the Prophet), initially performed as an operetta in 2005 and published in 2010. Mansur Rhabani was a well-known composer-dramatist and poet, who together with his brother Assi Rahbani (famously known as the Rahbani Brothers) and the iconic singer Fairuz revolutionised the Arab musical scene in the second half of the twentieth century. The work of the Rahbani Brothers has been critically acclaimed, seen as arguably the most influential in the Middle East in the twentieth century.[139] Rahbani's operettas include, among others, *Ākhir ayyām Suqrāt* (The Last Days of Socrates, 1998) and *Ākhir yūm* (The Last Day, 2004), an Arabic adaptation of Shakespeare's *Romeo and Juliet*.[140] *Gibran and The Prophet* is the last of his operettas. It is based partly on Gibran's life and partly on *The Prophet*. It brings together, in an intriguing and imaginative manner, real characters including Gibran, Mary Haskell, Mikhail Naimy, Abdelmassih Haddad[141] and Gibran's publisher Alfred Knopf, on the one hand, and *The Prophet*'s fictional characters such as Almustafa, Almitra and the people of Orphalese on the other. All these characters are engaged in an intense dialogue that animates the main ideas and concerns of Gibran in *The Prophet*, revealing at once their insightfulness and limitations. In other words, Gibran's vision in the book meets its necessary worldly limitations as a human vision. What emerges is a theatrical rejuvenation of Gibran that mixes life and fiction, biography and *oeuvre*, idealism and realism, present and future, in a manner that shows or reimagines the dialectical and arduous process of writing concealed by the text itself, 'the struggle, at once theatrical and dialectical, between Gibran and Almustafa, between the real personality and the fictional one, between Orphalese the age and Orphalese the dream'.[142] In other words, this is the afterlife of the text as experienced and imagined in the lifeworld of some of its *creative* readers.

In his preface to the written edition, Usama Rahbani states that, by writing and performing this operetta, the aim was to infuse the Gibranian life with a new pulse, where Orphalese, Almustafa and Gibran are animated with the living spirit of the age, not losing sight, all the while, of the struggle that the *Mahjari* poet had undergone in writing *The Prophet*, 'until he submitted it to the publisher, in a moment that no one had guessed would be immortal in the history of Gibran and world literature'.[143] There are specific conditions of reading that occasioned this theatrical engagement. Already part of the modern Lebanese heritage, Gibran is inherited, *therefore available* (for Mansur Rahbani) as Lebanese cultural, literary and symbolic capital, which is its social function in Lebanon. One should also mention the broader Arabic literary field to which Gibran is seen as an influential and canonical modern contributor. Thanks to these conditions, the Arab-American Gibran returns from the *Mahjar* in Rahbani's operetta: he returns to speak Arabic, to perform and be performed in an Arabic tinged with a Lebanese dialect, thereby consolidating his identity as Arab Lebanese. This fictional return derives its discursive force from the *Mahjari* status of Gibran, for without his immigration to the US, which amounted to a territorial and metaphysical exile, a text such as *The Prophet* would have never seen the light of day. Gibran's exilic status, further testified by the numerous translations of *The Prophet* and some of his other works into many languages on a global scale, has cemented his symbolic and cultural significance *inside* Lebanon and the Arab world. That is, Gibran is seen to have made it to world literature, understood as a network of texts that circulate globally, *as* an Arab Lebanese writer. It is this *Mahjari* Arabness that serves as an implicit but essential mediator between his Anglophone writings and a theatrical resuscitation of his life and *chef d'oeuvre* such as Rahbani's.

In this specific context, the fact that Gibran wrote in English remains something marginal but important, to the extent that it is a sign of his departure towards the foreign language/culture that necessarily entails – for the Arab interpretative community – a return to his native language. This innovative instance of receiving the Anglophone Gibran in Arabic is unknown in the Euro-American world, where only by way of translation into English can it draw attention and recognition.[144] But since it is an Arabic engagement with Gibran's Anglophone work, it is itself an instance of world literature that, however provincial, *eo ipso* provincialises his reception in the US. In other words, as an example of world literature in Arabic, it serves to disrupt the implicit correlation between 'world' and 'English' in the academic discourse of 'world literature'. Gibran's text moves from English into Arabic creatively, and this movement forces us to think beyond English, even as we paradoxically do write in it. Yet this is precisely the task: moving beyond English while writing in it, activating the plurality of the world in this imperial language in order to contain its cultural imperialism.

If Rahbani resuscitates Gibran's English text theatrically, Fethi Meskini rejuvenates it philosophically. This philosophical engagement is significant in that it attests, on the one hand, to the multiple readings to which Gibran's work lends itself and, on the other, to its capacity to generate alternative perspectives on local and universal concerns from an Arab vantage point. Before delving into Meskini's essay, it would be helpful to contextualise my discussion of it by sketching out his philosophical enterprise. For the Tunisian philosopher and translator,[145] the horizon of contemporary Arab thought should be at once local and universal. It is local in that it derives from what he calls, after Charles Taylor, the 'sources of our old selves': *al-Muʿallaqāt* (the famous suspended odes or the hanging poems of pre-Islamic Arabia), the Qurʾān and the rich philosophical, Sufi, poetic, theological and jurisprudent repertoire of texts now referred to as *turāth* (heritage), which Meskini takes as an '*a priori* hermeneutical situation'[146] that belongs to the modern Arabs. And it is universal in that philosophy, however locally situated, should be concerned with the universal that finds its meaning in 'the shared' – which is normative, therefore multiple – not in 'the one' of science as the Greeks conceived of it.[147] This movement from the local to the universal begins with reclaiming, in a liberated and liberating manner,[148] those sources of the self from the inside in a way that reinvents them beyond *turāth*, a critical orientation that must be firmly distinguished from the so-called 'return of the religious'.[149] Such a reinventive movement has the aim of simultaneously dislodging those sources from Islamist and *turāthist* monopoly, on the one side, and from Euro-oriented dogmatic dismissal in the name of Western modernity, on the other. Philosophising this way, for Meskini, is the necessary trajectory that contemporary Arab thought should follow in order to go beyond local debates about modernity and tradition and offer a universal, de-colonised contribution to contemporary philosophy within its own 'post-secular' and 'post-religious' horizon. This summary of Meskini's philosophical enterprise is important to understand his hermeneutical movement from the local to the universal in his essay 'Barāqiʿ al-ʿaql, aw Jubrān wa-l-anā al-majnūn' (The Veils of Reason, Or Gibran and the Mad I).[150]

In Meskini's reading, Gibran's *The Madman* is seen 'to revolve around the liberation of the [Arab] Eastern self from its maladies',[151] yet with no claims to *Nahḍa qua* Enlightenment. In so doing, Meskini implicitly and strategically 'Arabises' Gibran's English text by inserting it within a tradition of Arab self-critique, in the sense of exposing and attempting to transcend the normative structures governing, in advance, the Arab Eastern self. This (self)-critique, enacted in the Arab geo-epistemic location, bespeaks an agential affirmation of the self that is aware of the capacity of its own hermeneutical situation to foster, *from the inside*, 'a new ethics of belonging'.[152] What is perplexing in Meskini's reclamation of the 'I' as Arab Eastern, however, is that, while he reminds us at the outset of the essay that *The Madman* is published in English, he pays no attention to the fact that it was initially addressed to an American or Anglo-Saxon audience in the aftermath of World War I. This strategy of recontextualising Gibran and his English work is occasioned by a certain horizon of expectation that transforms the reading experience of the Arab Anglophone text, as this horizon dictates certain 'norms, questions, values, and problems'[153] pertinent to the Arab cultural geography.

Thus, Gibran's English text in the Arab discursive universe remains Arab in essence; that it is originally written in English is an unimportant element for an Arab philosopher such as Meskini. But if this should constitute a certain blindness *vis-à-vis* the text's initial context and linguistic choice, it is nevertheless a blindness that enables the possibility of insight, to invoke Paul de Man, as attested by the interpretative rigour and depth that Meskini's essay displays. Put differently, this recontextualisation has recuperated the text's visibility which the Euro-American context, for reasons to do with its own conditions of reading and reception, has veiled. Furthermore, the 'I' in Gibran's parable is not an *essentially* Eastern one; this was a discursive strategy of reclamation conditioned by local questions of Arab modernity and tradition. Meskini's reading, as I discuss below, becomes a phenomenological reflection on the human face as such as elicited by Gibran's parable – that is, a universal philosophical thinking that is nonetheless culturally situated in its application.

In this parable, the speaker tells us how he became a madman: waking up one day from a 'deep sleep', he discovers that all his masks, 'the seven masks [he has] fashioned and worn in seven lives', were stolen. Running masklessly and loudly cursing the thieves, a youth on top of a house cries out, 'he is a madman', whereupon he looks up and 'the sun kiss[es his] own naked face for the first time', and '[his] soul is enflamed with love for the sun'. He does not want his masks anymore; instead, he blesses his thieves. In his madness, thus, he finds the 'freedom of loneliness and the safety from being understood, for those who understand us enslave something in us'.[154] The parable, however, ends with a sceptical note: 'But let me not be proud of my safety. Even a thief in a jail is safe from another thief'.[155] For Meskini, the stolen masks are the veils of reason, for to become a madman is to be and think outside 'the dominant institution of reason'.[156] Yet madness here is not the antithesis of reason, as Meskini argues, but 'the capacity of reason itself to be liberated by way of its own madness'[157] – that is, by doing away with its own 'masks'. The madman is a reasonable man narrating his own story of madness. Although the theft here is 'an event' that has befallen him, it is 'an outside' that nevertheless compels him to tell his own story from within, an outside that radically alters his mode of reason and being in the world: the mask-lessness, or the nakedness of the face, entails breaking away with the past insofar as it designates 'the seven masks I have fashioned and worn in seven lives'.[158] It becomes clear at this point that what is at stake here is 'Awakening' – and this is why Meskini reads the parable by initially situating it within the Arab Eastern context – a concept that he considers, insofar as it entails the violent enlightening of the dark minds (*al-īqāẓ*), to be vertical and authoritarian.[159] This is because it presupposes a laziness – or, for that matter, a 'decadence' – in the self, while Gibran's insight, for him, is that madness *qua* Awakening occurs to the self as an event by virtue of which it embraces its own nakedness, its radical being outside pre-destined or pre-fashioned identitarian veils.[160] One might add that the theft becomes emblematic of an age – the modern times – from which we cannot run. Contemporaneity turns out to be a condition of resistance rather than a sign of defeat or deficiency: by blessing the thieves one reveals their incognizance of what their very theft has enabled, rather than disabled. This mask-less face is the mode of being that resists the interference and enslaving understanding of others, those who stole the masks included – since they mistook the masks for the face. 'Madness becomes in effect a mode of adjoined "freedom and safety"': the freedom of 'subjectification' (*tadhawwut*) and the

safety from being appropriated by the Other.[161] Unlike the masks, therefore, the face cannot be stolen: 'we do not owe our faces or faciality to any other'.[162] The theft is a blessing in disguise.

Meskini picks up on this element and transforms it philosophically; he writes:

> The Other is, above all, visual. The Other appears, at face value, in the guise of a thief or an inquisitive, robbing our veils and stripping our masks. Otherness is a kind of anger induced by the initial theft of our boundaries and sanctities. Nevertheless, without this originary thievery of the Other, the inquisitive, and without the abrupt theft of our old masks, we would never experience the sense of nakedness in front of some mirror, a mirror that – invisible to us – contains us; and there would be no 'faces', that is, distinctive or personal modes of subjectification, which we often call our 'selves', and to which we attribute vague but necessary names such as 'I', 'you', . . . etc., without any other specific demarcation.[163]

What is interesting in this reflective interpretation is that the Gibranian text becomes not only a *source* for an alternative outlook on the *Nahḍa* in the Arab literary and philosophical field, one that conceives of it as an inevitable event rather than a 'violent enlightenment' seeking to reform the 'decadent' minds. It also becomes an *occasion* for a phenomenological reflection on faciality (*al-wajhiyya*), which posits the originary thievery of the Other as a necessary double event: one that strips us of our self-fashioned sanctity while awakening the face that lies beneath a history of masking – that is, beneath a history of a particular kind of reason that forms and narrates who we are. To reside outside these masking narratives of the institution of reason is therefore to become or, rather, to be seen by others as a madman. The latter becomes a condition of possibility for a subjectification that the Other, as a thief or a veil, is not able to comprehend.

This hermeneutical application of the Gibranian text should not be regarded as an over-interpretation. What we see here, to invoke Gadamer, is a 'fusion of horizons'.[164] This fusion, however, does not aspire to an 'aesthetic truth' as much as it enables a movement towards a universal horizon that lies beyond this recontextualisation. Meskini's engagement indicates the capacity of the Gibranian text to invite new ways of thinking in the Arab world and beyond. However situated the notion of the 'Eastern self', what matters most here is not East or West, but the possibility of being and thinking around and beyond them:

> The face [*al-wajh*] is the space of being specific to each one of us, yet we do not owe our faces nor our faciality [*wajhiyya*] to any other. The being of the Other itself is possible only insofar as it acquires a 'face' or a faciality. And the Other must look for a mirror in order to look at me. Yet what hangs over mirrors, their beauty notwithstanding, is to metamorphose into veils, that is, into visual hurdles that forestall our faces [. . .] But my face is not my doing. It is the trace of a sun's kiss, a sun that 'enflamed my soul with love', that is, with a truthful estrangement that consists in belonging to my own self without veils.[165]

The encounter with the face of the Other can only take place by virtue of a mask-less faciality, but not without a mirror, an invisible mirror that contains the self and the Other, whereby the Other is seen by the self and the self is seen by the Other; that is, no immediate encounter is possible without this *mutual representation*. It is the susceptibility of this mirror to turn into a fixed identitarian veil, simultaneously masking one to oneself and to the Other, against which Meskini's phenomenological hermeneutics of the face warns. Only by virtue of a radical Outside or a wholly Other – the metaphor of the sun – can one recognise one's own naked face.

Gibran's mask-less madman is thus unmasked hermeneutically only by masking the original language of the text, and this is possible because the text itself was 'born-translated'.[166] This is an indication of the extent to which translation bears on how texts are constituted, imagined, categorised, configured, reconfigured and open or limited in terms of the interpretative capacity they can generate. Translation can simultaneously mask and unmask. It can either exoticise or de-exoticise, depending on the normative, cultural and epistemic framework in which translation takes place; on the language that enunciates the text and the language that reenunciates it, as it were; on the conditions of reading and the horizons of expectations that shape the value and pertinence of what is read; as well as the identity of the enunciator. This identitarian element is inescapable, yet the way in which it is deployed in multiple discursive and evaluative practices across different but inter-related cultural geographies is something that we should always expose, reflect upon, interrogate and learn from, and Gibran's case as a bilingual writer is illustrative in that regard.

As discussed earlier, Gibran's Oriental identity, understood in essentialist terms, often precedes and predefines his texts and the ways in which they are received, read and appropriated in the American cultural and literary field. That *The Prophet* is (still) popular in the US is not an issue – it is also popular elsewhere. The issue, rather, resides in the conditions and mechanisms of value-coding and legitimation that assign a particular value and meaning to it – and to his other works – without paying close attention to its own textual difference. In an American literary field dominated by the modernist poetics of T. S. Eliot and New Criticism, this difference was either unacknowledged as such or regarded as essentially Eastern, mystical and (therefore) exotic. Even after attempts to revise the canon in the 1970s and 1980s, the continuous popularity of *The Prophet* since its publication and its appropriation as an essentially spiritual and Oriental book, especially in and after the New Age movement, has left Gibran uncanonised and decontextualised in the US. Yet these American conditions of reading and reception – in Bourdieu's sense – form one side of the bilingual picture. Because a new hermeneutic life is given to Gibran's Anglophone text when translated into Arabic, this translational movement is equally significant in any appraisal of it, precisely because it renders visible what is veiled by its American reception while rendering invisible translation itself. In highlighting the bilingual trajectory of this text, another world to which it culturally belongs has been *un*forgotten and problematised, not romanticised or taken simply as 'different'. While Gibran's work is spiritually appropriated and institutionally neglected in one field, it is creatively, philosophically and discursively reappropriated in another, as the cases of Adonis, Yusuf al-Khal, al-Rahbani and Fethi Meskini demonstrate. This is a paradox that reflects what is lost and gained in (cultural) translation in an irreducibly heterogeneous world. Remembering and reactivating that irreducible heterogeneity, while exposing and critiquing what mystifies it, is an ethical imperative in the age of 'world literatures'.

Notes

1 This is from a preface by Amin Maalouf to a new translation of *The Prophet* into French: Khalil Gibran, *Le Prophète*, trans. Janine Levy (Paris: Editions de la Loupe, 2003), 10. The original reads: Je ne connais pas d'autre exemple, dans l'histoire de la littérature, d'un livre [*The Prophet*] qui ait acquit une telle notoriété, qui soit devenu une petite bible pour d'innombrables lecteurs, et qui continue cependant à circuler en marge, comme sous le manteau, sous dizaines de millions de manteaux, faudrait-il dire, mais sous le manteau quand même, comme si Gibran était toujours écrivain sacré, un écrivain honteux, un écrivain maudit.

2 Abdelkebir Khatibi, *Plural Maghreb*, trans. P. Burcu Yalim (London; New York: Bloomsbury, 2019), 21–22.

3 Insofar as it is enunciated, situated and received in the US, Gibran's Anglophone work belongs to American literature, or at least it is 'Arab-American' (even if uncanonised), without losing its fundamental status as Arabic literature in English, which is the condition of its becoming 'American'.

4 Damrosch, *What is World Literature?*, 4–5.

5 For more on this, see, for instance, Pierre Bourdieu, *The Field of Cultural Production*, trans. and ed. Randal Johnson (Cambridge: Polity Press, 1993), especially the 'Editor's Introduction' and 'Part I: The Field of Cultural Production'.

6 John Frow, *Cultural Studies and Cultural Value* (Oxford: Clarendon Press, 1995), 5.

7 Hans Robert Jauss, *Toward an Aesthetic of Reception*, trans. Timothy Bahti (Brighton: Harvester, 1982), 22–28.

8 Bourdieu calls for 'a sociology of art and literature [that] has to take as its object not only the material production but also the symbolic production of the work, i. e. the production of the value of the work or, which amounts to the same thing, of belief in the value of the work'. Bourdieu, *The Field*, 37.

9 This change – which devalued writers such as Benjamin Franklin, Washington Irving and William Dean Howells, to name but a few, while valuing others like Henry Melville, Mark Twain and Henry James – was reinforced by an institutional configuration that consisted in 'the professionalization of the teaching of literature, the development of an aesthetic theory that privileged certain texts [New Criticism], and the historiographic organization of the body of literature into conventional "periods" and "themes"'. Paul Lauter, *Canons and Contexts* (New York; Oxford: Oxford University Press, 1991), 24–27.

10 This formation excluded black, female and working-class writers. Ibid., 27–32.

11 T. S. Eliot, 'Tradition and the Individual Talent', *Selected Essays* (London: Faber and Faber, 1932), 15.

12 Ibid., 16.

13 Eliot talks about the 'perfected medium in which special, or very varied, feelings are at liberty to enter into new combinations'. Ibid., 18

14 Ibid., 21.

15 Ibid., 22.

16 Lauter, *Canons and Contexts*, 34.

17 'Formalist criteria of excellence developed in the 1920s by critics like John Crowe Ransom, Cleanth Brooks, R. P. Blackmur, and Tate, have emphasized complexity, ambiguity, tension, irony, and similar phenomena; such standards are by no means casual. They place a premium on the skills of the literary interpreter: *He* shall unpack the ambiguities and tensions to the uninitiated students, the products of a degraded "mass education"'. Ibid., 35 [emphasis in the original].

18 Ibid., 36.

19 Gibran and Gibran, *Kahlil Gibran: Beyond Borders*, 304.

20 'English is not the language for parables, but one is apt to find faults with his tools when he cannot use them well. The fault lies within me. But I *will* learn how write in English'. KG to MH, 16 May 1916 [emphasis in the original].

21 Joseph Gollomb, 'An Arabian Poet in New York', *N. Y. Evening Post* (29 March 1919), 10.

22 Hassan, 'The Gibran Phenomenon', 67–68.

23 Gibran and Gibran, *Kahlil Gibran: Beyond Borders*, 304.

24 Ibid., 305; *The Nation* 107 (28 December 1918), 510.

25 Ibid.

26 The genocides inflicted on the indigenous people of the land and the doctrine of 'Manifest Destiny' attest to this imaginary.

27 Marguerite Wilkinson, *New Voices: An Introduction to Contemporary Poetry* (New York: Macmillan, 1919), 27, 95.

28 Said, *The World*, 39.

29 To the best of my knowledge, this remains, along with Gregory Orfalea and Sharif Elmusa (eds), *Grape Leaves: A Century of Arab-American Literature* (Salt Lake City: University of Utah Press, 1988), the only two serious anthologies of American literature to include Gibran's work.

30 Gibran and Gibran, *Kahlil Gibran: Beyond Borders*, 353.

31 I use the present tense here because the text itself – the way in which we understand, reconstruct and interpret it – is still an open process, but that process is one that should be critically accounted for. What is unchangeable is the actual materiality of the text, not the text itself.

32 Jauss, *Toward an Aesthetic of Reception*, 146 [emphasis mine].

33 Hans-Georg Gadamer, *Truth and Method*, trans. Joel Weinsheimer and Donald G. Masrhall (New York: Continuum, 2004), 306–7.

34 *CWs*, 47–48.

35 Waterfield, *Prophet*, 216.

36 Ibid.

37 See Stephen William Forster, 'The Exotic as a Symbolic System', *Dialectical Anthropology* 7, no. 1 (September 1982): 21–30.

38 Waterfield, *Prophet*, 216.

39 Ibid.

40 'And we, sun and earth, are but the beginning of a greater sun and a greater earth. And always shall we be the beginning'. *CWs*, 53. See also Jennifer Ratner-Rosenhagen's brief discussion of Gibran in her *American Nietzsche* (Chicago: University of Chicago Press, 2012), 164.

41 *CWs*, 54.

42 Ibid.

43 Ibid., 55.

44 Ibid.

45 Ibid.

46 Ibid., 55–56.

47 For more on the specificity and function of the parable as a form in ancient and modern literature, see James Champion, 'The Parable as an Ancient and a Modern Form', *Literature and Theology* 3, no. 1 (March 1989): 16–39.

48 Derrida's reflections on hospitality instantly come to mind, as he ponders the question of absolute hospitality, which, in its absoluteness, is not offered as a 'right' or 'duty' to a known foreigner (conditional hospitality), but to the foreigner who is unnamed, anonymous and, therefore, an absolute Other. See Anne Dufourmantelle and Jacques Derrida, *Of Hospitality*, trans. Rachel Bowlby (Palo Alto: Stanford University Press, 2000), 24–26.

49 The first wave of Syrian (from Greater Syria) immigrants to the US (1880–1924) were classified as Turks, not as Syrians, because the area was still part of the Ottoman Empire then. The immigrants, however, identified themselves as Syrians and loathed the Ottoman repression of the Syrians. See Tanyss Ludescher, 'From

Nostalgia to Critique: An Overview of Arab American Literature', *MELUS* 31, no. 4 (Winter 2006), 39.

50 Derrida refers to a chain of signification that links the *hostis* to the *hospis* when reflecting on the etymology of ipseity, the 'I can', rather than 'the capacity to say I', that precedes any identity of the subject. See Derrida, *Monolingualism*, 14.

51 Bushrui and Jenkins, *Kahlil Gibran*, 203.

52 Adonis produces a different reading of the parable. For him, the parable shows how the law is exposed and overcome by applying it literally, 'as though punishment were the condition that makes forbidden pleasure possible'. Adonis, 'Jubrān Khalīl Jubrān', 183.

53 This is how Gibran described the book to his friend Mikhail Naimy. Naimy, '"A Strange Little Book"', *Aramco World* 15, no. 6 (November/December 1964), https://archive.aramcoworld.com/issue/196406/a.strange.little.book.htm

54 Waterfield, *Prophet*, 260–61.

55 Gibran and Gibran, *Kahlil Gibran: Beyond Borders*, 358.

56 The cover of the first edition was a very simple one: dark brown with a small circle below the title that apparently contains one of Gibran's drawings – an open hand from which bodies are floating upwards. In other words, there was no marketing that supposedly capitalised on the imagined identity of Gibran as an exotic Easterner. Joan Acocella notes that '[a]part from a brief effort during the twenties, "The Prophet" has never been advertised'. See Joan Acocella, 'Prophet Motive: The Kahlil Gibran Phenomenon', *The New Yorker*, 30 December 2007, https://www.newyorker.com/magazine/2008/01/07/prophet-motive

57 'I have just one rule in writing – to say it in the simplest way I can'. MH Journal, 20 August 1920.

58 Marjorie Allen Seiffert, 'Foreign Food', *Poetry* 24, no. 4 (January 1924): 216–18 [emphasis mine].

59 Waterfield also notes, contrastingly, the favourable review of the Chicago *Evening Post*, in which the book was hailed as a 'little bible', praising Gibran for daring to be idealist in a cynical age. I am referring to Waterfield because unfortunately I could not get hold of the review. See Waterfield, *Prophet*, 261. Mary Haskell notes that Gibran informed her about this review, 'in which all of his "Work" was quoted'. MH Journal, 26 November 1923.

60 This totalising contrast of Orient and Occident in relation to *The Prophet* can be also discerned in the brief review of *The Bookman* (1923): 'Oriental philosophy holds a strange fascination for occidental minds. And doubly attractive is this philosophy when couched in the beautifully simple poetic prose of Kahlil

Gibran's "The Prophet" (Knopf). A modern, mystic touch is imparted to the book by the twelve drawings with which the author ornaments his text – highly artistic drawings of graceful nudes rising from chaos, as if to illustrate the striving toward clarity of more or less complicated ideas'. 'Recent Books in Brief Review', *The Bookman* (February 1924): 673–74.

61 Walter Benjamin, 'The Task of the Translator', in *Illuminations*, trans. Harry Zohn (London: Collins/Fontana Books, 1973), 71.

62 George William Russell, *The Living Torch* (New York: Macmillan, 1937), 169.

63 Ibid.

64 Ibid., 170.

65 See Raymond Schwab, *The Oriental Renaissance*, trans. Gene Patterson-Black and Victor Reinking (New York: Columbia University Press, 1981), and especially Edward's Said's remarkable foreword to the book.

66 By which is meant a de-institutionalised Christianity that conceives of Jesus in Nietzschean terms – that is, as a man who champions power rather than weakness and as a poet who embodies Gibran's notion of the 'Greater Self'. This Christianity manifests itself, formally, in Gibran's own fascination with the biblical style in English, which for him is reminiscent, as discussed in Chapter Two, of its old Syriac version.

67 Khatibi, *Plural Maghreb*, 21.

68 Waterfield, *Prophet*, 260.

69 MH Journal, 26 November 1923.

70 KG to MH, 2 October 1923.

71 Waterfield, *Prophet*, 224.

72 See my reading of some passages from the book in Chapter One.

73 Said, *Orientalism*, 156 [emphasis added].

74 'In 1957, the millionth copy [of *The Prophet*] was sold and by 1965 the book had passed the 2.5 million mark. By the 1970 *The Prophet* was continuing to sell at a rate of approximately 7000 a week, its total sales having grown to more than 4 million copies in America alone'. Bushrui and Jenkins, *Kahlil Gibran*, 330 (note 107).

75 The *Transcript* review of the book (Boston, December 1926) described it as 'a mixture of pungent observations, absurdities and meaningless mysticism'. In another Gibran was praised as a 'Syrian Humanist'. See Hawi, *Kahlil Gibran*, 233. Gibran himself described the book as a 'stop-gap between *The Prophet* and the next book'. See Naimy, *Kahlil Gibran*, 207.

76 Waterfield, *Prophet*, 264–65.

77 'Aye, He was a poet whose heart dwelt in a bower beyond the height, and His songs though sung for our ears, were sung for other ears also, to men in another land where life is for ever young and time is always dawn [. . .] the Poet who is the sovereign of all poets'; 'Master, Master Poet, Master of our silent desires, the heart of the world quivers with the throbbing of your heart. But it burns not with your songs'. *CWs*, 304–5, 411.

78 Naimy, *Kahlil Gibran*, 207–8 [emphasis mine].

79 For an account of the differences between Gibran's Jesus and Jesus of the Gospel, see ibid., 210–12.

80 *CWs*, 287.

81 Ibid., 271

82 Ibid., 294.

83 The book was reviewed together with Walter Russell Bowie's *The Master: A Life of Jesus Christ*, published in the same year. See P. W. Wilson, 'Jesus was the Supreme Poet: That is the Conception Animating These Two Books about Him'. *New York Times*, 23 December 1928, https://archive.nytimes.com/www.nytimes.com/books/98/12/13/specials/gibran-jesus.html

84 Ibid.

85 Gibran and Gibran, *Khalil Gibran: Beyond Borders*, 294–97. Claude Bragdon went as far as talking about 'Gibranism'. See Claude Bragdon, *Merely Players* (New York: A. A. Knopf, 1929), 141.

86 Gibran's Syrian origin was deemed an element crucial to the uniqueness of the book, given that the 'holiness' of Lebanon and beauty of its cedars, which Gibran invokes, are well-known in the Bible. For this reason, Gibran was not perceived in this case as an Oriental whose mode of thought and writing is radically different, exotic or incomprehensible. In other words, his Christianity, however unorthodox or subversive, and not his exoticism, has bridged the gap of his Oriental distance.

87 Galen Kalem, 'Translations of *The Prophet*', in *Gibran in the 21st Century: Lebanon's Message to the World* (Papers of the 3rd Khalil Gibran International Conference) (Beirut: Lebanese American University, 2018), 105.

88 Irfan Shahid, 'Gibran and the American Literary Canon: The Problem of *The Prophet*', in *Tradition, Modernity, and Postmodernity in Arabic Literature*, ed. Kamal Abdel-Malek and Wael Hallaq (Leiden: Brill, 2000), 321–34.

89 This is how the early review of the Chicago *Evening Post* described the book. See Waterfield, *Prophet*, 261.

90 This is the section in which I found Kahlil Gibran's *The Collected Works* at the Waterstones bookshop in the UK, for instance. Poet D. H. Melhem tells us that *The Prophet* is categorised as 'Eastern religions' at the bookstore Barnes & Noble in the US.

91 This is quoted from Barbara Young, a late friend of Gibran, in her biography (or hagiography) titled *This Man from Lebanon: A Study of Kahlil Gibran* (New York: A. A. Knopf, 1945). It is indeed a strange comment, for how could the whole book 'be entirely of the East'? What does the East stand for here, and where do we hermeneutically locate it in the text? Comments such as these have done a big disservice to Gibran's English-language works.

92 Graham Huggan, *The Postcolonial Exotic: Marking the Margins* (New York: Routledge, 2001), 20.

93 Motifs such as 'I am God', 'Higher Self', 'holism', 'reincarnation' and 'universal interconnectedness' prevalent in the New Age movement resonate with Gibran's notion of the Greater Self and the evolutionary religious vision that underpins it. For a remarkable scholarly account of New Age thought, see Wouter J. Hanegraaff, *New Age Religion and Western Culture: Esoterism in the Mirror of Secular Thought* (Utrecht: Universiteit Utrecht, 1995), especially 176–90, 222–31.

94 Huggan, *The Postcolonial Exotic*, 16–17.

95 Irfan Shahid argues that '*The Prophet*, whatever its limitations, is a work of literary art in the strictest sense of the *belles-lettres*', its religious character notwithstanding. See Shahid, 'Gibran and the American Literary Canon', 325. Poet D. H. Melhem makes a similar point but calls for an invention of a category in the absence of one. As one possibility, she mentions 'holistic poetry' as opposed to 'Eastern religions', which is its category at the bookstore Barnes & Noble. D. H. Melhem, 'Gibran's "The Prophet" Outside the Canon of American Literature', *Al Jadid* 8, no. 40 (Summer 2002), https://www.aljadid.com/content/gibran%E2%80%99s-%E2%80%98-prophet%E2%80%99-outside-canon-american-literature

96 John Guillory, *Cultural Capital: The Problem of Literary Canon Formation* (Chicago; London: University of Chicago Press, 1993), 294–95.

97 Liesl Schillinger, 'Pioneer of the New Age', *New York Times*, 13 December 1999, https://www.nytimes.com/1998/12/13/books/pioneer-of-the-new-age.html

98 Waterfield, *Prophet*, 261.

99 Stanley Fish, *Is There a Text in This Class? The Authority of Interpretative Communities* (Cambridge, MA: Harvard University Press, 1980), 11.

100 Guillory, *Cultural Capital*, 336.

101 These adaptations are mostly reworkings of the classical Orientalist translations of Rumi by Arthur John Arberry and Reynold Allen Nicholson. See Ziad Elmarsafy, 'User-Friendly Islams: Translating Rumi in France and the United States', in *Between the Middle East and the Americas: The Cultural Politics of Diaspora*, ed. Ella Shohat and Evelyn Alsultany (Ann Arbor: University of Michigan Press, 2013), 264–67.

102 Ibid., 265, 272.

103 See Amira El-Zein, 'Spiritual Consumption in the United States: The Rumi Phenomenon', *Islamic and Christian-Muslim Relations* 11, no. 1 (2000): 71–85.

104 Huggan, *The Postcolonial Exotic*, 24.

105 Bourdieu, *The Field*, 37.

106 Another cultural geography to which Gibran's work has travelled in translation, without being 'exoticised', is the Chinese one. Ma Zheng notes that all of Gibran's writings have been translated into Chinese between the 1920s and 1990s, and a burgeoning scholarly interest in his work from a cross-cultural perspective has been flourishing since the 1990s. For a detailed account of the study of Gibran in China see Ma Zheng, 'The Study of Kahlil Gibran in Contemporary China: New Developments and Influences', in *The Enduring Legacy of Kahlil Gibran* (Papers delivered at the Second International Conference on Kahlil Gibran: 'Reading Gibran in the Age of Globalisation and Conflict', 3–6 May 2012), ed. Suheil Bushrui and James Malarkey (College Park: University of Maryland, 2012), 227–34. Also see Glen Kalem, 'The Spread and Influence of Gibran in China', *Kahlil Gibran Collective*, 12 October 2019, https://www.kahlilgibran.com/latest/80-the-spread-and-influence-of-gibran-in-china.html

107 Bourdieu, *The Field*, 20.

108 This is manifest in the absence of Gibran from anthologies and especially from syllabi of American literature. As Guillory points outs, '[t]he canonicity of works is [. . .] another name for their institutional mode of reception and reproduction, but it is the name by which the concrete instrumentality of the syllabus in the formation of the transhistorical canon is typically misrecognized'. Guillory, *Cultural Capital*, 269.

109 Pierre Bourdieu and Loic J. D. Wacquant, *An Invitation to Reflexive Sociology* (Chicago: University of Chicago Press, 1992), 84–85 [emphasis in the original].

110 Jacob Berman argues that, '[b]ecause of its abstract representation of Oriental identity, Gibran's writings do not adequately comply with the paradigm of

inclusion required for entrance into the pluralistic pantheon masquerading as American's multicultural canon. The sacrifice of vernacular specificity and ethnic consciousness in Gibran's writings has resulted in sacrificing a place in American literature's ethnic canon'. Berman does not tell us how the text exhibits or represents this 'Oriental identity', but rather refers to Gibran's articulation of 'abstract universals' and one review that 'highlights Gibran's reception as an "Eastern" mystic who appealed to Bohemian artistic sensibilities'. Berman, moreover, does not quote anything from Gibran's English texts. Berman, '*Mahjar* Legacies', 72–73.

111 Compare with Naimy's '"A Strange Little Book"', where he discusses the arduous personal labour and literary and intellectual trajectory of Gibran, which for him peaks with the writing of *The Prophet*. See https://archive.aramcoworld.com/issue/196406/a.strange.little.book.htm

112 Shu-Mei Shih has expressed her exasperation of what she calls 'the return of the systemic' in theories of world literature (Moretti, in particular) and the lack of close attention to which the Third-World text is condemned when it travels to the West and, more specifically, when its polysemic reality is filtered through Western systemic theories: 'The gap between the ideal of polysemia and the practice of monosemia is, perhaps, an allegory of the relation between the First World theorist and the Third World text'. Shu-Mei Shih, 'Global Literature and the Technologies of Recognition', *PMLA* 119, no. 1 (January 2004), 22.

113 See Mustafa Sadiq al-Rafiʿi, *Taḥta rāyat al-Qurʾān: al-Maʿraka bayna al-qadīm wa-l-jadīd* (Under the Banner of the Qurʾān: The Battle between the New and the Old) (Qairo: Hindāwi, 2014 [1926]), 15–16.

114 See Gibran, 'al-ʿAhd al-jadīd', in *al-Badāʾiʿ wa al-ṭarāʾif*, *CWs in Arabic*, 323–26.

115 For an overview and modernist critique of al-Rafiʿi's stance on the question of the new and the old, see Adonis, *al-Thābit wa-l-mutaḥawwil*, 123–31.

116 For more details on the polemics between Gibran and al-Manfaluti, see John Daye, *Lakum Jubrānukum*, 57–59.

117 Gibran, *al-Nabiyy*, trans. Tharwat ʿOkasha, 9th edition (Qairo: Dār al-shurūq, 2000).

118 Adonis, *al-Thābit wa-l-mutaḥawwil*, 160–211.

119 Ibid., 18.

120 Ibid., 157.

121 Ibid., 170.

122 Ibid., 179.

123 Ibid., 203.

124 For more on this, see Muhammad Jamal Barut, 'al-Ḥadātha al-'ūla: Mushkilāt qaṣīdat al-nathr min Jubrān ilā majallat *Shi'r*' (The First Modernity: The Problem of the Prose Poem from Gibran to the Journal of *Shi'r*), *al-Ma'rifa*, no. 283–84 (1 September 1985) and no. 285 (1 November 1985): Parts I and II, respectively. See also Huda J. Fakhreddine, *The Arabic Prose Poem: Theory and Practice* (Edinburgh: Edinburgh University Press, 2021), Chapter One: 'Precursors, Terms and Manifestos between Theory and Practice'.

125 Adonis, *al-Thābit wa-l-mutaḥawwil*, 243.

126 For more on this, see Fakhreddine, *The Arabic Prose Poem*, 3–6.

127 Yusuf al-Khal, 'Jubrān: Fikr munīr fī qālib fannī', *Shi'r* no. 38 (1 April 1968), 134.

128 'By "significant geographies" we mean the *conceptual*, *imaginative*, and *real* geographies that texts, authors, and language communities inhabit, produce, and reach, which typically extend outwards without (ever?) having a truly global reach.' This notion is 'a way of ensuring sensitivity to the richness and plurality of spatial imaginings that animate texts, authors, and publics in the world'. Karima Laachir, Sara Marzagora and Francesca Orsini, 'Significant Geographies in Lieu of World Literature', *Journal of World Literature*, no. 3 (2018): 293–94 [emphasis in the original].

129 To the best of my knowledge, only one researcher in Arabic, Leyla al-Malih al-Sabuni, has drawn critical attention to the question of the language of writing in Gibran, in an article that highlights and scrutinises what readers of Gibran in Arabic – be they critics or poets – often overlook, namely, the reason why he wrote in English. Seeing Gibran from the perspective of 'world literature written in English', or Anglophone world literature, al-Sabuni argues that Gibran saw himself as a universal poet, not just as an Arab one, and that partly explains why he wrote in English. What explains his adoption of English as a language of writing, furthermore, is that the new world did not strip him of his self-confidence as an Arab, Eastern writer, in that in the US he was free from the relationship between a colonising West and a colonised East. This crucial point is either forgotten or obfuscated in post-colonial readings of Gibran. What made Gibran's style in English unique and successful, al-Sabuni argues, is his peculiar revival of Romanticism, coupled with the way in which he transformed this style by virtue of his personal experience. See Leyla al-Malih al-Sabuni, 'Jubrān nabiyyu man?' (Gibran: Whose Prophet?), *al-Ma'rifa* no. 252 (1 December 1983): 187–200.

130 A comparative study of *The Prophet*'s translations into Arabic and French has been recently published by Najwa Salim Nassir, under the title *The Prophet, Arabic and French Translations: A Comparative and Linguistic Analysis* (Beirut: Librairie de Liban, 2018). French translations of Gibran's English and Arabic works are also numerous. See https://gibranchair.umd.edu/news/new-analysis-arabic-and-french-translations-prophet

131 Gibran, *al-Aʿmāl al-kāmila muʿarraba*, trans. Nadim Naimy (Beirut: Nawfal, 2015).

132 Geoffrey Nash, *The Arab Writer in English: Arab Themes in a Metropolitan Language, 1908–1958* (Brighton: Sussex Academic Press, 1998), 13

133 Hassan, 'The Gibran Phenomenon', 70.

134 Gadamer points out that '[i]nterpretation is not an occasional, post facto supplement to understanding; rather, understanding is always interpretation, and hence interpretation is the explicit form of understanding'. Gadamer, *Truth and Method*, 306.

135 I draw on Ayman El-Desouky's emphasis on the irreducible specificity of the Qur'ānic *Nazm* or voice as a language experience particular to Arabic and, by extension, on the language experience of non-European literary and theoretical traditions as that which anchors, hermeneutically, 'the line of conceptual negotiation of difference in textual traditions and their histories of reception'. This leads El-Desouky to propose as 'critical method' in world literature the 'possibilities of abstracting method from concepts naming specific practices in non-European literary, intellectual and aesthetic traditions', where 'untranslatability [. . .] is not only *that irreducible of difference* in acts of understanding, translation and circulation that allows for the imaginative [but is] also theorizable as that which allows to emerge, through critical hermeneutical rigour, the conceptual on the other side of Western metaphysics, beginning with *the danger in the dialogue*'. See Ayman A. El-Desouky, 'Theorizing the Local and Untranslatability as Comparative Critical Method', in *Approaches to World Literature, Volume 1, Weltliteraturen/World Literatures Series*, ed. Joachim Küpper (Berlin: Akademie Verlag, 2013), 59–86 [emphasis in the original].

136 Fethi Meskini deems Gibran's *The Prophet* and Naimy's *The Book of Mirdad* (1948), both of which are originally published in English, part of contemporary Arab thought that stretches back to the *Nahḍa*. For him, both are seen as Arab Romantic restatements of the notion of 'the prophet' which, under the secularising conditions of modernity, has become available as an icon for public use in the modern nation-state. This is in contrast to its redeployment

as a political, military and moral icon in some strands of Islamist thought in the twentieth century (Sayyid Qutb and al-Maududi). Both the Romantic and the Islamist deployments of the notion of the prophet are 'post-religious', Meskini argues, in that 'the prophet' would not be available as an icon/symbol of public use were it not for the profound normative transformation of this notion in modernity. See Meskini, 'al-Nabiyy al-mustaḥīl', in *al-Īmān al-ḥurr*, 381–410.

137 Naimy states in the introduction to the book that, 'unless one is bound to, it is not appropriate to add or cut out anything when translating a writer such as Gibran'. Gibran, *al-Nabiyy*, trans. Mikhail Naimy (Beirut: Nawfal, 2013), 34–35.

138 It is not possible to discuss the Arabic translations in English, as this would require an (impossible) double translational effort in which literalness is all that matters. But perhaps one example would evince the difference between these two translations. 'A fragment of Life's heart' is translated by Naimy as '*ba'ḍ min qalb al-ḥayāt*', a literal translation except for '*ba'ḍ*', which means 'some' or 'a bit of' but could be used to translate 'fragment'. 'Okasha, in contrast, translates the phrase as '*fildha min qalb al-wujūd*'. '*Fildha*', in my view, is a word that translates 'fragment' more poetically than '*ba'ḍ*' (it also means fraction, a shattered piece, a part broken off and so on). What is more, 'Okasha translates Life as existence or Being (*al-wujūd*), which is also, in my opinion, more appealing that the literal translation of Life, as the latter, especially when capitalised, was often synonymous with Being for Gibran (see my discussion in Chapter One).

139 Yvette K. Khoury, '*Akhir Yom* (The Last Day): A Localized Arabic Adaptation of Shakespeare's *Romeo and Juliet*', *Theatre Research International* 33, no. 1 (2008): 52–53.

140 Yvette K. Khoury, 'Mansour Rahbani: Dramatist and Writer of the Classic Songs of a Lebanese Golden Age', *The Guardian*, 17 April 2009, https://www.theguardian.com/music/2009/apr/17/obituary-mansour-rahbani

141 Another *Mahjari* writer who was a member of *Arrabitah*.

142 Mansur Rahbani, *Jubrān wa-l-nabiyy* (Gibran and the Prophet) (Beirut: M al-Raḥbāni, 2010), 13.

143 Ibid., 14.

144 Shu-Meh Shih reminds us of 'an obvious and often displaced statement: what precedes recognition, and is more devastating than the politics of recognition, is *sheer ignorance or feigned negligence*. Negligence and ignorance are fundamental to the neo-colonial production of knowledge and the global division of intellectual labour'. Shih, 'Global Literature and the Technologies of Recognition', 17 [emphasis added].

145 Meskini has translated into Arabic German philosophical works such as Heidegger's *Being and Time*, Nietzsche's *The Genealogy of Morals* and Kant's *Religion within the Limits of Reason Alone*.

146 Meskini, *al-Īmān al-ḥurr*, 385.

147 Meskini, *al-Huwiyya wa-l-ḥurriya*, 167–68.

148 *Liberated*, on the one hand, from Islamist reclamations of 'tradition' (or a certain version of it) and, on the other hand, from the dismissal of this long and rich tradition in the name of a Eurocentric understanding of modernity, of which Orientalism was a potent epistemological force. In other words, this is an enactment of a *liberating* 'epistemic de-linking', to invoke Walter Mignolo upon whom Meskini draws, in order to go beyond this bifurcated mode of thinking that shackles contemporary Arab thought. See Meskini, *al-Īmān al-ḥurr*, 20–25.

149 Ibid., 25.

150 Meskini, *al-Kujīto al-majrūḥ: As'ilat al-huwiyya fi-l-falsafa al-muʿāṣira* (The Wounded Cogito: Questions of Identity in Contemporary Philosophy) (Algiers: Editions el-ikhtilef; Riyadh, Beirut: Dhifāf Publishing, 2013), 191–96.

151 Ibid., 191.

152 Ibid.

153 Petr Zima, 'Problems of Reader-Response Criticism: From Hermeneutics to Phenomenology', in *The Philosophy of Modern Literary Theory* (London: Athlone Press, 1999), 59.

154 *CWs*, 5.

155 Ibid.

156 Fethi Meskini, *al-Kujīto al-majrūḥ*, 194.

157 Ibid., 192.

158 *CWs*, 5; Meskini, *al-Kujīto al-majrūḥ*, 193.

159 Ibid., 193.

160 Ibid., 192–93.

161 Ibid.

162 Ibid.

163 Ibid., 195.

164 Gadamer, *Truth and Method*, 306–7.

165 Meskini, *al-Kujīto al-majrūḥ*, 195–96.

166 I borrow this elegant phrase from Rebecca L. Walkowitz's *Born-Translated: The Contemporary Novel in an Age of World Literature* (New York: Columbia University Press, 2015).

Epilogue

Rereading Gibran and the Question of Reading

What emerges in the process of reading? What emerges from it? The question of emergence is tied to its process and, more precisely, to what anchors, presupposes and enables that process. In other words, what emerges in and from reading depends on the mode of reading. This is of course well-known, but not always self-evident. To read is to 'understand something in a particular way', as the *Oxford Dictionary* tells us. And understanding is a complex procedure that requires, as much as possible, a conscious and rigorous method. This book has tried to read Gibran and understand his work in a particular way in order for a new, critical picture of Gibran to emerge – has it emerged? Whether it has or not is not for me to tell. But I can say that the journey of reading Gibran anew, of re-reading Gibran, has demonstrated to the reader that his writings elicit creative and attentive reading, one which is worldly at the same time as it bears out the literary particularity of his work. Whatever was said about Gibran before does not exhaust what his work is saying, and neither is my attempt in this book an exhaustive one. But this does not mean that one abstains from judgment – is judgment not what results from understanding, irrespective of the mode of that understanding? By judgment, I do not mean a verdict, but a critical intervention that reveals the value or, to use a less loaded term, the multiple and interlaced dimensions of Gibran's work in our present moment. I say dimensions because reading is a way of seeing. And I say our present moment because reading is always subject to its historical juncture, however much it tries to outlive that juncture.

Our age is that of 'world literatures'. To read Gibran as Arab world literature is to see his work in a way that reveals how its local and universal dimensions, as a modern Arab writer, are configured and reconfigured: configured in their textual manifestations and reconfigured in their readerly reception. This ties the question of the historicity of reading to that of location, which more readily reflects the meaning of world literature. The journey of reading is therefore one that crosses place and time, one that is 'chronotropic' to use Bakhtin's term. The chronotropic journey which this book has taken demonstrates that the manifoldness and dynamics of the Gibranian text resist its reduction, consciously or not, to any monocultural pigeon-holing. By monocultural, I mean that kind of reading or judgement that is confined to, or informed by, one cultural location. Gibran belongs to two literary and cultural fields at once, the Arab and the American, not to mention his influence elsewhere. To lay bare and probe the modalities and difference of that dual reception is to bear witness to his work as world literature, and to accentuate how the value and relevance of his work is produced depending on the world in which it is read and received.

To say that Gibran's work is 'spiritual', as is often the case in Euro-America, is of course valid and meaningful, given that multiple readers found in it a spiritual power and resonance not found elsewhere. But what is forgotten here is that the spiritual is enabled by the poetic, not the other way around. And the poetic, in Gibran, is the stamp that marks his whole literary enterprise, irrespective of language, genre, context and audience. Moreover, the poetic for him is essentially prophetic, in that the poet speaks in an Abrahamic register in an age dominated by a technological or scientific regime/paradigm of knowledge. Within this regime of knowledge, in which 'the countless things that pass in the dim twilight of neither sin nor virtue are recorded and catalogued', to quote one more time from Gibran's poem '"The Perfect World"',[1] the poet assumes the role of a post-religious prophet who reinvents the religious by virtue of the poetic. The poet, in this world, enables the possibility of 'other worlds – remote, lonely, silent, far – of strange delicious life',[2] to use Gibran's own words. But it is within this regime of knowledge that we must understand that reinvention, whose meaning and purpose it acquires only in relation to the attempt of that regime to impose one way of looking at and experiencing the world.

The deeper implication, in this respect, is that poetry expresses that which defies 'perfection', completion and closure, celebrating the poetic state of the world: that which remains irreducible to positivism and rationalisation, that which remains open for experience and expression. Hence '*quwwat al-ibtikār*' or the 'power of invention' that Gibran attributes to poetry. Poetry (re)invents the world or, to draw on Derrida, it makes possible 'other worlds' by 'preparing for [their] coming'.[3] The paradox here is that the invention of such a world is impossible, and therefore it is the only possible reinvention.[4] The poetic, insofar as it is prophetic, is concerned with that reinvention. Adonis writes that Gibran sounds 'at once modern and classical, realist and mystical, nihilist and revolutionary'.[5] His poetic reinvention of the religious, which is occasioned by the epistemic paradigm of modernity at the same time as it resists its calculative and identitarian modes of reason, is precisely what renders him difficult to classify. This worldly dimension of Gibran's prophetic imagination is key to understanding its significance and relevance in the twentieth and twenty-first centuries: Gibran is a modern writer who is critical, as a poet, of modernity in its local and global manifestations.

Another key implication of looking at Gibran as Arab world literature lies in the fact that, across his Arabic and English writings as well as across the different genres with which he experimented, his prophetic imagination remains the overarching motif. As such, it does not lend itself to culturalist readings of bilingual writers that confound poetics with politics. While Gibran's *The Prophet* is generally deemed 'Oriental' and 'spiritual' in the US, this is an issue that pertains to the cultural politics of reception, to which the problem of identity is central. Hence, it is the context of reception, and the mode of that reception, that prompts an analytical focus on how 'identity' is constructed and operative as a filter of reading and valuation. Reception itself is conditioned by its cultural location, by the notions of the world and the Other that are imagined and produced within that location. We must be wary, therefore, of privileging certain places and neglecting others when we talk about reception and valorisation, all the while acknowledging that some locations are more influential, attractive and decisive than others – because of power, accumulated prestige and institutional value. This is of critical importance when we read from the perspective of 'world literature' today. Gibran's case illustrates that the Arabic reception, while oblivious to the peculiarity of his Anglophone work as work written in a foreign language, illuminates aspects of his text that go unnoticed in the US. This is because the text's meaning is contingent on the linguistic, cultural, normative and historical conditions of reading, on a particular configuration of the world that makes the text readable, relatable and meaningful in ways that are different from other locations. It bears reminding that the degree of that difference is contingent and, of course, allows for overlap.

The political focus on identity should not foreshadow the poetics of the literary text. Rather, the text's poetics should be examined in a way that demonstrates how it intervenes, in its capacity as literature, in politics. Different levels of analysis should not be confused with one another. Otherwise, we risk flattening out the complexity of literature by looking at it through the lens of what the author's identity represents in its relation to the dominant one, a disposition into which the 'Third World' literary text has been often forced and thereby robbed of its literary richness or polysemy. As my discussion throughout has tried to show, the poetic in Gibran is not meant to express minoritarian identity or ethnicity, but to reinvent the notions of God, the self and the world, to suggest a different way of dwelling in the world – that it is still resonant today means that, its limitations aside, it strikes a deep human chord. Moreover, this poetic reinvention stems from the particular, from Gibran's condition as a man of his times and *Mahjari* circumstances, a product of the *Nahḍa* and imperial modernity, and an Arab, bilingual writer and inheritor of a long tradition. What escapes attention here is that Gibran considered himself a poet with a universal vision, partly because the complexity of colonial psychology did not concern or affect him as an *émigré* in the US at the time.[6] His bilingualism as a writer, therefore, does not lend itself to the sort of colonial discourse analysis applied to later post-colonial writers who adopted the language of the former coloniser. And this is precisely what calls for attentive and careful rereading, for another way of seeing, experiencing and evaluating his work.

This bilingual movement has nevertheless eclipsed the singularity of Gibran's poetic vision, producing a cultural chasm that generated divergent functions of Gibran. Yet, by reading his *oeuvre* bilingually, one recognises that the prophetic is the poetic motif that permeates it, and that the chasm is therefore essentially interpretative and only secondarily cultural. Both Selma Kerama in *al-Ajniḥa al-mutakassira* and Almustafa in *The Prophet*, as shown in Chapter One, speak prophetically; both posit the notion of Love as sacrifice; both push the experience of being in the world to its limits, albeit in different ways. And they do so because the poetic power of their words enables them to do so. To draw on Jacques Rancière, poetry here expresses rather than represents: it no longer signifies the production of poetry as much as it designates the power of language itself to see the 'poeticity' of things,[7] the power of language to invent new modes of relation and perception.

Gibran's movement from Arabic into English reveals, furthermore, a strained endeavour to write creatively in English while thinking in Arabic. And that movement is interestingly mediated by his fascination with the Syriac Bible, a trace of which is carried for him in the English Bible. This bilingual movement, which is in fact trilingual, is also exilic. For Gibran would write in a manner that resonates with the nineteenth-century Romantics, rendering him – in style and not just in identity and experience – an exile in Euro-American 'high' culture. But that exilic condition is what makes him vaguely relevant in the twentieth century. It has been one of the aims of this book to clear up that vagueness, to demonstrate that Gibran is a writer subject to his time but, in equal measure, resistant to it.

Gibran's importance as a modern Arab writer also lies in his national *Nahḍawī* commitment. A staunch, but reluctant, nationalist, Gibran expresses and stresses an ethics of belonging that conceives of the Syrian *waṭan* or homeland (in Greater Syria) as the sole unifier of its diverse inhabitants. The national in Gibran is essentially ethical in its emphasis, on the one hand, on the insightful and strenuous effort and dedication that love for the nation necessarily requires and, on the other, on the awareness and activation of the 'moral independence' necessary for the formation of the nation and the realisation of a true *Nahḍa*. Investigating this facet of Gibran was essential to my argument for two reasons. The first has to do with laying bare the breadth and complexity of Gibran's literary enterprise, of which this national facet is an essential element. Gibran, in this regard, emerges as a 'decolonial' intellectual who stresses moral independence as a foundational condition for an original Arab *Nahḍa* to materialise. The second lies in the fact that Gibran, in his national commitment as a *Mahjari* intellectual, thought of himself as essentially a poet. This would not have a crucial importance here, were it not for the fact that the poetic for Gibran is synonymous with the universal, which is implied in his short essay 'Ilā al-sharqiyyīn' (To the Easterners), as discussed in Chapter Three, not to mention his explicit reference to this disposition elsewhere. Which is to say that it is *as a poet* that Gibran moves between the nation and the world, between Arabic and English, between the Arab East and the US (and the rest of the world). That this universal vocation of the poet, what he calls '*al-tafkīr bi-l-ḥayāt*' or 'life-thinking', is expressed in both languages – his *al-'Awāṣif* and *al-Badā'i' wa al-ṭarā'if* illustrate this life-thinking impulse in tandem with a critical-nationalist concern – means that the poetic, to reiterate, is not amenable to readings that begin and end with the political. Not that the politics of writing or reception do not matter. On the contrary, the last chapter has exposed and interrogated the culturalist presuppositions that inform various modes of reading and domestication in the US, which are enmeshed in practices of cultural (mis)translation, according to which Gibran's literary texts – as texts written by an Oriental – are read through the discursive and evaluative lens of exoticism. My point is that *as* poetic, this text invites a hermeneutic of alterity that begins with the text itself, one that attempts to approach it hospitably but responsibly. As I have emphasised throughout, this hermeneutic movement locates this text in its context of enunciation and reception, without subsuming it under that context.

This ethics of reading is therefore not averse to the politics of culture. It rather attempts to be more conscious of the nuanced inter-relatedness of aesthetics and politics without confusing one with the other, especially when we talk about modern Arab(ic) literature or literature more generally. Identity, in this respect, is one circumstantial and discursive element that informs the act of reading, but it neither exhausts it, nor does it mirror its poetics. Rather, creative poetics helps us see that very identity – whether the author's, the Other's, or in general – in a different and perhaps unexplored manner. Even if poetics seems to corroborate the ideological identitarian constructions of the dominant culture, it can still tell us something about politics that politics does not; sometimes, it can even contradict it from the inside while consolidating it on the surface.[8]

As Arabic literature (in English), Gibran's work is not only important because of its poetics and the way in which it engages with local and universal issues. In its travelling beyond and back to the Arab transnational scene, it carries the mark of Arabic literature, even if it is articulated in English or translated into other languages. As Arab world literature, in other words, it retains the indelible trace of Arabic as language, literature and culture. To appreciate such a text, therefore, is to be at once aware of its worldly genealogy and movement, of its bi- or multi-lingual making and remaking. Which is to say that this awareness is vital in approaching and evaluating the 'different' on the global literary scene in which world literatures are not evenly visible and equally influential in their appeal beyond the national. The power relations that underlie the circulation and (in)visibility of literature on a planetary scale cannot be overstated in this respect. That English is *the* imperial language that directly or tacitly bears on what kind of literature we read today and, mostly importantly, *how* we do so, is an indisputable fact that cannot be challenged by foregrounding intractable particularisms. The very question of difference requires, instead, a critical negotiation that makes visible the particular in its specificity and multiplicity without falling prey to exoticism in its implicit but powerful forms. For to assume that the Other is culturally intractable or impenetrable presupposes a radical, incommensurable difference that simultaneously absolves the Other of criticism and exoticises it. On the other hand, it entails a relentless ethical effort that lies in bracketing, to the extent that it is possible, the normative and imaginative sphere of the same in the encounter with the culturally different Other, but without negating the same in its potential transformation by this encounter. This attitude is one that foregrounds *al-mushtarak* or the shared, which makes translation both impossible and necessary,[9] precisely because the shared is both fragile and infinitely necessary.[10]

Gibran's enterprise – and its legacy – is one that illustrates this inevitable but creative tension between the particular and the universal, between the linguistic and cultural particularity of the Arabic language and its rich cultural memory, and the universal horizon towards which this particularity in its Gibranian instantiation aesthetically and translationally orients itself. This book, in its emphasis on the ethics of reading that this bilingual movement requires, is a contribution, however small and limited, to contemporary debates about 'world literature' in its inevitable inter-connection with Arabic literature and, more precisely, to debates about the way(s) in which we can better understand and approach the latter in our post-colonial world. How to read, appreciate and critique Arab literary works, and particularly those that have emerged in the modern and contemporary period, is of the utmost importance here. I hope that this contribution will elicit or inspire further debates around or related to this critical concern, which is ultimately and simultaneously about poetics, ethics and politics as inter-related realms that are nevertheless irreducible to one another.

Notes

1 *CWs*, 47.
2 MH Journal, 20 June 1914.
3 Derrida, *Psyche: Inventions of the Other, Volume I*, trans. Peggy Kamuf and Elizabeth Rottenberg (Palo Alto: Stanford University Press: 2007), 45.
4 Ibid., 44–45.
5 Adonis, 'Jubrān Khalīl Jubrān', 210.
6 al-Sabuni, 'Jubrān nabiyyu man?' 192.
7 Rancière, *Mute Speech*, 58–61.
8 This is brilliantly manifest in Said's reading of Joseph Conrad's *Heart of Darkness* in *Culture and Imperialism*, for instance, where the empire and its project are at once confirmed and shown as limited, and where the novel as a narrative reflects the imperialist project as an unavoidable system at the same time as it conveys, through its formal devices, its contingency, functionality and inevitable weaknesses. See Said, *Culture and Imperialism*, 24–34.
9 Derrida, *Monolingualism*, 57.
10 The shared (*al-mushtarak*) is understood as that which is opposed, not to the private, but to the identitarian (*al-ḥuwawī*). See Meskini, *al-Huwiyya wa-l-ḥurriya*, 174.

Bibliography

Works by Gibran in Arabic

al-Majmūʿa al-kāmila li muʾallafāt Jubrān Khalīl Jubrān bi-l-ʿarabiyya (The Collected Works in Arabic). Beirut: Kitābuna li-l-Nashr, 2014.

al-Majmūʿa al-kāmila li muʾallafāt Jubrān Khalīl Jubrān: Nuṣūs khārij al-majmūʿa (The Collected Works in Arabic: Texts outside the Main Collection). Edited by Antoine al-Qawwal. Beirut: Dār al-Jīl, 1994.

Iqlib al-ṣafḥa yā fatā: Makhṭūṭāt lam tunshar (Turn the Page: Hitherto Unpublished Manuscripts). Edited by Waheeb Keeruz and Antoine Khouri Tuq. Beirut: Gibran's National Committee, 2010.

'Wathāʾiq' (Manuscripts). In *ʿAqīdat Jubrān* (The Doctrine of Gibran), 225–429. Edited by John Daye. London: Dār Surāqia, 1988.

'al-Wathāʾiq' (The Manuscripts). In *Lakum Jubrānukum wa lia Jubrānī* (You Have Your Gibran and I Have Mine), 241–358. Beirut: Qub Elias Press, 2009.

Works by Gibran in English

Beloved Prophet: The Love Letters of Kahlil Gibran and Mary Haskell. Edited by Virginia Hilu. London: A. Knopf Inc., 1972.

Kahlil Gibran: An Illustrated Anthology. Edited by Ayman A. El-Desouky. London: Spruce, 2010.

Lazarus and his Beloved. New York: Graphic Society, 1973.

The Collected Works. New York: Everyman's Library, 2007.

Works by Gibran Translated into English

The Broken Wings. Translated by A. R. Ferris. London: Heinemann, 1959.

'The Future of the Arabic Language'. Translated by Angela Giordani. *The Arab Renaissance: A Bilingual Anthology of the Nahda*. Edited by Tarek El-Aris, 50–67. New York: The Modern Language Association of America, 2018.

The Love Letters of Kahlil Gibran to May Ziadah. Translated and edited by Suheil Bushrui and Selma H. al-Kuzbari. Oxford: Oneworld, 1995.

The Storm. Translated by John Wallbridge. Santa Cruz, CA: White Cloud Press, 1993.

Works by Gibran Translated into Arabic

al-A'māl al-kāmila mu'arraba, trans. Nadim Naimy. Beirut: Nawfal, 2015.

al-Nabiyy (The Prophet). Translated by Mikhail Naimy. Beirut: Nawfal, 2013.

al-Nabiyy (The Prophet). Translated by Tharwat 'Okasha. Cairo: Dār al-Shurūq, 2009.

Other Sources

'Abbas, Ihsan and Muhammad Yusuf Najm. *al-Shi'r al-'arabī fi-l-mahjar: Amīrca al-shamāliyya* (Arabic Poetry in the *Mahjar*: North America). 3rd edition. Beirut: Dār Ṣādir, 1982.

'Abbud, Marun. *Ruwwād al-nahḍa al-ḥadītha* (The Pioneers of the Modern Renaissance). Qairo: Hindawi, 2015 [1952].

——. *Saqr Lubnān: Baḥth fi-l-nahḍa al-'adabiyya al-ḥadītha wa rajulihā al-awwal Aḥmad Fāris al-Shidyāq* (Lebanon's Falcon: A Study of the Modern Arab Renaissance and its First Man: Ahmad Faris al-Shidyaq). Beirut: Dār al-Makshūf, 1950.

'Abd al-Hayy, Muhammad. *Tradition and English and Romantic Influence in Arabic Romantic Poetry: A Study in Comparative Literature*. London: Ithaca, 1982.

Abdel-Malek, Kamal and Wael Hallaq, eds. *Tradition, Modernity, and Postmodernity in Arabic Literature*. Leiden: Brill, 2000.

Abu-Deeb, Kamal. 'The Collapse of Totalizing Discourse and the Rise of Marginalized/Minority Discourses'. In *Tradition, Modernity, and Postmodernity in Arabic Literature*. Edited by Kamel Abdel-Malek and Wael Hallaq, 335–66. Leiden: Brill, 2000.

Aboul-Ela, Hosam. 'Is There an Arab (Yet) in This Field? Postcolonialism, Comparative Literature, and Middle Eastern Horizon of Said's Discourse Analysis'. *MFS Modern Fiction Studies* 56, no. 4 (Winter 2010): 729–50.

al-'Aqqad, 'Abbas Mahmud. *al-Fuṣūl*. Cairo: Hindāwi, 2014 [1922].

Al-Azm, Sadiq Jalal. 'Orientalism and Orientalism in Reverse'. In *Orientalism: A Reader*. Edited by A. L. Macfie, 217–38. New York: New York University Press, 2000.

Al-Azmeh, Aziz. *Islams and Modernities*. London; New York: Verso, 2009.

Acocella, Joan. 'The Prophet Motive: The Kahlil Gibran Phenomenon'. *The New York Times*, 7 January 2008. https://www.newyorker.com/magazine/2008/01/07/prophet-motive.

Adonis. *An Introduction to Arab Poetics*. London: Saqi Books, 1990.

———. 'Jubrān Khalīl Jubrān, aw al-ḥadātha al-ru'yā' (Gibran, or Modernity as Vision). In *al-Thābit wa-l-mutaḥawwil: Baḥth fi-l-ittibā' wa-l-ibdā' 'inda al-'arab: Ṣadmat al-ḥadātha* (The Fixed and the Changing in Arabic Poetics: The Shock of Modernity), 160–211. Beirut: Dār al-'awdah, 1978.

———. Preface to Khalil Gibran. *Le Prophète*, 7–23. Translated by Anna Wade Minkowski. Paris: Gallimard, 1992.

———. *al-Thābit wa-l-mutaḥawwil: Baḥth fi-l-ittibā' wa-l-ibdā' 'inda al-'arab: Ṣadmat al- ḥadātha*. Beirut: Dār al-'Awda, 1978.

Appiah, Kwame Anthony. 'There is No Such Thing as Western Civilisation'. *The Guardian*, 9 November 2016. https://www.theguardian.com/world/2016/nov/09/western-civilisation-appiah reith-lecture.

Apter, Emily. *Against World Literature: On the Politics of Untranslatability*. London: Verso, 2013.

Arberry, A. J. *Sufism: An Account of the Mystics of Islam*. London: Unwin Brothers, 1972.

Asad, Talal. *Formations of the Secular: Christianity, Islam, Modernity*. Palo Alto: Stanford University Press, 2003.

Attridge, Derek. *The Singularity of Literature*. London: Routledge, 2004.

———. 'Innovation, Literature, Ethics: Relating to the Other'. *PMLA* 114, no. 1 (January 1999): 20–31.

Bakhos, Carol. *The Family of Abraham: Jewish, Christian, and Muslim Interpretations*. Cambridge, MA: Harvard University Press, 2014.

Barakat, Halim. *Ghurbat al-kātib al-'arabī* (The Exile of the Arab Writer). London: Saqi Books, 2011.

———. 'Explorations in Exile and Creativity: The Case of Arab-American Writers'. In *Tradition, Modernity, and Postmodernity in Arabic Literature*. Edited by Kamal Abdel-Malek and Wael Hallaq, 304–20. Leiden: Brill, 2000.

Barthes, Roland. 'The Death of the Author'. In *Image, Music, Text*, 142–48. Translated by Stephan Heath. London: Fontana Press, 1977.

Barut, Muhammad Jamal. 'al-Ḥadātha al-'ūla: Mushkilāt qaṣīdat al-nathr min Jubrān ilā majallat *Shi'r*, al-juz' al-'awwal' (The First Modernity: The Problem of the Prose Poem from Gibran to the Journal of *Shi'r*, Part I). *al-Ma'rifa* no. 283–84 (1 September 1985): 119–77.

———. 'al-Ḥadātha al-'ūla: Mushkilāt qaṣīdat al-nathr min Jubrān ilā majallat *Shi'r*, al-juz' al-thāni' (The First Modernity: The Problem of the Prose Poem from Gibran to the Journal of *Shi'r*, Part II). *al-Ma'rifa* no. 285 (1 November 1985): 79–122.

Bawardi, Hani J. *The Making of Arab Americans*. Austin: University of Texas Press, 2014.

Benhabib, Seyla. *The Rights of Others: Aliens, Residents and Citizens*. Cambridge: Cambridge University Press, 2005.

Benjamin, Walter. 'The Task of the Translator'. In *Illuminations*, 69–82. Translated by Harry Zohn. London: Collins/Fontana Books, 1973.

Berman, Jacob. '*Mahjar* Legacies: A Reinterpretation'. In *Between the Middle East and the Americas: The Cultural Politics of Diaspora*. Edited by Ella Shohat and Evelyn Alsultany, 65–79. Ann Arbor: University of Michigan Press, 2012.

Beshara, Adel. 'A Rebel Syrian: Gibran Kahlil Gibran'. In *The Origins of Syrian Nationhood: Histories, Pioneers and Identity*. Edited by Adel Beshara, 143–62. London; New York: Routledge, 2011.

Blanchot, Maurice. 'Prophetic Speech'. In *The Book to Come*, 79–85. Translated by Charlotte Mandell. Palo Alto: Stanford University Press, 2003.

Bourdieu, Pierre. *The Field of Cultural Production*. Translated and edited by Randal Johnson. Cambridge: Polity Press, 1993.

Bourdieu, Pierre, and Loic J. D. Wacquant. *An Invitation to Reflexive Sociology*. Chicago: University of Chicago Press, 1992.

Bragdon, Claude. *Merely Players*. New York: A. A. Knopf, 1929.

Bushrui, Suheil and Joe Jenkins. *Kahlil Gibran, Man and Poet: A New Biography*. Oxford: OneWorld, 1998.

Champion, James. 'The Parable as an Ancient and a Modern Form'. *Literature and Theology* 3, no. 1 (March 1989): 16–39.

Chaouki Zine, Muhammad. 'Tafkīkiyyat Ibn 'Arabī: al-Ta'wīl, al-ikhtilāf, al-kitāba' (Ibn Arabi's Deconstruction: Hermeneutics, Difference, Writing). *Kitābāt Mu'āṣira* 36, no. 9 (March 1999): 53–59.

———. 'Al-Hijra, al-maskūnia, al-manzil al-mafqūd: 'Anāṣir fī hājis al-gharāba' (Migration, Habitability and the Lost Home: Elements in the Apprehension of *Unheimlich*). *Majallat Yatafakkarūn*, no. 11 (2017): 14–31.

Chittick, William. *Imaginal Worlds*. Albany: State University of New York Press, 1994.

———. *The Sufi Path of Knowledge: Ibn Arabi's Metaphysics of Imagination*. Albany: State University of New York Press, 1989.

Corbin, Henry. *Alone with the Alone: Creative Imagination in the Sufism of Ibn Arabi*. Translated by Ralph Manheim. Princeton: Princeton University Press, 1997.

Damrosch, David. *What is World Literature?* Woodstock: Princeton University Press, 2003.

Dawn, C. Ernest. 'The Origins of Arab Nationalism'. In *The Origins of Arab Nationalism*. Edited by Rachid Khalidi et al., 3–30. New York: Columbia University Press, 1991.

Daye, John. *'Aqīdat Jubrān* (The Doctrine of Gibran). London: Dār Surāqia, 1988.

———. *Lakum Jubrānukum wa lia Jubrānī* (You Have Your Gibran and I Have Mine). Beirut: Qub Elias Press, 2009.

De Man, Paul. *Blindness and Insight: Essays in the Rhetoric of Contemporary Criticism*. New York: Oxford University Press, 1976.

Derrida, Jacques. *Adieu to Emmanuel Levinas*. Translated by Pascale-Anne Brault and Michel Naas. Palo Alto: Stanford University Press, 1999.

———. 'Différance'. In *The Margins of Philosophy*, 1–29. Translated by Alan Bass. Brighton: Harvester Press, 1982.

———. *Dissemination*. Translated by Barbara Johnson. London: The Athlone Press: 1981.

———. *Giving Time: I. Counterfeit Money*. Translated by Peggy Kamuf. Chicago; London: University of Chicago Press, 1992.

———. *Monolingualism of the Other, or the Prosthesis of Origin*. Translated by Patrick Mensah. Palo Alto: Stanford University Press, 1998.

———. *Psyche: Inventions of the Other, Volume I*. Translated by Peggy Kamuf and Elizabeth Rottenberg. Palo Alto: Stanford University Press, 2007.

———. *The Gift of Death and Literature in Secret*. Translated by David Wills. Chicago; London: University of Chicago Press, 2008.

Dufourmantelle, Anne and Jacques Derrida. *Of Hospitality*. Translated by Rachel Bowlby. Palo Alto: Stanford University Press, 2000.

El-Aris, Tarek. ed. *The Arab Renaissance: A Bilingual Anthology of the Nahda*. New York: The Modern Language Association of America, 2018.

El-Desouky, Ayman A. 'Theorizing the Local and Untranslatability as Comparative Critical Method'. In *Approaches to World Literature, Volume 1,*

Weltliteraturen/World Literatures Series. Edited by Joachim Küpper, 59–86. Berlin: Akademie Verlag, 2013.

El-Zein, Amira. 'Spiritual Consumption in the United States: The Rumi Phenomenon'. *Islamic and Christian-Muslim Relations* 11, no. 1 (2000): 71–85.

Eliot, T. S. 'Tradition and the Individual Talent'. In *Selected Essays*, 13–22. London: Faber and Faber, 1932.

Elmarsafy, Ziad. *The Enlightenment Qur'an: The Politics of Translation and the Construction of Islam* (Oxford: OneWorld, 2009).

———. 'User-Friendly Islams: Translating Rumi in France and the United States'. In *Between the Middle East and the Americas: The Cultural Politics of Diaspora*. Edited by Ella Shohat and Evelyn Alsultany, 264–81. Ann Arbor: University of Michigan Press, 2013.

Elshakry, Marwa. *Reading Darwin in Arabic, 1860–1950*. Chicago: University of Chicago Press, 2013.

Fakhreddine, Huda J. *The Arabic Prose Poem: Theory and Practice*. Edinburgh: Edinburgh University Press, 2021.

Fawaz, Leila Tarazi. *A Land of Aching Hearts: The Middle East in the Great War*. Cambridge, MA: Harvard University Press, 2014.

Fish, Stanley. *Is There a Text in This Class? The Authority of Interpretative Communities*. Cambridge, MA: Harvard University Press, 1980.

Forster, Stephen William. 'The Exotic as a Symbolic System'. *Dialectical Anthropology* 7, no. 1 (September 1982): 21–30.

Foucault, Michel. *The Order of Things: An Archaeology of the Human Sciences*. New York: Vintage, 1973.

———. 'What is an Author?' In *The Foucault Reader*. Edited by Paul Rabinow, 101–20. London: Penguin, 1984.

Frazer, T. G. *The First World War and Its Aftermath: The Reshaping of the Middle East*. London: Gingo Library, 2015.

Freud, Sigmund. *The Standard Edition of the Complete Psychological Works*. Translated by Alix Strachey et al. New York: Norton, 1961.

Frow, John. *Cultural Studies and Cultural Value*. Oxford: Clarendon Press, 1995.

Frye, Northrop. *Fearful Symmetry: A Study of William Blake*. Princeton: Princeton University Press, 1974.

Gadamer, Hans-Georg. *Truth and Method*. Translated by Joel Weinsheimer and Donald G. Marshall. New York: Continuum, 2004.

Gibran, Jean and Khalil G. Gibran. *Kahlil Gibran: His Life and World.* New York: Interlink Books, 1991.

———. *Kahlil Gibran: Beyond Borders*. New York: Interlink Books, 2017.

Gollomb, Joseph. 'An Arabian Poet in New York'. *New York Evening Post*, 29 March 1919.

Guillory, John. *Cultural Capital: The Problem of Literary Canon Formation*. Chicago; London: University of Chicago Press, 1993.

Habib, Masʿud. *Jubrān ḥayyan wa mayyitan* (Gibran in his Life and Death). Beirut: Dār al- Rihāni, 1966.

Haddad, Qassim. 'Jubrān Khalīl Jubrān: Namūdhaj al-usṭūra al-wāqiʿiyya' (Gibran as a Model of Realistic Myth). *al-Quds al-ʿArabī*, 10 April 2021. https://www.alquds.co.uk/جبران-خليل-جبران-نموذج-الأسطورة-الواق/

Hafez, Sabry. *The Genesis of Arabic Narrative Discourse: A Study in the Sociology of Modern Arabic Literature*. London: Saqi Books, 1993.

Hallaq, Boutros. *Gibran et la refondation littéraire arabe: Bildungsroman, écriture prophétique, transgénérisme*. Arles: Sindbad-Actes Sud, 2008.

———. 'Love and the Birth of Modern Arabic Literature'. In *Love and Sexuality in Modern Arabic Literature*. Edited by Roger Allen et al., 16–23. London: Saqi Books, 1995.

Hallaq, Wael B. *The Impossible State: Islam, Politics and Modernity's Moral Predicament*. New York: Columbia University Press, 2012.

Hamzah, Dyala, ed. *The Making of the Arab Intellectual (1880–1960): Empire, Public Sphere and the Colonial Coordinates of Selfhood*. London: Routledge, 2013.

Hanegraaff, Wouter J. *New Age Religion and Western Culture: Esoterism in the Mirror of Secular Thought*. Utrecht: Universiteit Utrecht, 1995.

Hassan, Waïl S. 'The Gibran Phenomenon'. In *Immigrant Narratives: Orientalism and Cultural Translation in Arab American and Arab British Literature*, 59–77. Oxford: Oxford University Press, 2011.

Hawi, Khalil. *Kahlil Gibran: His Background, Character and Works*. Beirut: The Arab Institute for Research and Publishing, 1972.

Heidegger, Martin. *Being and Time*. Translated by John Macqurrie and Edward Robinson. Oxford: Blackwell, 1962.

———. 'Letter on Humanism'. In *Basic Writings*. Edited by D. F. Krell, 189–242. London: Routledge: 1978.

———. 'On the Essence of Truth'. In *Pathmarks*. Edited by William MacNeill, 136–45. Cambridge: Cambridge University Press, 1998.

———. *Poetry, Language, Thought*. Translated by Albert Hofstadter. New York: Harper and Row, 1971.

———. 'The Question Concerning Technology'. In *The Question Concerning Technology and Other Essays*, 3–35. Translated by William Lovitt. London; New York: Harper and Row, 1977.

Hishmeh, Richard E. 'Strategic Genius, Disidentification, and the Burden of *The Prophet* in Arab-American Poetry'. In *Arab Voices in Diaspora: Critical Perspectives on Anglophone Arab Literature*. Edited by Layla Al-Maleh, 93–119. Amsterdam; New York: Rodopi, 2009.

Hourani, Albert. *Arabic Thought in the Liberal Age*. Oxford: Oxford University Press, 1983.

Huggan, Graham. *The Postcolonial Exotic: Marking the Margins*. New York: Routledge, 2001.

Ibn al-ʿArabi, Muhy al-Din. *al-Futūḥāt al-makkiyya* (The Meccan Openings), Vol 3. Edited by Ahmad Shams al-Din. Beirut: Dār al-Kutub al-ʿIlmiyya, 1999.

Jauss, Hans Robert. *Toward an Aesthetic of Reception*. Translated by Timothy Bahti. Brighton: Harvester, 1982.

Jayyusi, Salma Khadra. ed. *Modern Arabic Poetry: An Anthology*. New York: Columbia University Press, 1987.

———. 'Modernist Poetry in Arabic'. In *Modern Arabic Literature*. Edited by M. M. Badawi, 132–79. Cambridge: Cambridge University Press: 1992.

———. *Trends and Movements in Modern Arabic Poetry*. Leiden: Brill, 1977.

Kalem, Galen. 'The Spread and Influence of Kahlil Gibran in China'. *Khalil Gibran Collective*, 12 October 2019. https://www.kahlilgibran.com/latest/80-the-spread-and-influence-of-gibran-in-china.html

———. 'Translations of *The Prophet*'. In *Gibran in the 21st Century: Lebanon's Message to the World* (Papers of the 3rd Khalil Gibran International Conference), 146–51. Beirut: Lebanese American University, 2018.

Kayruz, Wahib. *'Ālam Jubrān al-fikrī II* (The Intellectual World of Gibran II) Beirut: Basharīyā, 1983.

Kellman, Steven G. *The Translingual Imagination*. Lincoln: University of Nebraska Press, 2000.

al-Khal, Yusuf. 'Jubrān: Fikr munīr fī qālib fannī' (Gibran: Enlightened Thought in Artistic Form). *Shiʿr* no. 38 (1 April 1968): 132–34.

Khatibi, Abdelkebir. *Plural Maghreb*. Translated by P. Burcu Yalim. London; New York: Bloomsbury, 2019.

——. *Love in Two Languages*. Translated by Richard Howard. Minneapolis: University of Minnesota Press, 1990.

Khoury, Yvette K. '*Akhir Yom* (The Last Day): A Localized Arabic Adaptation of Shakespeare's *Romeo and Juliet*'. *Theatre Research International* 33, no. 1 (2008): 52–69.

——. 'Mansour Rahbani: Dramatist and Writer of the Classic Songs of a Lebanese Golden Age'. *The Guardian*, 17 April 2009. https://www.theguardian.com/music/2009/apr/17/obituary-mansour-rahbani

Kierkegaard, Soren. *Fear and Trembling*. Translated by Sylvia Walsh. Cambridge: Cambridge University Press, 2006.

Kilito, Abdelfattah. *Je parle toutes les langues, mais en arabe.* Arles: Sindbad-Actes Sud, 2013.

——. *The Author and His Doubles*. Translated by Michael Cooperson. Syracuse: Syracuse University Press, 2001.

——. *The Tongue of Adam*. Translated by Robyn Creswell. New York: New Directions Paperwork: 2016.

——. *Thou Shalt Not Speak My Language*. Translated by Waïl S. Hassan. Syracuse: Syracuse University Press, 2017.

Kleingeld, Pauline. *Kant and Cosmopolitanism: The Philosophical Ideal of a World Citizenship.* Cambridge: Cambridge University Press, 2012.

Laachir, Karima, Sara Marzagora and Francesca Orsini. 'Significant Geographies in Lieu of World Literature'. *Journal of World Literature* no. 3 (2018): 290–310.

Laroui, Abdallah. *The Crisis of Arab Intellectuals: Traditionalism or Historicism?* Translated by Diarmid Cammell. Berkley; London: University of California Press, 1976.

Lauter, Paul. *Canons and Contexts*. New York; Oxford: Oxford University Press, 1991.

Levinas, Emmanuel. 'Ethics as First Philosophy'. In *The Levinas Reader*. Edited by Sean Hand, 75–85. Oxford: Basil Blackwell, 1989.

——. *Totality and Infinity: An Essay on Exteriority*. Translated by Alphonso Lingiss. The Hague; London: Nijhoff, 1979.

Ludescher, Tanyss. 'From Nostalgia to Critique: An Overview of Arab American Literature'. *MELUS* 31, no. 4 (Winter 2006): 93–114.

Maalouf, Amin. Preface to Khalil Gibran. *Le Prophète*, 7–15. Translated by Janine Levy. Paris: Editions de la Loupe, 2003.

Massad A, Jospeh. *Desiring Arabs.* Chicago: University of Chicago Press, 2007.

Medici, Francesco. 'Tracing Gibran's Footsteps: Unpublished and Rare Material'. In *Gibran in the 21st Century: Lebanon's Message to the World*. Edited by Henry Zoghaib and May Rihani, 93–145. Beirut: Centre for Lebanese Heritage, LAU, 2018.

Melhem, D. H. 'Gibran's "The Prophet" Outside the Canon of American Literature'. *Al-Jadid* 8, no. 40 (Summer 2002). https://www.aljadid.com/content/gibran%E2%80%99s-%E2%80%98 prophet%E2%80%99-outside-canon-american-literature

Meskini, Fethi. *al-Huwiyya wa-l-ḥurriya: Naḥwa anwār jadīda* (Identity and Freedom: Towards a New *Aufklärung*). Beirut: Dār Jadāwil, 2011.

———. *al-Huwiyya wa al-zamān: Ta'wīlāt finuminulujia li mas'alat al-naḥn* (Identity and Time: Phenomenological Interpretations of the 'We' Question). Beirut: Dār al-Ṭalīʿa, 2001.

———. *al-Īmān al-ḥurr aw mā baʿda al-milla: Mabāḥith fī falsafat al-dīn* (Free Faith, or Post-*Milla*: Studies in the Philosophy of Religion). Rabat: Mominoun Without Borders, 2018.

———. *al-Kujīto al-majrūḥ: As'ilat al-huwiyya fi-l-falsafa al-muʿāṣira* (The Wounded Cogito: Questions of Identity in Contemporary Philosophy). Algiers: Editions el-ikhtilef; Riyadh, Beirut: Dhifāf Publishing, 2013.

———. *Falsafat al-nawābit* (The Philosophy of *Nawabit*). Beirut: Dār al-Ṭalīʿa, 1997.

Mignolo, Walter. *Local Histories/Global Designs: Coloniality, Subalterns Knowledges, and Border Thinking*. Princeton; Oxford: Princeton University Press, 2012.

Mufti, Aamir. *Forget English! Orientalisms and World Literatures*. Cambridge, MA: Harvard University Press, 2016.

Musa, Salama. 'From *What is the Renaissance*?' Translated by John Barskerville. *The Arab Renaissance: A Bilingual Anthology of the Nahda*. Edited by Tarek El-Aris, 32–49. New York: The Modern Language Association of America, 2018.

Naimy, Mikhail. *Kahlil Gibran: A Biography*. New York: Philosophical Library, 1988.

———. '"A Strange Little Book"'. *Aramco World* 15, no. 6 (Nov/Dec 1964). https://archive.aramcoworld.com/issue/196406/a.strange.little.book.htm.

Naimy, Nadim. 'The Mind and Thought of Kahlil Gibran'. *Journal of Arabic Literature* no. 5 (1974): 55–71.

Nash, Geoffrey. *The Arab Writer in English: Arab Themes in a Metropolitan Language, 1908–1958*. Brighton: Sussex Academic Press, 1998.

Nassar, Eugene Paul. 'Cultural Discontinuity in the Works of Kahlil Gibran'. *MELUS* 7, no. 2 (Summer 1980): 21–36.

Nassir, Najwa Salim. *The Prophet, Arabic and French Translations: A Comparative and Linguistic Analysis*. Beirut: Librairie de Liban, 2018.

Nicholson, Reynold Alleyne. *Studies in Islamic Mysticism*. Cambridge: Cambridge University Press, 1921.

Nietzsche, Fredrich. *The Will to Power*. Translated by Walter Kaufmann and R. J. Hollingdale. New York: Random House, 1967.

———. *Thus Spoke Zarathustra*. Translated by Walter Kaufmann. New York: Penguin, 1966.

Noorani, Yaseen. 'Hard and Soft Multilingualism'. *Critical Multilingualism Studies* 1, no. 2 (2013): 7–28.

Omri, Mohamed-Salah. 'Notes on the Traffic between Theory and Arabic Literature'. *International Journal of Middle East Studies* 43, no. 4 (November 2011): 731–33.

Orfalea, Gregory and Sharif Elmusa, eds. *Grape Leaves: A Century of Arab-American Literature*. Salt Lake City: University of Utah Press, 1988.

Patel, Abdulrazzak. *The Arab Nahḍah: The Making of the Intellectual and Humanist Movement*. Edinburgh: Edinburgh University Press, 2013.

Phillip, Thomas. 'Jurji Zaydan's Role in the Syro-Arab Nahda: A Re-evaluation'. In *The Origins of Syrian Nationhood: Histories, Pioneers and Identity*. Edited by Adel Beshara, 79–99. London; New York: Routledge, 2011.

Qandil, Fatima. *Al-Rāwī al-shabaḥ: Shiʿriyyat al-kitāba fī nuṣūṣ Jubrān Khalīl Jubrān* (The Spectral Narrator: The Poetics of Writing in the Texts of Gibran Khalil Gibran). Cairo: Dār al-ʿAyn li-l-Nashr, 2015.

Rahbani, Mansur. *Jubrān wa-l-nabiyy* (Gibran and the Prophet). Beirut: M al-Raḥbāni, 2010.

al-Rafiʿi, Mustafa Sadiq. *Taḥta rāyat al-Qurʾān: al-Maʿraka bayna al-qadīm wa-l-jadīd* (Under the Banner of the Qurʾān: The Battle between the New and the Old). Qairo: Hindāwi, 2014 [1926].

Rancière, Jacques. *Mute Speech: Literature, Critical Theory, and Politics*. Translated by James Swenson. New York: Columbia University Press: 2011.

———. 'The Politics of Literature'. *SubStance 103* 33, no. 1 (2004): 10–24.

Ratner-Rosenhagen, Jennifer. *American Nietzsche: A History of an Icon and his Ideas*. Chicago; London: University of Chicago Press, 2012.

'Recent Books in Brief Review'. *The Bookman* (February 1924): 673–74. https://www.unz.com/print/Bookman-1924feb-00673a05/

Ricoeur, Paul. 'Religion, Atheism, and Faith'. In *The Conflict of Interpretations: Essays in Hermeneutics*, 440–67. Translated by Charles Freilich. Edited by Don Ihde. Evanston: Northwestern University Press, 1974.

Rowner, Ilai. *The Event: Literature and Theory*. Lincoln: University of Nebraska, 2015.

Russell, George William. *The Living Torch*. New York: Macmillan, 1937.

al-Sabuni, Leyla al-Malih. 'Jubrān nabiyyu man?' (Gibran: Whose Prophet?). *al-Ma'rifa* no. 252 (1 December 1983): 187–200.

Said, Edward. *Culture and Imperialism*. London: Vintage, 1993.

———. *Orientalism*. London: Penguin, 2003.

———. *On Late Style: Music and Literature against the Grain*. New York: Pantheon Books, 2006.

———. *Reflections on Exile, and Other Literary and Cultural Essays*. London: Granta Books, 2012.

———. *The World, the Text, and the Critic*. London: Vintage, 1991.

Sayigh, Tawfiq. *Aḍwā' jadīda 'alā Jubrān* (Gibran under New Spotlights). London: Riad el Rayyes, 1990.

Schillinger, Liesl. 'Pioneer of the New Age'. *New York Times*, 13 December 1998. https://www.nytimes.com/1998/12/13/books/pioneer-of-the-new-age.html

Schulze, Reinhard. 'Mass Culture and Islamic Cultural Production in the Nineteenth Century Middle East'. In *Mass Culture, Popular Culture and Social Life in the Middle East*. Edited by George Stauth and Sami Zubaida, 189–222. Frankfurt; Boulder: Westview Press, 1987.

Schwab, Raymond. *The Oriental Renaissance*. Translated by Gene Patterson-Black and Victor Reinking. New York: Columbia University Press, 1984.

Seiffert, Marjorie Allen. 'Foreign Food'. *Poetry* 24, no. 4 (January 1924): 216–18.

Shahid, Irfan. 'Gibran and the American Literary Canon: The Problem of *The Prophet*'. In *Tradition, Modernity, and Postmodernity in Arabic Literature*. Edited by Kamal Abdel-Malek and Wael Hallaq, 321–34. Leiden: Brill, 2000.

Sharabi, Hisham. *Arab Intellectuals and the West*. Baltimore: The Johns Hopkins Press, 1970.

Sheehi, Stephen. *Foundations of Modern Arab Identity*. Gainesville: University of Florida Press, 2003.

———. 'Modernism, Anxiety and the Ideology of Arab Vision'. *Discourse* 28, no. 1 (Winter 2006): 72–79.

———. 'Towards a Critical Theory of *al-Nahḍah*: Epistemology, Ideology and Capital'. *Journal of Arabic Literature* 43, no. 2/3 (2012): 269–98.

Shehadeh, Lamia Rustum. 'The Name of Syria in Ancient and Modern Usage'. In *The Origins of Syrian Nationhood: Histories, Pioneers and Identity*. Edited by Adel Beshara, 17–29. London; New York: Routledge, 2011.

Shih, Shu-Mei. 'Global Literature and the Technologies of Recognition'. *PMLA* 119, no. 1 (January 2004): 16–30.

Siddiqui, Mona. *Hospitality and Islam: Welcoming in God's Name*. New Haven and London: Yale University Press, 2015.

Smith, Anthony D. *Nationalism: Theory, Ideology, History*. Cambridge: Polity, 2010.

Spivak, Gayatri. *Death of a Discipline*. New York: Columbia University Press, 2003.

Taylor, Charles. *Sources of the Self: The Making of the Modern Identity*. Cambridge, MA: Harvard University Press, 2001.

The Koran Interpreted. Translated by A. J. Arberry. Oxford: Oxford University Press, 1983.

Tihanov, Galin. 'Narratives of Exile: Cosmopolitanism Beyond the Liberal Imagination'. In *Whose Cosmopolitanism? Critical Perspectives, Relationalities and Discontents*. Edited by N. Glick Schiller and A. Irving, 141–59. New York and Oxford: Berghahn, 2015.

Walbridge, John. 'Gibran: His Aesthetic, and His Moral Universe'. *Al-Hikmat* no. 21 (2001): 47–66.

Walkowitz, Rebecca L. *Born-Translated: The Contemporary Novel in an Age of World Literature*. New York: Columbia University Press, 2015.

Waterfield, Robin. *Prophet: The Life and Times of Kahlil Gibran*. London: Allen Lane, 1998.

Wilkinson, Marguerite, ed. *New Voices: An Introduction to Contemporary Poetry*. New York: Macmillan, 1919.

Williams, Raymond. *Keywords: A Vocabulary of Culture and Society*. New York: Oxford University Press, 1983.

Wilson, P. W. 'Jesus Was the Supreme Poet: That Is the Conception Animating These Two Books About Him'. *New York Times*, 23 December 1928. https://archive.nytimes.com/www.nytimes.com/books/98/12/13/specials/gibran-jesus.html

Wrathall, Mark A. 'Introduction: Metaphysics and Onto-theology'. In *Religion after Metaphysics*. Edited by Mark A. Wrathall, 1–6. Cambridge: Cambridge University Press, 2003.

Young, Barbara. *This Man from Lebanon: A Study of Khalil Gibran*. New York: A. A. Knopf, 1945.

Zheng, Ma. 'The Study of Kahlil Gibran in Contemporary China: New Developments and Influences'. In *The Enduring Legacy of Kahlil Gibran*

(The Second International Conference on Kahlil Gibran: 'Reading Gibran in the Age of Globalisation and Conflict', 3–6 May 2012). Edited by Suheil Bushrui and James Malarkey, 227–34. College Park: University of Maryland, 2012.
Zima, Petr. 'Problems of Reader-Response Criticism: From Hermeneutics to Phenomenology'. In *The Philosophy of Modern Literary Theory*, 55–80. London: Athlone Press, 1999.

Index

Abbasid poetry, 13, 14
ʿAbd al-Hamid, Ottoman Sultan, 13
ʿAbd al-Hayy, Muhammad, 28n
Abrahamic, 11, 22–3, 33–6, 42, 45, 49, 58, 62, 67, 69–71, 73, 75, 80, 82n, 120, 242
Abu-Deeb, Kamel, 2
Abu Madi, Ilia, 12
Abu Nuwas, 133n, 212
Abu Tammam, 133n, 212
Adonis (Ali Ahmad Said Esber), 2, 24, 25n, 102, 133n, 211–15, 218, 227, 231n, 236n, 237n, 243, 248n
agency, 15, 120, 126, 147, 159, 223
al-Ajniḥa al-mutakassira (Broken Wings), 9, 44, 61, 137n, 244
American literary field, 204–5
al-ʿAqqad, ʿAbbas Mahmud, 111, 211
Arabic poetry, 20, 101–2, 111, 133n, 212, 219
Arabism, 142, 157, 174n, 175n
ʿArāʾis al-murūj (Nymphs of the Valley), 9
al-Arwāḥ al-mutamarrida (Spirits Rebellious), 9, 211
ʻal-ʿĀṣifaʼ (The Tempest), 169–70.
Attridge, Derek, 4, 5, 20
al-ʿAwāṣif (The Tempests), 9, 28n, 37, 39, 74, 79, 109, 139n, 149, 246
al-Azm, Sadiq Jalal, 29n

Badʾ thawra (The Beginning of a Revolution), 144–8
al-Badāʾiʿ wa al-ṭarāʾif (Marvels and Masterpieces), 9, 67, 109, 121, 236n, 246
baqāʾ (subsistence/persistence in God), 43, 46
Barakat, Halim, 2
Barthes, Roland, 7
al-Barudi, Mahmud Sami, 13
al-barzagh (the isthmus or the imaginal), 98
baṣīra (disclosing insight), 6
Bayna layl wa ṣabāḥ (Between Night and Morn), 151–5, 164
Benjamin, Walter, 199
bilingualism, Gibran's, 109–10, 112–21, 126–8, 130, 185–6
Blake, William, 35, 111, 114
Blanchot, Maurice, 11, 35–6, 63–4, 82n
Boulus, Sargon, 217
Bourdieu, Pierre, 187, 188, 197, 209, 227, 288n

Britain, imperial, 13, 124, 139n, 141, 148, 156, 161–2, 30n, 148, 155, 160, 177n
al-Buhturi, 13
Bushrui, Suheil, 4, 26n, 196
al-Bustani, Butrus, 13, 30n, 135n, 142, 172, 175n
al-Bustani, Salim, 13, 184n

Chaouki Zine, Muhammad, 118, 199
Chittick, William C., 44
Christianity, 11, 56, 58, 67, 88n, 92n, 135n, 145–7
  civilisation, 200, 203
  Jesus, 232n, 233n
Conrad, Joseph, 248n
cosmopolitan patriotism, 103–8
crucifixion, 44, 46, 56–7, 79

Dam'a wa ibtisāma (A Tear and A Smile) 9, 37, 98, 103, 132
Damrosch, David, 27n, 186
Darwin, Charles, 13, 22, 24, 30n, 36, 38–40, 48, 82n, 143, 155
Darwinism *see* Darwin
De Man, Paul, 106, 223
Derrida, Jacques, 7, 22, 75, 82n, 95, 97, 106, 115, 117, 131n, 134n, 230n, 231n, 243
El-Desouky, Ayman, 36, 338n
despotism, 18, 156, 163
al-dhāt al-ma'naqiyya/al-waḍ'iyya (ethical or innate self), 43, 58, 63

The Earth Gods, 9, 77–80, 109
Eliot, T. S., 110, 188, 189, 199, 202, 227, 229n
Elshakry, Marwa, 15, 38
event, as epiphany, 33, 49, 56, 58–60, 81–2n, 98, 224–5
evolutionism, 16, 22, 36, 38–41, 45–6, 80, 122
exoticism, 193–4, 197, 233n, 246, 247

fanā' (annihilation/extinction in God), 43, 46
Fawaz, Leila Tarazi, 151
The Forerunner, 9, 58, 67, 70, 74, 109, 126, 137n, 193–5, 197
France, imperial, 13, 124, 100n, 139n, 141, 148, 156, 160–2, 181n
freedom, Gibran on, 71–3, 91n
Freud, 63, 82n, 89n, 92n, 190
Frye, Northrop, 35
'The Future of the Arabic Language', 121–6

Gadamer, Hans-Georg, 192, 225, 238n
The Garden of the Prophet, 9, 68, 85n
ghurba (exile or estrangement), 65–6
Gibran's worldview, 37–46
giving, Gibran on, 75–6, 103
'God' (poem), 46–8
God, Gibran on, 37–46, 47–8, 50, 54–6, 68–71, 74, 75–6, 83n, 85n, 90n
Greater Self, 45, 55, 57, 58, 67, 79, 202, 232n, 234n
Greater Syria, 5, 13, 23, 102, 121, 124, 141, 143, 148, 150, 155, 162, 173, 230n, 245
Guillory, John, 206

Haddad, Abdelmassih, 220
Haddad, Qasim, 25n
'Ḥaffār al-qubūr' (The Grave Digger), 50–3, 78, 86n, 87n
al-Hallaj, 44
Hallaq, Boutros, 2, 42n, 59, 89n
Hallaq, Wael, 176n
Haskell, Mary, 10, 17, 37, 42, 44, 77, 82,

88n, 93n, 95, 112, 113, 116, 137n, 175n, 177n, 178n, 201, 220, 231n
Hassan, Waïl S., 26n, 190, 218
Hawi, Khalil, 3–4
Hegel, 32n, 82n, 124
Heidegger, Martin, 42, 49, 53–4, 55, 82n, 86n, 87n, 240n
hospitality, 76, 97, 195–5, 199
as concept, 117–19, 134n, 230n
as right or ethical imperative, 105–6, 134n
Hourani, Albert, 30n, 178n, 179n

Ibn al-ʿArabi, 44, 67, 68–9, 71, 76, 83n, 91n, 100
ibtikār (invention or innovation), 122–4, 134, 166, 170, 172
identity
collective or national, 32, 116, 119, 123, 144, 165, 171–2, 175n, 221
conceptual, 246, 231n, 248n
East–West, 15–19, 23, 31n, 96, 119–20, 127, 130, 137n, 166, 189, 193, 197, 227, 231n, 235–6n
as mode of reason or institution, 21–2, 34, 49, 53, 81, 120, 130, 243
personal, 128–9, 164, 231n
politics of, 102, 210, 243–4
as veil, 49, 97, 120, 121, 127–8, 166, 224, 226
'Ilā al-sharqiyyīn' (To the Easterners), 164–6
inḥiṭāṭ (decadence), 13, 29n, 162, 177n
insight (*baṣīra*, *ru'yā*), 64–6, 70, 98–9
Iram dhāt al-ʿimād (Iram, City of Lofty Pillars), 48, 64–6, 85n
Islam, 11, 44, 64, 67, 90, 134n, 141, 145–7, 154, 158, 176n, 177n, 207
Islamist, 222, 239n, 240n

'al-Jabbār al-ri'bāl' (The Lonely Giant), 86n
Jauss, Hans Robert, 187, 192
Jayyusi, Salma Khadra, 102
Jesus the Son of Man, 9, 109, 188, 202

Kant, Emmanuel, 82n, 104, 105, 240n
kashf (disclosure, revelation), 49, 65
Keats, John, 39, 114
al-Khal, Yusuf, 24, 133n, 211, 212, 214–15, 217, 218, 227
Khatibi, Abdelkebir, 95, 114, 185, 200
Kierkegaard, Soren, 71
Kilito, Abdelfattah, 102, 113–14, 132n, 133n
al-kulliya (universality), 146, 177n

'Lakum lubnānukum wa lia lubnānī' (You Have Your Lebanon and I Have Mine), 102, 143–4, 174–5n
'Lakum lughatukum w lia lughatī' (You Have Your Language and I Have Mine), 101, 211
Laroui, Abdallah, 182n
Lazarus and his Beloved, 91n
Lebanon, 3, 5, 9, 39, 49, 59, 63, 65, 83n, 102, 121, 136n, 138n, 143–4, 169, 174–5n, 211, 221, 233n
Levinas, Emmanuel, 20, 92n, 97, 106, 117, 134n
Loti, Pierre, 17–18
love (*mahabba*), Gibran's notion of, 58–61, 63, 79–80, 81, 88n, 107–8, 244–5

Maalouf, Amin, 185, 228n
'Maḍjaʿ al-arūs' (The Bridal Couch), 58–9

The Madman, 9, 37, 46, 49–50, 57, 74, 84n, 95, 109, 116, 128, 137n, 188, 189–93, 197, 205, 213, 223–4
Mahjari school *see* Romanticism
al-Mala'ika, Nazik, 215
al-Manfaluti, Mustafa Lutfi, 125, 139n, 211, 236n
'Mārtha', 58–9
Marx, Karl, 30n
al-mas'ala al-sharqiyya (The Eastern Question), 16, 30n, 40, 148
'Māta ahlī' (Dead are My People), 151
al-Mawākib (The Processions) 9, 59, 109, 110, 112, 169, 211
Melhem, D. H., 234n
Meskini, Fethi, 21–2, 32n, 33, 50, 75, 81n, 87n, 156, 179n, 222–7, 238–9n, 240n
Michelangelo, 29n
the Mist, Gibran's notion of, 67–70, 91n
moral independence (*al-istiqlāl al-ma'nawī*), 14, 23, 125, 143, 159, 161, 166, 171, 173, 245
Mubarak, 'Ali, 13, 83n
Muhammad, Prophet, 28n, 90n, 177n, 92n, 182n
al-Mulk, Nizam, 90n
Musa, Salama, 83, 172, 183n
mushāhda (witnessing), 65, 90n
al-mushtarak (the shared), 247, 248n
al-Mūsīqā (On Music), 9, 100–1, 135
al-Mutanabbi, 13
al-Muwaylihi, Muhammad, 13
'My Friend', 97, 128–30, 190

al-Nadim, 'Abdallah, 13
Nahḍa, 6, 12–17, 29n, 30n, 31n, 35, 38, 40, 46, 63, 102, 119, 121–5, 135n, 136n, 142–3, 149, 156, 162, 164, 166–73, 174n, 175n, 176n, 178n, 179n, 181n, 183n, 200, 210, 212, 223, 225, 238n, 244, 245
'Nahḍat al-sharq al-'arabī' (The Awakening of the Arab East), 167–8, 170
Naimy, Mikhail, 12, 84n, 202, 217, 219–20, 231n, 238n, 239n
al-nāmūs al-kullī (universal nomos/ law), 49, 58, 62, 89n
Napoleon, invasion of Egypt, 12, 142, 172
nation, Syria *see* nationhood
nationalism
  Arab, 174n, 175n
  as concept and/or ideology, 13, 28n, 104, 144, 174n, 175n
  Gibran's, 23, 125, 142, 150–1, 155–62, 172, 181n
  Syrian, 148, 150, 172, 174n, 175n
nationhood, Syrian, 10, 142, 143, 148, 151, 155–7, 180n
New Age, 1, 8, 202, 204–7, 227, 234n
New Criticism, 188–9, 199, 202, 227, 228n
Nietzsche, 9–10, 22, 33, 36–7, 39, 41–2, 47–8, 50, 53, 57–8, 71, 74, 77, 80, 82n, 84n, 88n, 92n, 93–4n, 146, 190, 194, 200, 205, 232n, 240n
nihilism, 10, 51, 53, 213
al-nushū' wa-l-irtiqā' (evolution and progress) *see* evolutionism

'Okasha, Tharwat, 211, 217, 239n
ontotheology, 42, 71
Orientalism, 15–19, 29n, 30n, 146–7, 210, 240n
the Other, 15, 97, 107–8, 118, 128–9, 147, 194, 199, 213, 243–6
  as absolute or wholly, 36, 55

as concept, 20–1, 95, 117, 119, 225–6, 247
as culturally different, 15–17, 55n
Ottoman, 13, 41, 107, 141, 142, 144, 148, 151–2, 155–6, 160, 162–3, 175n, 177n, 230n

'"The Perfect World"', 54–6, 116, 192–3, 242
Phoenician, 29, 60, 61
poet, role of the, 14, 36, 46–7, 51–4, 103, 107, 122–3, 212, 242, 246
poetic genius, 61–2
poetic prose, 97–8, 101
poet-prophet, 9, 11, 35, 37, 104, 204, 218
post-colonialism, 5, 19–20, 217, 237n, 244
The Prophet, 8, 9, 10, 24, 26n, 63, 73–4, 76–7, 80, 93n, 103, 109, 112, 185, 186, 188, 191, 194, 197–202, 204–6, 209–11, 213, 214–21, 227, 228n, 231–2n, 234n, 236n, 238n, 243, 244
the prophetic
as mode/form of writing, 11, 26n, 33–7, 46, 49–50, 58, 77, 81, 82n, 120, 126, 244
as *the* impossible/Outside, 67, 120

Qandil, Fatima, 100–1
Qur'ān, 22, 64, 68, 90n, 138n, 211, 222, 238n
quwwat al-ibtikār (the power of invention), 11, 40, 121–2, 124, 126, 167

al-Rābiṭa al-Qalamiyya (*Arrabitah*, the Pen Bond), 12, 28n
al-Rafiʿi, Mustafa Sadiq, 211, 236n
Rahbani, Mansur, 10, 220–1
'Ramād al-ajyāl wa al-nār al-khālida' (The Ashes of Generation and Eternal Fire), 42, 60
Rancière, Jacques, 138n, 164, 245
reincarnation, 41, 42, 60–1, 69, 85n, 234n
reinvention
of God and/or the self, 45, 57, 172, 255
of the religious, 10, 22, 34, 37, 56, 74, 83n, 172, 244, 272
religion, Gibran on, 49, 52, 56, 74–5, 145–7
Ricoeur, Paul, 32n, 33, 71, 74, 88n, 92n
Rihani, Ameen, 12, 39, 102, 160, 175n
Romanticism, 14, 35, 122, 123, 138n, 182n, 183n, 184n, 212, 214, 237n
Arab *Mahjari*, 11, 12–14, 28n, 135n, 238n
Egyptian, 211
Gibran's, 37, 59, 73, 77, 102, 104, 106–7, 132, 169–71, 174n, 204
Rousseau, Jean-Jacques, 144, 182n
Rumi (Jalal ad-Din Muhammad al-Rumi), 207–8
Russell, George William, 199–200

Said, Edward, 3, 6, 15–16, 18–20, 31n, 80, 131n, 165, 191n, 232n, 248n
Sannuʿ, Yaʿqub, 13
'Ṣawt al-shāʿir' (The Voice of the Poet), 103–8, 177n
Schwab, Raymond, 200
al-shawq (longing), 43, 48, 65
Shawqi, Ahmad, 13
Sheehi, Stephan, 14, 168–9, 181n, 182n
al-Shidyaq, Ahmad Faris, 13, 135n, 136n

Shih, Shu-Mei, 236n
Shumayyil, Shibli, 38–9, 83n
Socrates, 199
Spencer, Herbet, 40
the spiritual, 22, 63–4, 66, 100, 242
Spivak, Gayatri, 5
sufism (Islamic mysticism), 11, 28n, 44, 46, 60, 65–5, 69, 85n, 86n, 90n, 90, 91n, 170, 200
'Sūria 'alā fajr al-mustaqbal' (Syria on the Dawn of the Future), 155–60, 162–4
survival of the fittest *see* evolutionism
Sykes-Picot Agreement, 139n, 148, 160, 177–8n
Syriac, 116, 119, 122, 136n, 245

Tagore, Rabindranath, 28n, 110, 189–90, 199
al-Tahtawi, Rifa'a Rafi', 13, 178n
Taylor, Charles, 32n, 61, 222
Thus Spoke Zarathustra see Nietzsche
tradition (*turāth*), 12, 14, 32, 58, 62, 102, 139n, 167, 182n, 222–3, 240n, 244
  T. S. Eliot on, 188, 202
transcendence, 36, 42, 44–6, 48, 74–5, 80, 86n
translation
  and Arabic literature, 113, 149, 125, 132n, 149
  of the Bible, 116–17
  cultural, 24, 127, 186, 208
  and Gibran's work/reception, 118, 132n, 187, 192, 199, 208, 210, 211, 213–21, 227, 288n, 235n, 238n, 239n, 246
  of Rumi, 207, 235n
  self-translation, 23, 126, 208
  and the untranslatable, 132n, 238n
  and world literature, 27, 186, 226–7, 247

Voltaire, 144, 182n

unhomeliness, 63
the universal, as concept or horizon, 3, 5–6, 10, 11, 22, 32n, 96, 130, 173, 178n, 207, 214, 216, 222, 245, 247

Walbridge, John, 27n
'Warda al-Hāni', 58–9
Waterfield, Robin, 4, 25n, 193, 206, 131n
Wilson, Woodrow, 160, 180n, 181n
worldliness, 1, 24, 191, 197, 201
world literature, 5, 8, 10, 24, 27n, 186–7, 214–16, 218, 221–2, 227, 236n, 237n, 238n, 241–3, 246–7
World War I, 23, 37, 107, 139n, 141, 144, 148–9, 151, 161, 168, 178n, 188, 189, 223

al-Yajizi, Ibrahim, 13
'Yūḥanna al-majnūn' (Yuhanna the Mad), 58–9

Zaydan, Emile, 159, 161, 180n, 181n
Zaydan, Jurji, 13, 83n, 122, 142, 174n
Ziadeh, May, 10